T0277699

"Welty takes up the sensitive matter of suffering and evil, and it is ⟨...⟩ book is characterized by biblical fidelity, careful reasoning, hum⟨...⟩ those who espouse different points of view. At the same time, I fou⟨...⟩ persuasive since they are so well supported by the Scriptures and by rigorous reasoning. ⟨...⟩ the book is wonderfully clear and accessible to general readers. Interested laypersons, students, and pastors will all be helped by this insightful work."

—Thomas Schreiner,
Professor of New Testament Interpretation and Professor of Biblical Theology,
The Southern Baptist Theological Seminary

"If God is good, why is there so much evil and suffering in the world? It's a question that every Christian must face at some point. In *40 Questions About Suffering and Evil*, Greg Welty deals fairly with a multiplicity of perspectives and possibilities, refusing to resort to simple or reductive responses. The result is a serious yet practical work that will be useful to anyone who trusts in the unerring truth of God's Word."

—Timothy Paul Jones,
Chair of the Department of Apologetics, Ethics, and Philosophy,
The Southern Baptist Theological Seminary

"This book is an extraordinary resource, and I am thrilled to see it published. The problem of evil is as important a topic as it has ever been, but it is often very difficult to know where to begin. As such, the subject matter is well served by the 40 Questions approach, and Greg Welty is the perfect person to write it. His exhaustive work, attention to detail, wisdom, and theological depth are once again on full display as he treats the various facets of the problem of evil. Without hesitation, this will be the very first volume I point people to as they explore the theological and philosophical questions surrounding evil and suffering."

—Jamie Dew,
President and Professor of Christian Philosophy,
New Orleans Baptist Theological Seminary

"You will not find a more biblically based, thoroughly researched, and carefully reasoned treatment of the philosophical questions of suffering and evil. It is well organized with many helpful summaries. Some of the best things about this book are what the author doesn't do: He doesn't duck any of the hardest questions about suffering and evil. He doesn't go beyond what can be deduced from Scripture in answering these questions. He doesn't merely use the Bible for proof texts, but carefully expounds the Scriptures. He doesn't claim to have all the answers. He doesn't go over the heads of ordinary readers, even though he is a brilliant philosopher. He doesn't merely present abstract philosophical concepts but offers many helpful illustrative examples. He doesn't merely deal with theory but provides practical, gospel-focused counsel to those who suffer."

—Jim Newheiser,
Professor of Christian Counseling and Pastoral Theology,
Director of the Christian Counseling Program, Reformed Theological Seminary

"Greg Welty writes with insight and clarity on what is, and always has been, the primary objection to Christian faith: *Why doesn't God do more to stop suffering?* The book *40 Questions About Suffering and Evil* is helpfully arranged with clear questions matched to easily accessible answers. Whether considering how best to respond to a questioning friend, preparing to preach or teach, guiding your kids, or finding encouragement for your own faith, Dr. Welty's book is one you'll want close at hand."

—J. D. Greear, PhD,
Pastor, The Summit Church

"Biblically saturated, historically attuned, philosophically and theologically astute, and pastorally sensitive, this is an excellent entryway into one of the most difficult topics in Christian doctrine. While readers may not agree with every conclusion, this is well worth your attention and consideration. I highly recommend it!"

—Matthew Y. Emerson,
Co-Provost, Dean of Theology, Arts, and Humanities, Professor of Religion, Oklahoma Baptist University

"Dr. Welty tackles a substantial problem in the Christian faith with substantial arguments. The problem of suffering and evil remains difficult for all who trust and believe in the true and triune God. The apologetic dimensions of this discussion are considerable, as are the pastoral implications. Dr. Welty has addressed these and other aspects of this problem in an accessible and encouraging way, for believer and unbeliever alike. His discussion of inscrutability is a promising, even if often ignored, addition to this entire debate. This volume should be added to the library of any Christian who desires to think deeply about suffering and evil."

—K. Scott Oliphint,
Professor of Apologetics and Systematic Theology,
Westminster Theological Seminary

"When I first learned that Greg Welty would be writing this book, I knew it would be good. But having read the finished work, I find myself struggling to find words that adequately convey how truly exceptional it is. Saturated with Scripture, theologically robust, philosophically incisive, lucidly written, comprehensive in scope, brimming with compassionate realism and pastoral wisdom, *40 Questions About Suffering and Evil* is nothing short of a masterclass in how to reason responsibly about what God has (and has not) revealed in his Word. For more than three decades, Dr. Welty has been reflecting on the challenges of evil and suffering, drinking deeply from the whole counsel of God and the accumulated stock of Christian wisdom through the centuries, and we are blessed to be the beneficiaries of his labors. I do not exaggerate when I say that every pastor, teacher, elder, and counselor should add this extraordinarily rich, insightful, and rewarding book to their library. Indeed, if every Christian were to read and meditate on just one chapter a week, it would do the church a power of good. Without hesitation, this will be my first recommendation for believers looking for solid biblical answers and practical counsel on the topics of suffering and evil."

—James N. Anderson,
Carl W. McMurray Professor of Theology and Philosophy,
Academic Dean, Reformed Theological Seminary

"This is an outstanding addition to Kregel's 40 Questions series. Greg Welty is a superb guide through the labyrinth of issues that emerge from the experience of suffering and evil. Grounded in up-to-date scholarship, this volume is a gold mine of wisdom from Scripture, theology, and philosophy, yet is marked throughout by accessibility, pastoral sensitivity, and a bold willingness to face the hard questions with humility and honesty. This book is an excellent resource for pastors, counselors, teachers, small groups, Sunday school classes, discipleship ministries, and anyone seeking answers to the tough, perennial questions about God and evil. My own faith in Christ has been bolstered by reading it. I highly recommend it to all!"

—John C. Wingard,
Professor of Philosophy and Dean of Humanities,
Covenant College

"There are a lot of books on the so-called 'problem of evil.' There are none quite like this one by Greg Welty. Many books on this subject approach it from a purely philosophical perspective and leave out, almost entirely, any biblical perspective. The books that include a biblical perspective are often bereft of relevant philosophical approaches. *40 Questions About Suffering and Evil* hits the sweet spot! It presents a clear and persuasive account of the Bible's relevance, power, and beauty in responding to sin and suffering while simultaneously weaving in philosophical material that can help illuminate the biblical account. I rarely read a book that I think needs to be read by all my friends, family, and academic colleagues. At least one of the groups would be very frustrated if I convinced them to purchase every book I read. Not so with this book. I will recommend it to everyone I know and you will too."

—David E. Alexander,
Vice President for Academic Affairs, Associate Professor of Philosophy,
Providence Christian College

40 QUESTIONS ABOUT
Suffering and Evil

Greg Welty

Benjamin L. Merkle, Series Editor

40 Questions About Suffering and Evil
© 2024 Greg Welty

Published by Kregel Academic, an imprint of Kregel Publications, 2450 Oak Industrial Dr. NE, Grand Rapids, MI 49505-6020.

This book is a title in the 40 Questions Series edited by Benjamin L. Merkle.

For a complete list of titles in the 40 Questions series, go to 40questions.net.

All rights reserved. No part of this book may be reproduced, stored in a retrieval system, or transmitted in any form or by any means—electronic, mechanical, photocopy, recording, or otherwise—without written permission of the publisher, except for brief quotations in printed reviews.

Italics in Scripture quotations indicate author's added emphasis.

All Scripture quotations, unless otherwise indicated, are from The ESV® Bible (The Holy Bible, English Standard Version®), © 2001 by Crossway, a publishing ministry of Good News Publishers. Used by permission. All rights reserved.

Scripture quotations marked CEV are from the Contemporary English Version Copyright © 1991, 1992, 1995 by American Bible Society. Used by Permission.

Scripture quotations marked NASB 1995 are from the (NASB®) New American Standard Bible®, Copyright © 1960, 1971, 1977, 1995 by The Lockman Foundation. Used by permission. All rights reserved. www.Lockman.org

Scripture quotations marked NIV are taken from the Holy Bible, New International Version®, NIV®. Copyright © 1973, 1978, 1984, 2011 by Biblica, Inc.™ Used by permission of Zondervan. All rights reserved worldwide. www.zondervan.com. The "NIV" and "New International Version" are trademarks registered in the United States Patent and Trademark Office by Biblica, Inc.™

ISBN 978-0-8254-4799-0

Cataloging-in-Publication Data is available from the Library of Congress

Printed in the United States of America

24 25 26 27 28 / 5 4 3 2 1

To my parents,
Richard and Virginia Welty

Contents

Part 4: Practical Questions About Suffering and Evil

Introduction

What This Book Is Trying to Do

This book provides a biblically informed intellectual toolkit for answering significant questions about suffering and evil. We will think through what our definitions will be and to which authorities we will listen (part 1), what the Bible and mature theological reflection have to say about suffering and evil (part 2), how we can defend the Christian faith from those who would use suffering and evil as an argument against our faith (part 3), and how we can respond to suffering and evil in our own lives, and counsel others and ourselves in the midst of it (part 4).

Any reader who peruses these chapters will discover that I argue for a specific set of views when it comes to thinking about and responding to suffering and evil. I think my answers are the most biblically faithful and theologically orthodox ones, but of course everyone says that about their own views. Along with making my own case, an equally important aim of the book is to expose readers to a wide range of important and influential views that have been articulated by many different Christians over the past two millennia. Though we all read the same Bible, no consensus has emerged in the Christian community about how to precisely answer each of these forty questions. Rather, quite a few different sets of answers have been influential in church history, for better or for worse, and those who wish to work out for themselves the answers worth having should be willing to enter this historical conversation among their Christian peers, if only to avoid naivete, narrowness, and intellectual isolation.

So, while I seek to guide you through the contours of the debate, referring to good theology whenever and wherever it speaks to the issue at hand, I try to recognize throughout that Christians more thoughtful, learned, and godly than me may take a different view. Their valuable perspectives will therefore gain a hearing. Yes, all truth is God's truth, and the truth is what it is, quite independently of me or anyone else. We either get it right or we do not. But the Christian tradition of making sense of and responding to suffering and evil reveals there is at least some flexibility among the theologically orthodox about which themes to emphasize and which themes to leave less prominent. I have chosen to make the goodness of God's purpose, the sovereignty of his providence, and the hiddenness of his ways front and center, because I believe the Bible repeatedly makes them front and center. Other Bible-believing Christians may place their accents elsewhere, but I have no doubt we will still end up having much more in common than not.

This book draws upon my experience of regularly teaching a class on suffering and evil at two different Southern Baptist seminaries for the past twenty years. I am grateful for the influence of my own philosophy and theology teachers who carefully addressed this subject in the classroom, exposing me to a variety of thoughtful alternatives on many difficult questions. These teachers include Robert and Marilyn Adams (UCLA), John Frame (Westminster Seminary), and Richard Swinburne (University of Oxford). I am also grateful for writers—in addition to those just named—who have taken the time to write especially penetrating analyses of the subject, from either a biblical or philosophical point of view: William Alston, Michael Bergmann, Jerry Bridges, D. A. Carson, Paul Helm, Daniel Howard-Snyder, C. S. Lewis, Alvin Plantinga, Eleonore Stump, Nicholas Wolterstorff, and Stephen Wykstra. Over the years my perspectives on various individual matters have been influenced, developed, strengthened, challenged, and sometimes changed by interacting with what they have to say. Deserving special mention is Michael Peterson's production of an excellent anthology on "the problem of evil," which I continue to assign to students today because of the historical relevance and intellectual depth of his selections.[1]

I appreciate the trustees and administration of Southeastern Seminary, who granted me sabbatical leave for 2022, during which I wrote much of this book. Thanks also to my wife, Rose, who read the chapters as I wrote them and gave discerning feedback, and to my good friend James Anderson (at Reformed Theological Seminary, Charlotte), who provided feedback on some chapters.

I dedicate this book to my parents. Richard Welty (d. 2009) served on an aircraft carrier in the Pacific in WWII, and Virginia Welty (d. 2021) served with the Red Cross in Tokyo, Japan, during the Korean War. In their own ways, their lives were aimed at meaningfully confronting and overcoming the suffering and evil they found in the world.

---

1. Michael Peterson, ed., *The Problem of Evil: Selected Readings*, 2nd ed. (Notre Dame, IN: University of Notre Dame Press, 2016).

PART 1

General Questions About Suffering and Evil

What Is at Stake in How We Respond to Suffering and Evil?

Why spend time considering and answering the forty questions which compose this book? Suffering and evil are undoubtedly something to be endured, but why must they be seriously considered? Some people answer the questions in this book one way, and others answer differently, but why seek to offer answers at all? What difference does it make? *What is at stake in responding to suffering and evil?* Simply put, providing answers to these questions promotes Christian apologetics (defending the faith to a watching world), fosters Christian discipleship (equips Christians to persevere when tempted to apostasy), and reinforces the Great Commission (confirms the fundamental message of the gospel). Let us consider these points in turn.

Suffering and Evil Are a Challenge to Christian Apologetics

First, Christians must offer answers to the questions in this book because by doing so we fulfill the basic Christian duty to offer a reasoned defense for distinctive Christian claims. The Greek word for "reasoned defense" is *apologia*, and it is chiefly found throughout the New Testament in two contexts: in Paul's defense against the accusations of his enemies, and in Peter's command for believers to give a defense for their hope.

As seen in the use of *apologia* in the book of Acts (22:1; 24:10 [*apologoumai*]; 25:8 [*apologoumenou*]; 16 [*apologias*]; 26:1 [*apelogeito*]; 2 [*apologesthai*]; 24 [*apologoumenou*]) and in the epistles (1 Cor. 9:3; Phil. 1:7, 16; 2 Tim. 4:16), Paul not only defended himself from the false accusations of unbelieving Jews and Gentiles, but he defended the claims of the gospel itself. Because Paul's example was to be imitated as a norm for basic Christian life (Phil. 4:9), his pervasive commitment to "reasoned defense" (*apologia*) should convince Christians to have and make their own reasoned defense. Paul reasons, persuades, and disputes with Jews in the synagogue and with Greeks in the marketplace day by day (Acts 17:1–4, 17). He is particularly anxious to answer their questions (Acts 17:18–19), and it is obvious to all that his ultimate goal is not only to defend himself from the charges made against him, but more importantly to persuade them of the gospel itself (Acts 26:27–29).

Given the first-century context of outright hostility to and persecution of those who named the name of Christ (2 Cor. 6:4–10; 11:22–33), the willingness of these early Christians to continually endure the suffering and evil inflicted by others against them must have provoked many questions from skeptical onlookers about *why* they were willing to do so. "Why voluntarily suffer the loss of social privileges, possessions, and even life itself, just to maintain loyalty to Jesus? Why not restore comfort and ease by simply abandoning your strange, new creed?" "Why worship a Jewish man who suffered and died at the hands of the Romans? Could such a man be worthy of worship? How could such a sufferer be God himself?" "How could God be for you when you face such painful consequences for remaining in his service?" Surely from the very beginning, Christian *apologia* was forced to reckon with multiple questions about suffering and evil, and such questions remain today. For this reason, about a third of the questions in this book occur in part 3, "Apologetic Questions About Suffering and Evil."

In addition to the extended example of the apostle Paul, there is also the apostle Peter, whose first epistle is largely devoted to developing a theology of suffering and trial for Christians dispersed among hostile regions (1 Peter 1:6–7; 2:18–25; 3:8–22; 4:1–2, 12–19; 5:1, 9–11). It is while Peter is equipping them against the world's evil that he gives his well-known command for Christians to "make a defense":

> Now who is there to harm you if you are zealous for what is good? But even if you should suffer for righteousness' sake, you will be blessed. Have no fear of them, nor be troubled, but in your hearts honor Christ the Lord as holy, *always being prepared to make a defense to anyone who asks you for a reason for the hope that is in you*; yet do it with gentleness and respect, having a good conscience, so that, when you are slandered, those who revile your good behavior in Christ may be put to shame. For it is better to suffer for doing good, if that should be God's will, than for doing evil. (1 Peter 3:13–17)

In this brief passage, which contains the *locus classicus* for Christian apologetics in verse 15 (italicized above), the reality of suffering and evil is mentioned no less than eight times: "harm you," "suffer for righteousness' sake," "fear," "troubled," "slandered," "revile your good behavior in Christ," "suffer for doing good," and "suffer . . . for doing evil." It therefore makes sense that the problem of evil ranks so high on the apologetic agenda, for Peter makes clear that suffering and evil are *the* principal context in which Christian faith is challenged, whether intellectually or practically. So, if we are to obey Peter's command and follow Paul's example, we must equip ourselves and others with God-informed answers to questions about suffering and evil.

In fact, the so-called problem of evil is probably the number-one reason unbelievers give for rejecting the God of the Bible, or a good God of any sort (see Question 17). It is thus no surprise that Jesus anticipates and addresses his own disciples' questions about the evils inflicted by other people and the suffering produced by natural disasters (Luke 13:1–5). Nor is it a surprise that Paul's imaginary objector to the gospel raises a version of the problem of evil: How can God blame us for our evil if we cannot resist his sovereign plan (Rom. 9:19)? Given Paul's example and Peter's command, if the critic of God's existence has made an argument, then it is incumbent on the Christian to say *something* in response (rather than avoid unbelievers or merely pray for them).

This also follows from more general commands which God gives. For example: "Walk in wisdom toward outsiders, making the best use of the time. Let your speech always be gracious, seasoned with salt, so that you may know how you ought to answer each person" (Col. 4:5–6). We need divine "wisdom" to equip us for the wide range of questions "each person" can ask, for they "ought" to receive an "answer." Indeed, Jesus often took the time to listen to and then relevantly respond to the arguments of those who were opposed to his beliefs, and we see an extended account of this in Luke 20:27–40.

Suffering and Evil Are a Challenge to Living the Christian Life

Second, Christians must offer answers to the questions in this book because this will equip Christians to persevere when they are tempted to abandon the faith. This point is related to the previous one, since unbelievers are not the only people who ask questions which need answering. Atheists widely claim that the suffering and evil in the world gives them good reason to reject God's existence, but that same suffering and evil gives many *Christians* great temptation to doubt God's existence (or at least his love, his power, or his wisdom). So "the problem of evil" is a question which has "intra-faith" application, which means that Christian answers must not only be directed to the world but to the church. The Scriptures are full of faithful believers who are genuinely perplexed by the evils that they or their community suffer. The psalmist cries out, "How long, O LORD?" (Ps. 13:1), the prophet is bewildered that God sets iniquity before him and fails to judge the wicked (Hab. 1), and the righteous man faces unexpected counsel to "curse God and die" because of the evil he has suffered (Job 2:9). What answers did they seek, and which did they find?

This issue is important because, as we will see in answer to Question 30, experiencing suffering and evil can unsettle our faith in God's promises, distort our perception of God's character, weaken our loyalty to God's purposes, and harden our hearts so that we are bitter toward God and others. The repeated apostolic counsel that we should forgive each other (2 Cor. 2:7; Eph. 4:32; Col. 3:13) presupposes that Christians can be the source of suffering and evil for other Christians, threatening to cause a "root of bitterness" to spring up, cause trouble, and defile many (Heb. 12:15). For the sake of perseverance in Christian discipleship, what should be our perspective on these evils which come our way? Our own hearts can whisper to us: "Does God care more about the free will of others than about my own well-being?" "Is he oblivious to my pain?" "Is he aware but apathetic?" "Is he a cosmic sadist?" "Does he have a moral code utterly alien to my own?" It is no secret that these questions genuinely torment Christians and tempt them to apostasy, and so suffering and evil forms an insidious internal threat to Christian existence. How shall Christians answer the forty questions in this book, not for the world but *for themselves*?

Biblically informed intellectual resources are needed here, as we remind one another of the character of God (Question 37), his works in history (Questions 38–39), and the relevance of the gospel (Question 40). The world would conform us to its unbelief, but we are to be transformed by the renewal of our minds (Rom. 12:2), avoiding the darkened understanding and futile mindset that is caused by hardness of heart (Eph. 4:17–18), which if left unchallenged will further harden our own hearts. We are to "have mercy on those who doubt" (Jude 22) by helping them with the answers they need, rather than harshly dismissing them as unspiritual. And Christians are to think through these challenges ahead of time, putting on the whole armor of God before "the evil day" arrives (Eph. 6:13), storing up God's word in their heart so that they do not sin against him (Ps. 119:11). New Testament scholar D. A. Carson offers his excellent book on the problem of evil as "a book of preventative medicine" for Christians, and his advice here on *when* we should work out answers for ourselves is worth quoting in full:

> One of the major causes of devastating grief and confusion among Christians is that our expectations are false. We do not give the subject of evil and suffering the thought it deserves until we ourselves are confronted with tragedy. If by that point our beliefs—not well thought out but deeply ingrained—are largely out of step with the God who has disclosed himself in the Bible and supremely in Jesus, then the pain from the personal tragedy may be multiplied many times over as we begin to question the very foundations of our faith.[1]

---

1. D. A. Carson, *How Long O Lord? Reflections on Suffering and Evil*, 2nd ed. (Grand Rapids: Baker Academic, 2016), 12.

Responding to Suffering and Evil Is at the Heart of the Christian Gospel

Finally, seeking answers to the questions in this book not only promotes Christian apologetics and fosters Christian discipleship, but also reinforces our most important mission in life: bearing witness to the gospel message (Matt. 28:18–20). The *message* of the cross reveals to us the marvelous, unexpected way in which God confronts and overcomes the evil of our hearts: by sending Jesus, the one who lived the life we ought to have lived, and who died the death we ought to have died (Rom. 3:24–25; 5:6–11, 18–19; 1 Peter 2:24). But the *method* of the cross reveals to us that God's overcoming the evil of our hearts rests upon God's using the evils of the world to bring about the cross (because he uses the evil decisions of Satan, Judas, the Jewish leaders, Pilate, and the Roman soldiers, all of which resulted in the suffering of the cross; see Acts 2:23; 4:27–28). The message and method of the cross is in effect God's double victory over evil, a double revelation of the powerful love of God in the midst of evil. Evil gets put in its place twice over, as God uses the evil of the world (the cross) to overcome the evil of our hearts (our sin).

This gospel perspective on how God relates to suffering and evil is central and not peripheral to the message of the Bible. The way God achieves victory over evil in the gospel affords us a fundamental insight into the *modus operandi* of divine providence, God's "way of working," since God's plan to redeem the world through Jesus has deep roots in the Bible's entire storyline, rather than being a side note in history. In the cross, God is a God who aims at great goods (as we shall see in later chapters, goods for us and for himself; see Question 7). In the cross, God aims at these great goods by way of suffering and evil. And in the cross, God works in ways that would be completely unknowable by us, if he had not specifically told us what he was doing (see Question 8). Future chapters will return to these gospel themes of divine goodness, sovereignty, and inscrutability again and again, as they provide a kind of model for what God is up to with respect to the rest of the suffering and evil in the world. (For instance, these same three themes come to the fore in the Job and Joseph narratives in the Old Testament, anticipating how God deals decisively with evil in the Jesus narrative; see Questions 7 and 8.)

Of course, it is also important not to overread gospel implications for matters of suffering and evil, as if John 3:16 gave us sufficient and precise answers to the full range of questions in this book. God gave us a whole Bible, and not simply John 3:16, and so the testimony of that whole Bible must be consulted. But as we seek to apply the fundamental wisdom of the Book to each of the questions in this book, we ought to be inspired, motivated, encouraged, and guided in our answers by the good news of God's decisive victory over suffering and evil. The Christian gospel means that we cannot stand mute before the suffering in the world, offering no God-informed commentary and perspective on it, for we not only proclaim this message of how God has responded (and will respond) to the world's suffering and evil, but we base our lives on that message.

Summary

Providing answers to questions about suffering and evil promotes Christian apologetics (defending the faith to a watching world), fosters Christian discipleship (equips Christians to persevere when tempted to apostatize), and reinforces the Great Commission (confirms the fundamental message of the gospel). To meet these ends, this book provides biblically informed intellectual resources for answering significant questions about suffering and evil, while exposing readers to a wide range of important and influential views which have been articulated by many different Christians over the past two millennia.

REFLECTION QUESTIONS

1. Do you agree that Christians of equal piety can reasonably disagree over precisely how to answer the full range of questions about suffering and evil (see Introduction)? If so, why might God allow this to take place?

2. How important is it to be aware of "the historical conversation among our Christian peers" about suffering and evil (see Introduction)? Can you list any benefits to such awareness?

3. Are there other examples of "apologetics" in the Bible, broadly speaking, beyond the example of the apostle Paul? Does Scripture ever speak to our own character qualifications as we engage in this activity?

4. Is Carson correct about the need for Christians to have "preventative medicine" on this subject? Have you personally seen, in your life or in the lives of others, what happens in the absence of such medicine?

5. Where do you believe the contemporary church is weakest in addressing questions about suffering and evil: apologetics, discipleship, or gospel witness?

What Is the Difference Between Moral Evil and Natural Evil?

In Question 1 we connected the topic of this book—suffering and evil—to Christian apologetics, Christian discipleship, and the gospel message. But how should "suffering" and "evil" be defined, and what is the relationship, if any, between them? These are surprisingly deep waters. Whatever definitional choices we make at the outset should be informed by Scripture, illuminate our everyday experience, and equip us to meaningfully address the full range of questions posed by the world and the church about all the "bad things" in life. With respect to these criteria, not all definitions are created equal. How shall we proceed?

It turns out that a simple, initial characterization of "evil" as "any significant case of pain and suffering" is enriched by a further distinction between "moral evil" and "natural evil." This goes a long way toward providing the definitions we need. The "moral evil" / "natural evil" distinction has a long history in church tradition and shows up in just about any textbook treatment of "the problem of evil."[1] My thinking about the topic for the past thirty-five years leads me to the definitions below as the most helpful starting point. In

---

1. The tradition is one of *concept*, not necessarily one of terminology. For example, the medieval theologian Thomas Aquinas divides "evil" into the evil of pain (or penalty) and the evil of fault (or defect of will). As we will see, this distinction maps rather well onto what I will say under the "natural evil" / "moral evil" terminology. See Thomas Aquinas, *Summa Theologica* 1.48.5–6, and 1.49.2 (reply 1). For the "moral evil" / "natural evil" distinction in contemporary treatments of the problem of evil, see Alvin Plantinga, *God, Freedom, and Evil* (Grand Rapids: Eerdmans, 1977), 30; John Feinberg, *The Many Faces of Evil: Theological Systems and the Problems of Evil*, rev. and exp. ed. (Wheaton, IL: Crossway, 2004), 22; and Michael Peterson, *God and Evil: An Introduction to the Issues* (New York: Routledge, 2018), 10–13. Peterson argues that "the distinction between natural and moral evil runs through most great literature" (p. 12), citing William Blake and Fyodor Dostoyevsky as examples.

this chapter we will define "evil," "moral evil," and "natural evil" and begin to consider whether Old Testament word usage supports this distinction. In Question 3 we'll continue this biblical grounding of the distinction by considering New Testament usage as well, and then examine several reasons why the distinction is of immense practical importance.

What Is "Evil"?

Christian apologist C. S. Lewis's influential book on the problem of evil is entitled *The Problem of Pain* rather than *The Problem of Evil*, precisely because he regards the terms "evil" and "pain" as interchangeable for his purposes.[2] I follow him in this decision, defining "evil" as *any significant case of pain and suffering*. Of course, this invites the further question of what "pain and suffering" are, but we don't seem to have any difficulty in identifying those! Whenever we experience the loss of something of value, we experience pain and suffering. This valuable thing might be physical or psychological well-being, or one or more of the many things which contribute to that well-being (friendship, family, job, health). But the loss of any of that *just is* "pain and suffering." For the purposes of this book, our grip on what counts as "pain and suffering" is so intuitive that we do not need to go any deeper here.[3]

What is interesting is that when we survey the biblical usage of *ra'ah* (Hebrew), and *ponēros* and *kakia* or *kakos* (Greek)—the Hebrew and Greek words most commonly translated as "evil" in our English Bibles—we find that these terms typically refer either to the presence of pain and suffering (harm, injury, distress, misery), or to that which causes such pain and suffering (adversity, calamity; wicked choices, actions, or words). Amid the overwhelming diversity among cases of evil in the Bible (due to bad weather, poisonous herbs, wild beasts, defeat in battle, murder, adultery, theft; see Question 6), this is what most uses of the terms seem to have in common: evil deprives us of physical or spiritual well-being. (We will see several specific examples in the next two sections.)

If we were to survey all the "bad things" talked about in Scripture (and which we regularly experience in life), we would see that evils can be additionally described in terms of *their immediate cause*. Why this is something worth noting will be discussed at the end of this chapter, but the distinction

---

2. See C. S. Lewis, *The Problem of Pain* (San Francisco: HarperOne, 2015).
3. If one wanted to "go deeper," a first step would be to consider Aquinas's *privation* definition of "evil": evil is the privation of good. This is not the mere negation or absence of good, but the depriving of a good that something ought to have by nature. So, on the privation theory, it is not evil that a rock cannot see, but it *is* evil if a human being cannot see. That is, blindness is an evil for humans but not for rocks, since it is in the nature of humans to see. Whether or not an "evil" in this sense should be further categorized as a "moral evil" or a "natural evil" depends on its *cause*, as we are about to see in the next two sections of this chapter. See Thomas Aquinas, *Summa Theologica* 1.48.3 (*respondeo*).

itself seems obvious once you think about it. As we will now see, the terms "moral evil" and "natural evil" distinguish evils in terms of their immediate cause.

What Is "Moral Evil"?

For the purposes of this book and in accordance with much traditional thinking on the topic, "moral evil" will be defined as *any evil*—that is, any significant case of pain and suffering—*which is caused by free persons through defect of will, either intentionally or through culpable neglect of their respon-sibilities*. Christians sometimes call these "sins of commission" and "sins of omission." It is doing what ought not to be done, and leaving undone what ought to be done, such that the consequence is lots of pain and suffering.

So, moral evils are things like adultery (Deut. 22:22; Prov. 6:24), lying (Deut. 19:18–20; Ps. 34:13), murder (Judg. 9:56–57; 2 Sam. 12:9), slavery (Gen. 50:15, 17, 20; Deut. 24:7), rape (Judg. 20:12–13), rebellion against parents (Deut. 21:18–21), theft (Gen. 44:4–5), and so on. (Each of these texts uses the Hebrew word *ra'ah*.) In these cases, and in many more, people are abusing their free will, intentionally and deliberately inflicting pain and suffering on each other, in a way that is contrary to or neglectful of their moral responsi-bilities. And the suffering does not have to be restricted to that endured by humans. Many advocates of the problem of evil emphasize the problem of animals suffering needlessly at the hands of humans. That is moral evil too.[4]

Many more cases of moral evil occur through culpable neglect. If I am sitting by a swimming pool reading the news on my phone and I see a toddler go by and topple into the pool, then see her flail her arms around helplessly, then hear her gurgling as she drowns—and I do absolutely nothing when it is in my power to act—I have neglected my responsibilities in this situation, and I am guilty of adding to the moral evil in the world. It was up to me whether I prevented this pain and suffering, and I did not prevent it. One might even go so far as to say I partially caused it, since causes are what "make a difference" in the course of events from what they would otherwise be, and my depraved indifference *made* a difference as to the pain and suffering in the world.[5] A large proportion of moral evil is of this type, that is, sins of omission.

---

4. Many uses of the term "evil" in Scripture are broader than those cited above, referring to habits, attitudes, or thoughts that *dispose* someone to engage in the kinds of deeds named in this paragraph. Consider Jesus's characterization of "evil thoughts": "For out of the heart come evil [*poneros*] thoughts, murder, adultery, sexual immorality, theft, false witness, slander" (Matt. 15:19).

5. "We think of a cause as something that makes a difference, and the difference it makes must be a difference from what would have happened without it. Had it been absent, its effects—some of them, at least, and usually all—would have been absent as well" (David Lewis, "Causation," in David Lewis, *Philosophical Papers: Volume II* [Oxford: Oxford

So, what is essential to "moral evil" is that it is a type of pain and suffering which occurs through a defect of will, an abuse of free will. Sin is "missing the mark" of what you *ought* to have aimed at (Rom. 3:23).

What Is "Natural Evil"?

The second kind of evil is "natural evil." Simply put, natural evil is any evil caused by impersonal objects and forces, rather than by people's defect of will. It involves significant pain and suffering in the world that are not caused by free persons either intentionally or through culpable neglect of their responsibilities. Where does it come from, then? For lack of a better phrase, natural evil comes from "how nature goes on," which is quite independent of human choices. So natural evils are the pain and suffering produced by bad water (2 Kings 2:19), birth defects in animals (Deut. 15:21; 17:1), disease (Deut. 7:15; 28:59; 2 Chron. 21:19), hunger (Num. 20:5), injurious boils on the skin (Deut. 28:35), poisonous herbs (2 Kings 4:39–40), rotten food (Jer. 24:2–3, 8), stormy weather (Jonah 1:7–8), wild or harmful beasts (Gen. 37:20, 33; Lev. 26:6), and so on. (As before, each of these texts uses the Hebrew word *ra'ah* or *ra*, but here the focus is different: it is on pain and suffering not immediately caused by human choice.)

Similar types of events can include tornados, hurricanes, earthquakes, tsunamis, (naturally occurring) plague, (most) genetic defects, (most) forest fires, falling trees and rolling boulders that crush all in their path, and so on. (The qualifications of "naturally occurring" and "most" are needed because at least some plagues, genetic defects, and forest fires can arise through scheming or neglectful humans, in which case they are moral evil, not natural evil.) And again, many natural evils involve the pain and suffering of animals, such as those which are grievously burned in naturally occurring forest fires. This widens the scope for natural evil considerably.

Thus, in the remainder of this book, "evil" will be referring to these two kinds of pain and suffering: one kind brought about by human beings choosing to inflict pain and suffering on each other (or culpably failing to prevent it) through defect of will, and the other kind brought about in virtue of "how nature goes on," regardless of human choices. Interestingly, Job 2:10–11 uses the term *ra'ah* quite broadly to refer to *all* the evil which Job suffered, which turns out to be a combination of moral evil (the Sabeans and Chaldeans stealing and murdering, and Satan inflicting ill health) and natural evil (the fire and wind destroying buildings, animals, and people). Likewise, Jeremiah 5:12 uses *ra'ah* for a kind of "disaster" that seems to cover both "sword" (moral evil) and "famine" (natural evil).

University Press, 1986], 161). See also the discussion of "absence causation" in Carolina Sartorio, *Causation & Free Will* (Oxford: Oxford University Press, 2016), 46–50.

Summary

"Evil" is defined in this book as "any significant case of pain and suffering." "Moral evil" is suffering which is caused by free persons through defect of will, either intentionally or through culpable neglect of their responsibilities. (Typical cases include murder, adultery, rape, theft, slavery, and lying.) "Natural evil" is suffering not caused by persons abusing their free will, and instead comes from "how nature goes on." (Typical cases include hunger, disease, bad weather, poisonous food, rampaging wild animals, birth defects, plague, earthquakes, and forest fires.) The Hebrew word for "evil" (*ra'ah*) has a semantic range which includes both meanings, and which meaning is intended by the author on any occasion will be largely determined by context.

REFLECTION QUESTIONS

1. Is your definition of "evil" different from the one provided in this chapter? Does it contain any advantages over the definition presented here? Does it have any drawbacks? (You might want to revisit this question at the end of the book.)

2. Aquinas's thoughts on defining "evil" were relegated to footnotes, whereas the scriptural material was central to the text. What are some of the dangers in reversing this emphasis? And what are some of the benefits in being familiar with church tradition, nevertheless?

3. Much moral evil occurs when we fail to do something. How can that rightly be understood as a *cause* of suffering for ourselves and others?

4. Some authors have contended that animal suffering—whether caused by humans or nature—is not much of an "evil," since (on their view) we have little reason to think that animals experience pain as we do. Is this a position a Christian should take? How would you argue against it?

5. Many of my students do not like the phrase "natural evil," contending that only "moral evil" is *truly* evil. Does the biblical usage of *ra'ah* indicate a broader understanding of "evil"?

QUESTION 3

Does the Bible Distinguish Moral Evil and Natural Evil?

Question 2 began to look at the difference between moral evil and natural evil, offering brief definitions of three terms:

- *Evil:* any significant case of pain and suffering
- *Moral evil:* evil caused by free persons through defect of will, either intentionally or through culpable neglect of their responsibilities
- *Natural evil:* any evil that is not moral evil; this is evil caused by "how nature goes on," quite independently of human choices

Our discussion subsequently focused on the Hebrew word *ra'ah* in the Old Testament, finding through a multitude of examples that it covered both moral and natural senses of "evil." Question 3 extends the discussion to the New Testament usage of key terms for "evil," thus completing the biblical grounding for the distinction. In addition, we will find that distinguishing moral evil and natural evil has practical significance for our effectiveness in apologetics, counseling, and gospel witness.

Does the New Testament Distinguish These Two Meanings of "Evil"?

In the entries for the two Greek words most frequently translated as "evil" (*ponēros*, and *kakia* or *kakos*), New Testament Greek lexicons repeatedly acknowledge the distinction between the "moral evil" and "natural evil" senses of the same Greek word in different contexts, with the former meaning focusing on defect of will, and the latter meaning focusing on the harm or pain suffered quite independently of any human source.

The "Moral Evil" Sense of Key New Testament Terms for "Evil"[1]

Lexicon	*ponēros* as "moral evil"	*kakia* or *kakos* as "moral evil"
Thayer	"in an ethical sense, *evil, wicked, bad*, etc."	"morally, i.e., of a mode of thinking, feeling, acting; *base, wrong, wicked*: of persons, *evil*, i.e. what is contrary to law, either divine or human, *wrong, crime*"
Danker	"deviation from an acceptable moral or social standard"	"morally/socially reprehensible . . . moral offensiveness"
Friberg	"in a moral sense of persons and things characterized by ill will *evil, wicked, malicious*"	"morally, of persons characterized by godlessness, *evil, bad* . . . as moral conduct, attitudes, plans of godless people, *evil, base, wicked* . . . *depravity, vice, wickedness*"
Louw-Nida	"pertaining to being morally corrupt and evil—'immoral, evil, wicked' . . . pertaining to guilt resulting from an evil deed—'guilty'"	"bad (moral): pertaining to being bad, with the implication of harmful and damaging . . . the quality of wickedness, with the implication of that which is harmful and damaging"
Gingrich	"in the ethical sense *wicked, evil, bad, vicious, degenerate*"	"*badness, faultiness* in the sense *depravity, wickedness, vice* . . . *Malice, ill will, malignity*"

---

1.   Lexicons referenced in this chart: Joseph Henry Thayer, *A Greek-English Lexicon of the New Testament*, abridged and rev. (Ontario: Online Bible Foundation, 1997); Frederick William Danker with Kathryn Krug, *The Concise Greek-English Lexicon of the New Testament* (Chicago: University of Chicago Press, 2009); Barbara Friberg and Timothy Friberg, eds., *Analytical Greek New Testament*, 2nd ed. (Grand Rapids: Baker, 1994); Johannes E. Louw and Eugene A. Nida, eds., *Greek-English Lexicon of the New Testament Based on Semantic Domains*, 2nd ed. (New York: United Bible Societies, 1989); F. Wilbur Gingrich, *Shorter Lexicon of the Greek New Testament*, 2nd ed., rev. Frederick W. Danker (Chicago: University of Chicago Press, 1983).

The "Natural Evil" Sense of Key New Testament Terms for "Evil"		
Lexicon	***ponēros* as "natural evil"**	***kakia* or *kakos* as "natural evil"**
Thayer	"in a physical sense, diseased or blind"	"*troublesome, injurious, pernicious, destructive, baneful,* an *evil,* that which injures; substantially equivalent to *bad,* i.e. distressing, whether to mind or body . . . evil things, the discomforts which plague one"
Danker	"*bad, poor,* 'in deteriorated or undesirable state or condition,' of physical circumstance, *bad* eyesight, *virulent* sore"	"causing harm, with focus on personal/physical injury, *harmful* . . . of misfortune, *bad* . . . troublesome circumstance"
Friberg	"what is physically disadvantageous *bad, harmful, evil, painful* . . . as adverse circumstances *evil, trouble, misfortune*"	"of circumstances and conditions that come on a person, *harmful, evil, injurious* . . . *ruin, harm, misfortunes, evils*"
Louw-Nida	"a state of being sickly or diseased"	"pertaining to having experienced harm . . . a state involving difficult and distressing circumstances— 'difficulties, evil'"
Gingrich	"in the physical sense *in poor condition, sick*"	"*trouble, misfortune*"

Notice how the first chart brings out the relevance of human defect of will as the cause of pain and suffering, whereas the second chart focuses on suffering which may occur "naturally" (such as blindness, disease, sickness, or overall misfortune). Which meaning is intended by the scriptural author will depend on various contextual factors, but the basic distinction is unmistakable. As in the Old Testament, so in the New Testament: moral evils are things like adultery (Luke 3:19), blasphemy (Matt. 9:4), boasting (James 4:16), crime (Matt. 27:23; Mark 15:14; Rom. 13:3–4), false accusations (3 John 10), greed for money (Acts 8:22), insults (Matt. 5:39), malice (Rom. 1:29; Eph. 4:31; Col. 3:8; Titus 3:3; 1 Peter 2:1), mercilessness (Matt. 18:32), rash oaths (Matt. 5:37), sinful unbelief (Heb. 3:12), slander (Matt. 5:11), suicide (Acts 16:28), unjust persecution (Acts 9:13), and so on. (Each of these texts uses the Greek word *ponēros, kakos,* or *kakia.*) Natural evils are the pain and suffering produced by bad eyesight (Matt. 6:23; Luke 11:34), bad health (Mark 5:26), impoverishment (Luke 16:25), malignant sores on the body (Rev. 16:2), poisonous snakebites (Acts 28:5), unfruitful trees (Matt. 7:17–18), and so on. (As before, each of these texts uses the Greek word *ponēros*, *kakos*, or *kakia*, but here the focus is different: it is on pain and suffering not immediately caused by human choice.[2])

Why Is It Important to Distinguish Between These Two Kinds of Suffering and Evil?

There are at least four reasons why the definitions in these last two chapters are important. First, the definition of "evil" as "significant case of pain and suffering" generates perhaps the most discussed version of "the problem of evil" within Christian apologetics today (see part 3, and Question 17 in particular). It is the basic definition used in the most widely anthologized atheist piece of writing on the topic in the second half of the twentieth century.[3] William Rowe's argument directly connects the presence of "intense suffering" to two of God's attributes: his power and his goodness. A powerful God would be *able* to prevent such suffering, and a good God would *want* to prevent such suffering. Atheists claim that if we deny that God's attributes have these two implications, then we hardly know what the terms "power" and "goodness" mean. (Could I claim that I was "good" if my goodness gave me *no* motivation to prevent the suffering of the drowning toddler mentioned earlier in Question 2?) Given that God's attributes seem to have these implications, Rowe argues that the widespread existence of intense suffering is considerable evidence against there being a God with such attributes. Rowe's article has generated a veritable cottage industry of imitations and replies over the past forty years.

Second, distinguishing "moral evil" from "natural evil" will affect the ways the problem of evil can be both raised and answered. The central case of evil discussed by Rowe is of a fawn that burns to death in a forest fire, suffering terrible agony for several days before expiring.[4] As an atheist, Rowe chooses to highlight this case of natural evil precisely because he knows that many of the traditional ways of defending God in the face of evil only work for moral evil, not natural evil, or only work for human suffering, not animal suffering. It seems unlikely that God allows the fawn's suffering because the fawn is being punished for its sins, or is abusing its free will, or is getting its character shaped through trial, or is getting its attention alerted to the need for the gospel. (As we will see in Questions 21–25, these are all answers Christians have posed for why human beings suffer.) None of this applies to animal

---

2. Readers are encouraged to look up each entry to see the specific biblical texts cited by the lexicons for each kind of word usage and make up their own minds. Providing that wealth of material is beyond the scope of this brief chapter.
3. William Rowe, "The Problem of Evil and Some Varieties of Atheism," *American Philosophical Quarterly* 16, no. 4 (1979): 335–41.
4. Rowe, "The Problem of Evil and Some Varieties of Atheism," 337.

suffering, and Rowe knows this. Christians will have to be alert to these kinds of distinctions if we are to offer reasoned defenses of the faith that are *relevant* to the questions being asked. Not just any reason God could have for permitting evil will apply to every evil, it seems. God could have different reasons for allowing different kinds of evil, and Christians should search the Scriptures and develop replies with this in mind.

Third, familiarizing ourselves with the wide range of "moral evils" and "natural evils" will broaden our understanding of the kinds of evil people can suffer, therefore deepening our sympathy for such people and provoking wisdom in our response. Sometimes we suffer because human beings are against us, and sometimes we suffer because "nature" is against us, as it were. What is characteristic of each kind of suffering? What are the kinds of answers we console ourselves with? What intellectual dead-ends can we fall into when thinking about these two categories of suffering? Are humans and nature the *ultimate* cause of our suffering, or are they instead means in the hands of an all-wise, provident, and good God? And could some natural evil like hurricanes and disease be like moral evil, in that it is caused by *nonhuman* persons abusing their free will (that is, fallen angels)? Does this ever happen, and if so, to what degree? Distinguishing moral evil from natural evil leads us to consider these differences and possible similarities. Good biblical counseling often depends on recognizing the importance and limitations of various distinctions we make (see part 4, "Practical Questions About Suffering and Evil").

Fourth, the "moral evil" / "natural evil" distinction conveys a fuller picture of just how fallen the world is, and just how far God's salvation extends. Traditionally, Christians have traced natural evils like disease and natural disasters to the effects of the fall of man (though some Christians have other views; see Question 25). Humanity seems to have suffered a disharmonious relationship with nature ever since God "subjected" the world to "futility" and "bondage to corruption," so that we look forward to the very "redemption of our bodies" (Rom. 8:20–23). How awful must human rebellion have been if the world includes pervasive natural evils as well as moral evils. And how great must be the promise of full, cosmic redemption (Col. 1:15–20), this setting free of "creation itself" (Rom. 8:21), when God puts "all things in subjection" under Christ's rule (1 Cor. 15:27). Clear thinking on the full range of evils in the world will help us sing with more feeling and understanding, both now and especially in the life to come: "No more let sins and sorrows grow, nor thorns infest the ground. He comes to make his blessings flow, far as the curse is found, far as the curse is found."[5]

---

5.   Isaac Watts, "Joy to the World," verse three. (Notice the reference to both moral and natural evil.)

Summary

Like the Hebrew word *ra'ah*, the common Greek words for "evil" (*ponēros, kakia, kakos*) have a semantic range which include "moral evil" and "natural evil," and which meaning is intended by the author on any occasion will be largely determined by context. The moral evil/natural evil distinction thus seems biblically grounded in both Old Testament and New Testament word usage. In addition, the distinction is important for contemporary Christian apologetics, for counseling those who suffer, and for conveying a fuller picture of both the fallenness of the world and the extent of God's salvation.

REFLECTION QUESTIONS

1. The same biblical word can refer to "pain and suffering caused by human defect of will" in one context but refer to "pain and suffering caused by nature" in another context. Have you ever had a fruitless conversation about "the problem of evil" because key words were being taken out of context? What are some practical ways we can overcome this (all-too-common) feature of human conversation and dialogue?

2. Has someone ever given you a version of William Rowe's "problem of evil" before, which tries to set pain and suffering in opposition to God's attributes? If so, how did you respond? Has your thinking changed in any way since then?

3. Could God "have different reasons for allowing different kinds of evil"? Some Christians think God has just *one* reason for everything: his own glory. Do these answers conflict? How could they both be true?

4. The second full paragraph on page 29 above asked six different questions. Pick one and give your best answer to it. (You might want to revisit your answer at the end of the book to see if it has changed.)

5. The chapter ended by reminding us that thinking about the "bad" things can help us appreciate the "good" things even more. Can you think of any scriptural concepts or passages that would encourage this line of application?

What Is the Bible's Role in Helping Us Understand Suffering and Evil?

So far, we have seen that several important things are at stake in how we respond to suffering and evil (Question 1) and that we can give simple, straightforward definitions of "evil," "moral evil," and "natural evil" that are grounded in the scriptural usage of key terms. These definitions enhance our ability to intellectually respond to suffering and evil (Questions 2 and 3).

These humble beginnings lead us to a very large question: Which authorities will we listen to as we reflect upon this difficult topic? Where will we get our *answers* to our "40 Questions"? As Christians navigate this terrain, the impression is often given that the choice is clear, fundamental, and exclusive: either we can listen to God or we can listen to ourselves. Put a bit more sharply, we can rely solely on statements of Scripture in figuring out what to believe, or we can go *beyond* God's wisdom and seek to supplement it with some wisdom of our own. Put even more sharply, we can be those who consult God's Word and are satisfied with what God expressly declares—about suffering, evil, or any other topic—or we can be the people about whom God laments: "My people have committed two evils: they have forsaken me, the fountain of living waters, and hewed out cisterns for themselves, broken cisterns that can hold no water" (Jer. 2:13).

If God's Word is the exclusive repository of inspired, inerrant, and infallible truth from God, why mingle that with uninspired, errant, and fallible speculations of our own, especially when considering matters of great significance? Good question! As I seek to show in this chapter and the next, *the answer is not either/or but both/and*. The Bible does indeed tell us many things which we cannot figure out on our own and does so with the highest authority possible. That is the focus of this Question. However, the possession and use of human reason is a gift from God that is needed to interpret and apply the Bible, to identify and ward off inappropriate inferences from the Bible, and to helpfully confirm what we already know by way of the Bible. Reason can be of *service* in these ways, subordinate to Scripture while magnifying its voice. That is the focus of the next Question. So these next two chapters will provide a foundation for the use of Scripture and reason that will guide us in the rest of this book.

General Revelation Is Not Enough

Christians believe the world was created by God and is providentially sustained by him for his glory and our good. Nevertheless, the suffering associated with both moral evil and natural evil is pervasive throughout creation, and things have been like this from (almost) the very beginning, right up to the present day. Why does it occur? Why is there so much of it? Did God plan this evil? Or is he merely allowing it while wishing it were not here? Or, even more disturbingly, does divine "allowing" have nothing to do with it at all? Does evil creep up on God and his creative project in a way that is unanticipated and out of his control?

These are good questions, but creation stands mute before them. While the sciences are an extraordinarily successful cooperative enterprise that has made plain many truths about the physical universe, no rock, test tube, or telescope will divulge the answers to *these* questions, or even tell us if there are any answers to be had. For that we need divine testimony, both about what God has been up to in human history and what he intends to do in the future. Since God is a personal being, like any person he has plans, purposes, and goals, and whether these are revealed to anyone else is up to God, as it is always up to the person possessing them. "For who knows a person's thoughts except the spirit of that person, which is in him? So also no one comprehends the thoughts of God except the Spirit of God" (1 Cor. 2:11).

So, in the very nature of the case, because of the *kinds* of questions we are wondering about in this book, we are wholly dependent upon divine testimony if we are to get reliable answers. The familiar distinction made by systematic theologians between general revelation and special revelation seems biblically grounded and especially relevant here. General revelation is what we can know about God from nature, is nonverbal, is available to all, and has a very general content: God exists, and we are under his moral law (Ps. 19:1–6; Rom. 1:18–20, 32; 2:14–15). So even people who have never seen a Bible or heard a preacher nevertheless live in an environment of "speech" from God, that is, testimony from nature about God and his moral law. By way of contrast, special revelation is what we can know about God from his Word (whether spoken or written), is verbal, is only available to some, and has a very specific content (all that we find in the sixty-six books of the canon; see Pss. 19:7–11; 119:1–176). The Bible is God's laws, testimonies, precepts, statutes, commandments, rules, words, ways, promises, decrees, and judgments, given initially to Israel and then increasingly made available to the rest of the world through the efforts of God's people via replication, translation, and distribution.[1]

We Need Scripture as Divine Testimony

It is precisely because the contents of general revelation are so limited that we are dependent on further, much more detailed revelation from God about his specific plans and purposes in his world. General revelation speaks to God's nature (including its moral aspects), while special revelation speaks to God's will (including the purposes he aims at, and why). We are especially dependent on special revelation when it comes to God's relation to the various evils in the world. We can take Paul's point at the end of Romans chapter 11 as an example.

Faced with the apostasy of his Jewish kinsmen who rejected Jesus, Paul was confident in chapters 9 through 11 of Romans that God had a plan, even for these evils, and he explains that divine plan in those chapters. But he only *knew* that plan by God's special revelation to him. When he learned that "God has consigned all to disobedience, that he may have mercy on all" (Rom. 11:32), it led Paul to cry out:

> Oh, the depth of the riches and wisdom and knowledge of God! How unsearchable are his judgments and how inscrutable his ways! "For who has known the mind of the Lord, or who has been his counselor?" "Or who has given a gift to him that he might be repaid?" For from him and through him and to him are all things. To him be glory forever. Amen. (Rom. 11:33–36)

We will return to this passage in Question 8 when we reflect upon its twin themes of divine sovereignty over evil and divine inscrutability in the midst of evil. But Paul's exclamation can also be seen as his confession that unless God had revealed to him the contents of chapters 9 through 11, he also would stand mute before the evils of the world, unable to say much of anything about God's providential plan concerning them. This makes it even more extraordinary that God *has* given us such a rich and detailed repository of divine testimony about "what he is up to" in creation, providence, redemption, and

---

1. For further investigation of this view of the Bible, see Robert L. Plummer, *40 Questions About Interpreting the Bible*, 2nd ed. (Grand Rapids: Kregel Academic, 2021). Plummer's book also contains quite a bit of helpful material about the "interpretive" use of reason that I consider in the next Question. On the canon of Scripture, see L. Scott Kellum and Charles Quarles, *40 Questions About the Text and Canon of the New Testament* (Grand Rapids: Kregel Academic, 2023).

future glory, and so the rest of this book will be heavily dependent upon this divine wisdom in formulating answers to the "40 Questions."[2]

The Danger of a Radically Limited Viewpoint

It is easy to miss how fundamental this point is when it comes to the topic of suffering and evil. Whether or not God has spoken, and if so, *what* he has said, is of supreme relevance in interpreting the significance of the world and its suffering. In her insightful and rewarding volume on the problem of suffering, philosopher of religion Eleonore Stump likens atheists who insist that no sense whatsoever can be made of the evils in the world to

> Martians whose sole knowledge of human life on earth comes just from videotape footage of medical treatments taking place within a large city hospital. Imagine how the doctors who run the hospital must look to such a Martian. The Martian sees patients being given drugs that make them sick and wretched. He sees patients having their limbs amputated or their internal organs cut out, and he hears the groans of those recovering from surgery. He sees patients dying in the hospital, including those dying as medical teams are doing things to them, and he observes the grief of their families and friends. This litany of miseries could continue ad nauseam. The Martian seeing all this will be filled with horror and with moral indignation at the doctors who plainly allow the suffering when they are not in fact actively causing it.
>
> Any suggestion that the doctors are actually benevolent toward their patients will be met by the Martian with scorn and with incredulity that we would have the face to try advancing such a claim. The Martian knows what he has seen.[3]

By likening our world to a hospital that continually administers antidotes (to remove deadly disease) and therapeutic procedures (to restore flourishing), Stump is taking a stand on how best to interpret the suffering in the world: it has a kind of medicinal value that is aimed at human good, despite the pain. But by only looking at the videotape footage and refusing to countenance a

---

2. This is not to say that the Bible answers every question we would like to get answers about. Which questions are answered are up to the one testifying, after all, and God's declining to address a topic of interest to us may itself be a kind of indirect testimony of his priorities, as to what is most important for us to know. This also should be treasured information. For more on that topic, see Question 27.
3. Eleonore Stump, *Wandering in Darkness: Narrative and the Problem of Suffering* (Oxford: Oxford University Press, 2010), 17.

larger context in which hospitals make sense (such as the motivations of the doctors, the existence of life beyond the hospital, and why there are hospitals at all), the Martians deprive themselves of the only available means of making sense of the suffering they observe. Indeed, they would be *expected* to misunderstand, given their radically limited viewpoint. Likewise for those who ignore the light that is shed on our circumstances by the Bible, which is divine testimony. Suffering and evil are best understood from the perspective of the only being who sustains and governs the universe (to the extent that he chooses to make his will on these matters known to us).

As we will see, the Bible does not answer every question we might have. But it says a lot: about the goods that God aims at, about the means that God uses to accomplish his good ends, and about how he often leaves us in the dark about what he is up to. These themes of divine goodness, sovereignty, and inscrutability can shed much light on our situation, even if it is not all the light we might like to have. We would be foolish to ignore these revealed truths, even as we would be foolish to make firm conclusions about how *anyone* relates to a difficult situation if we do not even consider what that person has expressly declared about his intentions, goals, methods, and so on.

Summary

General revelation from nature about God's existence and moral law is not nearly enough to provide illuminating insight on the suffering and evil that concerns and perplexes us. For that we need the testimony of the only being who sustains and governs the universe, God himself. In particular, the Bible is divine testimony that gives us specific information about the goodness of God's purposes, the sovereignty of his providence, and the inscrutability of his ways. However, although the Bible plays an essential role in helping us understand suffering and evil, the next Question continues this discussion by considering how reason is a threefold tool that serves to magnify the voice of Scripture in these areas.

REFLECTION QUESTIONS

1. The terms "inspired" (breathed out by God), "inerrant" (asserting no falsehood), and "infallible" (being incapable of error) were used to describe the Scriptures. Although defending this characterization of Scripture is not the main focus of this book, what do you think is at stake in addressing suffering and evil if we do not regard Scripture as having these three characteristics?

2. "General revelation" was distinguished from "special revelation." Are the natural sciences—as a source of knowledge—at fault or somehow defective

if they cannot answer our deepest questions about suffering and evil? If someone said these questions simply did not *have* an answer, because science cannot answer them, how would you respond?

3. As was mentioned, in Romans 9–11 Paul defended the faithfulness of God in the face of Jewish unbelief by appealing to a divine purpose he could only know through revelation. Are there other topics Christians comment on that we should similarly regard as "unsearchable" and "inscrutable" (Paul's terms) unless God has spoken about them?

4. Eleonore Stump's illustration of the "world as a hospital" is evocative of her particular strategy on the problem of suffering. Are there other metaphors for the world (e.g., temple, stadium, barracks) that are similarly useful in this context? What point are they trying to convey?

5. Are there other topics, besides that of suffering and evil, that seem hopeless for anyone to understand unless we consider God's testimony about them? Why does God's testimony seem *especially* relevant to the topic of this book?

Does the Bible or Reason Help Us Better Understand Suffering and Evil?

The Need for Reason

As we learned in the previous Question, the Bible tells us things we cannot figure out on our own. But does the Bible answer *every* question we might have? Consider that consulting the teaching of the Bible could possibly make the problem of suffering and evil *worse*. After all, the Bible presents God as having an extraordinary, unrivaled degree of goodness, knowledge, and power. Indeed, he is perfect in all three of those attributes, and in every other aspect of his character. So, it certainly seems he would want to get rid of evil (given his goodness), he would know how to do it (given his knowledge), and he would be able to do it (given his power). And yet there is evil, including all the pain and suffering recorded for us in the Bible itself. So, by being very clear about the perfection of God's character, the Bible presents us materials for a case *against* God, as it were. Rather than shedding light for us, it seems to increase our darkness.

One of the burdens of this book is to make a sustained case that this initial appearance, while seductive, is deceiving. We would be unwarranted to conclude from God's attributes that the evil in the world poses an intellectual obstacle to believing in him. But I will have to use *reason* to make that case. Reason puts the *logos* into *theologos*, or theology. It is a God-given tool that equips us to apply the Scriptures to human need, including our need to have our questions answered.[1]

---

1. For a defense of this idea of "theology as application" to human need, with special attention to the use of reason in generating that application, see John Frame, *The Doctrine of the Knowledge of God* (Phillipsburg: P&R, 1987), especially chapters 3 and 8.

The fact of the matter is that it is entirely natural, and trivially easy, to pose serious, thoughtful questions that the Bible does not explicitly answer, questions that need answers if we are to make use of the Bible in even the most ordinary of contexts. How is the Hebrew and Greek text to be translated and interpreted? For any text, which other texts in the canon (if any) are to be given more weight when interpreting that text, and why? How is apparent conflict between the teaching of two or more texts to be resolved, among the many ways available to do this? Can we summarize the Bible's teaching using terms and general claims that are not themselves found in the Bible? What licenses us to do this if the Bible itself does not do this or tell us to do it? And, to come back to the topic of this book, if someone gives a bad or weak argument against the Bible's teaching, *where* is the argument weak, and why should we think this?

It turns out that the Bible does not directly answer any of these questions. We are therefore faced with a choice: give up on getting answers to these and any similar questions, restricting ourselves to merely reading the text of the Bible to each other, or use plausible, defensible principles of reason to apply the Bible to these questions. When it comes to matters of suffering and evil, the rest of this book will assume that reason has at least three fundamental roles to play in helping apply the Bible to matters of human concern: *interpretive*, *evaluative*, and *confirmative*.

The Interpretive Use of Reason

The Bible implies that the Holy Spirit is a personal being. The Bible does not say this in so many words. But it is quite reasonable for us to believe this based on what the Bible does say. The Holy Spirit is referred to by way of personal pronouns (John 14–16), he can be lied to (Acts 5:3), he can be grieved (Eph. 4:30), and he intercedes for us (Rom. 8:26–27). Given these and many other passages, it is reasonable to believe that the Holy Spirit is a person, a claim that is quite crucial to formulating and defending the doctrine of the Trinity. Here, reason helps us interpret the Bible.

Similarly, the Bible does not say any of the following things explicitly. But we can use reason to construct good arguments that the following are implications of biblical teaching:

- "God aims at good things by way of evil things, while often leaving us in the dark that he is doing this." (implied by the Job, Joseph, and Jesus narratives; see Questions 7 and 8)
- "Quite possibly, suffering can be due to God's goals in punishment, or chastisement, or character shaping, or getting our attention, or producing various other 'greater goods.'" (implied by reflection on various biblical texts; see Questions 21–26)

- "It is to be expected that some of the reasons God has for doing the things he does cannot be reliably guessed by us." (implied by reflection on various biblical texts; see Questions 8, 20, and 31)

The idea is that the Scriptures are best interpreted as implying these claims and many more besides, though we must use reason—the interpretive use of reason—to show this.

The Evaluative Use of Reason

Arguments are tools to persuade ourselves and others that we have good reason to accept a claim. They bring us intellectually from point A to point B, from the premises (the claims that we already accept) to the conclusion (the claim we wish to support by appealing to the premises). But not all arguments are created equal. Bad arguments either have premises that are false or unsupported, or they use inference forms that are suspect, or they suffer both these flaws. It is often the task of reason to *evaluate* arguments by pointing out these flaws, something that will be on display throughout this book.[2]

For example, reason can show us that some premises are false:

- "God would never permit pain and suffering he could easily prevent."
- "God does not know ahead of time how we would use our free will."
- "No event can be intended by humans for evil and intended by God for good."
- "No event can be brought about by both humans and God."
- "God would never include an evil event in his plan for the universe."

Again, you will not find the Bible expressly *saying* that these claims are false, but as many Questions in this book will contend, reason can help us see that the Bible *implies* that these claims are false.

Reason can also show us that some premises, whether they are true or false, are *unsupported*. That is, the following claims might be true, but we have no good reason to think they are true:

- "My sufferings are likely because I am being punished for some reason." (Question 21)
- "Christians should always attempt to figure out the reason why they are suffering or have suffered." (Question 31)

---

2. For a clear, accessible, and affordable introduction to how reason can be used to do all three of the things below, and many more things besides, see Lee Hardy, Del Ratzsch, Rebecca K. DeYoung, and Gregory Mellema, *The Little Logic Book* (Grand Rapids: Calvin College Press, 2013).

- "God could have created a world with the same amount of good as our world has, but with less evil." (Question 20)
- "Free will and the laws of nature explain all moral evil and natural evil, respectively." (Questions 24 and 25)

The fact that we have no good reason to think that any of the previous claims are true can be *highly* significant when it comes to how we should relate to the suffering and evil in the world.

Finally, reason can show us that even if someone's premises or assumptions are good ones (they are both true and supported), the inference one makes from those premises might be *invalid* or *very weak*. That is, there is no reason to think that, in the following pairs of claims, the first claim gives us a good reason to accept the second claim:

- "God intends the whole. *Therefore*, he must intend every part of that whole." (Question 15)
- "God is sovereign 'in the details.' *Therefore*, I cannot have free will." (Questions 14 and 32)
- "I know some of the ways that goods can depend on evils. *Therefore*, I must know all the ways that goods can depend on evils." (Question 20)
- "I know some of the things that are valuable for God and for human beings. *Therefore*, I must know all the things that are valuable for God and for human beings." (Question 20)
- "I cannot come up with a good reason why God would do something. *Therefore*, God does not have a good reason." (Questions 8 and 20)
- "God includes suffering and evil in his providential plan for the world. *Therefore*, God is 'doing evil that good may come.'" (Question 14)
- "God uses evil for a greater good. *Therefore*, I should never seek to eliminate evil." (Question 33)

In each case, biblical teaching implies that the above inferences are bad ones, but it may take reason to see this.

Like the interpretive use of reason, the threefold evaluative use of reason magnifies the voice of Scripture, in this case by steering us away from inappropriate assumptions or inferences people make *about* God's Word (or about God's world, for that matter).

The Confirmative Use of Reason

Human reason can also confirm for us what we already know by way of the Bible. It can be quite intellectually healthy, not to mention emotionally satisfying, to find further support for views we already accept. Strictly speaking, we may not *need* this support, but obtaining it is a kind of indirect testimony that we have been on the right track all along. Reason performs this function quite well. It is one of the many reasons why a firm grasp of philosophy can be salutary rather than destructive of Christian faith.

For example, based on the Bible, I can know that the same God who is all-powerful is also all-knowing. God speaks clearly to each of these aspects of his character. (Of course, I might need reason in its interpretive and evaluative functions to come to a full conviction that this is indeed the biblical teaching. See above.) But I can also know, based on reason quite apart from the Bible, that if God is all-powerful then he must also be all-knowing. If God is all-powerful, he has the maximum degree of power we can conceive. But then he would have maximal *cognitive* power, and that implies that he is all-knowing. Put intuitively, a being who has power but who does not know all the *ways* he could use his power and does not know all the *circumstances* in which he could use his power is not nearly as powerful as we thought. So maximal power implies maximal knowledge. It "comes along for the ride," as it were.[3]

Of course, my faith in God's omniscience does not *depend* on the ability of reason to argue this, or even on my awareness that someone, somewhere has argued this in a clever philosophy book. I can simply trust God's own testimony that he is both all-powerful and all-knowing, and that is that. Still, there is something immensely satisfying about the fact that what we can know from one source (divine testimony) entirely agrees with and finds corroboration from what we can know from another source (reasoned argument independent of Scripture). This confirmative use of reason will be on display several times in this book.

For example, over the past twenty-five years one of the most discussed and potentially powerful philosophical responses to the intellectual problem of evil is "skeptical theism," which stresses our finitude in discerning justifications God might have for allowing or bringing about suffering. This philosophical position makes no special reference to the Bible. But it seems wholly anticipated by what we already know about divine inscrutability by way of the Bible, especially in the book of Job and in the epistles of Paul (see Question 20). It is as if philosophers have been scaling a mountain and when they arrive at the summit, they are greeted by a band of biblical exegetes and theologians who have been there all along.[4]

---

3. For two philosophers of religion (among many) who argue along similar lines, see Joshua Rasmussen, "For a Personal Foundation," in ch. 8 of Joshua Rasmussen and Felipe Leon, *Is God the Best Explanation of Things? A Dialogue* (Cham, Switzerland: Palgrave Macmillan, 2019), esp. 112–13; and Richard Swinburne, *The Coherence of Theism*, 2nd ed. (Oxford: Oxford University Press, 2016), 152, 196, 226, 244, 253 n. 5.
4. Apologies to Robert Jastrow, the astronomer and physicist from whom this (now proverbial) illustration is swiped and adapted. See Robert Jastrow, *God and the Astronomers*, 2nd ed. (New York: W. W. Norton, 1992), 107.

These Three Uses of Reason Are in Scripture

Those who accept the Bible as the Book of books, the only literature in the world which speaks with divine authority, should be reassured to learn that nothing in the Bible says that reason cannot or ought not be used in any of the ways just described. On the contrary, much in the Bible implies that this is how God intended reason to be used. Consider the following:

- New Testament authors often use reason to bring out the implications of the Old Testament for the question they are addressing. The apostle Paul makes an inductive argument from a catena of Old Testament texts for the general conclusion that all mankind is completely depraved, from head to toe (Rom. 3:9–20). He follows this up by arguing, from the lives of Abraham and David, that justification by faith alone has always been God's method of salvation (Rom. 4:1–12).
- On the day of Pentecost, the apostle Peter used reason to ward off incorrect interpretations of recent historical events: those speaking in tongues cannot be drunk because it is only nine in the morning. The better explanation is that the phenomena fulfill Joel's prophecy (Acts 2:14–21). And Psalm 16 cannot be speaking of David, because he is still in his tomb; the better interpretation is that it speaks of the risen Christ (Acts 2:22–32).
- Jesus uses reasoned argument to expose the lack of cogency in the Sadducees' own argument against the resurrection, first refuting their argument as a straw-man argument (Luke 20:34–36) and then composing an argument for the resurrection from a biblical text the Sadducees accepted (Luke 20:37–38).
- Through the prophet Isaiah, God invites his people to "reason together" with him by asking them to consider the obvious evidence for two things: their own guilt (Isa. 1:2–15) and his own disposition to show mercy to repentant sinners (Isa. 1:16–20).
- Paul reasons with imaginary objectors to show that certain objections to his views are not credible, given other things Paul says (Rom. 3:5–8; 9:14–24).
- Reason is also a tool with profoundly pastoral implications: the psalmist often reasons with himself as a way of overcoming bouts of depression, anger, and fear (see Pss. 42:5; 43:5; 77:10–11, and countless other psalms). Part 4 of this book, Questions 29–40, puts this use on display.

Careful examination of these and other biblical examples will reveal the use of reason in its interpretive, evaluative, and confirmative modes. Since these three uses of reason are themselves confirmed by the testimony of Scripture, we have now come full circle in our investigation—begun in Question 4—of which authorities we will listen to as we consider the matter of suffering and evil. Yes, the scriptural narrative and its theology "makes sense" in light of the resources of reason, as this book will seek to show. But this use of reason also "makes sense" in light of that scriptural narrative and theology, because Scripture commends these uses of reason.

Summary

God's voice in Scripture is magnified rather than muted when we use reason to interpret it, evaluate arguments against it, and confirm its teaching. This threefold use of reason is confirmed by how the scriptural writers themselves use reason and will therefore be on display in the rest of this book. Evidently, one must presuppose reason to argue (by way of reason!) that we can do without it. So rather than opt out of the reasoning game altogether, commit yourself to play the *good* reasoning game, rather than the *bad* reasoning game.

REFLECTION QUESTIONS

1. The claim was made that "reason puts the *logos* into *theologos*, or theology." Do you agree with how the author unpacked this claim? Is there a better way to understand the difference between simply reading Scripture and doing theology?

2. The formula "theology is application" seems rife for postmodern misunderstanding. But then again, what else does theology *do*, strictly speaking, except to answer our questions?

3. Do you agree that we need the interpretive use of reason, applied to the Bible, if we are to accept claims such as "the Holy Spirit is a person"? Another route to accepting this claim is to simply accept what Christian creeds say. What are the advantages of the former approach?

4. Could there be another way an argument could be defective, apart from its premises and its inferences?

5. How significant is it for us today that multiple biblical authors seem to rely on various uses of reason?

PART 2

Biblical and Theological
Questions About Suffering and Evil

Questions Related
to the Bible

What Kinds of Suffering and Evil Occur in the Bible?

So "evil" is significant cases of pain and suffering, and this is either "moral evil" (if brought about by free persons through defect of will) or "natural evil" (if caused by impersonal forces and objects and not by free persons). As this chapter will show, the Scriptures are filled with examples of moral evil (e.g., idolatry, blasphemy, murder, immorality, theft, and deception) and natural evil (e.g., famine, drought, rampaging wild animals, disease, illness, birth defects, plague, bad weather, and death). *Whether* these evils occur is not controversial, but Christians often disagree as to *why* they occur, and much of this book is devoted to considering this last question.

It might seem needless to describe in detail the range of evils that specifically occur in the Old and New Testaments. Why not simply start with the suffering of the modern world? But as we will see, coming to grips with the diversity of evil on display throughout the Bible—including the nature, sources, victims, and consequences of these evils—will give us a biblical realism about evil, a biblical context for understanding evil, and a biblical preparation for responding to evil. These lessons will fundamentally affect how we approach the remaining Questions in this book.

There Are Diverse Kinds of Evil in the Bible

Moral Evils Range Across All Ten Commandments

The Ten Commandments (Exod. 20:1–17; Deut. 5:1–21) are ordinarily seen as a kind of summary of God's moral standards for human life and are themselves summarized in a twofold law of love for God and neighbor (Matt. 22:34–40; Mark 12:28–34). Since sin is either transgression of God's law (1 John 3:4) or failure to obey God's law (James 4:17), it is no wonder that such defects of human will—and therefore the diversity of moral evil—can be illustrated with respect to each of these commandments. Moral evils ranging across all Ten Commandments include:

Worshiping other gods: Israelites worshiping false Moabite gods at Peor (Num. 25:2–3), Philistines worshiping Dagon their god (Judg. 16:23–24), Manasseh king of Judah worshiping Baal and all the host of heaven (2 Kings 21:1–5; 2 Chron. 33:3–5), and Gentiles worshiping images rather than God (Rom. 1:22–23; Acts 17:29; 19:26–27).

Idolatry, or worshiping the true God in an unauthorized way: Israelites worshiping the golden calf (Exod. 32:1–6), Nadab and Abihu offering up unauthorized fire before the Lord (Lev. 10:1), and Jeroboam king of Israel building golden calves, inventing a religious feast, ordaining his own priests, and devising his own offerings (1 Kings 12:25–33; 13:33–34; 2 Chron. 11:14–15).

Blasphemy, or taking God's name in vain: the son of an Israelite woman and Egyptian father blaspheming God (Lev. 24:10–11), Eli's sons blaspheming God (1 Sam. 3:13), and Goliath blaspheming the name of God (1 Sam. 17:43).

Sabbath-breaking—that is, doing work on the Sabbath day or otherwise not keeping it holy: a man gathering sticks on the Sabbath (Num. 15:32), Israelites treading winepresses and selling food on the Sabbath (Neh. 13:15–18), and Israelites worshiping God in an unholy manner on the Sabbath (Isa. 1:12–14).

Disobedience to parents: Samson refusing to listen to his parents (Judg. 14:1–3), and Eli's sons refusing to listen to their father (1 Sam. 2:25).

Murder: Cain murdering his brother Abel (Gen. 4:8), Joab murdering Abner (2 Sam. 3:26–30), and David murdering Uriah the Hittite by arranging his defeat in battle (2 Sam. 11:14–17).

Adultery, and other sexual sin: Shechem son of Hamor raping Dinah daughter of Leah (Gen. 34:1–2), Judah sleeping with his daughter-in-law, Tamar, thinking she is a prostitute (Gen. 38:15–18), and David committing adultery with Bathsheba (2 Sam. 11:2–4).

Theft: Micah stealing 1,100 pieces of silver from his mother (Judg. 17:1–2), Benjaminites stealing the daughters of Shiloh at the yearly feast (Judg. 21:20–23), and Ahab king of Israel stealing Naboth's vineyard (1 Kings 21:15–16).

Lying, and other forms of deception: Rebekah and Jacob deceiving Isaac about Jacob's identity (Gen. 27:5–25), Aaron lying to Moses about where the golden calf came from (Exod. 32:24), and Ziba deceiving David about Mephibosheth's loyalty (2 Sam. 19:27).

Coveting—that is, desiring what is not rightfully yours: Joseph's brothers being jealous of Joseph and hating him (Gen. 37:4, 8, 11), Achan coveting for himself some of the silver and gold devoted to destruction (Josh. 7:1, 20–21; 1 Chron. 2:7), and Saul coveting David's fame in battle (1 Sam. 18:8–9).

Natural Evils Range Across the Entirety of Nature
     Just as moral evil is as broad as the ways that humans will it, natural evil is as broad as nature itself, since just about any aspect of nature can cause pain and suffering for any sentient creature. For example:

Bad food and water: the undrinkable, bitter water of Marah (Exod. 15:23), the manna filled with worms (Exod. 16:20), and poisonous stew (2 Kings 4:38–40).

Bad weather: fire burning up animals and servants (Job 1:16), a great wind collapsing a house on a family (Job 1:18–19), and a storm causing shipwreck (Acts 27:13–41).

Birth defects: the man born blind (John 9:1), the man lame from birth (Acts 3:2), and the man crippled from birth (Acts 14:8).

Disease: Naaman, commander of Syria's army, suffering leprosy (2 Kings 5:1), Asa king of Judah being diseased in his feet (2 Chron. 16:12), and Jehoram king of Judah suffering from a bowel disease (2 Chron. 21:18–19).

Earthquakes: an earthquake during the reign of Uzziah king of Judah (Amos 1:1; Zech. 14:5), an earthquake at the crucifixion of Jesus (Matt. 27:51, 54), and an earthquake during Paul and Silas's imprisonment in Philippi (Acts 16:26).

Famine: the seven-year famine in Joseph's day (Gen. 41:53–57; 42:5; 43:1; 47:13), the famine in the days of the judges (Ruth 1:1), and the seven-year famine in Elisha's day (2 Kings 8:1–3).

Wild or harmful animals: plagues of frogs, gnats, flies, and locusts (Exod. 8:1–32; 10:1–20), bears mauling children (2 Kings 2:23–24), and lions killing the inhabitants of Samaria (2 Kings 17:24–26).

There Are Diverse Sources and Victims of Evil in the Bible

     A broader survey of the biblical record reveals diverse sources of moral and natural evil, ranging across genders, age groups, religious communities, nations, and multiple aspects of nature.

Both genders commit moral evil: the men of Sodom seek to gang-rape Lot's visitors (Gen. 19:1–11), Jacob's sons revenge-kill all the men in the city of Shechem (Gen. 34:25–29), and the men of Gibeah abuse and murder the Levite's concubine (Judg. 19:25–26). But Potiphar's wife falsely accuses Joseph of attempted rape (Gen. 39:13–18), Jezebel threatens the prophet Elijah's life (1 Kings 19:2), and Athaliah murders the entire royal family (2 Kings 11:1–2; 2 Chron. 22:10).

Every age group commits moral evil: youths mock the prophet Elisha (2 Kings 2:23), younger men give foolish advice to Rehoboam king of Judah (1 Kings 12:6–14), adults sell Joseph into slavery (Gen. 37:25–28), and the old prophet in Bethel lies to another prophet to occasion his death (1 Kings 13:11–18).

Multiple religious communities commit moral evil: among ancient pagans, Baal-worshiping Canaanites and Adrammelech-worshiping Sepharvites burn their children in the fire (Deut. 12:31; 2 Kings 17:31). Among Jews, Ahaz king of Judah burns his son as an offering (2 Kings 16:1–4; 2 Chron. 28:1–3), as does Manasseh king of Judah (2 Chron. 33:6). Some Jews in the Gospels seek to kill an innocent Jesus (Matt. 26:3–4), and some Jews in Acts seek to kill Jesus's followers (Acts 6:8–15; 7:57–60; 14:19; 21:27–31; 23:12–15). Among Christians, members of the church at Corinth engage in jealousy and strife (1 Cor. 3:3), commit incest (1 Cor. 5:1–2), and defraud each other (1 Cor. 6:8).

Multiple nations commit moral evil: the Egyptians oppress the Israelites with slave labor (Exod. 1:13–14; 2:23; 5:4–18), and Pharaoh commands infanticide for Israelite males (Exod. 1:15–16). Ancient Persia decrees all Jews be put to death (Esther 3:8–15). Assyria arrogantly seeks to destroy and plunder Israel (Isa. 10:5–19, 27–34). The sinful violence of Damascus, Gaza, Tyre, Edom, Ammon, and Moab is judged by God (Amos 1:1–2:3), and Judah and Israel also come under God's judgment (Amos 2:4–9:10).[1] Among Roman rulers, Herod Antipas beheads an innocent John the Baptist (Matt. 14:1–11), Pontius Pilate delivers an innocent Jesus to be crucified (Matt. 27:26), and Herod Agrippa I executes the apostle James (Acts 12:1–5).

Multiple aspects of nature generate natural evil: this includes suffering produced by diverse weather phenomena across geographical regions and seasons (storms, drought, famine, earthquakes), by multiple species of insect (hornets, locusts, gnats, flies) and animals (frogs, bears, lions), and by

---

1. At least twenty-four different nations come under the explicit judgment of God in the Old Testament, in addition to Israel and Judah. See the references in the one-page chart "Oracles against Nations in the Prophets," *ESV Study Bible* (Wheaton, IL: Crossway: 2012), 1264.

weaknesses in human nature (susceptibility to disease, frail age, and genetic defects such as blindness and deafness).

The victims of evil match the diversity of the sources of evil: both men and women are on the receiving end of moral evil: Cain kills his brother (Gen. 4:8) and Amnon rapes his sister (2 Sam. 13:29). Youth, adults, and the elderly can all be preyed upon by malevolent actors: the sons of Judah burn their sons and daughters in the fire (Jer. 7:30–31), Joab murders Abner (Saul's military general) (2 Sam. 3:26–30), and Joseph's brothers deceive their elderly father Jacob (Gen. 37:31–33). Diverse religious communities and nations all experience similar kinds of suffering. Famine afflicts Egypt (Gen. 41:53–57; 42:5; 43:1; 47:13), Israel (Ruth 1:1), and Syria (2 Kings 6:25). Pagan sailors face mighty tempests (Jonah 1:4–6) and Roman sailors suffer shipwreck (Acts 27:13–41). Victims of murder include Jewish priests (1 Sam. 22:16–19), Jewish prophets (2 Chron. 24:20–22), a Syrian king (2 Kings 8:15), a Hittite warrior (2 Sam. 11:14–17), and an Assyrian king (2 Chron. 32:21; Isa. 37:37). None of these communities are exempt from the ravages of moral and natural evil.

There Are Diverse Consequences of Evil in the Bible

Defining "evil" as "significant cases of pain and suffering," as was done in Questions 2 and 3, was not meant to be a reductive but an *expansive* characterization of the evilness of evil. While "pain" might indicate highly unpleasant physical sensations, "suffering" indicates the deprivation of anything that would have intrinsic value for the victim. For individuals, this includes not merely physical pain, but also psychological scarring and social isolation. As an example of psychological scarring, Jacob's sons reflect on how their betrayal of Joseph caused "the distress of his soul, when he begged us and we did not listen" (Gen. 42:21). Or consider the anguish brought on by Peninnah's treatment of Hannah: "And her rival used to provoke her grievously to irritate her, because the LORD had closed her womb. So it went on year by year" (1 Sam. 1:6–7). As an example of social isolation, moral and natural evil combine to isolate Job from his wife, from his (now nonexistent) family, and from his broader community.[2]

While Joseph, Hannah, and Job suffer as individuals, the Bible does not support an exclusively individualistic picture of the consequences of evil, though no doubt individuals as individuals do bear the brunt of the suffering. Beyond this, evil brings consequences for every sector of society.

For families: think of the grief endured by Aaron's family at the loss of Nadab and Abihu (Lev. 10:1–7), and the chaos into which David's family is plunged because of David's adultery (2 Sam. 12:10).

---

2. On Job's social isolation, see Eleonore Stump, *Wandering in Darkness: Narrative and the Problem of Suffering* (Oxford: Oxford University Press, 2010), 181–83.

For the business sector: when the wages of laborers and harvesters are fraudulently held back, their cries as a group reach the ears of the Lord of hosts (James 5:4; Mal. 3:5).

For the courts: when Jezebel uses false witnesses to help Ahab steal Naboth's vineyard, a system of justice is converted into an oppressor of the poor (1 Kings 21:8–14).

For the marketplace: the greed and deception behind unequal weights, unequal measures, and false balances corrupt the very environment of buying and selling (Prov. 20:10, 20:23, 11:1; Deut. 25:13–15; Lev. 19:35–36).

For religious communities: the idolatry of the son of Eliashib the high priest and others "desecrated the priesthood and the covenant of the priesthood and the Levites" (Neh. 13:28–29).

For the military: the moral cowardice of political leaders can lead whole groups of Roman soldiers to mock and crucify an innocent man while letting the guilty go free (Luke 23:11, 25, 33, 36–37).

For the economically marginalized: nobles and officials in the land can oppress the poor, exacting interest and enslaving debtors (Neh. 5:1–13).

For the environment: though details are not given, it seems clear that the wickedness of humans can result in the land being "polluted" and "defiled" (Num. 35:33–34), so that "the earth mourns and withers" and "the earth lies defiled under its inhabitants" (Isa. 24:4–5). God is committed to "destroying the destroyers of the earth" on the final day of judgment (Rev. 11:18).

It seems obvious, then, that while the consequences of evil start with individuals, they easily spread to every available social structure named above, and even to the physical environment if left unchecked.

Lessons for Us from the Diversity of Evil in the Bible

Biblical Realism: Do Not Be Surprised!
Ancient Israel was surrounded by nations which worshiped other gods, so the contemporary phenomenon of "religious plurality" would be no surprise to them. Likewise, the biblical characters experienced the pervasiveness of evil in all its kinds, sources, victims, and consequences, fashioning the very environment in which they lived and breathed. A thoughtful reader of the Bible would not be *surprised* to learn of the diversity of evil today, even as she would not be surprised to learn of the diversity of religions that

exist today. The biblical history, as it pertains to evil, is a kind of microcosm of the world ever since. If faith must endure a shock when grappling with contemporary evil, it will not be because the Book of faith has kept this hidden from us. Indeed, there is a kind of biblical realism when it comes to the kinds of evil that exist in the world. The depth of depravity on display is shocking: torture, dismemberment, child sacrifice, cannibalism, incest, rape, brutal executions, and so on, each of which finds a counterpart in the modern world.

John Calvin called the Psalms "An Anatomy of All the Parts of the Soul."[3] This was in reference to the full range of human emotion on display in that biblical book, for it is hard to find an important feeling in life that is *not* represented in the passionate prayers of the ancient psalmists. Likewise, we now see that biblical history presents a kind of "anatomy of evil," and it is only with difficulty that we find an evil in the modern world which is not *in principle* represented in the Old or New Testaments. While modern readers are sometimes shocked by the "Good Book's" graphic depiction of pain and suffering, the biblical characters would not be similarly surprised by the modern world. Knowing that the biblical portrait of evil "rings true" in all these diverse respects can be an aid to faith, in an age that increasingly regards the Bible as too culturally distant from us, and too alien to our experience, to serve as a wise counselor amid suffering.

Biblical Context: Do Not Be Cynical or Despairing!
Though this chapter has not explicitly shown it, the specific passages referenced all bear witness to a single truth: none of the moral evil in the Bible is presented in a positive context. Not a single perpetrator is praised for his bloodlust, or immorality, or thieving, or deception, or exploitation of the poor. There is not a shred of amorality in the Bible, no divine approval of Nietzschean supermen trampling the weak with impunity.

As this book will go on to emphasize, God of course *uses* various evils to bring about great goods, and this is a mystery that future Questions will investigate. But not a single time are human beings encouraged to "go and do likewise." Apparently, we are *not* to imitate God in his sovereign use of evils. Even in those cases in which God commands humans to bring about pain and suffering on a limited scale, this is completely at God's discretion and by his explicit instruction, not something we are ever permitted or encouraged to do on our own initiative, much less with wicked and selfish intention. The Bible is completely one-sided in its portrayal of those who commit moral evil: they are blameworthy and without excuse. The pervasiveness of the biblical

---

3. John Calvin, "Preface to the *Commentary on the Psalms* (1557)," in *A Reformation Reader*, 2nd eds., eds. Denis Janz and Sherry E. Jordon (Minneapolis: Fortress Press, 2008), 247.

portrait of evil should not be confused with the normalization of evil. If any-thing, what is normalized is divine condemnation of moral evil.[4]

Biblical Preparation: Do Be Sensitive to the Stories of Others!
Christians can tend to become isolated in their local church communities, or in gender-segregated social groups, or in the level of economic and social comfort provided by their job and community. But the Scriptures sensitize us to the range of possible evil beyond our own lives, to forms of suffering that are likely alien to us, exposing us to the full range of how the *rest* of the world regularly suffers. The apostle Paul recognized that his own affliction equipped him to comfort others who were similarly afflicted (2 Cor. 1:3–7). There is a kind of solidarity in grief that is pastorally useful. But simple *awareness* that the totality of suffering in the world does not begin and end with us can give us a much-needed perspective on our own circumstances, while leading us to discern the cries of others that we would otherwise miss.

Summary
Diversity characterizes the biblical portrait of evil in the world at every point. Moral evil ranges over disobedience to all Ten Commandments, while natural evil is as broad as nature itself. Those who perpetrate evil, and those who are the victims of evil, include both genders, every age group, and mul-tiple religious communities and nations. And the consequences of evil regu-larly include physical pain, psychological scarring, and social isolation, not just for individuals but for families, businesses, the courts, the marketplace, religious communities, the military, the economically marginalized, and even the environment. But the diversity of this portrait fuels a kind of biblical re-alism about evil (so that we are not surprised by the depravity of the world), a biblical context for evil (so that we, like God, are one-sided in our condemna-tion of evil), and a biblical preparation for evil (so that we are better equipped to discern the limitations of our own experience of suffering and are more sensitive to the suffering of others).

REFLECTION QUESTIONS

1. At first glance, some moral evil does not seem categorizable as violation of, or failure to obey, one of the Ten Commandments—for instance, Noah's drunkenness (Gen. 9:21–22), Israel's repeated grumblings against God (Exod. 16:2–3; 17:2–3; Num. 11:1–6), or Saul consulting the medium of

---

4. Natural evil by definition has impersonal nature—not human will—as its cause, so there is no question as to whether humans should "bring it about."

Endor (1 Sam. 28:7–14; 1 Chron. 10:13). How could these, nevertheless, be violations of the Ten Commandments?

2. Think of the three cases of moral evil mentioned in the previous question. If "pain" is "highly unpleasant physical sensations," and "suffering" is "the deprivation of anything that would have intrinsic value for the victim," then how are these cases of moral evil cases of "significant pain and suffering"? Does that give you a better perspective on why they are so bad?

3. Some might argue that there are moral or natural evils today that are not represented, even in principle, by what occurs in biblical history. Are they right?

4. Imagine they *are* right (see previous question). To what degree would that undermine the applications presented at the end of this chapter?

5. The diversity of evil in the Bible was analyzed via four aspects: kind (moral vs. natural), source, victims, and consequences. Are there any further ways we can categorize the diversity of evils in the Bible?

How Does God Bring About Good Through Suffering and Evil?

Having familiarized ourselves with the diverse range of evils in the Bible (Question 6), it is now time to reflect on how God relates to the suffering and evil in the world, including the kinds of evils we have just surveyed. Does God bring about good through suffering and evil? Is that what God is aiming to do? If so, how does he do that? This chapter and the next argue that multiple biblical narratives repeatedly weave together three themes that together reveal the goodness of God amid the world's evils:

- The goodness of God's purpose—God aims at great goods.
- The sovereignty of God's providence—God often intends these great goods to come about by way of various evils.
- The inscrutability of God's ways—God typically leaves created persons in the dark (either about *which* goods he is aiming at, or about *how* these goods depend on the evils which occur, or both).

By examining how these three themes come together in the Job, Joseph, and Jesus narratives, we will see a kind of divine *modus operandi* when it comes to diverse kinds of evil in the world. The three themes above do not lie hidden in obscurity; they are right there on the surface of the biblical text. And they can help Christians develop an overall perspective on evil that is biblically faithful and that forms a foundation for answering the apologetic and practical questions in parts 3 and 4 of this book.

In this chapter (Question 7) we will look at God's purposes and methods: the goodness of his purpose and the sovereignty of his providence. In the next chapter (Question 8) we will consider our lack of access to God's purposes and methods: the inscrutability of his ways.[1]

Good Purposes and Sovereign Providence: The Job Narrative

The Goodness of God's Purpose
    In the opening chapters of Job, the "prologue" before the main events, Satan accuses Job of serving God out of mercenary motives:

- "But stretch out your hand and *touch all that he has*, and he will curse you to your face" (Job 1:11). (Accusation: Job serves God for *possessions*.)
- "But stretch out your hand and *touch his bone and his flesh*, and he will curse you to your face" (Job 2:5). (Accusation: Job serves God for *health*.)

    In response, God seeks to refute Satan's charges and frustrate Satan's predictions, and thereby vindicate God's own worthiness to be served for who he is, rather than for the earthly goods which he supplies. He does this by giving Job an opportunity to display great perseverance amid great suffering. Although the text does not explicitly reveal why the vindication of God's name is such a great good, and thereby *worth* the evil which Job suffers, other chapters of Scripture are quite clear as to its value (Ps. 99:1–3; Isa. 48:10–11; Ezek. 20:9, 14, 22; 36:21–23; Matt. 6:9).

The Sovereignty of God's Providence
    In the subsequent narrative, Job's great suffering is a *means* for him to display great faithfulness, and that suffering is a combination of moral evils and natural evils:

    Moral evils:
- The Sabeans attacked, stealing Job's oxen and donkeys, and striking down his servants (Job 1:15). The Chaldeans attacked, stealing Job's camels, and striking down more of his servants (Job 1:17).
- Satan himself "struck Job with loathsome sores from the sole of his foot to the crown of his head" (Job 2:7).

    Natural evils:
- "The fire of God fell from heaven and burned up the sheep and the servants and consumed them" (Job 1:16).

---

1.   Should these lessons gleaned from the Job, Joseph, and Jesus narratives be *generalized* to all evil whatsoever? Or would that be a hasty generalization lacking credibility? This important question will be considered in Question 11.

- "A great wind came across the wilderness" and destroyed Job's house and family (Job 1:19).

Job's display of faithfulness while suffering these evils fulfills God's good purpose of vindicating God's worthiness to be served for who he is rather than for what he gives. But just as extraordinary, there are at least four indications in the text that *God* is the one who was behind the suffering and who ultimately brought it to pass in Job's life.

First, while not denying that the Sabeans, Chaldeans, fire, and wind were the means of his suffering, Job says, "The LORD gave, and the LORD has taken away" (Job 1:21). In thus attributing his suffering to God, "Job did not sin or charge God with wrong" (Job 1:22).

Second, in responding to his wife's faithless admonition to "curse God and die," Job says, "Shall we receive good from God, and shall we not receive evil [*rā*]?" (Job 2:10). On Job's view, it would be foolishly inconsistent to think that only goods come from God and not evils as well. Again, by attributing his suffering to God, "Job did not sin with his lips" (Job 2:10).

Third, when God passes judgment on the various speeches made about him, whereas Job's friends fare badly, Job's theology fares well: "My anger burns against you and against your two friends, for you have not spoken of me what is right, as my servant Job has" (Job 42:7).

Fourth, at the end of the book, Job's siblings and friends seem to share Job's view of the matter: "And they showed him sympathy and comforted him for all the evil (*ra'ah*) that the LORD had brought upon him" (Job 42:11). They confirm Job's interpretation of his own suffering and its ultimate cause.

Good Purposes and Sovereign Providence: The Joseph Narrative

The Goodness of God's Purpose

In the Joseph narrative (Gen. 37–50), God aims at the great good of preserving his people in a time of famine, so that they can survive to be a great nation in the land of Canaan, and ultimately bring Jesus into the world as the Savior of the world (Jesus himself was a descendent of the Israelites who existed in Joseph's day [Matt. 1:1–17; Luke 3:23–38]). The good at which God is aiming is nothing less than redemption for all who would place their faith in this Savior who would come from the future Israelites.

Because of the famine in Egypt and Canaan that threatens Abraham's descendants (Gen. 47:13), God's redemptive purposes are *hanging by a thread*. To spare his people starvation, God raises up Joseph to be Pharaoh king of Egypt's "right-hand man" (Gen. 41:37–45), administering a wise plan to stockpile and then distribute sufficient food in time of need (Gen. 41:46–49; 53–57; 47:13–26).

The Sovereignty of God's Providence

But the narrative also reveals that God intends the great good of the preservation of his people to come *by way of* the various evils that propel Joseph to his official status:

- His brothers betray him, conspire to kill him (Gen. 37:18–20), leave him for dead (Gen. 37:21–24), and finally sell him into slavery (Gen. 37:25–28).
- Slavers sell him to Potiphar, an officer of Pharaoh in Egypt (Gen. 39:1).
- Potiphar's wife falsely accuses him of attempted rape (Gen. 39:7–18).
- Potiphar imprisons him based on this false charge (Gen. 39:19–20).
- Pharaoh's cupbearer, Joseph's fellow prisoner, fails to remember Joseph's request to bring Joseph's case before Pharaoh (Gen. 40:14–15, 23).

After God brings great good out of these evils, exalting Joseph and delivering Jacob's sons from famine, Joseph's brothers are terrified that he will take revenge for the "evil" (*ra'ah*) they inflicted on him earlier (Gen. 50:15–18). But Joseph comforts and instructs his brothers with the sovereign providence of God amid their evil:

> But Joseph said to them, "Do not fear, for am I in the place of God? As for you, *you meant evil* [ra'ah] *against me, but God meant it for good* [tov], to bring it about that many people should be kept alive, as they are today. So do not fear; I will provide for you and your little ones." Thus he comforted them and spoke kindly to them. (Gen. 50:19–21)

So we have *one set of events*: the betrayal of Joseph by his brothers, his being left for dead, and his being sold into slavery. But we have *two sets of intentions* with respect to these events: human and divine. The brothers "meant evil" *(ra'ah)*—that was their intent, their goal. But God meant these same events with another intention or purpose in mind: great "good" (*tov*), "to bring it about that many people should be kept alive, as they are today." Similarly, there are two sets of intentions behind the moral evil in the Job narrative: the (bad) intentions of Satan, the Sabeans, and the Chaldeans to either demean God's name or pillage Job's possessions, and the (good) intentions of God to vindicate his name.

Further confirmation of the (good) divine intentionality behind the (bad) events suffered by Joseph is found in two additional passages. First, there are Joseph's earlier words to his brothers:

> Do not be distressed or angry with yourselves because you sold me here, for *God sent me* before you to preserve life. . . . And

> *God sent me* before you to preserve for you a remnant on earth, and to keep alive for you many survivors. (Gen. 45:5, 7)

Joseph's view is that *God* ultimately sent him to Egypt, though this sending was by way of the bad events listed above. Second, there is the psalmist's retelling of God's "wondrous works":

> When he summoned a famine on the land and broke all supply of bread, *he had sent a man ahead of them, Joseph, who was sold as a slave.* (Ps. 105:16–17)

Again, *God* ultimately sent Joseph into Egypt for his good purposes, though the earthly means of that divine sending was the brothers and the Midianite traders. God is not a passive bystander who merely allows Joseph to be sent by others. Rather, he sends him.[2]

Good Purposes and Sovereign Providence: The Jesus Narrative

The Goodness of God's Purpose

In the passion narratives of the Gospels, God aims at the great good of redeeming the world by the atonement of Christ. The sacrificial death of the God-man who lived a righteous life turns aside the wrath of God for all who trust in him. Because Jesus's cross perfectly solves the worst problem we could possibly have—being liable to God's just judgment against our sin—God's aiming at the cross is his aiming at the best good we could possibly receive.

But the cross also exalts God in all his attributes: his justice (for judging our sin in Jesus), love, grace, and mercy (for providing an atonement for undeserving sinners), wisdom (for devising this perfect plan of redemption), and power (for orchestrating historical events over millennia to fulfill this plan). Insofar as his glory is his highest good, God's aiming at the cross is his aiming at the best good *he* could possibly have.

The Sovereignty of God's Providence

These same passion narratives also reveal that God intends these great goods to come *by way of* various evils:

- Jewish leaders plot against Jesus (Matt. 26:3–4, 14–15).
- Satan prompts Judas to betray Jesus (John 13:21–30).

---

2. Curiously, this text from Psalms also reveals that God was the one who "summoned a famine on the land and broke all supply of bread," which is exactly what Genesis 41:32 says. This certainly seems to extend God's sovereign providence to natural evil as well, and we saw a similar extension in the Job narrative with respect to the wind and fire.

- Judas betrays Jesus (Matt. 26:47–56; 27:3–10).
- Unjust "show trials" wrongly convict Jesus of blasphemy (Matt. 26:57–68).
- Pilate cowardly condemns a clearly innocent man to death (Matt. 27:15–26).
- Roman soldiers carry out this unjust sentence (Matt. 27:27–44).

This is a perplexing chain of perverse moral evil, and the removal of any link would have robbed the world of the highest good for both man and God.

When Peter and John were imprisoned for testifying to the cross, their friends' prayer for them gives crucial insight into how early Christians viewed Jesus's sufferings:

> "Why did the Gentiles rage, and the peoples plot in vain? The kings of the earth set themselves, and the rulers were gathered together, against the Lord and against his Anointed"— for truly in this city there were gathered together against your holy servant Jesus, whom you anointed, both Herod and Pontius Pilate, along with the Gentiles and the peoples of Israel, *to do whatever your hand and your plan had predestined to take place.* And now, Lord, look upon their threats and grant to your servants to continue to speak your word with all boldness. (Acts 4:25–29)

So the early Christians believed God planned that the responsible human beings who perpetrated these moral evils would in fact do so. *They* intend it for evil, but *God* intends it for good, to the (spiritual) saving of many lives. The early Christian believers' view of the sufferings of Jesus was therefore like Job's view of his sufferings and Joseph's view of his sufferings. *God* is the one who fulfills his promise and his plan in these events, even though the Jewish leaders, Satan, Judas, the Sanhedrin, Pilate, and the Roman soldiers are the historical actors on the scene (Acts 2:23; 3:18). God's "handing over" Jesus to death was by way of many others "handing over" Jesus to death, though the motives or intentions differ between the creaturely and the divine. Steven C. Roy helpfully summarizes this point:

> This dual responsibility for the handing over of Jesus to death can also be seen in biblical texts that use the verb "hand over" *[paradidōmi].* The gospels point to three individuals or groups that have special responsibility for handing Jesus over to be crucified: Pilate (Mt 27:26), the Jewish religious leaders (Mt 27:18) and Judas Iscariot (Mt 26:14–16). John Stott summarizes: "First, Judas 'handed him over' to the priests (out

of greed). Next, the priests 'handed him over' to Pilate (out of envy). Then Pilate 'handed him over' to the soldiers (out of cowardice), and they crucified him" (*The Cross of Christ* [Downers Grove: InterVarsity Press, 1986], p. 58). Yet God was not passive and uninvolved in the handing over of his Son to death. Rom. 8:32 says that God the Father "did not spare his own Son but gave him up *[paradidōmi]* for us all." Thus it was the will of the Father to surrender him over to death "for us all." And this was as well the voluntary self–surrender of God the Son. In Gal 2:20, Paul speaks of Jesus Christ as "the Son of God who loved me and gave *[paradidōmi]* himself for me."[3]

Summary

In each of the Job, Joseph, and Jesus narratives there is *one set of events*, but *two sets of intentions* behind the events: creaturely and divine. The creaturely intentions were evil (involving greed, envy, cowardice, hatred, covetousness, etc.), whereas the divine intentions were good (aiming at goods for both man and God).

Of course, it is one thing to discover that God *has* aimed at great goods by way of significant evils. It is quite another to hold that we can always *discern* the goods he is aiming at by way of evils, that he wills *all* the evils there are (and not just some), that God *commands* that we inflict suffering and evil, that God *causes* the evils he uses as means to goods, or that God *intends* that evils occur. The remaining Questions in this part of the book will address these topics.

REFLECTION QUESTIONS

1. This chapter considered both "the goodness of God's purpose" and "the sovereignty of God's providence." It seems important to defend both claims at the same time. How would your view of each claim change, if you came to believe that the other claim was not true?

2. Is it possible for Job (or anyone else) to "display great perseverance amid great suffering" without there being great suffering? If not, then at least *some* goods cannot be the goods they are, unless they incorporate evils (because they are a response to the evils). Is this a problematic view to take?

3. Consider the social and psychological suffering that attended Joseph's involuntary separation from his own family (including separation from his

---

3.   Steven C. Roy, *How Much Does God Foreknow? A Comprehensive Biblical Study* (Downers Grove, IL: IVP Academic, 2006), 74 n. 3.

own parents), as well as the physical suffering endured during his "lost years" in Pharaoh's dungeons. Does Joseph ever indicate that God's sovereign providence made that suffering "disappear" or become "unreal"? Does he deny the "evil" of his brothers' intentions, or does he instead affirm that those intentions were in fact evil?

4. The passion narratives repeatedly appeal to prophecy as being fulfilled by these historical events. What if God repeatedly *predicted* the evils suffered by Jesus, but he did not *plan* them? Is that a plausible view to take?

5. "Planned evil" has struck many people as a simply awful view to take of God, inevitably turning him into a "moral monster." We will return to this question later. But even at this early stage in the book, what are some helpful guidelines that would lead us to resist the "moral monster" conclusion?

Does God Hide His Reasons for Why He Permits Suffering and Evil?

The previous chapter (Question 7) claimed that two themes come together in the Job, Joseph, and Jesus narratives: the goodness of God's purpose and the sovereignty of God's providence. This chapter finds a third and final theme in the narratives just mentioned: the inscrutability of God's ways. Left to our own powers of discernment, we simply lack access to God's purposes and methods in any case of suffering. This perspective is confirmed when we consider Paul's doxology in Romans 11, and the dismal record in Scripture of humans attempting to divine God's purposes. As will be seen in future Questions, recognizing this third and final theme of divine inscrutability has extraordinary relevance for how we relate to God, how we counsel others, and how we answer "the problem of evil."

Divine Inscrutability: The Job Narrative

The Prologue and Epilogue of Job

We who read the book of Job have access to the story's prologue in Job chapters 1–2. We witness Satan's charges against God and God's intention to refute those charges. But Job himself is privy to none of this illuminating material. Job does not know *which* goods God aims at by Job's sufferings. And Job does not know *how* the goods depend on the evils he's suffered. Indeed, even at the end of the book—the "epilogue"—God never reveals to Job *why* he suffered. He is left completely in the dark on these matters.

This fact has immediate pastoral relevance for our lives. Though we are unlike Job in that we have access to the prologue of his story whereas he does not, when we put down the book of Job and reflect on our own suffering, we may wish for a similar prologue to our life's story, something that will inform and illuminate our experiences of suffering. But, like Job, we are typically left wholly in the dark as to the particulars. Job is an everyman. In being privileged to see his prologue we are not like him, but in remaining ignorant of our own prologue we are just like him.

God's Speeches to Job and His Friends

God's speeches in Job chapters 38–41 reinforce this theme of divine inscrutability. The repeated focus is on Job's ignorance of the physical world. According to God, Job "darkens counsel by words without knowledge" (38:2). He is woefully ignorant of how God brought about and governs any aspect of created reality: the foundation and expanse of the earth, the doors of the sea, the dawn of the morning, the storehouses of snow and hail, the rain, stars, lightning, lion, raven, goat, donkey, ox, ostrich, horse, hawk, eagle, Behemoth, and Leviathan (38:4–39:30; 40:6–41:34).

The import seems to be that if Job is so ignorant about how God created and sustains his world in all its impressive diversity and complexity, how can he possibly guess rightly the reasons for why God does what he does? As theologian John Frame puts it: "The point is that if Job is so ignorant concerning God's works in the natural world, how can he expect to understand the workings of God's mind in distributing good and evil?"[1]

Job's friends do not escape God's assessment either. They are condemned for their ignorance, for making mistaken claims about divine providence: "My anger burns against you and against your two friends, for you have not spoken of me what is right, as my servant Job has" (42:7). As we saw in Question 7, their mistaken assumption was not that the Lord ultimately brought the suffering to pass. The prologue and epilogue both seem to make clear that the *ra'ah* was ultimately from God (1:21–22; 2:10; 42:7). Rather, the mistake of Job's friends was in thinking that the Lord did it *to punish Job for his sins*. This speculation about the divine motivation, repeated by each of Job's friends, is sheer ignorance on their part, a contradiction to the facts of Job chapters 1–2, and an example of hurtful counseling.[2]

Job's Response to God

Finally, divine inscrutability is precisely what Job acknowledges at the end of the book. In response to God's speaking to him out of the whirlwind, Job confesses his utter ignorance of God's ways. Job acknowledges that God is right to focus on Job's lack of knowledge. First, Job says:

---

1. John Frame, *Apologetics: A Justification of Christian Belief* (Phillipsburg: P&R, 2015), 175. Frame adds an instructive reference to John 3:12: "If I have told you earthly things and you do not believe, how can you believe if I tell you heavenly things?"
2. In Question 21 we will return to the many ways this "punishment theodicy" gets sadly misapplied.

> Behold, I am of small account; *what shall I answer you? I lay
> my hand on my mouth.* I have spoken once, and *I will not
> answer*; twice, but I will proceed no further. (40:4–5)

Job puts his hand on that part of his body by which he would express
knowledge, if he had any: his mouth. He simply has no answer to give, in
response to God's display of knowledge. There is no competition here, only
silence. Here finally is something Job knows—that he does not know. Second,
Job says:

> *I know that you can do all things, and that no purpose of yours
> can be thwarted.* "Who is this that hides counsel without
> knowledge?" Therefore *I have uttered what I did not un-
> derstand, things too wonderful for me, which I did not know.*
> "Hear, and I will speak; I will question you, and you make it
> known to me." I had heard of you by the hearing of the ear,
> but now my eye sees you; therefore I despise myself, and re-
> pent in dust and ashes. (42:2–6)

Job's response combines the second and third themes we have been examining in Questions 7–8: the sovereignty of God's providence ("no purpose
of yours can be thwarted") and the inscrutability of God's ways ("I have ut-
tered what I did not understand"). The first theme—the goodness of God's
purpose—is not something Job can comment on, given that he lacks access
to the prologue and therefore to God's dispute with Satan. Its absence only
reinforces this theme of divine inscrutability.

Divine Inscrutability: The Joseph Narrative
In the Joseph narrative, God aims at great goods: preserving his people
from famine so that they can flourish in Canaan and ultimately bring the
Savior into the world. But God leaves various human beings in the dark that
these great goods are his reason for the evils suffered by Joseph, or even that
there is any reason for the evils. To be sure, in some way that is not explained
to us, *Joseph* ultimately gains knowledge that God intended these events for
good. Otherwise, he would not say, "you meant evil against me, but God
meant it for good" (Gen. 50:20). Perhaps Joseph has this knowledge by special divine revelation to him. Or perhaps this is just part of his overall view
of God, his theology of God's character, as it were, a lens through which he
interprets the world.
But it is quite plausible to think that when various evils were committed against Joseph, neither Joseph's brothers, nor the Midianite traders,
nor Potiphar's wife, nor the cupbearer knew the role that their blameworthy
actions would play in preserving God's people in a time of danger. Jacob,

Potiphar, and Pharaoh would be similarly in the dark, both with respect to the goods God aimed at and the dependence of the goods on the evils. Consider the timing of Joseph's release from prison. If the cupbearer, upon being released from prison, had promptly remembered Joseph's plight, and fulfilled Joseph's request to bring that plight before Pharaoh (Gen. 40:14–15), rather than forget him (Gen. 40:23), then Joseph would have been released earlier in the narrative, prior to the arrival of Pharaoh's dreams and their need for interpretation (Gen. 41:1–8). For all anyone knew, an unneeded and earlier-released Joseph would have been "lost in the crowd," seeking to make his way home to Canaan. How could anyone on the scene know that it was the cupbearer's *failure* to remember Joseph which enabled his remembering of Joseph two years later, precisely when Pharaoh needed an interpretation of his dreams, and thus an event well-timed for Joseph's elevation to a position of authority?

Or again, consider Joseph's own dreams as a child, the sharing of which provoked resentment and jealousy in his brothers (Gen. 37:5–11), which in turn provided them with evil motivation to betray him and sell him abroad (Gen. 37:18–28). No one at the time would have had a clue as to what momentous outcomes turned on childhood dreams. If the analysis in Question 7 was correct—that there can be two sets of intentions behind painful, unsettling, and even morally questionable events—then apart from divine revelation the only intentions available to humans are the human ones. God's method of providence, then, virtually guarantees that the third theme follows closely in the wake of the first two themes. God is not inscrutable despite being good and sovereign. He is inscrutable because of these things.

Divine Inscrutability: The Jesus Narrative

In the Jesus narrative, God aims at great goods: redeeming the world by the atonement of Christ, and displaying his own justice, love, grace, mercy, wisdom, and power. But God leaves various human beings in the dark that these great goods are his reason for the perplexing chain of perverse moral evil suffered by Jesus in the passion narratives, or even that there is any reason for the evils. To be sure, *Jesus* seems to have a firm grasp of the divine providential plan for his suffering and crucifixion:

- "From that time Jesus began to show his disciples that he *must* go to Jerusalem and suffer many things from the elders and chief priests and scribes, and be killed, and on the third day be raised" (Matt. 16:21; cf. Mark 8:31; Luke 9:22; 17:25; 24:6–7).
- "The Son of Man will *certainly* suffer at their hands" (Matt. 17:12).
- "Do you think that I cannot appeal to my Father, and he will at once send me more than twelve legions of angels? But how then should the Scriptures be fulfilled, that it *must* be so?" (Matt. 26:53–54).

- "For I tell you that this Scripture *must* be fulfilled in me: 'And he was numbered with the transgressors.' For what is written about me has its fulfillment" (Luke 22:37).
- "Was it not *necessary* that the Christ should suffer these things and enter into his glory?" (Luke 24:26).
- "Then he said to them, 'These are my words that I spoke to you while I was still with you, that everything written about me in the Law of Moses and the Prophets and the Psalms *must* be fulfilled'" (Luke 24:44).
- "And as Moses lifted up the serpent in the wilderness, so *must* the Son of Man be lifted up" (John 3:14).

But the Jewish leaders, Satan, Judas, Pilate, and the soldiers are all ignorant of the role they play in fulfilling God's redemptive purpose by the cross of Christ. Rather, they have other purposes in mind: the Jewish leaders intend to end Jesus's alleged blasphemy of claiming to be equal to God; Satan intends that Jesus's ministry be an utter failure; Judas intends to earn his silver; Pilate intends to quell growing Jewish discontent before it reaches unmanageable proportions; the soldiers intend to earn their pay. As in the Job and Joseph narratives, so here in the Jesus narrative: considerable access to blameworthy creaturely intentions offers no access at all to divine intentions.

In the Jewish synagogue at Pisidian Antioch, the apostle Paul preached on this theme of creaturely ignorance about the significance of the cross:

> Those who live in Jerusalem and their rulers, because *they did not recognize him nor understand* the utterances of the prophets, which are read every Sabbath, *fulfilled them by condemning him.* And though they found in him no guilt worthy of death, they asked Pilate to have him executed. And when *they had carried out all that was written of him*, they took him down from the tree and laid him in a tomb. (Acts 13:27–29)

By God's good purpose, atonement was provided. By God's sovereign providence, the prophets were fulfilled. But these were accomplished without the *recognition* or *understanding* of the (non-divine) participants. Indeed, without the Gospels, Acts, and New Testament letters, we would be just as ignorant of God's purposes and methods as were the people in Jesus's day.

Paul's Doxology in Romans 11
According to what the apostle Paul teaches in Romans chapter 11, the evil of unbelief—in this case the widespread failure of many first-century Jews to place their faith in Jesus, God's "anointed one" or promised Messiah—is something God intends to work for good. And this good would be unknown even by Paul except for God's revealing it to him. When he learned that "God

has consigned all to disobedience, that he may have mercy on all" (Rom. 11:32; see also Gal 3:22), it led Paul to cry out:

> Oh, the depth of the riches and wisdom and knowledge of God! How unsearchable are his judgments and *how inscrutable his ways!* "For who has known the mind of the Lord, or who has been his counselor?" "Or who has given a gift to him that he might be repaid?" *For from him and through him and to him are all things. To him be glory forever.* Amen. (Rom. 11:33–36)

Here the themes of God's good purpose ("To him be the glory forever"), sovereign providence ("from him and through him . . . are all things"), and inscrutable ways ("how inscrutable his ways!") blend together, just as they do in the Job, Joseph, and Jesus narratives. And by stressing the divine inscrutability in this context, Paul is implying that he would know nothing of this divine plan (explained at length in Romans chapters 9–11) unless it had been revealed to him by God. Certainly the unbelieving Jews, in their refusal to accept Jesus as the Messiah, had no inkling of how God would turn these circumstances to good.

The Dismal Record of Human Guesswork

Imagine you were one of Job's friends or Joseph's brothers or Jesus's tormentors. Would you have guessed correctly as to God's purposes in each of these circumstances? Indeed, we *know* that Job's friends were on the wrong track, as their repeated attempt to trace Job's suffering to his sins is rebuked by God as not speaking rightly of him (Job 42:7).

In fact, on multiple occasions in the Bible, people on the historical scene try to guess as to why a particular evil—whether moral evil or natural evil—has occurred, and they invariably *get it wrong*. Here are three examples. First, Jesus's disciples were mistaken when they speculated that the man born blind was that way because God was punishing either the man or his parents for their sin. Jesus flatly denies their explanation and affirms a higher divine purpose in that case (John 9:1–3). Second, Jesus sharply corrected first-century guessers who suspected, in specific cases, that some people suffered because they "were worse sinners" than others (Luke 13:1–5). Third, when the pagan Maltese natives saw a poisonous viper slither out from a campfire and fasten itself to the apostle Paul's hand, they immediately concluded Paul was being punished by the gods for his sin. In this they were mistaken (Acts 28:3–6).

Summary

God often hides his reasons for why there is suffering and evil. Job, and Job's counselors, were in the dark. Joseph's brothers, Jacob, Potiphar, and

Pharaoh were in the dark. Jesus's tormentors, and even his disciples, were in the dark. But their inability to discern God's reasons was no reason to think he did not have reasons. It is clear to readers of these narratives that God knew what he was doing, even if the participants did not know what that was. Paul's doxology at the end of Romans 11 reinforces these themes of divine goodness, sovereignty, and inscrutability. Finally, when human observers try to guess at God's reasons, they typically get the facts wrong.

REFLECTION QUESTIONS

1. The Job narrative is one of the most extended treatments of God's relation to evil in the entire Bible. Do you agree with the argument given above that Job is intended to be an "everyman," whose circumstances of ignorance are meant to mirror our own?

2. Human scientific knowledge has expanded considerably since God's exposure of Job's ignorance of the natural realm in Job 38–41. Imagine that Job had a PhD in biology, chemistry, physics, geology, zoology, or the like. Would God's speeches still apply to him?

3. Genesis 50:20 indicates that Joseph had *some* sense that God was purposing the evils in his life for good. On the one hand, this is surely a significant piece of knowledge. On the other hand, it is still a limited kind of knowledge. Can you come up with a list of things that Joseph would not know, even granting his faith in the goodness of God's character and the sovereignty of his ways?

4. Bible students regularly claim, rightly, that the message of the cross spans the entire Bible, rather than being restricted to the texts of the Gospels themselves. In that sense, the "Jesus narrative" is the Bible's narrative. How might this affect our understanding of God's *modus operandi* (his "way of working") when it comes to pursuing great goods for his creation? Is the Jesus narrative peripheral or central to how God relates to the world?

5. Is it really true that God can aim at goods for himself? If he is perfect in every way, then what goods can be "added" to him? Is this a misguided way of thinking?

Is Natural Evil Ever "of the Lord"?

Where Are We Going in This Question and the Next?

We are halfway through part 2A of this book, "Questions Related to the Bible." The main goal has been to get the biblical "data" about several topics out there on the table, in full view, so that we have something to work with when we proceed to theology (part 2B), apologetics (part 3), and pastoral practice (part 4). The biblical data so far have been in three categories: the kinds of suffering and evil that occur in the Bible (Question 6), God's aiming at great goods by way of suffering and evil (Question 7), and our lack of access to God's purposes and methods in any particular case of suffering and evil (Question 8).

Some extraordinarily delicate questions remain for us on the horizon. As a means of comforting Christians that "God is in control," texts like Genesis 50:20 from the Joseph narrative may seem to be overused: "You meant evil against me, but God meant it for good." Who said such texts apply to all evil? Perhaps the Job, Joseph, and Jesus narratives, examined at length in the preceding two Questions, are a kind of biblical anomaly. Perhaps we are not meant to develop a biblical theology of suffering and evil from such meager data points. Are there any other cases where natural evil and moral evil can be traced back to God, even in some hazy, yet to be defined sense? That is, does the Bible ever say that numerous cases of suffering and evil are "of the Lord"?

This Question and the next argue that the occurrence of natural evil and moral evil not only *can* come within the providential purpose of God but seem to do so repeatedly. This is simply how the Bible often speaks when relating God to the suffering and evil in the world. What we learned in the Job, Joseph, and Jesus narratives is not an exception to but several instances of a broader teaching about God spread liberally through the Bible. This chapter will focus on natural evil, while the next will focus on moral evil.

Can Various Natural Evils Be Traced Back to Divine Purposes?

Questions 2 and 3 distinguished "natural evil" and "moral evil" by their *causes*, where these causes are "how nature goes on" (quite independently of human willing) and "human defect of will" (quite independently of how nature goes on). It is important to point out that we are speaking here of *immediate* causes. Various pains and sufferings having immediate causes seems compatible with having God as their "ultimate" cause. It appears that many biblical passages suggest that God is "behind" various natural evils (and moral evils) in a way that is "above" their merely earthly causes.

Paradigm examples of natural evil include famine, drought, rampaging wild animals, disease, birth defects like blindness or deafness, plague, stormy weather, and even death itself. But in many cases, it seems that these effects are not *merely* due to "how nature goes on" but—as with the fire, wind, and disease visited upon Job, his family, and his livestock—can be traced back to God himself.

Famine
> And *I will heap disasters upon them*; I will spend my arrows on them; *they shall be wasted with hunger*, and devoured by plague and poisonous pestilence; I will send the teeth of beasts against them, with the venom of things that crawl in the dust. (Deut. 32:23–24)

Additionally:
- The famine "is fixed by God, and God will shortly bring it about" (Gen. 41:32).
- God "has called for a famine" (2 Kings 8:1).
- God "summoned a famine" (Ps. 105:16).
- God "is taking away . . . all support of bread" (Isa. 3:1).
- God "will break the supply of bread" (Ezek. 4:16; 14:13).
- God will send "deadly arrows of famine" (Ezek. 5:16).
- God "will send famine" (Ezek. 5:17; 14:21).
- God "will take back my grain" (Hos. 2:9).
- God "gave you . . . lack of bread" (Amos 4:6).
- God "struck you with blight and with mildew" (Amos 4:9; Hag. 2:17).

Drought
> And *I have called for a drought on the land and the hills*, on the grain, the new wine, the oil, on what the ground brings forth, on man and beast, and on all their labors. (Hag. 1:11)

Additionally:
- God "will strike . . . you with drought" (Deut. 28:22).
- God will "shut up" heaven so "there is no rain" (1 Kings 8:35).

- God "shut up the heavens so that there is no rain" (2 Chron. 7:13).
- God "turns rivers into a desert, springs of water into thirsty ground" (Ps. 107:33).
- God "is taking away . . . all support of water" (Isa. 3:1).
- God commands "the clouds that they rain no rain" (Isa. 5:6).
- God can "make her like a parched land, and kill her with thirst" (Hos. 2:3).
- God "withheld the rain from you" and sent "no rain on another city" (Amos 4:7).

Rampaging Wild Animals
> And *I will let loose the wild beasts against you*, which shall bereave you of your children and destroy your livestock and make you few in number, so that your roads shall be deserted. (Lev. 26:22)

Additionally:
- God "will send hornets before you" (Exod. 23:28; Deut. 7:20; Josh. 24:12).
- God "sent fiery serpents among the people" (Num. 21:6).
- God "will send the teeth of beasts against them" (Deut. 32:24).
- God "has given him to the lion, which has torn him and killed him, according to the word that the LORD spoke to him" (1 Kings 13:26).
- God "sent lions among them, which killed some of them" (2 Kings 17:25).
- God sends "among you serpents, adders that cannot be charmed, and they shall bite you" (Jer. 8:17).
- God sends "wild beasts against you" (Ezek. 5:17).
- God causes "wild beasts to pass through the land, and they ravage it" (Ezek. 14:15).
- God sends "upon Jerusalem . . . wild beasts" (Ezek. 14:21).
- God will give "whoever is in the open field . . . to the beasts to be devoured" (Ezek. 33:27).

Disease and Sickness
> Behold, *the LORD will bring a great plague* on your people, your children, your wives, and all your possessions. (2 Chron. 21:14)

Additionally:
- God "afflicted Pharaoh and his house with great plagues" (Gen. 12:17).
- God "sent a plague on the people" (Exod. 32:35).
- God "will visit you . . . with wasting disease and fever" (Lev. 26:16).
- God "will send pestilence among you" (Lev. 26:25).
- God "struck down the people with a very great plague" (Num. 11:33).

- God "will strike them with the pestilence" (Num. 14:12).
- God "will make the pestilence stick to you" (Deut. 28:21).
- God "will strike you with wasting disease and with fever" (Deut. 28:22).
- God "will strike you with the boils of Egypt, and with tumors and scabs and itch" (Deut. 28:27).
- God "will bring upon you again all the diseases of Egypt" (Deut. 28:60).
- God "afflicted the child . . . and he became sick" (2 Sam. 12:15).
- God "sent a pestilence on Israel" (2 Sam. 24:15; 1 Chron. 21:14).
- God "touched the king, so that he was a leper to the day of his death" (2 Kings 15:5; see 2 Chron. 26:19–20).
- God will "send pestilence among my people" (2 Chron. 7:13).
- God "struck him . . . with an incurable disease" (2 Chron. 21:18).
- God "sent a wasting disease among them" (Ps. 106:15).
- Lazarus's illness "is for the glory of God, so that the Son of God may be glorified through it" (John 11:4).

Birth Defects (such as blindness and deafness)
> Then the LORD said to him, "Who has made man's mouth? Who makes him mute, or deaf, or seeing, or blind? *Is it not I, the LORD?*" (Exod. 4:11)

> As he passed by, he saw a man blind from birth. And his disciples asked him, "Rabbi, who sinned, this man or his parents, that he was born blind?" Jesus answered, "It was not that this man sinned, or his parents, *but that the works of God might be displayed in him.*" (John 9:1–3)

Ten Egyptian Plagues
These include:
- turning the Nile river to blood (Exod. 7:14–24)
- swarms of frogs from the Nile river (8:1–15)
- swarms of gnats (8:16–19)
- swarms of flies (8:20–32)
- death of Egyptian livestock (9:1–7)
- boils on the skin of men and animals (9:8–12)
- hailstones (9:13–35)
- swarms of locusts (10:1–20)
- total darkness (10:21–29)
- the death of firstborn Egyptians (11:4–10; 12:12–13, 27–30)

Stormy Weather
> Whatever the LORD pleases, he does, in heaven and on earth, in the *seas* and all deeps. He it is who makes the *clouds* rise

at the end of the earth, who makes *lightnings* for the rain and brings forth the *wind* from his storehouses. (Ps. 135:6–7)

Additionally:
- God "will send rain on the earth forty days and forty nights, and every living thing that I have made I will blot out from the face of the ground" (Gen. 7:4).
- God "threw the Egyptians into the midst of the sea" (Exod. 14:27; Ps. 136:15).
- "The crash of your thunder was in the whirlwind" and "your lightnings lighted up the world" (Ps. 77:18).
- "Pursue them with your tempest and terrify them with your hurricane" (Ps. 83:15).
- God's "lightnings light up the world" (Ps. 97:4).
- God "makes his messengers winds, his ministers a flaming fire" (Ps. 104:4).
- God "raised the stormy wind, which lifted up the waves of the sea" (Ps. 107:25).
- God "prepares rain for the earth" (Ps. 147:8).
- God "gives snow . . . frost . . . ice . . . cold . . . wind . . . waters" (Ps. 147:16–18).
- "Praise the LORD . . . fire and hail, snow and mist, stormy wind fulfilling his word" (Ps. 148:7–8).
- God "hurled a great wind upon the sea" (Jonah 1:4).
- God's "way is in whirlwind and storm . . . he rebukes the sea and makes it dry; he dries up all the rivers" (Nah. 1:3–4).
- God "scattered them with a whirlwind" (Zech. 7:14).

Death Itself
> The LORD kills and brings to life; he brings down to Sheol and raises up. The LORD makes poor and makes rich; he brings low and he exalts. (1 Sam. 2:6–7)

Additionally:
- "I kill and I make alive; I wound and I heal" (Deut. 32:39).
- "It was the will of the LORD to put them to death" (1 Sam. 2:25).
- "The LORD struck Nabal, and he died" (1 Sam. 25:38).
- "God struck him down there because of his error" (2 Sam. 6:7).
- God "will make him fall by the sword in his own land" (2 Kings 19:7).
- "The LORD put him to death" (1 Chron. 10:14).
- "The LORD struck him down, and he died" (2 Chron. 13:20).
- God "killed the strongest of them" (Ps. 78:31).
- God "struck down every firstborn in Egypt" (Pss. 78:51; 105:36; 135:8; 136:10).
- God "killed mighty kings" (Pss. 135:10; 136:18).

What Are Three Cautions in Interpreting These Passages?

These Passages Don't Teach That Every Natural Evil Is a Punishment for Sin

Clearly, a broad swath of natural evils can be traced back to the will of God. But we must be careful here. On the one hand, most of the cases above are clearly instances of divine punishment or chastisement for sin (once one consults the surrounding context). God seems to use natural disasters and painful effects of nature as a way of rebuking or punishing humans for their sin. There is no way around this, and if God is judge of all, it seems fitting that he is in control of how he brings about his judgment.

But it is equally clear that these texts, by themselves, do not support the idea that every or even most instances of "natural evils" in the world are an individual punishment of some sort from God. As we saw at the end of the last Question, the Bible repeatedly warns against the temptation to make that inference in any individual case. We are simply too ignorant of the divine intentions, of the range of divine providential purposes, to make a reliable guess. The blind man was not born blind because of his sin (John 9:1–3), Jesus did not let Lazarus die because of his sin (John 11:1–6), and Paul was not attacked by the snake because of God's judgment (Acts 28:3–5). Yes, the above lists of verses covering multiple categories of natural evil do seem to establish that no one would go wrong in tracing natural evils back to "the will of God." But whether "the will of God" behind natural evils is one of punishment is something we simply cannot read off from the events themselves. Where God has not spoken, we must remain silent.

These Passages Do Not Explicitly Answer All the Questions We May Have

These texts do not answer every question. The sooner we recognize this, the better. How exactly does God relate to natural evils? Yes, many natural evils are being traced back to God, but the details are rather vague. Are these passages best interpreted as teaching:

- God *wills* suffering and evil to exist, or
- God *causes* suffering and evil to exist, or
- God *intends* suffering and evil to exist, or
- God is *responsible* for the suffering and evil that exists?

Many quite reasonable and pious Bible students would find it difficult to accept all the claims on this list. At the very least, all should agree that it is not entirely clear what these passages are specifically teaching. In subsequent Questions, all these possible interpretations will be further considered. The point of this chapter and the next is simply to get these puzzling passages out in the open so that we can subsequently reflect on them. According to the apostle Paul, "Whatever was written in former days was written for our instruction, that through endurance and through the encouragement of the

Scriptures we might have hope" (Rom. 15:4). Surely these passages fall into the category of being "written in former days" and "written for our instruction," and therefore deserve our attention, though the "encouragement" and "hope" they offer might not be clear until later discussion. This is why we must proceed to theology (in part 2B), which is a form of rational reflection that must always *start with* the biblical data. Further theological reflection is needed to answer some of our questions.

These Passages Can Have Pastoral Value for Us If Properly Interpreted

Knowing that painful circumstances produced by nature are merely instruments in the hands of a good God, who knows what he is doing, may make all the difference in the world to whether we can bear up against such evils. The events are not random events, unanticipated by God, pockets of his creation not subject to his providential purpose. Rather, the highest and most ultimate explanation of why the event occurred is in terms of God's wise and good intentions. This is not a perspective foisted on the text via *a priori* philosophical maneuvering. Rather, it arises naturally from a consideration of the very details of the text, again and again. It is an evident and repeated fact that even the worst of natural disasters can be included in the broader purposes of a good God.

The context of divine judgment, so prevalent in the passages summarized above, provides a striking and perhaps unexpected illustration of pastoral value. Christians are rightly accustomed to thinking about the final day of judgment, and about the gospel as God's means to avoid that judgment (since the gospel brings the gracious message of one who was judged in our place). But that day is a unique and final day, and no judgment that precedes it should be equated with it. So, what is God up to when he "judges sin" *prior* to that great and terrible day? The fact of the matter is that any divine judgment that falls short of final judgment can be taken as a warning to repent while the day of gospel mercy is still here. Local and limited judgments, terrible as they are, indicate that God is not done with us yet. It is a large part of the message of the Old Testament prophets to present earthly judgments in that way. So not only would we be unwise to assume that all or most natural evils are God's judgment. We would also be unwise to assume that the natural evils which *may* be God's judgment are therefore evidence that God has abandoned us. The opposite is the case: God draws near in judgment *because* he cares about salvation. Harbingers of the final day are a kind of mercy meant to lead us to repentance before that final day (Rom. 2:4).

Summary

Theology, apologetics, and pastoral practice should always begin by examining the biblical data, even if they do not end there. The Scriptures seem to teach that many cases of natural evil—famine, drought, rampaging wild animals, disease and sickness, birth defects like blindness and deafness, plague, stormy weather, and even death itself—can be traced back to God. Though many of these cases constitute God's punishment for sin, these texts do not teach that every or even most natural evils are in this category. Nor do these texts, by themselves, answer every question we might have about how precisely God relates to these evils. Finally, these passages can have pastoral value for us if they are rightly interpreted.

REFLECTION QUESTIONS

1. Should theology, apologetics, and pastoral practice always begin by consulting Scripture? Why is it so bad if we begin elsewhere, as long as we consult the Scriptures somewhere in this process?

2. Some might think that natural disasters are either caused by nature *or* caused by God, but not both. How might the passages in this chapter imply otherwise?

3. Can you think of any other areas where it is important to accept that "where God has not spoken, we must remain silent"? And is this *always* the case, for any topic whatsoever?

4. Why might someone think it is *better* to believe that some events are "random events, unanticipated by God, pockets of his creation not subject to his providential purpose"? What important concerns drive their belief here? Even if nothing is ultimately random, could it still be true that such people are *right* to have the concerns they do?

5. The passages about the blind man (John 9:1–3) and Lazarus (John 11:1–6) seem to give us a glimpse of other purposes for natural evil, beyond punishment. What might those purposes be? (We will return to this topic in Questions 22–26.)

Is Moral Evil Ever "of the Lord"?

Reviewing Our Two-Part Definitions of "Natural Evil" and "Moral Evil"

As we saw in Question 2 and again in Question 9, the phrases "natural evil" and "moral evil" each have two-part definitions, corresponding to the two words in each phrase. In each phrase, "evil" refers to *the suffering itself*—e.g., physical pain, psychological scarring, social isolation, and so on. And in each phrase, "natural" or "moral" refers to *the immediate cause* of the suffering: nature or defect of will. We can say something about each part of these definitions.

First, with respect to pain and suffering, presumably God is *opposed* to it. There is nothing good about suffering, in and of itself. All things being equal, no one would prefer to suffer. But as we saw in Questions 7 and 9, that does not preclude God including the pain and suffering of natural evil within his providential purposes. Whether God has good reason for doing so—for instance, because of what suffering leads to—is something we will investigate when we get to "apologetics" in part 3 of this book.

Second, with respect to the immediate cause of suffering, God is well able to use *nature* to bring about pain and suffering. This was the import of the passages considered in the previous Question. But is God also able to use *defective human will* to bring about pain and suffering? To ask this is to ask whether moral evil can in some significant sense be traced back to the providential purpose of God. That is the "biblical data" to be investigated in the current Question.

Paradigm cases of moral evil include disobeying God's law, disobeying parents, committing adultery, rejecting wise counsel, murdering kings and their families, deceiving others as a false prophet, and tempting innocent people to sin. Could the occurrence of any of these events ever be "of the Lord"? If the earlier question of natural evil was delicate, this is more so, since bringing God into too close a relation to moral evil would seem to generate a double challenge: God's character might be impugned, and human freedom might be denied. The main burden of Questions 13–15 will be to address these very important concerns. Still, as surprising as it may seem, the Bible presents God as having such meticulous control over the course of human history that moral evils in the categories just named can be regarded as "of the Lord." Even as God does not *merely* permit nature to "do its thing," so he does not *merely* permit humans to "do their thing." Without erasing or suppressing the intentionality of creatures—and this includes their deliberations, their reasoning, their choosing between alternatives they consider and reflect upon—God's own intentionality stands above and behind the responsible choices of his creatures.

Though moral evil was already represented in the Job narrative (the Sabeans' murder and theft), the Joseph narrative (Joseph's brothers betraying and selling their brother into slavery), and the Jesus narrative (the morally evil role of some Jewish leaders, Judas, and Pilate in the crucifixion of an innocent man), Scripture reveals several further examples of the occurrence of moral evil being due to divine providence. In each case, the sinful intentions of humans are to be distinguished from the righteous intentions of God.

Can Any Moral Evils Be Traced Back to Divine Purposes?

Samson's Request for a Foreign Wife (Judg. 14:1–4)
Samson was one of the last deliverers that God raised up in the period of the "judges," temporary leaders in the transitional period between Joshua's generalship and Saul's kingship. At this time, Israelites were clearly forbidden from marrying non-Israelites, not for racial reasons but religious ones: pagan outsiders would corrupt and undermine the religious devotion of their Israelite spouses (Exod. 34:16; Deut. 7:3–4; cf. 1 Kings 11:1–8). But Samson sinfully desired a foreign wife for himself, contrary to God's command:

> Samson went down to Timnah, and at Timnah he saw one of the daughters of the Philistines. Then he came up and told his father and mother, "I saw one of the daughters of the Philistines at Timnah. Now get her for me as my wife." But his father and mother said to him, "Is there not a woman among the daughters of your relatives, or among all our people, that you must go to take a wife from the uncircumcised Philistines?" *But Samson said to his father, "Get her for me, for she is right in my eyes." His father and mother did not know that it was from the LORD*, for he was seeking an opportunity against the Philistines. At that time the Philistines ruled over Israel. (Judg. 14:1–4)

The narrative never portrays Samson's request here as anything but sinful—besides being contrary to God's law, it led to quite a few tragic events, involving much bloodshed and destruction. But while this was a sinful request on the part of Samson, the Bible reveals something that Samson's parents could not possibly have discerned in their situation: Samson's request "was from the Lord," to carry out God's larger purposes at that stage in Israel's history.

Eli's Sons' Disobedience to Their Father (1 Sam. 2:23–25)

Eli the priest rightly rebuked his sons Hophni and Phinehas (also priests) for they "treated the offering of the LORD with contempt" (1 Sam. 2:17). Eli's parental concern was too little, too late: "But they would not listen to the voice of their father, for it was the will of the LORD to put them to death" (1 Sam. 2:25). The "for" clause indicates an explanation for what precedes. Rather than saying that God put the sons to death because of this sin, the passage says the reverse: their sinful rejection of their father's pleading happened because of "the will of the LORD" to put them to death. Obviously, the choice of Hophni and Phinehas to reject their father was grounded in the human will of Hophni and Phinehas. That was the choice *they* made. But their actions themselves are explained in light of a higher purpose of God: God planned to put them to death (1 Sam. 2:34), and he eventually did so by way of battle with the Philistines (1 Sam. 4:11).

Absalom's Adultery (2 Sam. 12:11–12; 16:22)

David commits adultery with Bathsheba and kills her husband Uriah the Hittite, and God sends the prophet Nathan to rebuke David for his sin and pronounce his chastisement against David:

> Thus says the LORD, "Behold, *I will raise up evil against you out of your own house.* And I will take your wives before your eyes and give them to your neighbor, and he shall lie with your wives in the sight of this sun. For you did it secretly, but I will do this thing before all Israel and before the sun." (2 Sam. 12:11–12)

The "evil" (*ra'ah*) God promises to raise up against King David is the evil of David's concubines being given to his son Absalom to lie with, which is indeed what happened (2 Sam. 16:22). Concubinage is a form of marriage (see Judg. 19:9), which is why this episode was so odious to the Israelites (2 Sam. 16:21). Standing behind the sinful human intentions ("Absalom went in to his father's concubines in the sight of all Israel") are the righteous divine intentions ("I will raise up evil against you out of your own house").

Absalom, Rehoboam, and Amaziah Rejecting Wise Counsel (2 Sam. 17:14; 1 Kings 12:15; 2 Chron. 25:20)

Presumably it is a sin not to listen to wise counsel, as the book of Proverbs indicates multiple times (Prov. 11:14; 12:15; 13:10; 19:20). But three kings (Absalom, Rehoboam, and Amaziah) each reject wise counsel because such rejection was "ordained" by the Lord, "brought about by the Lord," or "was of God":

> Absalom and all the men of Israel said, "The counsel of Hushai the Archite is better than the counsel of Ahithophel." *For the* LORD *had ordained* to defeat the good counsel of Ahithophel, so that the LORD might bring harm upon Absalom. (2 Sam. 17:14)

> So the king [Rehoboam] did not listen to the people, *for it was a turn of affairs brought about by the* LORD that he might fulfill his word, which the LORD spoke by Ahijah the Shilonite to Jeroboam the son of Nebat. (1 Kings 12:15)

> But Amaziah would not listen [to Joash], *for it was of God*, in order that he might give them into the hand of their enemies, because they had sought the gods of Edom. (2 Chron. 25:20)

Assassination of Jeroboam's House (1 Kings 14:10), and of Sennacherib King of Assyria (2 Kings 19:7)

Because of Jeroboam's sin in making the golden calves (1 Kings 12:26–33), God says that he "will cut off from Jeroboam every male" (1 Kings 14:10). Four verses later, we learn *how* God will do this: "The LORD will raise up for himself a king over Israel [Baasha] who shall cut off the house of Jeroboam today" (1 Kings 14:14). And this is exactly what Baasha does: "And as soon as he was king, he killed all the house of Jeroboam" (1 Kings 15:29). So God cuts off the descendants by way of Baasha cutting off the descendants. *God* does not commit murder, but he does cut off the descendants *by way of* Baasha's murders. Baasha's actions were not righteous; indeed, Baasha's own descendants are destroyed precisely because Baasha murdered Jeroboam's descendants (1 Kings 16:7, 11). God purposes that these means shall be used, but the one who murders is Baasha, not God.

Likewise, God says regarding Sennacherib king of Assyria: "Behold, I will put a spirit in him, so that he shall hear a rumor and return to his own land, and I will make him fall by the sword in his own land" (2 Kings 19:7). How does God "make him fall by the sword"? Sennacherib's sons assassinate him: "And as he was worshiping in the house of Nisroch his god, Adrammelech and Sharezer, his sons, struck him down with the sword and escaped into the land of Ararat. And Esarhaddon his son reigned in his place" (2 Kings 19:37). As surprising as it might seem, the moral evil of the sons is how "the LORD saved Hezekiah and the inhabitants of Jerusalem from the hand of Sennacherib king of Assyria" (2 Chron. 32:22). There is divine intentionality ("I will make him fall by the sword in his own land") *and* human intentionality ("his sons struck him down with the sword"), and neither erases the other.

The Lying Spirit in the Mouths of the Prophets (1 Kings 22:20–23)
     In the presence of Ahab king of Israel, the prophet Micaiah recounts God's purpose to "entice Ahab, that he may go up and fall at Ramoth-gilead" (1 Kings 22:20). The Lord considers "by what means" that enticement shall take place, and a spirit answers to God, "I will entice him" (1 Kings 22:21–22). As Micaiah tells it, divine intentionality and creaturely agency combine for a righteous purpose: "Now therefore behold, the LORD has put a lying spirit in the mouth of all these your prophets; the LORD has declared disaster for you" (1 Kings 22:23). That is, God assures disaster for this wicked king *by way of* false prophets deceiving Ahab about Ahab's prospects for battle victory. God's purpose is that Ahab fails, while the lying spirit's purpose is to deceive.

The Death of Saul (1 Chron. 10:4–6, 13–14)
     Saul was rejected by God as king of Israel because of his sin, and he was eventually wounded in battle by the Philistines. Saul then commits suicide when his armor-bearer won't finish the job:

> Then Saul said to his armor-bearer, "Draw your sword and thrust me through with it, lest these uncircumcised come and mistreat me." But his armor-bearer would not, for he feared greatly. *Therefore Saul took his own sword and fell upon it.* And when his armor-bearer saw that Saul was dead, he also fell upon his sword and died. Thus Saul died; he and his three sons and all his house died together. (1 Chron. 10:4–6)

Who killed Saul? The answer is perfectly straightforward: Saul killed Saul, by deliberately falling on his own sword. But to leave the answer there would be telling only one side of the story, for the narrative goes on to say:

> So Saul died for his breach of faith. He broke faith with the LORD in that he did not keep the command of the LORD, and also consulted a medium, seeking guidance. He did not seek guidance from the LORD. *Therefore the LORD put him to death* and turned the kingdom over to David the son of Jesse. (1 Chron. 10:13–14)

Who killed Saul? Again, the answer is perfectly straightforward: "Therefore the LORD put him to death." God killed Saul. Of course, we can combine the teaching of both passages by saying that God killed Saul *by means of* Saul killing Saul. The moral evil of Saul's suicide—that is, Saul's responsible human agency—was how God put him to death. The account would be incomplete if we left out either of these claims.

Satan Tempting Jesus (Matt. 4:1–11)

When Matthew recounts the circumstances of Jesus being tempted by Satan, his description is perhaps more precise than many interpreters realize:

> Then Jesus was led up by the Spirit into the wilderness to be tempted by the devil. (Matt. 4:1)

Who led Jesus into the wilderness? The Spirit, that is, God himself. And for what purpose was he led there by the Spirit? "To be tempted by the devil." Of course, *Satan* is the tempter here (Matt. 4:1, 3, 5–6, 8–9), not God. God tempts no one (James 1:13)! Nevertheless, *that* Jesus should be tempted by Satan comes within the purpose of God (it is *why* the Spirit led Jesus into the wilderness). God's purpose is a good purpose: Jesus's temptations were a crucial ingredient in his living a perfectly righteous life, thus fitting him to be our perfect substitute upon the cross (Heb. 2:10; 5:7–10), and a perfect help in time of need (Heb. 2:18; 4:15–16). The three themes of Questions 7–8 emerge again. God *aims at a great good*: Jesus's perseverance amid temptation. God intends that great good to come about *by way of various evils* (here, Satan's evil solicitations to Jesus that he sin). And God *leaves humans in the dark* regarding his reason for the evils. (We only know of God's intention here by way of special divine revelation in Matthew 4:1.)

Again, to be clear: God does not tempt Jesus, but he does test Jesus by way of Satan's temptations. God purposes that these means shall be used (Satan's temptations), but the one who uses them is Satan, not God. There could not be a clearer case of two sets of intentions entirely opposed to each other: God's (righteous) intention that Jesus succeed, and Satan's (wicked) intention that Jesus fail.

Three Observations About These Passages

The Goodness of God Is Highlighted in Each of These Passages

The defeat of God's enemies, God's judgment on sin, God's chastisement for sin, the defeat of foolish or idolatrous kings, the equipping of Jesus to be our Savior—these are all *good* things which God intends by way of the occurrence of the moral evils considered in this chapter. The goodness of God's intentions is to be contrasted with the wickedness of the creaturely intentions that (unwittingly) bring about the good things God intends. There is a depth to divine providence that is fitting for how a transcendent being governs the universe. But that providence is always on behalf of good purposes through and through.

Most of the Cases Considered Are from the Old Testament

The Old Testament is often caricatured as a dry collection of genealogies and obsolete law codes. Nothing could be further from the truth. The Old Testament narratives present a God who is worthy to be trusted even in the worst of times, especially by those who do not have "the whole story" about what God is up to. A large part of the literary power of the Bible's narrative, and the spiritual encouragement it offers, rest upon this interplay between the ignorance of the human actors and the wisdom of divine providence, and nowhere is this seen more clearly than in the historical portions of the Old Testament.

We Ultimately Have Nothing to Fear from the Most Fearsome People in the World and in Our Lives

Proverbs 21:1 says, "The king's heart is a stream of water in the hand of the LORD; he turns it wherever he will." Especially in ancient times, a king's decree could adversely affect the welfare of thousands. If God has control over these unrivaled potentates, how much more over the less powerful people with whom we interact every day? Their intentions for evil cannot compete with God's ability to accomplish his good ends. There is nothing shameful about our very real and understandable emotions of fear and dismay in the face of evil people. But we should find encouragement in the fact that their machinations cannot ultimately thwart God's care for us.

Summary

Even as God can use nature to bring about pain and suffering for his good purposes, God can use defective human will to accomplish the same. Creaturely intentions, no matter how wicked, are not able to thwart (and, indeed, they often carry out) more ultimate divine intentions, which are always good. Scripture seems to indicate that paradigm cases of moral evil—including disobeying God's law, disobeying parents, committing adultery, rejecting wise counsel, murdering kings and their families, deceiving others as a false prophet, and tempting innocent people to sin—can be traced back to the providential purpose of God. The goodness of God, revealed especially in Old Testament narratives, can be the means of quelling our fear and encouraging us in our circumstances today.

REFLECTION QUESTIONS

1. Have any of the passages in this chapter explained *how* God "ordains" or "brings about" these events that are said to be "the will of the Lord"? Or are they silent on that point?

2. Of the two dangers explicitly noted in this chapter—"impugning God's character" and "denying human freedom"—which do you think would have the worse consequences for our faith, and why? (If you think the dangers are roughly equal, make a case for that view instead.)

3. One main goal of this Question and the previous one was to show that the Job, Joseph, and Jesus narratives are not anomalies but part of a broader teaching of Scripture about how divine providence relates to evil. Did these chapters make their case? What doubts remain?

4. The case of Sennacherib king of Assyria seems to indicate that God's providence extends beyond Israelites, to pagan rulers and the rest of the world. Why might that be an important thing for contemporary Christians to consider?

5. The Bible can sometimes give two or more answers to a single question (e.g., "Who killed Saul?"). Must this mean that truth is contradictory, or can it instead mean that reality is more complicated than it first appears? What is the difference?

Does God Will *All* Suffering and Evil?

Should We Universalize These Particulars?

Our survey of biblical data in the last four Questions has given us a lot of particulars: about the various evils in the Job, Joseph, and Jesus narratives (Questions 7–8), and about many natural evils and moral evils which occur in the scriptural history beyond those narratives (Questions 9–10). This biblical data seems to indicate that the cases of pain and suffering so far discussed can be traced back to the will of a good God whose good intentions are to be distinguished from the bad intentions of creaturely perpetrators. That conclusion would be surprising to many in our increasingly secular culture. But an even more surprising (and perhaps unwelcome) conclusion is on the horizon: it might be that all evils whatsoever can be traced back to and explained by the providential purpose of God.

But is that idea not an unwise and irresponsible hasty generalization from specific, discrete particulars? That is an important concern—surely we do not want to go *beyond* the scriptural testimony, especially on so sensitive a topic, and one fraught with many implications for our view of God and human beings. But it might be that this universal conclusion about all suffering and evil is properly supported by many genuinely "universal" Scripture texts that address the topic. If so, then perhaps the particular texts we have seen so far are best understood as a kind of illustration of what these more general texts are teaching. The three kinds of "universal" Scripture text considered in this chapter pertain to how God relates to all calamity, to all human decision-making, and to all events whatsoever. After considering these categories in turn, we will close with some appropriate cautions and application.

God's Relation to All Calamity (Eccl. 7:13–14; Isa. 45:7; Lam. 3:37–38; Amos 3:6)

The "plain vanilla," common, straightforward Hebrew terms for "good" and "evil" in the Old Testament are *tov* and *ra'ah*, respectively. And the Bible is not silent about whether *tov* (as a category) and *ra'ah* (as a category) can be traced back to the work of God's providence:

> *Consider the work of God*: who can make straight *what he has made crooked?* In the day of prosperity [*tov*] be joyful, and in the day of adversity [*ra'ah*] consider: *God has made the one as well as the other,* so that man may not find out anything that will be after him. (Eccl. 7:13–14)

"The day of adversity" covers the full range of natural evils and moral evils that occur in God's world. (A search on *ra'ah* will reveal this.) And this is said to be "the work of God" and that which "God has made"—where "work" and "made" are the Hebrew *asah*, often used to speak of God's work of creation (Gen. 1:7, 16, 25–26, 31; 2:2–4, 18; 3:1). With respect to "the day of prosperity [*tov*]" and "the day of adversity [*ra'ah*]," "God has made the one as well as the other." Thus, Job was right to rebuke his faithless wife: "Shall we receive good [*tov*] from God, and shall we not receive evil [*ra'ah*]?" (Job 2:10).

Does the use of such "creation" language imply that God *directly* and *immediately* brings about both *tov* and *ra'ah*? Not necessarily. God's work of creation may involve, to a greater or lesser degree, God's use of *means*. The fruit is "made" (*asah*) by the fruit trees, even as vegetation is "sprouted" by the earth and seed is "yielded" by the plants (Gen. 1:11–12). God "gives light" on the earth by way of the sun and moon (Gen. 1:14–18), and the earth "brings forth" living creatures according to their kinds (Gen. 1:24–25). Even as God's work of creation may in these ways involve him using means, rather than bringing about everything directly or immediately, so God's work of providence (with respect to *tov* and *ra'ah*) may also involve him using means. The use of "creation" language does not require *or* rule out the use of means. But it does trace these elements of the world ultimately back to God.[1]

The wording in Ecclesiastes is not an anomaly. We find similar "creation" language in Isaiah, applied again to *ra'ah*:

> I form light and create darkness;
> I make well-being [*shalom*] and create calamity [*ra*];
> I am the LORD, who does all these things. (Isa. 45:7)

---

1. Whether God's work of creation in the Genesis narrative involved, to a greater or lesser degree, God's use of means is profitably considered in Questions 6, 12–13, and 38 of Kenneth D. Keathley and Mark F. Rooker, *40 Questions About Creation and Evolution* (Grand Rapids: Kregel Academic, 2014). In addition, God is the Creator of every human being since Adam and Eve, including us. But he used the means of our parents to create us.

Here, the Hebrew words "form" (*yatsar*, Gen. 2:7–8, 19), "create" (*bara*, Gen. 1:1, 21, 27; 2:3–4; 5:1–2; 6:7), and "make"/"does" (*asah*, see prev. references) are all creation-words used in the Genesis narrative, and Isaiah connects *bara* to *ra*. There are no qualifications here; the references are to light as such, darkness as such, well-being and calamity as such. God speaks similarly through Jeremiah:

> Who has spoken and it came to pass, unless the LORD has commanded it? *Is it not from the mouth of the Most High that good [tov] and bad [raʾah] come?* (Lam. 3:37–38)

God's "command" as a King comes from his "mouth"—it is his declaration that such-and-such *shall be*. This is God's command as "decree," as when he commands "Let there be light" (Gen. 1:3). Again, what Ecclesiastes, Isaiah, and Lamentations are saying via their creation language is that *tov* and *raʾah* are willed by God; they are not commenting on *how* God brings his will about.

Notice that the implied answers to these two rhetorical questions in Lamentations 3 are: "no one" and "yes." Nothing happens except if God has decreed it. Calamities (in general) and good things (in general) come from the Lord. There are no contextual qualifiers here, and we should be reluctant to arbitrarily impose them. Finally, Amos:

> Is a trumpet blown in a city, and the people are not afraid? *Does disaster [raʾah] come to a city, unless the LORD has done it?* (Amos 3:6)

Again, "done" in "the LORD has done it" is *asah*, a creation-word. There is no doubt that the four texts just cited are mysterious, particularly in their refusal to divulge *how* God brings his will to pass. But they are not *completely* mysterious: God has made the day of *raʾah*, God creates *raʾah*, it is from his mouth that *raʾah* comes, and it is the Lord's doing that *raʾah* comes to a city. Each text seems to be tracing calamities as such back to the will of God.

God's Relation to All Human Decision-Making (Prov. 16:9; 19:21; 20:24; 21:1; Jer. 10:23)

The second category of "universal" Scripture text pertains to how God relates to all human decision-making—whether these creaturely decisions aim at good, evil, or are relatively neutral. In some way, even these decisions are "established" by God or "from the Lord" or subject to God's "purpose" or "turned" by his will:

> The heart of man plans his way, but the LORD establishes his steps. (Prov. 16:9)

> Many are the plans in the mind of a man, but it is the purpose
> of the LORD that will stand. (Prov. 19:21)

> A man's steps are from the LORD; how then can man under-
> stand his way? (Prov. 20:24)

> The king's heart is a stream of water in the hand of the LORD;
> he turns it wherever he will. (Prov. 21:1)

> I know, O LORD, that the way of man is not in himself, that it
> is not in man who walks to direct his steps. (Jer. 10:23)

Again, there is mystery here, and it is important not to treat these texts
like a wet dishrag that we twist to squeeze out what may not be there. *How*
does the Lord establish the steps of a man who plans his way? *How* does God's
purpose still "stand" when a man's actual plans are for evil? *How* are the steps
"from" the Lord? *How* does he "turn" the heart "wherever he will"? These
scriptures are completely silent on these points. Presumably God's method of
providence preserves our identity as creatures distinct from him, and is more
sophisticated than a divine hand coming down out of heaven that pushes Saul
down on his sword (1 Chron. 10:13–14), or slaps the Egyptians silly until they
burn with hatred toward the Israelites (Ps. 105:23–25). Secret voices were not
whispering in the ears of Joseph's brothers, "Do it! Do it!" (Gen. 50:20). The
Roman soldiers were not dragged along by a Death Star–like tractor beam
and forced to drive in the nails (Acts 4:27–28).

The Anglican theologian Austin Farrer was therefore on to something
when, in his book *Faith and Speculation*, he expressed skepticism about the
means of the divine causation, saying that it is essentially hidden from us:
"Both the divine and the human actions remain real and therefore free in
the union between them; not knowing the modality of the divine action we
cannot pose the problem of their mutual relation."[2] But not *everything* is
hidden. The all-embracing character of divine providence is not hidden.

God's Relation to All Events Whatsoever (Ps. 115:3; Prov. 16:33; Isa. 46:9–10; Rom. 8:28; 11:36; Eph. 1:11)

The third category of "universal" Scripture text pertains to how God relates to all events whatsoever, whether or not these involve evil or even creaturely decision-making:

> Our God is in the heavens; he does all that he pleases. (Ps.
> 115:3)

---
2.   Austin Farrer, *Faith and Speculation* (London: A&C Black, 1967), 66.

The lot is cast into the lap, but its every decision is from the LORD. (Prov. 16:33)

For I am God, and there is no other; I am God, and there is none like me, declaring the end from the beginning and from ancient times things not yet done, saying, "My counsel shall stand, and I will accomplish all my purpose." (Isa. 46:9–10)

And we know that for those who love God all things work together for good, for those who are called according to his purpose. (Rom. 8:28)

For from him and through him and to him are all things. To him be glory forever. Amen. (Rom. 11:36)

In him we have obtained an inheritance, having been predestined according to the purpose of him who works all things according to the counsel of his will. (Eph. 1:11)

This last passage is particularly instructive. God works or accomplishes "all things" (not just some things), effecting them according to the purpose, intention, or plan of his will. So, the "all things" are not an afterthought, God's making the best of a bad situation after the fact. In fact, Paul understands and accounts for the particular, spiritual "predestination" of individuals in light of this broader, more general truth: God's providential plan for all things ("the counsel of his will").

How the Particular and General Passages Illuminate Each Other

While the evils considered in Questions 7–10 were a limited set of particular evils, the three main points above (taken together) seem to indicate that it is not a "hasty generalization" to trace all evils back to the will of God. These more general texts—extending divine providence to all calamities, all human decision-making, and all events—give us a broader vision that we can integrate with the particulars of Questions 7–10. God speaks about the specifics in individual cases so that we can repeatedly *see* that God's providence *does* work out in individual cases. He is the God who aims at goods through particular evils. At the same time, God assures us of a more general perspective in the texts now before us, in light of which the otherwise surprising, particular texts make more sense. When you put these two perspectives together—the particular providences examined in Questions 7–10 and the general providential perspective given here in Question 11—it is a very strong case that we are to take the particulars as instances of the more general view taught elsewhere.

In short, if God *cannot* aim at goods through evils—if doing so is beyond his power or contrary to his character—then what is going on in the earlier texts in Questions 7–10? But if God *can* do this in the particular cases we have considered, why can he not do so in all, exactly as the more general texts suggest here in Question 11? So the particular and general perspectives illuminate and mutually support each other.

Some Cautions and Applications

What About Contrasting Texts, or Different Christian Interpretations?
This is a good question. I have tried to avoid triumphalism in making my case. It is possible I have misinterpreted some of the particular texts, and/or have overread the general texts. There are other positions argued by Christians that differ from where I have landed here, particularly those that focus on texts I have not considered (such as texts seemingly indicating divine failure, divine change of plans, and so on). This book focuses on suffering and evil, so while I have made the best case I can in the space provided to explain where I have landed, this book does not try to adjudicate long-standing debates among Christians about the nature of divine providence.[3]

Still, I can offer a suggestion. Consider a contrary view, one that says that all evils cannot be traced back to the will of God. Then try to come up with an overall interpretation of the particular *and* the universal texts, such that they are best understood in this alternative way. What would that alternative look like? I have tried to do that many times and have not been successful, which is why I commend my view as a natural characterization of the biblical data. But I could be wrong. This chapter is not laid down as a gauntlet to intimidate detractors; it is more of an invitation for all of us to wrestle with the Scriptures. Coming up with a convincing way to relate texts about particular events to texts teaching general principles, as I have sought to do, helps avoid simplistic, isolated "proof texting" for one's pet doctrines.

What About the Goodness of God?
It would be fundamentally depressing for a reader's takeaway from these past several Questions to be: "I did not know that God was connected to so many *evils* in the world! What about the *goodness* of God?" But reading these passages in their context enables us to see them in their proper perspective.

---

3.   For some very helpful resources on this broader topic, consider Shawn Wright, *40 Questions About Calvinism* (Grand Rapids: Kregel Academic, 2019); J. Matthew Pinson, *40 Questions About Arminianism* (Grand Rapids: Kregel Academic, 2022); Paul Helm, *The Providence of God* (Downers Grove, IL: InterVarsity Press, 1993); Roger Olson, *Arminian Theology: Myths and Realities* (Downers Grove, IL: InterVarsity Press, 2006).

God both declares and exercises his control over these evils *to bring to pass his good purposes*. In quite a few of the "particular" passages, God is:

- *fulfilling his promise* to those who love and trust him, that he will protect them from their enemies.
- *displaying his unrivaled power* over the natural and human realms, to provide a firm basis for trusting him and to indicate that he knows what he is doing and can bring it to pass.
- *displaying his justice* in the face of many human sins so that we can more easily believe that he will justly and with finality visit the rest of human sin.
- *encouraging us to be thankful* for the life we have received, by reminding us that life is a precious gift and privilege from him that can be removed at any moment.

For these and many more reasons, the passages that relate God to various evils should lead us to marvel at the *goodness* of God. Additionally, as the Puritan Thomas Watson points out, God works all *good* things for good, as well as all bad things.[4] That is further testimony to the goodness of God. As the preacher might put it, "the day of prosperity" is just as much "the work of God" as "the day of adversity" (Eccl. 7:13–14). This includes the goods of family, friendship, cooperation in social endeavor, food, drink, and health. All those good things are worked for good by God as well.

Why Does This Matter?

Does it matter whether all, or just some, evils fall within the providential purpose of God? I would say "yes," because of what we considered at the end of the last Question: "We ultimately have nothing to fear from the most fearsome people in the world and in our lives." Subordinating *all* natural and moral evils to the providential purposes of a good God potentially makes a difference in how we bear up in dark times. Do we have reason to *always* trust God in these circumstances? The current argument supports the answer: yes! Or are there pockets of God's universe with significant cases of pain and suffering, due either to nature or other people, that are not subject to the good purpose of God's will? Again, the current argument seems to indicate "no."

Summary

The idea that all evils whatsoever can be traced back to and explained by the providential purpose of God seems to be the best way to make sense of two kinds of Scripture text: the "particular" cases of evil considered in previous Questions, and the "universal" Scripture texts considered in this Question.

---

4. Thomas Watson, *All Things for Good*, 2nd ed. (Carlisle: Banner of Truth, 2021), 7–20.

The latter relate God to all calamity, all human decision-making, and all events, while the former illustrate these relations in specific cases. Although the particular and general passages seem to illuminate and mutually support each other in this way, this is not the only interpretation offered by Christians. But this perspective can be seen to display rather than obscure the goodness of God, and it might matter for the comfort we can find in our own painful circumstances. Finally, the difference between "willing evils," "causing evils," and "intending evils" has not been broached here, and awaits theological discussion in part 2B.

REFLECTION QUESTIONS

1. Were you surprised by the texts in Genesis 1 that seemed to indicate that God might have used *means* to bring about various aspects of the creation? Would the latter be any *less* God's work because of that?

2. Reread the Scripture texts given in this chapter, but now imagine that they were written to *you* (as one of the original hearers or readers of Ecclesiastes, Lamentations, Amos, etc.). What practical purpose could God have in telling you these things?

3. This chapter repeatedly notes that the Scriptures are silent about *how* God accomplishes his will through calamity, human decisions, and so on. This might strike many readers as a "cop-out," a failure to tell us the most important things, the things we ought to know. But is it a cop-out?

4. The doxology of Romans 11:36 comes at the end of (and therefore seems to summarize) a three-chapter discussion. What is the topic, and how is it relevant to the topic of this book?

5. Since we are justified by faith alone, and not by our theology of divine providence, Christians can indeed disagree about the case made in this chapter. What can Christians *not* disagree about and still be Christians, in your view?

QUESTION 12

Does God Command Suffering and Evil in the Bible?

In the Bible, God repeatedly commands that some people end the earthly lives of other people. Three representative examples are God's commanding Israel to enforce capital punishment (Gen. 9:5–6; Exod. 21:12–14), God's commanding Israel to engage in holy war against the Canaanites (Deut. 20:16–18; Josh. 6:16–17, 21), and God's commanding Abraham to sacrifice his son Isaac (Gen. 22:2). Is God commanding *murder*, and therefore commanding moral evil, when he gives these commands? This chapter articulates and applies three plausible ethical principles that help us see that, far from compromising God's goodness, these commands might *display* God's goodness.

Three Principles for Interpreting These Commands

The Reality of the Divine Right to Take Life

According to this principle, as the creator and author of life (Gen. 1:1, 26–27; 2:7, 21–23; Ps. 100:3), only God has the intrinsic right to take back the life he has given if he so chooses. Every creature is God's possession, first existing by God's creative power, and then sustained moment by moment by God's providential power. This applies to all human beings: "He himself gives to all mankind life and breath and everything. . . . In him we live and move and have our being" (Acts 17:25, 28). It also applies to all nonhuman animals: "For every beast of the forest is mine, the cattle on a thousand hills. I know all the birds of the hills, and all that moves in the field is mine" (Ps. 50:10–11).

It is important to stress that this divine right is unique. No creature has this intrinsic right to take the life of another creature. No mere creature *could* have this authority because no creature sustains this unique, divine relationship of creation and providence to any other creature. While there is an analogy between God's work of creation and providence, and the work of parents in bringing about and raising children, the disanalogies must be equally recognized. Parents only do these things with divine permission and enablement and are entirely dependent on preexisting materials. By way of contrast, God needs no permission or enablement from anyone for anything he does, and he creates "from nothing" (*ex nihilo*). Indeed, the very power and opportunity of parents to do anything at all comes from God. If "from him and through him and to him are all things" (Rom. 11:36), then God will have prerogatives that no one else has. The unlawful taking of human life, ordinarily called "murder," is the taking of life in the absence of this divine authority. But it is not murder for God to take a life.

One reason why God might end a human life is to exercise his justice in response to those who disobey him. God does not *owe* further earthly life to those who disobey him, since life is a privilege granted by a good Creator. But God might have reasons to shorten a human life that have little if anything to do with that person being a sinner. In ways we are not likely to discern, God's complex and long-term providential purposes might be best furthered if that particular person has a life that is shorter than that of others. God does not wrong people if he distributes his gifts unequally, including the gift of length of life.

The Permissibility of Divine Delegation

According to this principle, if God has the right to do something, he also has the right to delegate that task to someone else. For God to take life is not murder, and for someone to take life *if expressly commanded by God to do so* is also not murder. I can have a delegated right to do what I have no intrinsic right to do.

This ethical principle is easily illustrated because it is a principle we already accept. If I have the right to take my younger children out of school for a day (perhaps to visit grandparents), then I have the right to delegate that task to my older son, sending him to get my children. If I have the right to restrict television watching when my children misbehave, then I can give the babysitter the right to impose that punishment. If the state has the right to imprison a violent offender, then the state has the right to send the sheriff to see that it happens. Nothing in these delegations is generalizable. It would not follow from the permissibility of delegation that *just anyone* has the right to remove my children from school, or to discipline them, or to imprison anyone. Rather, the relevant circumstances must be satisfied. Someone must have the right to do the task *and* a right to delegate the task, and then the task must be delegated *by* the one who has the right to do the task.

The Irrelevance of Human Fallibility

According to this principle, doubts over whether God *has* delegated a task to someone else do not undermine the ethical principle that God *has* the right to delegate the task. At a popular level, some argue that if "all it takes" to have the right to kill someone is that "God told me," then anyone could claim this, and who are we to doubt the person? Since we cannot be sure, in any particular case, that God has not delegated to someone his right to kill, then we will have to allow everyone to exercise this right if they claim it. Since that leads to societal chaos, we must hold that God cannot delegate that right, and so he has never done so. All those in history claiming to have this right would be deluded at best, immoral evildoers at worst.

But this reasoning is deeply flawed, and in relevantly similar contexts we reject it. For it confuses epistemology (theory of knowledge) with ethics (theory of value). It is one thing to doubt whether we know enough to responsibly apply an ethical principle. It is another thing to doubt the ethical principle itself. Our fallibility in arresting, trying, convicting, and sentencing violent offenders does nothing to undermine the ethical principle that violent offenders should be identified and removed from society. If anything, the importance of this ethical principle should lead us to be *more* vigilant about reforming the process so that it targets the guilty and not the innocent. The state does have the right to imprison violent offenders, even if it is possible the state is mistaken in identifying these offenders.

So if God has delegated to a person his right to kill, then it would not be immoral for that person to exercise it (as a delegated right). To show otherwise, one must do more than raise abstract doubts; one must make a case. After all, it is always *possible* that the person arresting me is not really a policeman duly authorized by the state. But that mere possibility, all by itself, does not prove he is not a policeman. Likewise, what reason do we have to think that God did not give the commands discussed in this chapter? In our practical moral reasoning as in all else, we do not treat mere possibilities as probabilities.[1]

These three principles of "reality of divine right," "permissibility of delegation," and "irrelevance of fallibility" can be applied to the three divine commands earlier mentioned, to defend the character of God in giving these commands.

Applying the Principles: Capital Punishment (Gen. 9:5–6; Exod. 21:12–14)

God first commanded capital punishment in the days of Noah:

> And for your lifeblood I will require a reckoning: from every beast I will require it and from man. From his fellow man I will require a reckoning for the life of man. Whoever sheds

---

1. In other words, the question of this chapter is not a historical one ("Did God give this command?") but an ethical one ("Would the command be murderous, immoral, or otherwise against the goodness of God?")

the blood of man, *by man shall his blood be shed*, for God made man in his own image. (Gen. 9:5–6)

These words to Noah are only implicitly in the form of a command. But God later gives an explicit and unambiguous command for capital punishment in the Mosaic Law:

Whoever strikes a man so that he dies *shall be put to death*. But if he did not lie in wait for him, but God let him fall into his hand, then I will appoint for you a place to which he may flee. But if a man willfully attacks another to kill him by cunning, *you shall take him from my altar, that he may die.* (Exod. 21:12–14)

Likewise, for the rest of the capital crimes listed, "*shall be put to death*" (or its equivalent) is repeated nine more times (Exod. 21:15, 16, 17, 20, 23, 29; 22:18, 19, 20).

Here the principles of divine right, delegation, and fallibility come together to vindicate the moral permissibility of capital punishment. It could not be intrinsically immoral for God to end the life of evildoers because he has the right to end life. And it could not be immoral for someone to carry out this task if God asks him to. Beyond that, it is arguably a *good* thing for divine justice to be displayed against serious moral evil, for evildoers to be prevented from further serious moral evil, and for future evildoers to be deterred from contemplating serious moral evil.

Should there be a thorough investigation prior to carrying out this task? Certainly, and the need for testimony from multiple witnesses is not merely suggested but commanded in capital cases (Deut. 17:6; 19:15). Should we be vigilant in guarding such a practice against racial and economic bias, and be open to radically reforming current practices for that reason? Again, yes. "You shall not pervert the justice due to your poor in his lawsuit. Keep far from a false charge, and do not kill the innocent and righteous, for I will not acquit the wicked" (Exod. 23:6–7; see Deut. 25:1).[2]

Perhaps capital punishment is immoral simply because it is irreversible? This line of reasoning, however, proves too much, for *any* punishment of any sort—whether death or incarceration or restriction of societal privileges to any degree—is always irreversible. One can never get back time spent

---

2. For an argument that mass incarceration and capital punishment in the United States might be particularly susceptible to such bias, see Michelle Alexander, *The New Jim Crow: Mass Incarceration in the Age of Colorblindness*, 10th anniversary ed. (New York: The New Press, 2020); and R. J. Maratea, *Killing with Prejudice: Institutionalized Racism in American Capital Punishment* (New York: NYU Press, 2019).

in prison, or years spent impoverished due to excessive fines, or time lived without various privileges. But the irreversibility of punishment is no argument that punishment as such is intrinsically immoral. It is instead a call for carefulness, thoroughness, and impartiality in the application of punishment.

Does God's command "You shall not murder" (Exod. 20:13) conflict with his command for capital punishment in Exodus 21:12? But the "murder" in Exodus 20:13 is the *unlawful* taking of human life, unlike the *delegated and therefore lawful* taking of life in the next chapter, which is limited to very specific and divinely prescribed circumstances. Why posit a contradiction between these two chapters when a much more natural and charitable solution is on offer?

Applying the Principles: Holy War in Canaan (Deut. 20:16–18; Josh. 6:16–17, 21)

God's command for the destruction of the Canaanites first came to Moses:

> But in the cities of these peoples that the LORD your God is giving you for an inheritance, *you shall save alive nothing that breathes, but you shall devote them to complete destruction*, the Hittites and the Amorites, the Canaanites and the Perizzites, the Hivites and the Jebusites, as the LORD your God has commanded, that they may not teach you to do according to all their abominable practices that they have done for their gods, and so you sin against the LORD your God. (Deut. 20:16–18)

Moses's successor Joshua, the general who was to conduct the holy war, later repeats this command:

> And at the seventh time, when the priests had blown the trumpets, Joshua said to the people, "Shout, for the LORD has given you the city. *And the city and all that is within it shall be devoted to the LORD for destruction*. Only Rahab the prostitute and all who are with her in her house shall live, because she hid the messengers whom we sent. . . . Then they devoted all in the city to destruction, both men and women, young and old, oxen, sheep, and donkeys, with the edge of the sword. (Josh. 6:16–17, 21)

We can take these passages as representative of the other passages where God commands Israel to "devote to destruction" a group of people. The fundamental moral issue is no different in these other passages. But what, exactly, *is* the moral issue? It is tempting to simply assimilate this command to the previous one: it is capital punishment "writ large," God's taking back the gift of life from multiple wicked peoples all at once, and a kind of preview of the judgment day when the entire world will face God's just judgment. If so, the principles of divine right, divine delegation, and the irrelevance of human fallibility apply. Holy war *is* capital punishment, and the ethical defense is the same.[3]

No doubt the wickedness of the Canaanites was a reason for God's ending their lives. The passage above speaks of "their abominable practices that they have done for their gods" (Deut. 20:18), and an earlier passage expands on this: "For every abominable thing that the LORD hates they have done for their gods, for they even burn their sons and their daughters in the fire to their gods" (Deut. 12:31). God cuts off the Canaanites so that the Israelites will not be ensnared in their idolatrous religious practices, which apparently include child sacrifice. So judgment day came *early* for these peoples, but such a day was inevitable one way or another, as long as a just God rules the universe.

But what about the Canaanite children, who fall under the same destruction? Even if the Canaanites were corrupt and worthy of divine judgment, why should the Canaanite conquest involve the destruction of children who presumably were *not* guilty of sacrificing children, or of anything else, for that matter? So another reason must be given for why it is permissible that they die. Why did God's holy war have to include the death of children when (as we have just seen) God himself is on record as opposing the death of children? If this is "capital punishment," it is not very discriminating. This is a very good reason to avoid a reductive approach. Unlike capital punishment, holy war involves large groups of people, not all of whom seem guilty of capital crimes, and many (the children) seem incapable of capital crimes.

The principle of divine right can help here because it is very broad. God can end life early, for anyone, and his reason does not have to be grounded in just punishment. Other complex and long-term providential purposes come to the fore. Perhaps an early death spares these children from growing up and likely repeating the crimes of their parents on an ever-larger scale. Perhaps their continuing their parents' idolatrous practices would prove to be a snare to Israel, just as God warned. Perhaps leaving the children alive makes likely their later revenge on the Israelites for waging the holy war, and God wants to avoid this (because it is important that Israel have relative peace in the land if they are to fulfill God's redemptive purposes for the world). If so, then due to these good providential purposes on the part of God, the lives of these children end up being shorter than the lives of most other children in the world. But again, God has no *obligation* to make their gift of life the same length as

---

3. In considering whether to take the Old Testament holy war passages as historical or allegorical, Christian philosopher Richard Swinburne says, "I myself believe that a God who gives life has the right to take it away; and in that case he has the right to command someone else to take it away for him. So a historical interpretation of such passages seems in order" (*Revelation: From Metaphor to Analogy* [Oxford: Oxford University Press, 1992], 190 n. 43).

others. In the end, God simply sustains a different relationship to human life than we do: he is its ultimate author and sustainer, not us. So he does have authority to take life according to his purposes, even if we do not.

The principle of delegation provides a further ethical safeguard by establishing the *uniqueness* of holy war in biblical history. God is simply not in the business today of continuing such delegations and repeating Israelite history for no reason, since that history found its fulfillment and culmination in the coming of Jesus into the world. Through the Israelite conquest, there was now a people, a land, and a law, so that Jesus could come "to his own" (John 1:11) and fulfill covenant promises. Now that the Savior has come, there is no need to dislodge a region's inhabitants to make room for yet another physical theocracy.

Make no mistake: it would be horrible for human beings to do this on their own initiative without revelation from God. It would be *right* and *obvious* to label that a moral monstrosity, for human presumption rather than divine prerogative would be on display. But that is not the situation here. And assuming that this was a divine task delegated by divine prerogative, nothing about the Canaanite judgment in the history of redemption seems repeatable or imitable for any reason at all—establishing Israel as a theocracy in the land is simply no longer needed, ever.[4]

Applying the Principles: The Sacrifice of Isaac (Gen. 22:2)

Long before the Mosaic Law or holy war, God commanded Abraham to sacrifice his son:

> He said, "Take your son, your only son Isaac, whom you love, and go to the land of Moriah, and offer him there as a burnt offering on one of the mountains of which I shall tell you." (Gen. 22:2)

The story is familiar to most readers of the Bible, and space does not permit an extended examination of the narrative.[5] But reflection on the principles already discussed affords us some guidance in distinguishing this case

---

4. Among other points, Paul Copan argues that the destruction language is "clearly exaggerated," and that the focus is on Canaanite religion, not the Canaanites *per se*, in Paul Copan, *Is God a Moral Monster?* (Grand Rapids: Baker, 2011), chs. 15–17. Copan's analysis is extremely helpful, and finds further development in Paul Copan and Matthew Flanagan, *Did God Really Command Genocide?* (Grand Rapids: Baker, 2014). Another useful resource is Heath Thomas, Jeremy Evans, and Paul Copan, eds., *Holy War in the Bible: Christian Morality and an Old Testament Problem* (Downers Grove, IL: IVP Academic, 2013). However, in the text, I have decided to make an argument that does not depend on Copan's claims about exaggerated language.

5. For an excellent exposition of Genesis 22 and the surrounding narratives, and argument that God's command was a means of God aiming at Abraham's good, of God drawing Abraham closer to himself, and even of God giving Abraham "the desires of his heart," see

from one of "attempted murder." There is the divine right principle: God has the right to end Isaac's life early. No one has the right for more life from God since life of any extent is a gift from him. There is the delegation principle: Abraham does not act, or even intend to act, on his own authority; his is a divinely mandated task. In some respects, this episode is easier to defend: unlike capital punishment or holy war, no one actually died in this scenario. God had authority to command the sacrifice *and* authority to command that Abraham stay his hand (Gen. 22:11–12), and God does both.

But in one respect this episode is harder to defend. Is there not something ethically perverse about a God who hates child sacrifice *commanding* child sacrifice ("as a burnt offering") as a test of faith? Abraham was supposed to come out of the nations (Gen. 12:1), not ethically conform to the nations! If Abrahamic faith is the model for saving faith (Rom. 4:1–25; Gal. 3:6–9), how can its highest expression be indistinguishable from the faith of bloodthirsty pagans? Some perplexity may be alleviated if we distinguish between the strength of faith (how one believes) and the content of faith (what one believes). The Genesis 22 episode illustrates that Israelite faith—that is, the faith of all the redeemed—was to be as *strong* as the faith of zealous idolaters willing to sacrifice their children. As God tells him, "You have done this and have not withheld your son, your only son" (Gen. 22:16). God demands a loyalty that exceeds that given to any god. But what was the content of Abraham's faith? Did he really believe that God was asking him to end the earthly life of his son? No, his faith was not akin to pagan confidence in the power of death to manipulate or bind the gods. Rather, his faith was in *resurrection*, and in God's power to bring it about:

> By faith Abraham, when he was tested, offered up Isaac, and he who had received the promises was in the act of offering up his only son, of whom it was said, "Through Isaac shall your offspring be named." *He considered that God was able even to raise him from the dead*, from which, figuratively speaking, he did receive him back. (Heb. 11:17–19)

Or as Paul puts it, Abraham's faith regarded God as one "who gives life to the dead" (Rom. 4:16–17). God's earlier promises to Abraham—that the whole world would be blessed through Abraham's offspring (Gen. 12:3), and that "through Isaac shall your offspring be named" (Heb. 11:18; see Gen. 17:19, 21)—meant that Isaac's life would not—*could not*—ultimately be ended through Abraham's obedience to God's command. And Abraham understood this. One way or another, God would ensure that Isaac's life continue, and Abraham's faith and obedience were directed to that end, to the display of the

Eleonore Stump, *Wandering in Darkness: Narrative and the Problem of Suffering* (Oxford: Oxford University Press, 2010), ch. 11.

power of God over death. If Isaac were to be a "burnt offering," it would be unlike any other, including those made in pagan lands. God's command, far from being immoral, gave Abraham an opportunity to exercise a faith that was as *strong* as the faith of idolaters willing to sacrifice their children, but a faith with a radically different *content* and therefore outcome. It was good of God to offer Abraham that opportunity to place his faith in God's power of resurrection, and so become "the father of the faithful."

Summary

Though God has on occasion commanded suffering to occur, including the suffering of death, these have not been commands for people to commit moral evil. Rather, in these instances God has temporarily delegated to others his right to end life, a right they do not intrinsically have, in order to fulfill specific and good providential purposes (including, though certainly not limited to, the display of his justice). As flawed and limited human beings, it is possible we can make mistakes in this gravest of actions. But we already knew that: human attempts to administer justice or decide much of anything else are rarely attended with absolute certainty. Such fallibility, by itself, does not forbid human decision-making. Thus, there seems little reason to think that the divine commands considered in this chapter are immoral or contrary to the goodness of God.

REFLECTION QUESTIONS

1. Could the main argument of this chapter be extended to cover the case of God commanding animal sacrifice (e.g., Lev. 1)? Would Psalm 50:10–11 shed some light here? What additional points would you make about the permissibility of that command?

2. What are some reasons the following two questions can get confused? "Did God command someone to do something?" "Was the command evil?"

3. Are there circumstances in which capital punishment *would* be immoral? If so, how is that consistent with the argument of this chapter?

4. "It is *because* the biblical record can be trusted that there is no rationale for holy war today." Can you give a good argument for this inference?

5. According to a face-value reading of the text, Abraham told his servants that he would come back from Mount Moriah *with Isaac* (Gen. 22:5), and he told Isaac that *a lamb* would be sacrificed (Gen. 22:8). So, did Abraham think that Isaac would die at all?

Questions Related
to Theology

QUESTION 13

Does God Cause Evil?

What would be the problem with saying that God causes evil, moral evil as well as natural evil? Was that not the import of Questions 9–11 anyway, that both natural evil and moral evil are "of the Lord"? But here we must be careful. While the biblical data we looked at seems to indicate that in *some* sense, suffering and evil are "of the Lord," it does not *specify* that sense in any detail. Further theological reflection—articulating arguments that make rational inferences from the biblical data—is needed to answer these questions. (And there is no guarantee at the outset that these theological questions even *have* an answer that is worthy of our acceptance!)

Whether "God causes evil" depends on how we define "evil," and thankfully we have already done this in Questions 2 and 3 and applied these definitions further in Questions 9 and 10. Briefly, "evil" is any significant case of pain and suffering, and then "natural evil" and "moral evil" are distinguished by the immediate cause of that suffering: "how nature goes on" or "defect of will" (respectively). So each kind of evil involves *two* parts: the pain and suffering itself, and the immediate cause of that pain and suffering. This means the question "Does God cause evil?" subdivides into three further questions:

- Does God cause suffering?
- Does God cause suffering by causing nature to cause suffering?
- Does God cause suffering by causing the defect of will that causes suffering?

Any of these questions can count as "what we really mean" when we ask, "Does God cause evil?"

Does God Cause Suffering?

Of the three main questions, this is the easiest one to answer. Certainly God both can and does cause pain and suffering, and he can do so immediately,

bypassing natural causes and creaturely agency altogether. He can do this because he is all-powerful, and we know he does do it because of the biblical
record. He can immediately strike someone down in judgment and bring
earthly life to an end, as he did with Nadab and Abihu (Lev. 10:1–2), Nabal
(1 Sam. 25:38), and Uzzah before the ark (1 Chron. 13:10). He can cause leprosy to spontaneously break forth on the forehead of the wayward and presumptuous King Uzziah (2 Chron. 26:19–20).

Would God be *justified* in causing such suffering? That depends on two
things: his right and his reasons. Does God have the right to cause suffering?
Well, he is the creator of all, the providential sustainer of all, the giver of every
good and perfect gift, and the judge of all. He would certainly seem to have
the right. Does God have a good reason for doing it, one that morally justifies
him in doing it and that is compatible with his good character? This question
of moral justification is the question of *theodicy*: does God have a good reason
for causing or permitting significant cases of pain and suffering? This question is so important that Questions 21–26 are devoted to it.[1]

Does God Cause Nature to Cause Suffering?

Here we are not asking whether God causes suffering directly, but whether
he causes it *indirectly*, by causing nature to be the source of suffering. We are
asking whether God causes "natural evil." This main question is slightly harder
to answer than the previous one—but not *much* harder. And that is because
we have already covered this territory in Question 9 ("Is Natural Evil Ever 'of
the Lord'?"). The broad range of passages considered there seems to indicate
that, as a matter of biblical record, God *does* (on many occasions) cause nature to cause suffering. Examples include famine, drought, rampaging wild
animals, disease, birth defects like blindness or deafness, plague, and stormy
weather. Here we can make a point not made in that earlier chapter: ordinary
Hebrew verbs of *causation* are used to describe God's relation to these natural
phenomena: God "brings about," "takes away," "breaks," "sends," "takes back,"
"gives," "strikes," "shuts up," "makes," "withheld," "causes," "afflicts," "touches,"
"throws," "raises," "hurls," and "scatters." If this kind of language does not indicate causation, probably no language will. But this is exactly the kind of
language that we take to indicate *humans* causing things, so it is unclear why
it would have a completely different meaning when applied to God.

There is a slight worry here that if God causes nature to cause things,
then "nature" loses some of its integrity and inner coherence. But surely it
is fundamental to a biblical worldview that God is causally involved in the
workings of nature. In ordinary providence, he sustains our lives moment

---

1. "Theodicy" comes from two Greek words, *theos* (God) and *dikios* (justify). It means "a justification of the ways of God," and it typically involves specifying the reason God has that
   justifies him in bringing about or permitting pain and suffering.

by moment (Acts 17:25, 28), and in extraordinary providence, he works a broad range of spectacular miracles when and how he chooses (Acts 17:31; Heb. 2:4). "Nature" is not autonomous, somehow insulated or protected from the causal power of God. Deism, the view that God created nature but subsequently never intervenes in it, hardly seems reconcilable with the specifics of Scripture. So this concern seems unwarranted.[2]

As before, we are left with the moral question. Would God be *justified* in causing nature to cause suffering? But why should our answer here be any different from what it was before? In effect, natural evil would just be an *indirect* way to cause suffering (by nature). If God has the right to cause suffering directly, why would he not have the right to cause it indirectly? God owns nature. He created it and sustains it. He is not violating the "rights" of nature when he directs its often painful processes to his wise and good ends. So if God is justified in causing suffering directly, why wouldn't he be justified in causing it indirectly? Whether God *is* justified takes us to the question of theodicy, reasons God might have to use nature in this way. It takes us, again, to Questions 21–26.[3]

Does God Cause the Defect of Will That Causes Suffering?

Whereas the topic in the previous section was "natural evil," the topic here is "moral evil." And the questions of most concern are whether God can cause the defect of will that causes suffering, whether he does cause such defect of will, and whether he would be justified in causing such defect of will. For many people, this is *the* question; the others do not really matter (or matter as much). Our definitions have enabled us to focus on this question rather precisely, without irrelevant, distracting details getting in the way. *Does God relate to human free will in this way?*

Let us temporarily put aside the metaphysical question "Can God cause defect of will?" (we will return to it), and focus on the moral question. Let us say, for the sake of argument, that God *can* somehow cause defect of will (in a way that does not compromise our freedom or responsibility), a defect of will which then produces suffering. How could God be justified in doing this? The answer, surprisingly, is similar to the answers given for the last two main questions: God would be justified if he has the right to do this, and if he has a good reason for doing this, directing his efforts to a just and good end. After

---

2. For an excellent discussion of the various ways that special divine action in the universe can be reconciled with "the laws of nature" (biology, physics, etc.), see Alvin Plantinga, *Where the Conflict Really Lies* (Oxford: Oxford University Press, 2011), chs. 1–4. For a cogent case against deism, see Robert Larmer, *The Legitimacy of Miracle* (Lanham: Lexington Books, 2013), ch. 1.
3. Notice the similarity to the principles of "divine right" and "divine delegation" that we considered in Question 12. If God has the right to bring about suffering, then he has the right to *delegate* that task (as it were) to nature. There seems to be no intrinsic moral problem here.

all, if God has the right to use impersonal nature to bring about suffering, why would not he have the right to use human nature to bring about suffering? They are *both* instruments in his hands, and subject to his wise, good, and just providence.

At this point, such an answer may strike many readers as crazy. Surely there is a relevant moral difference between God using an earthquake to bring about suffering (perhaps as a judgment of some sort; see Num. 16:31–33) and God using a bloodthirsty, pagan soldier to bring about suffering (perhaps, again, as a judgment of some sort; see Isa. 5:26–30; 7:17–20; 8:5–9; 9:11; 10:5–12; 13:1–22). But as a matter of fact, the Scriptures present these as on a par, morally speaking. God has the right to use nature *or* human free will to bring about suffering, and I just gave examples of both. Further examples are not hard to find. In response to the sins of Manasseh, the wicked king of Judah, God says:

> I will appoint over them four kinds of destroyers, declares the
> LORD: the sword to kill, the dogs to tear, and the birds of the
> air and the beasts of the earth to devour and destroy. (Jer. 15:3)

Here, "sword" indicates human free will as the immediate cause of suffering, whereas "dogs," "birds," and "beasts" indicate nonhuman nature as the immediate cause of suffering.[4] God has the right to bring the suffering in any of these ways, by human persons *or* by nonhuman beasts. Indeed, when speaking of Manasseh's own capture, God's use of the instrumentality of human free will to bring about this suffering seems clear:

> Therefore *the* LORD *brought upon them* the commanders of
> the army of the king of Assyria, who captured Manasseh with
> hooks and bound him with chains of bronze and brought
> him to Babylon. (2 Chron. 33:11)

No doubt the commanders exercised their agency in bringing about this suffering for Manasseh. But just as clearly, God exercised *his* agency in bringing the commanders upon Manasseh in the first place. Or consider the threefold repetition of "God gave them up" in the wide-ranging list of freely willed sins noted in Romans 1:24–32. Here, the sins are both the *reason* for God's punishment and the *form* that God's punishment takes. Apparently, God is justified in using human wickedness toward his just ends, not as a

---

4. In the previous verse, "pestilence," "sword," "famine," and "captivity" indicate a similar
    mixture of free will and nature as the immediate cause of suffering, with "sword" and "cap-
    tivity" indicating free will, and "pestilence" and "famine" indicating nature.

merely passive observer but as the one who "gave them up" to sins because of earlier sins.[5]

Mystery abounds here, but it is important to locate that mystery in the right place. Is there not a relevant difference, some may ask, between soldiers and an earthquake, between human beings and a block of wood? I can cause wood to move or become wet without changing its nature as wood, but *no one* can cause a human to choose something without stripping him of his humanity. For God to get involved like *that* would change or violate the person's nature. This is an extremely good question—so good, in fact, that we will devote the next two Questions to it. But notice that it is the metaphysical question ("*Can* God cause defect of will?"), not the moral question upon which we are now focusing. Again, assuming that God *can* do this, we are wondering if he would be *justified* in doing it. And the answer seems similar to the earlier answers we gave for suffering in general, and for nature in particular: if God has the right, and a justified purpose, then there is no moral problem here. Whether God *would be* justified in causing all the suffering that does occur—directly, or indirectly—is a matter for theodicy, which we will consider in Questions 21–26.

How Shall We Proceed?

It is time to take stock. We have not given complete answers to the three main questions that together compose the "Does God cause evil?" question. But we have shed considerable light on these matters, and we can summarize our findings *and* their limitations from a biblical, metaphysical, and moral point of view.

Biblically speaking, the scriptural record clearly indicates that God causes suffering directly and causes suffering by way of impersonal nature. In addition, the scriptural record clearly indicates that God causes suffering by way of persons. But the Bible does not seem to clearly teach that God does the latter by *causing* the freewill choices of persons. Given the creation/causal language considered in Question 11, which seems to causally relate God to *ra'ah* in the world, the Scriptures seem to teach a causal relation of some sort between God and moral evil (Eccl. 7:13–14; Isa. 45:7; Lam. 3:37–38; Amos 3:6). But the Scriptures seem to fall short of claiming that God causes *the creaturely defect of will* that causes suffering. There are no texts which say that.[6] This is in stark contrast to the many texts which do seem to teach that God

---

5. Consider also what Solomon says: "The LORD has made everything for its purpose, even the wicked for the day of trouble" (Prov. 16:4).

6. Or, at the very least, there are no texts which say this is what God *usually* does. There is the specific case of God hardening Pharaoh's heart so that Pharaoh will disobey his command (Exod. 4:21; Rom. 9:17–18). On the other hand, there are no texts I am aware of that say God *does not* cause creaturely defect of will. The Scriptures do not seem to speak with such precision and explicitness *either way* on this question.

causes suffering directly or causes impersonal nature to bring about various kinds of suffering. So we should exercise some caution before saying that "the Scriptures teach God causes moral evil," if by the latter we mean "causes the defect of will that causes the suffering."

Metaphysically speaking, if God is all-powerful, why could he not cause suffering directly? For that matter, why could he not cause suffering indirectly by causing nature to cause it? Some people, perhaps, might have a weak intuition that God would "destroy" nature if he causally affected nature at all. But it seems hard to develop this into a cogent case against God's causal activity. A God who cannot affect his world without destroying it does not seem to be much of a God at all. But in contrast to this, *many* Christians have confessed to having a powerful metaphysical intuition that no one—not God or anyone else—can cause *acts of free will*, because then they would not be *free* acts, or even *acts* of the person who is so caused. If they are right, this seems to be a metaphysical "roadblock" against God causing moral evil (in addition to the biblical point made earlier, that the Scriptures do not explicitly teach this).

Morally speaking, assuming God *can* and *does* cause suffering, either directly or indirectly, how could God remain good in doing so? That is a concern common to all three main questions in this chapter. The answer depends on God's right to cause suffering and his reasons for causing it. It depends on the availability of *theodicy*.

These questions that remain will therefore be taken up in subsequent Questions in this book:

- Question 14 will consider whether a theological model of "dual-agency" can be plausibly derived from the Scriptures, so that the *biblical* question of God's relation to moral evil can be further addressed.
- Question 15 will consider two theories of free will ("compatibilist" and "libertarian") and two models of providence which apply them ("Calvinism" and "Molinism"), so that the *metaphysical* question of God's causing free will acts can be further addressed.
- Questions 21–26 will consider the range of justifying reasons God might have for bringing about suffering (whether directly or indirectly), so that the *moral* question of the availability of theodicy can be finally addressed.

Summary

So where do things stand on the "causation" question? God's causation of suffering directly, and his causation of natural evil, seem unobjectionable, from the biblical and metaphysical point of view. By way of contrast, God's causation of moral evil seems *underdetermined* from the biblical point of view, and *challengeable* from the metaphysical point of view. Finally, God's causing of *any* suffering, whether directly or indirectly, seems challengeable from the moral point of view, unless God has a justified reason for bringing about the suffering. This Question therefore paves the way for further development of these themes later in the book.

REFLECTION QUESTIONS

1. This chapter claimed that the earlier "of the Lord" language cannot *automatically* be interpreted as "causal" language, and that we should be cautious in doing so. What are some significant examples of Bible interpreters "overinterpreting" biblical language? What are some typical reasons this happens?

2. This chapter claimed that "there is no guarantee at the outset that these theological questions even *have* an answer that is worthy of our acceptance." Is it possible to ask a theological question for which God has not given an answer, or even the *materials* for constructing an answer? What are some guidelines for determining whether a question falls into this category?

3. Do you have rights over your children that other people do not have? What grounds those rights? Is there a useful theological analogy in the vicinity?

4. Is there a moral difference between God causing suffering directly and his causing it indirectly?

5. What is the difference between these two claims: "It would be impossible for God to cause defect of will" and "It would be immoral for God to cause defect of will"? Does the Bible address either claim?

Does God Relate to Moral Evil Through "Dual-Agency"?

According to Question 13, although "the Scriptures seem to teach a causal relation of some sort between God and moral evil (Eccl. 7:13–14; Isa. 45:7; Lam. 3:37–38; Amos 3:6)," these same Scriptures "seem to fall short of claiming that God causes *the creaturely defect of will* that causes suffering." How can these two sides of the biblical teaching—one positive, the other negative—be brought together?

This chapter considers whether a theological model of "dual-agency" can be plausibly derived from the Scriptures, a model that sheds further light on how God relates to the moral evil in the world. After noting the elements of the model and their biblical basis, several advantages of the model will be listed. The material of this chapter, while independently valuable, will also help us assess Calvinism and Molinism in the next Question, these being two contrasting perspectives on divine providence over evil that are popular among many Christians.

Introducing Dual-Agency

In Question 7 we first saw the phenomenon of "two sets of intentions" behind cases of moral evil in the Job, Joseph, and Jesus narratives: the selfish, immoral human intentions (which are evil), and the divine intentions (which are good). As a matter of fact, quite a few passages of Scripture seem to endorse this kind of distinction, which I will call the "dual-agency" passages. Responsible humans bring about through their agency the very thing God brings about through *his* agency. Apparently, the first part of the preceding statement does not cancel out the second part, or vice versa.

On the dual-agency model, one and the same event is described from two perspectives: as something (immediately) brought about by humans, and as something (ultimately) brought about by God. In each case, God accomplishes the outcome that the human is said to bring about. If David defeats the enemy, *God* is said to defeat him. If the king of Assyria is said to destroy Judah or bring her into exile, *God* is said to destroy Judah or bring her into exile. If Saul kills Saul, *God* is said to kill Saul. But because the human intentionality is not the divine intentionality, God incurs no blame from doing the same thing that the human does. His intentions are good, even if the human intentions are blameworthy. This is a very important distinction.

In the following we consider fifteen cases of "dual-agency" with respect to victory in war, defeat in war, and death. This is just a small selection of the passages which could be cited, as dual-agency seems to be a pervasive feature of the biblical text. There are examples of innocent human agency fulfilling God's good intentions (e.g., the death of Ahab, Hazael's defeat of Israel), followed by examples of murderous humans fulfilling God's good intentions (e.g., Zimri assassinating Baasha and his descendants, Sennacherib's sons assassinating him). So, one striking characteristic of these cases is that they range over human agency more generally, rather than being restricted to cases of moral evil more specifically. Dual-agency, it seems, is simply how God governs a universe that has *other persons* in it.

Examples of Dual-Agency

The Destruction of the House of Baasha King of Israel (1 Kings 16)

Who destroys the house of Baasha? God does: "Behold, *I* will utterly sweep away Baasha and his house, and *I* will make your house like the house of Jeroboam the son of Nebat" (1 Kings 16:3).

Who destroys the house of Baasha? Zimri does: "Thus *Zimri* destroyed all the house of Baasha, according to the word of the LORD, which he spoke against Baasha by Jehu the prophet" (1 Kings 16:12).

The Death of Ahab (1 Kings 22)

Who brings about Ahab's downfall? *God* does. Because of King Ahab's many sins, God says to him: "*I* will bring disaster upon you. *I* will utterly burn you up" (1 Kings 21:21). But the later historical details give us a different answer to the question, Who killed Ahab?:

> But a certain man drew his bow at random and struck the king of Israel between the scale armor and the breastplate. Therefore he said to the driver of his chariot, "Turn around and carry me out of the battle, for I am wounded." And the battle continued that day, and the king was propped up in his chariot facing the Syrians, until at evening he died. (1 Kings 22:34–35)

So God's purpose is that Ahab "may go up and fall at Ramoth-gilead" (1 Kings 22:20), and God says *he* will do it. But it is also true to say *the archer did it.* There is a distinction between God's intentions and the intentions of the agent whom God used to bring to pass his own intentions. The archer did not aim at and intend to kill Ahab—rather, he drew his bow at random. But by his undirected intention to just *shoot an arrow somewhere or other*, this human being accomplished the very thing which God intended: the death of Ahab.[1] So God brought the disaster on Ahab, by way of the archer bringing the disaster on Ahab.

God Cutting Off Parts of Israel (2 Kings 10)
   Sometimes the phenomenon of dual-agency is stated so concisely that we can miss it if we are not careful:

> In those days *the LORD* began to cut off parts of Israel. *Hazael* defeated them throughout the territory of Israel: from the Jordan eastward, all the land of Gilead, the Gadites, and the Reubenites, and the Manassites, from Aroer, which is by the Valley of the Arnon, that is, Gilead and Bashan. (2 Kings 10:32–33)

Who cut off parts of Israel? We are given two answers: "the LORD" did it, and "Hazael" did it. The extended historical process of shrinking Israel's real estate is said to be the work of both divine and creaturely agency. Even as what Scripture says, God says (2 Tim. 3:16; Heb. 3:7–11; 2 Peter 1:21), so what Hazael does, God does. Dual-agency equally characterizes divine inspiration and divine judgment, perhaps because it characterizes divine providence more generally.

The Assyrian Captivity (2 Kings 17)
   The Assyrian captivity is one of the saddest events in the history of Israel. But who was it who removed Israel out of the land? One answer to this question is: God himself.

> Therefore *the LORD* was very angry with Israel and *removed them* out of his sight. (2 Kings 17:18)

> And *the LORD rejected* all the descendants of Israel and *afflicted* them and *gave them* into the hand of plunderers, until *he had cast them out* of his sight. (2 Kings 17:20)

---

1. In Question 10, we already saw God putting lying spirits in the mouths of false prophets to entice Ahab to arrogantly *enter* the battlefield, confident of victory. But that by itself does not make Ahab *fall* on the battlefield, bringing about his downfall. For that, we need the lucky shot of the archer.

> *The LORD removed Israel out of his sight,* as he had spoken by all his servants the prophets. (2 Kings 17:23)

But there is another answer to this same question, one involving creaturely agency:

> In the ninth year of Hoshea, *the king of Assyria* captured Samaria, and *he carried the Israelites away* to Assyria *and placed them* in Halah, and on the Habor, the river of Gozan, and in the cities of the Medes. (2 Kings 17:6)

So, the Assyrian captivity is the work of God *and* the work of the king of Assyria. The work of this pagan king was ultimately the work of God in the world.

The Destruction of Judah (2 Kings 21, 24)
In response to the many sins of Manasseh king of Judah, God says that *he* will be the one who will destroy Judah:

> Behold, *I am bringing upon Jerusalem and Judah such disaster* that the ears of everyone who hears of it will tingle. (2 Kings 21:12)

But three chapters later we learn that it is roving bands of human beings who destroy Judah:

> And *the LORD sent against him* bands of the *Chaldeans* and bands of the *Syrians* and bands of the *Moabites* and bands of the Ammonites, *and sent them against Judah to destroy it,* according to the word of the LORD that he spoke by his servants the prophets. (2 Kings 24:2)

To leave out the work of these people groups against Judah would be to leave out the way God's work was accomplished in the world.

The Reubenites, Gadites, and Half-tribe of Manasseh War Victoriously over the Hagrites, Jetur, Naphish, and Nodab (1 Chron. 5)
What does God do? Bring about the war: "For many fell, because *the war was of God*" (1 Chron. 5:22).

How does God do it? Via the tribes named:

The *Reubenites,* the *Gadites,* and the half-tribe of *Manasseh* had valiant men who carried shield and sword, and drew the bow, expert in war, 44,760, able to go to war. *They waged war* against the Hagrites, Jetur, Naphish, and Nodab. (1 Chron. 5:18–19)

The Reubenites, Gadites, and Half-tribe of Manasseh Are Brought into Exile (1 Chron. 5)

What does God do? Take them into exile. What do Pul king of Assyria and Tiglath-pileser king of Assyria do? Take them into exile:

So *the God of Israel stirred up the spirit of Pul king of Assyria,* the spirit of Tiglath-pileser king of Assyria, *and he took them into exile,* namely, the Reubenites, the Gadites, and the half-tribe of Manasseh, and brought them to Halah, Habor, Hara, and the river Gozan, to this day. (1 Chron. 5:26)

David's Mighty Men Are Saved by a Great Victory (1 Chron. 11)

What does God do? Save them by a great victory: "And *the* Lord *saved them* by a great victory" (1 Chron. 11:14b).

How does he do it? Eleazar defended a plot of ground and killed the Philistines: "But *he* [i.e., Eleazar] took his stand in the midst of the plot and defended it and killed the Philistines" (1 Chron. 11:14a).

The Philistines Are Defeated at Baal–perazim (1 Chron. 14)

What does God do? Break through David's enemies. How does he do it? By David's hand:

And he went up to Baal-perazim, and *David struck them down* there. And David said, "*God has broken through* my enemies *by my hand,* like a bursting flood." Therefore the name of that place is called Baal-perazim. (1 Chron. 14:11)

David's Enemies Are All Defeated (1 Chron. 17–18)

What does God do? Cut off and subdue all of David's enemies:

I have been with you wherever *you* have gone and have cut off all your enemies from before you. . . . And *I* will subdue all your enemies. (1 Chron. 17:8, 10)

And *the* Lord *gave victory* to David wherever he went. . . . And *the* Lord *gave victory* to David wherever he went. (1 Chron. 18:6, 13)

How does he do it? By way of David, his mighty men, and his armies:

> *David* also defeated Hadadezer king of Zobah-Hamath. (1 Chron. 18:3)

> *David* took from him 1,000 chariots, 7,000 horsemen, and 20,000 foot soldiers. (1 Chron. 18:4a)

> And *David* hamstrung all the chariot horses. (1 Chron. 18:4b)

> *David* struck down 22,000 men of the Syrians. (1 Chron. 18:5)

> *David* put garrisons in Syria of Damascus. (1 Chron. 18:6)

> *Abishai*, the son of Zeruiah, killed 18,000 Edomites in the Valley of Salt. (1 Chron. 18:12)

The Assassination of Ahaziah King of Judah (2 Chron. 22)
Because he "walked in the ways of the house of Ahab" (2 Chron. 22:3), Ahaziah king of Judah faced the judgment of God.
What does God do? Ordain the assassination of Ahaziah:

> But *it was ordained by God* [Hebrew: "it was from God"] that the downfall of Ahaziah should come about through his going to visit Joram. For when he came there, he went out with Jehoram to meet Jehu the son of Nimshi, *whom the LORD had anointed to destroy the house of Ahab*. (2 Chron. 22:7)

How does he do it? Jehu puts him to death:

> *He* [Jehu] searched for Ahaziah, and he was captured while hiding in Samaria, and he was brought to Jehu and put to death. (2 Chron. 22:9)

120,000 Men of Judah Die in a Day (2 Chron. 28)
Why did they die? Pekah king of Israel killed them:

> For *Pekah the son of Remaliah killed* 120,000 from Judah in one day, all of them men of valor, because they had forsaken the LORD, the God of their fathers. (2 Chron. 28:6)

Why did they die? God gave them into Pekah's hand:

> Behold, because *the* LORD, the God of your fathers, was angry with Judah, *he gave them* into your hand. (2 Chron. 28:9)

The Assassination of Sennacherib King of Assyria (2 Chron. 32)
What does God do? He saves Hezekiah king of Judah from Sennacherib king of Assyria:

> So *the* LORD *saved Hezekiah* and the inhabitants of Jerusalem *from the hand of Sennacherib king of Assyria* and from the hand of all his enemies, and he provided for them on every side. (2 Chron. 32:22)

How does he do it? Sennacherib's sons assassinate Sennacherib:

> So he [Sennacherib] returned with shame of face to his own land. And when he came into the house of his god, *some of his own sons struck him down there with the sword.* (2 Chron. 32:21)

Famine, Drought, Pestilence, and Sword (Amos 4)
As we saw in Question 11, God asks a rhetorical question through the prophet Amos: "Does disaster [*ra'ah*] come to a city, unless the LORD has done it?" (Amos 3:6). In the very next chapter, God recounts various ways that he brings disaster through the "agency" of nature, as well as through human agency:

> I gave you cleanness of teeth in all your cities, and lack of bread in all your places. (Amos 4:6)

> I also withheld the rain from you when there were yet three months to the harvest. (Amos 4:7)

> I struck you with blight and mildew. (Amos 4:9)

> I sent among you a pestilence after the manner of Egypt. (Amos 4:10)

> I killed your young men with the sword. (Amos 4:10)

Obviously, God is distinct from the impersonal forces of nature and from creaturely agency. Nevertheless, what the latter do is repeatedly said to be something *God* does.[2]

Jonah Being Cast into the Sea (Jonah 1–2)

Who casts Jonah into the sea? God does: "For *you* cast me into the deep, into the heart of the seas" (Jonah 2:3).

Who casts Jonah into the sea? The sailors do: "So *they* picked up Jonah and hurled him into the sea, and the sea ceased from its raging" (Jonah 1:15).[3]

Five Advantages of the Dual-Agency Model

It Is a Natural Reading of the Biblical Text

One and the same event is produced by two agents (one divine and the other created). This seems to be the repeated testimony of Scripture. And the divine agency language is right there on the surface of the text, just as clear and straightforward as the human agency language. God is not a merely passive observer, or one who merely brings about circumstances and then steps away. Rather, he brings about what the creaturely agents *do* in those circumstances.

It Gives an Answer—Yes—to the Causation Question

Because it's *dual*-agency, the divine causation is just as real as the creaturely causation. The same verbs of causal agency regularly apply to both God and creatures: "sweep away," "make," "bring," "burn," "cut off," "remove," "afflict," "give," "cast out," "bring," "send," "stir up," "take," "save," "break through," "kill."[4] If humans cause things through their agency (and surely they do), then

---

2. Compare Amos 9:1, 3–4: "*I* will kill with the sword . . . *I* will command the serpent, and it shall bite them. . . . *I* will command the sword, and it shall kill them; and I will fix my eyes upon them for evil [*ra'ah*] and not for good."
3. Many more examples of dual-agency could be given. For example, the Sabeans, Chaldeans, fire, and wind took away Job's children, servants, and property (Job 1:13–19) and *God* took them away (Job 1:21). Saul killed Saul (1 Chron. 10:4–6) and *God* killed Saul (1 Chron. 10:13–14). Joseph's brothers sent Joseph into Egypt (Gen. 37:28), the Ishmaelite traders brought him there (Gen. 39:1), and *God* sent him into Egypt (Gen. 45:5, 7; Ps. 105:16–17). Pilate (Matt. 27:26), Jewish officials (Matt. 27:18) and Judas Iscariot (Matt. 26:14–16) give Jesus over to death and *God* "gave him up" to death (Rom. 8:32). Jesus was pierced by the Roman soldiers (John 19:34) and he was smitten, pierced, and crushed by *God* (Isa. 53:4–5, 10). The people of Israel destroyed 25,100 men of Benjamin and *the Lord* defeated Benjamin (Judg. 20:35).
4. The reader will recall a similar list of causal verbs in Question 13, describing God's relation to natural evil. Here, such verbs are applied to God, but with respect to events brought about by creaturely agency rather than impersonal nature.

it's hard to say that God does not cause things through *his* agency, since the same language describes both.

It Guarantees the Preservation of Human Freedom

Because it is *dual*-agency, we cannot reduce the human agency to the divine agency, or vice versa (that would be *single*-agency, which is precisely what the passages rule out). Rather, human agency is preserved, and there is no indication whatsoever that human freedom is removed in any of these cases. Everything about the human agent is "normal." There is never any hint of coercion, brainwashing, zapping, or physical pushing, pulling, dragging, or slapping. Everything you would *expect* in cases of free human choice is there.

It Allows for Human Blameworthiness and Divine Goodness

Because it is *dual*-agency, there can be asymmetry of intentions. So, the human intentions can be evil (and foolish and ignorant and risky), while the divine intentions are good (and wise and knowledgeable and without risk-taking). So in God's case, there can be responsibility without blameworthiness. Because of divine agency, he clearly has responsibility for the outcomes he effects. But because of good divine intentions, he is blameless. Indeed, this kind of asymmetry might be the reason *why* the Scriptures so often "pull back the curtain" to reveal the reality of the divine agency in human affairs. God's people are meant to be encouraged by a broader divine perspective that emphasizes God's good intentions and control even over cases of human wickedness.

It Encourages Caution in Developing Theological Models

It is precisely because there are two "levels" of agency in the world, neither ruling out the other, that this topic is so mysterious. Dual-agency comes as close as we can to establishing a causal relation between God and moral evil, while not answering all the questions we may have about how the two causal levels relate. One model that seems dead on arrival is the "links in a chain" model, where all causation is on the same level, where God acts "earlier" in time, and we act "later" in time. For what is subject to dual-agency is not just initial circumstances or final outcomes, but the totality of very complex and historically extended sequences of events (e.g., the destruction of a king's "house" or progeny, or the exile of Judah). God is not some cosmic billiards player who "gets the ball rolling" in the distant past and then watches for outcomes. Rather, he *effects* the outcomes. *He* defeats, destroys, raises up, and so on, although that is what the creaturely agent does as well.

Summary

By combining the dual-agency model with asymmetry of divine and human intentions, we have a lot of what we want in a theological model of how God relates to moral evil. A robust view of divine causation combines with human freedom and gives us "two sets of intentions" (see Question 7) that preserve human blameworthiness and divine blamelessness. The dual-agency model allows us to *liken* divine causation to human causation, *distinguish* divine causation from human causation, and *distinguish* divine intentions from human intentions. It therefore enables us to give a "yes" answer to each of the questions of divine causation, human freedom, and divine goodness. It is a good start.

Further theological reflection can help fill in some of these gaps in our understanding of the "how." To this end, the next Question will consider two theories of free will ("compatibilist" and "libertarian") and two models of providence which apply them ("Calvinism" and "Molinism"), so that the *metaphysical* question of God's causing free will acts can be further addressed. Important for assessing these models of divine providence is whether they satisfactorily account for the "dual-agency" discussed in this chapter.

REFLECTION QUESTIONS

1. Were you surprised by the language of dual-agency in the Scriptures? If this language is not hidden, why do we rarely talk about it?

2. Can you come up with an example where intentions (good or bad) make the difference between an act being good or being bad?

3. Most examples given in this chapter come from the darkest days in Israel's history. How could that be pastorally relevant to counseling those who suffer today?

4. Divine agency is behind bad things (Assyrian captivity) *and* good things (David's victories). Is that a reason to fear his judgments and be humble with his gifts?

5. Perhaps the divine agency language is just a bunch of poetry with no revelatory significance. Do you think this is a good reply to the argument of this chapter?

What Do Calvinism and Molinism Say About God's Providence over Evil?

Those familiar with contemporary theological debates will have already discerned that a "strong" doctrine of divine providence over evil is being supported in this book, primarily by way of interaction with Scripture. Whether through God's causation of natural evil (e.g., disease, famine, or natural disaster), or his "double-agency" with respect to moral evil (e.g., Job's sufferings, Joseph's betrayal, Jesus's cross), all cases of evil are "of the Lord" and included in his plan for the world. If this is the teaching of Scripture, then it should not be hidden. Rather, God's voice on these difficult matters should be heard and applied to our lives. However, such teaching ought to be carefully circumscribed and safeguarded from distortions. We should also continue to be cautious in the inferences we make from Scripture; my arguments are certainly fallible and open to correction!

This chapter reflects briefly on four models of divine providence that have been vigorously discussed by evangelical Christians:

- *Calvinism:* God plans that moral evil occurs and determines its occurrence.[1]

---

1. On Calvinism more generally, see Shawn Wright, *40 Questions About Calvinism* (Grand Rapids: Kregel Academic, 2019); and David N. Steele, Curtis C. Thomas, and S. Lance Quinn, *The Five Points of Calvinism: Defined, Defended, and Documented,* 2nd ed. (Phillipsburg, NJ: P&R, 2004). For what it is worth, my own attempt to explain why the Calvinistic doctrines of unconditional election and irresistible grace are biblically supportable and defensible from objections, see Greg Welty, "Election and Calling: A Biblical Theological Study," in *Calvinism: A Southern Baptist Dialogue,* eds. Brad Waggoner and E. Ray Clendenen (Nashville: B&H Academic, 2008), 216–43.

- *Molinism:* God plans that moral evil occurs and ensures its occurrence without determining it.[2]
- *Arminianism:* God never plans, determines, or ensures that moral evil occurs, but he does infallibly foreknow its occurrence.[3]
- *Open Theism:* God never plans, determines, ensures, or even infallibly foreknows that moral evil occurs.[4]

Admittedly, these characterizations are thumbnail sketches, and are not intended to represent *all* that is said within these rich, detailed traditions of theological inquiry. Rather, the focus is on how these models *differently relate God to moral evil*. Already we can see that Arminianism and Open Theism seem to be in considerable tension with the biblical data surveyed in Questions 7–11, 13–14. God does not merely allow evil to occur in a way that is entirely passive and unplanned, as in Arminianism, much less govern his universe without knowledge of what will occur, as in Open Theism. In saying this, I do not intend to alienate readers who are persuaded of these latter two views (persuaded perhaps by considerations that go beyond the scope of this book). Rather, I invite them to continue reading the book and see if the "stronger" doctrine of providence represented by Calvinism and Molinism can rise to the challenge of adequately addressing the apologetic and pastoral questions raised by suffering and evil.

Especially in light of the previous chapter (Question 14), what the dual-agency model gets us is a particular *stance* on how divine providence relates to

---

2. On Molinism, see Thomas Flint, *Divine Providence: The Molinist Account* (Ithaca, NY: Cornell University Press, 1998); Kenneth Keathley, *Salvation and Sovereignty: A Molinist Approach* (Nashville: B&H, 2010); and John Laing, *Middle Knowledge: Human Freedom in Divine Sovereignty* (Grand Rapids: Kregel Academic, 2018).
3. On Arminianism more generally, see J. Matthew Pinson, *40 Questions about Arminianism* (Grand Rapids: Kregel Academic, 2022); and Roger E. Olson, *Arminian Theology: Myths and Realities* (Downers Grove, IL: InterVarsity Press, 2006). On whether Arminianism should be distinguished from Molinism, Olson says, "Most classical Arminians are wary of this approach [e.g., Molinism]," and he argues strenuously that "Molinism leads to determinism and is therefore incompatible with Arminianism" (Olson, *Arminian Theology*, 196–97). Similarly, Thomas H. McCall and Keith D. Stanglin argue that there was a diversity of views among the Remonstrant Protestants, that "as a whole, these Protestants do not seem too attached to middle knowledge," and that there was even a "distancing from middle knowledge" among them (*After Arminius: A Historical Introduction to Arminian Theology* [New York: Oxford University Press, 2020], 52).
4. On Open Theism, see Gregory Boyd, *God of the Possible: A Biblical Introduction to the Open View of God* (Grand Rapids: Baker, 2000); William Hasker, *Providence, Evil, and the Openness of God* (New York: Routledge, 2004); John Sanders, *The God Who Risks: A Theology of Divine Providence*, 2nd ed. (Downers Grove, IL: IVP Academic, 2007); Thomas Jay Oord, *The Uncontrolling Love of God: An Open and Relational Account of Providence* (Downers Grove, IL: InterVarsity Press, 2015); and Richard Rice, *The Future of Open Theism: From Antecedents to Opportunities* (Downers Grove, IL: InterVarsity Press, 2020).

free human action. God is not some distant figure who "gets the ball rolling," much less a passive observer. Rather, he plans and *brings about* events involving humans, whether those events are good or bad (*tov* or *ra'ah*). That is not to say that distinct and even competing providential models cannot be developed from this foundation of strong and active providence, just that they must be developed from *this* foundation, for the latter constrains what any successful model will look like. In my view, Calvinism and Molinism are in, while (non-Molinist) Arminianism and Open Theism are out.[5]

Calvinism and Molinism: Differences

But do we have reason to be Calvinists rather than Molinists, or vice versa, when it comes to God's providence over evil? Molinist theologian Kenneth Keathley rightly cautions against investing too much in this debate:

> We are brethren, not adversaries, working in a mutual effort. Until we cross the veil, none of us has arrived on the journey of faith. So I look forward to this cooperative effort, convinced that the end result will be that we are better and more faithful witnesses of our common salvation. Calvinism and Molinism are much more similar than they are dissimilar, so I endeavor to avoid what might be called the narcissism of trivial differences.[6]

Nevertheless, as Keathley himself recognizes, most if not all Molinists advertise their way of relating God to the moral evils in the world as superior to the Calvinist approach. And my experience as a seminary professor for two decades confirms that this question is of considerable interest to many students of the Bible. So, for what it is worth, the remainder of this chapter will weigh in on that question, by first describing the key differences between the models, and then asking (and answering) two important questions about the models.

---

5. For thoughts on why, in my view, Open Theism does not really have an advantage over Calvinism or Molinism when it comes to the problem of suffering and evil, see Greg Welty, "Open Theism, Risk-Taking, and the Problem of Evil," in *Philosophical Essays Against Open Theism*, ed. Benjamin H. Arbour (New York: Routledge, 2018), 140–58. See also Greg Welty, "Review of *The Future of Open Theism: From Antecedents to Opportunities*. Richard Rice. IVP Academic, 2020," *Faith and Philosophy* 38, no. 2 (2021): 294–99. Further critical appraisals of Open Theism can be found in Arbour, *Philosophical Essays Against Open Theism*, as well as in Millard J. Erickson, *What Does God Know and When Does He Know It?* (Grand Rapids: Zondervan, 2003); John Frame, *No Other God: A Response to Open Theism* (Phillipsburg, NJ: P&R, 2001); Bruce Ware, *God's Lesser Glory: The Diminished God of Open Theism* (Wheaton, IL: Crossway, 2000); and John Piper, Justin Taylor, and Paul Kjoss Helseth, eds., *Beyond the Bounds: Open Theism and the Undermining of Biblical Christianity* (Wheaton, IL: Crossway, 2003).
6. Keathley, *Salvation and Sovereignty*, 14.

In Calvinism, God directly ordains evil, because he decides which free choices will be made in which circumstances—it is all ultimately up to him. But in Molinism, God *indirectly* ordains evil because (1) he knows what choices would be made in which circumstances, and (2) he decides which circumstances agents shall find themselves in. So, in Molinism, although *circumstances* are up to God's causal power, the *choices* in those circumstances are up to the agents themselves. God *knows* (by his "middle knowledge") what agents would do if he were to create them and place them in specific circumstances, but he does not *decide* that that is what they would do. What they would do is up to them, not God, and then God uses that knowledge to plan his universe accordingly. By way of contrast, Calvinists eschew this indirect way of doing providence, preferring instead to cut out the middleman of middle knowledge. As typical Reformed confessions put it, "Although God knows whatsoever may or can come to pass upon all supposed conditions, yet hath he not decreed anything because He foresaw it as future, or as that which would come to pass upon such conditions."[7]

The potential payoff for Molinists is threefold. First, humans have genuine *libertarian* free will. They can do otherwise in the same exact circumstances because what they do in those circumstances is up to them. On Calvinism, humans only have "compatibilist" free will, a freedom that is compatible with determinism. The second Molinist payoff is that God does not *cause* any evil choices in the world. For God does not ordain that an agent would choose evil rather than good, in a given circumstance. That is what agents do, not God. And the third Molinist payoff is that God does not *intend* any evil choices in the world, precisely because he is not the one causing the choices. It is up to agents what they choose to do, and then God (knowing what they would choose), incorporates those facts into his plan for the world.

What are we to make of these alleged advantages of Molinism over Calvinism? First, do we in fact have libertarian free will, and if we did, would it be a more valuable kind of free will to have? Unfortunately, such matters are beyond the scope of this book, which is about suffering and evil, not anthropology and philosophy of mind.[8] But even if libertarian free will were a valuable thing to have, it is not clear that Molinism preserves it for us. A libertarian agent must be free to do otherwise in the same exact circumstances. But if Molinism is true,

---

7. *Westminster Confession of Faith* (1647), 3.2. See the identical wording in the *Second London Baptist Confession of Faith* (1689), 3.2. It is the very last clause of the quoted sentence that is supposed to exclude a Molinist model of providence.

8. On Calvinist arguments for "compatibilist" free will, see Questions 8–12 of Wright, *40 Questions About Calvinism*. On Arminian arguments for "libertarian" free will, see Questions 16–17 of Pinson, *40 Questions About Arminianism*. For some philosophical introductions to this controversy, see John Martin Fischer, Robert Kane, Derk Pereboom, and Manuel Vargas, *Four Views on Free Will* (Malden: Blackwell, 2007); and Robert Kane and Carolina Sartorio, *Do We Have Free Will? A Debate* (New York: Routledge, 2022).

is there a possible world in which the agent does otherwise *in the same exact circumstances*? For if she does otherwise, then three things would be different, not just at that time but from all eternity: the *fact* about what she would do would be different, *God's beliefs* about what she will do would be different, and *God's decree* with respect to her would be different. So she could not do otherwise "in the same exact circumstances" after all. Molinists will understandably claim that matters are more complicated than my little argument indicates, but at the very least, it has not been clear to *everyone* who reflects on Molinism that it gives us a version of freedom superior to that had in Calvinism.[9]

Does God Cause Evil?

What are we to make of the second alleged advantage, that in Molinism, God does not *cause* any evil choices in the world? Well, if the philosopher David Lewis is right about our intuitive concept of causation, that "we think of a cause as something that makes a difference, and the difference it makes must be a difference from what would have happened without it," then surely God's decree within Molinism *does* make a difference as to what actually happens, down to the smallest detail.[10] Regardless of God's middle knowledge of what would happen, what will *in fact* happen—including all the evil in the world—does depend on what God decrees. In Molinism, it is up to God and no one else whether he includes any actual evil in his plan for the world, and no evil ever happens unless God decides to include it in that plan. What *else* would be needed for causation?

The following illustration reveals just how close Molinist providence is to ordinary causation. I pull a gun out of my pocket, aim it at a person at point-blank range, and pull the trigger, knowing what guns ordinarily do when fired at point-blank range. The person dies, and I caused his death. (If this is not a case of causation, then I do not know what is, and so I bow out of the discussion altogether.) But what, strictly speaking, did *I* do here? I pulled the trigger in circumstances in which I knew it was very likely that the person would die as a result. I knew this because I know the laws of nature, which are contingent truths about how nature would behave in various circumstances (inertia, explosions, human biology, etc.), truths over which I have no control.

---

9. As Thomas Morris puts it: "If there are truths and infallible divine beliefs about what I shall do, it is hard to see how they can really be beliefs and truths about what I shall do *freely*" (*Our Idea of God: An Introduction to Philosophical Theology* [Downers Grove, IL: InterVarsity Press, 1991], 97). Arminians have raised this concern about Molinism; consider Roger Olson's comments in n. 3 above. So have Open Theists: "But how can we meaningfully say that agents could have done otherwise if all they shall ever do, and all they would have ever done in any possible world, is an unalterable fact an eternity before they even exist?" (Gregory Boyd, in *Divine Foreknowledge: 4 Views*, eds. James Beilby and Paul Eddy [Downers Grove, IL: InterVarsity Press, 2001], 146).

10. The quote is from David Lewis, "Causation," *The Journal of Philosophy* 70 (1973): 557.

That is, I relied on truths that were not up to me (truths about nature), to bring about a particular result involving nature. I knew that in light of these facts about nature, my trigger-pull would result in death. Strictly speaking, my trigger-pull was not *sufficient* for the death, for nature had to cooperate with my trigger-pull in the ways I anticipated. But that does not get me off the hook, metaphysically speaking. Again, I caused the death. My action was sufficient *given other things*. (In general, that is how causation works: my striking a match is sufficient to cause a flame, *given* other things, such as the presence of oxygen and the absence of dampness in the match.)

How is this any different from what God does on Molinism? Here, God creates agents and places them in circumstances, knowing that it was not just likely but *certain* that they would choose what they choose if God so created and placed them. He knows this because he has middle knowledge, that is, knowledge of contingent truths about human nature over which God has no control. As in the gun case, so in Molinism: God relies on truths that are not up to him, to bring about a particular result (the agent's choice). Yes, God's creating agents and placing them in circumstances is not *sufficient* for their choice, strictly speaking. But then again, my trigger-pull was not sufficient for the death either. And yet I caused that death.

So Molinist providence *seems* just as causal as Calvinist providence, in which case the tough questions about causality and divine responsibility do not go away just because one has embraced Molinism. This does not seem to be an advantage that Molinism can credibly advertise.[11]

Does God Intend Evil?

What about the third alleged advantage, that in Molinism, God does not *intend* any evil choices in the world, precisely because he is not the one causing the choices? Well, if the preceding argument is correct, Molinism seems just as saddled with the question of divine causality as Calvinism is, and therefore with divine intentionality. But let us put that aside, and ask a more fundamental question: Do causality and intentionality go hand in hand? Even if divine providence is a kind of causality, does it have to involve God *intending* that all the evil in the world occur, or even that *any* evil occurs? Not at all, and both Calvinists and Molinists would be wise to incorporate this insight into their respective models. Perhaps surprisingly, causation and intention come apart in ways that are not only easy to understand, but which we already accept. As philosopher Heath White puts it:

---

11. There *might* be a way to block the inference to divine causation, but it involves appealing to a strategy that Calvinists themselves have perfected at a confessional level: *go apophatic*, just as Chalcedon does in its teaching about how Christ's two natures relate. For details, and further elaboration of the argument just presented in the text, see Greg Welty, "Molinist Gunslingers: God and the Authorship of Sin," in *Calvinism and the Problem of Evil*, eds. David E. Alexander and Daniel M. Johnson (Eugene, OR: Pickwick Publications, 2016), 56–77.

> Not everything I cause, even knowingly cause, do I intend. For example, I am constantly causing my shoe soles to wear down by walking around in them, but even though I know this is happening I do not, properly speaking, intend it. I would be perfectly happy if my shoe soles lasted forever.[12]

That is, what I *intend* is to take a walk. But while I know that my taking a walk involves wear and tear on my shoes—indeed, that it will *cause* such wear and tear—it seems implausible in the extreme to say that I intend to wear my shoes down every time I take a walk, even if that is what *happens* when I take a walk, and even if I *know* that it happens!

Another illustration of causation without intention comes from "the principle of double effect": in an act of self-defense, I can both save my life *and* kill the aggressor, while only intending the former and *not* the latter (even though I cause both and know I cause both). Thus Thomas Aquinas:

> Nothing hinders one act from having two effects, only one of which is intended, while the other is beside the intention. . . . Accordingly the act of self-defense may have two effects, one is the saving of one's life, the other is the slaying of the aggressor.[13]

These examples of shoes wearing down and of self-defense successfully illustrate causation without intention because they both make use of a basic moral fact: intentions are not closed under known entailment. If person S intends to bring about p, and S knows that p implies q (e.g., the shoes will wear down, or the aggressor will be slain), it does not follow that S thereby *intends* q. One does not intend everything which is implied by the occurrence of what one intends. So let us say that God intends the world he creates and providentially sustains and that he intends this whole in virtue of some property p that applies to the whole: the world's overall intrinsic value, or the fact that the world (will ultimately) tend to promote his glory or manifest the full range of his attributes. God intends the world in virtue of this property p, even though he knows that his creation of such a world implies sinful human act q occurring in its history. Since intentions are not closed under known entailment, it does not follow that God thereby intends q.[14]

---

12. Heath White, *Fate and Free Will* (Notre Dame: University of Notre Dame Press, 2020), 297.
13. Thomas Aquinas, *Summa Theologica* II.ii, q. 64, a. 7 *respondeo*.
14. To think otherwise would be to commit the fallacy of division, to think that what is true of the whole must be true of each of the parts. As Paul Helm puts it, "It is a fallacy to think that because some arrangement is wise, every detail of that arrangement, considered in isolation, is wise. It does not follow that every thread of my tartan tie is tartan" (Paul Helm, in eds. Beilby and Eddy, *Divine Foreknowledge*, 182). Similarly, we should not think that

Does Molinism Account for Dual-Agency?

Whether or not Calvinists can neutralize the three alleged advantages of Molinism in the ways I have indicated above, there is at least one respect in which the shoe seems to be on the other foot, where Calvinism seems to be preferable to Molinism. And that is, Molinism does not seem to come close to accounting for the pervasive scriptural language of dual-agency considered in the previous Question. That language seems to be the language of causation precisely because agency *is* causation. But Molinists are fond of the example of entrapment as an illustration of their view, and it is not hard to see why. Just as the DEA agent sets up circumstances in which he knows that the suspect is likely to sell drugs illegally (but the DEA agent does not *cause* this), so God, on the Molinist view, sets up circumstances in which he knows that persons will do bad things (but God does not *cause* this). But the entrapment metaphor seems to fall woefully short. In the dual-agency passages, God does not say, "I set up a circumstance in which I knew that *someone else* would kill you with the sword." Rather, God says, "*I* killed you with the sword." God does not just bring about circumstances. He brings about the events that take place in the circumstances. He does not just use other people to kill people. Rather, he kills them. To make God the subject of the action in this way is no doubt mysterious, and even unsettling. But the Molinist model does not seem to preserve the crucial scriptural details that generate the mystery. They just drop out.

As we saw in the previous Question, the model of providence that best accords with Scripture is not the "links in a chain" model, where God gets the ball rolling in the distant past and then passively observes outcomes in the present. It is not that God causes X to cause Y, which in turn causes Z, and so on. Rather, God brings about "X causes Y." The whole situation is his work. In the dual-agency passages, the entirety of "X causing Y" is *redescribed* as God's work. The right model here is not a game of pool, but Mars Hill. We not only have our being in God; our very living and moving is in God as well (Acts 17:28). All things are not only to him (redounding to his praise), but from him and through him (effected by his power) (Rom. 11:36). With respect to space and time, divine causality in providence is pervasive and intimate, not isolated and distant.

Summary

The current chapter has argued that the biblical data considered so far in this book is best accommodated by the Calvinist and Molinist models of providence, rather than the Arminian and Open Theist models. This is primarily because Calvinists and Molinists agree that God *includes* evil in his

---

because some arrangement is intended, every detail of that arrangement, considered in isolation, is intended.

providential plan and *ensures* its occurrence. As a secondary conclusion of this chapter, it is at least arguable that Molinism does not have the three advantages over Calvinism that are commonly advertised: preservation of libertarian free will, avoidance of divine causation of the occurrence of moral evil, or explaining how God does not intend evil. Finally, Molinism might have more problems than Calvinism in accounting for the dual-agency passages surveyed in the last Question.

But deciding between Calvinism and Molinism is not the main point of this book.[15] It is more than enough, for our remaining apologetic and pastoral concerns (parts 3 and 4 of this book), to focus not on where these views differ but on what they have in common: God acts in such a way that free human agency brings about results that God ultimately works for a greater good, in line with God's perfectly wise, good, and sovereign plan. So, unless noted otherwise, I have written this book in such a way that it accords with the Calvinist and Molinist views. Advocates of other views are welcome to benefit from this book despite my choices here. After all, the book covers quite a bit of the Bible, which is just as much their book as mine. I take the differences between Calvinism and Molinism to be a non-issue when it comes to equipping Christians with intelligent and defensible answers about suffering and evil in the world, and so these differences will not be making an appearance in the remainder of this book.

REFLECTION QUESTIONS

1. As evidenced by the footnotes in this chapter, the debate over models of divine providence is vigorous and detailed. Do you think Christians sometimes fall into what Keathley calls "the narcissism of trivial differences"? What principles can guide us away from this pitfall?

2. Molinists say their view preserves libertarian free will, whereas their detractors disagree. What is the best way for Calvinists and others to represent the Molinist point of view: saying that "Molinists do not *really* believe in libertarian free will," or saying that "Molinists might have problems *explaining* how we retain libertarian free will"? What is the difference between these representations?

3. Does being a cause require me to contribute *everything* that is needed for an outcome? If not, what does it require me to do?

---

15. It *is* the main point of the following book: John D. Laing, Kirk R. MacGregor, and Greg Welty, eds., *Calvinism and Middle Knowledge: A Conversation* (Eugene, OR: Pickwick Publications, 2019).

4. According to the shoes-wearing-down and self-defense examples, we can be causes of what we do not intend, even if we knowingly cause the outcome. Philosophical argument often proceeds by way of raising these kinds of counterexamples. Is it an effective strategy, in your view?

5. Arminians and Open Theists would not agree with the model of providence argued in the previous Questions and assumed in the remaining Questions. So what reasons could they have to finish this book anyway?

Does God Suffer?

Part 2 of this book ("Biblical and Theological Questions About Suffering and Evil") has been devoted to how God relates to the suffering and evil which we suffer as human beings. Does he aim at any goods by way of our suffering? Does he often keep us in the dark as to what he is up to? How does he relate, specifically, to natural and moral evils? What is the best way to understand his providence over the evils we suffer? And so on. The discussion has focused on God's transcendence, on how his goodness, sovereign power, and wisdom considerably exceed our own. But the Question of this current chapter, which finishes up part 2 of the book, is focused not on our suffering but God's. Do we have biblical or theological reason to think that God suffers? The question is important, because *if* God suffers, that could be of supreme relevance in helping answer some of the apologetic and pastoral questions that will be asked in parts 3 and 4 of the book, respectively. So it would be wise to consider this question before we move on.

In my view, God does suffer, but only *as a man*, that is, in Christ. I find it unhelpful from a theological point of view, and perhaps even counterproductive from an apologetic and pastoral point of view, to insist that God suffers *as God*, in and of himself and quite apart from the incarnation. Admittedly, the latter has become an increasingly popular view in our day, especially as a kind of response to the massive suffering endured by humanity in the twentieth century. Perhaps religion will not be relevant to contemporary humans unless God suffers at least as much as Holocaust sufferers did. And if he is not subject to enormous suffering, what use is he in our daily lives?[1]

---

1. Paul Fiddes (a defender of divine suffering) and Thomas Weinandy (an opponent of it) identify the suffering of the Holocaust and of Hiroshima as a catalyst for the contemporary popularity of a theology of divine suffering. See Paul Fiddes, *The Creative Suffering of God* (Oxford: Oxford University Press, 1998), 2–5, 21–22; and Thomas Weinandy, *Does God Suffer?* (Edinburgh: T&T Clark, 2000), 2–6. Both Oxford theologians in turn credit Jürgen Moltmann as one who (in Weinandy's words) "develops the need for a suffering God in the

The remainder of this chapter will weigh in on this question from several angles:

- Why think God *only* suffers as a man?
- Why think that God suffers as God?
- What are some problems with God suffering as God?
- How is scriptural language about divine suffering best interpreted?

The Traditional View: God Suffers as Man, But Not as God

The view of the ancient, medieval, and early modern church—that is, the church prior to the rise of Protestant liberalism—seemed to be that God, if he suffers, would only suffer as man and not as God. Of course, it would be extremely naïve to suppose that we should be suspicious of any new doctrine or practice merely because it came after the rise of Protestant liberalism. After all, Great Britain (1833) and the United States (1865) did not outlaw slavery until after the rise of Protestant liberalism, but that is no reason to lament this change rather than rejoice over it. In the end, arguments for any such change in theological view or church practice should be considered on their merits, rather than dismissed through historical association, and that is what this Question seeks to do.

One reason for thinking that God cannot suffer as God is because the perfection of the divine nature precludes it. Suffering seems to challenge divine aseity, immutability, and omnipotence. First, if God exists *a se* and so is self-existent, then he does not depend on anything distinct from him to be who he is. As Paul put it in his Mars Hill sermon, God is not a dependent being; rather, "he himself gives to all mankind life and breath and everything" (Acts 17:25). It is "in him we live and move and have our being" (Acts 17:28); God does not live and move and have his being in us or because of us. Or as Paul put it to the Romans, "From him and through him and to him are all things" (Rom. 11:36; see 1 Cor. 8:6). All things are ultimately from him, and this presumably includes his own experiences. God's providence may bring about suffering for us, but we do not bring about suffering for God. Second, if the nature of the Creator is that he "is blessed forever" (Rom. 1:25; 9:5; 2 Cor. 11:31), presumably the introduction of significant suffering into his experience would undermine that blessing, and so introduce change into his nature in a way that is unacceptable (Mal. 3:6; James 1:17). Third, it is typical of at least our significant sufferings that they are involuntary and not subject to our control, revealing our lack of power to avoid or immediately alleviate them. Attributing such lack of power to God seems improper (Jer. 32:17, 27; Matt. 19:26; Luke 1:37).

---

light of Auschwitz" (Weinandy, *Does God Suffer?*, 4; Fiddes, *The Creative Suffering of God*, 4). See Jürgen Moltmann, *The Crucified God* (London: SCM, 1974).

Of course, all these arguments are defeasible. (Notice my repeated use of the term "presumably.") They deserve to be defeated if stronger arguments are found for the other side. But these considerations at least help us understand why a traditional view of God might be held to exclude divine suffering.

Another reason for thinking that God cannot suffer as God is because the orthodox consensus that emerged in the early church about the two natures of Christ seems to presuppose this. According to the creed of Chalcedon (AD 451), "One and the same Son, our Lord Jesus Christ" has two natures: the divine nature (he is "perfect in Godhead" and "truly God") and the human nature (he is "perfect in manhood" and "truly man, of a reasonable soul and body"). Thus, he is "to be acknowledged in two natures, inconfusedly, un-changeably, indivisibly, inseparably; the distinction of natures being by no means taken away by the union, but rather the property of each nature being preserved."[2]

According to Chalcedon, different properties characterize different na-tures. Indeed, if this were not the case, the distinction of the natures could not be preserved. So, whereas the divine nature is "consubstantial with the Father according to the Godhead," the human nature is "consubstantial with us ac-cording to the Manhood." According to one nature, Jesus can be "begotten before all ages of the Father according to the Godhead," and according to the other nature, Jesus can be "in these latter days . . . born of the Virgin Mary . . . according to the Manhood." Presumably, Jesus "increased in wisdom and in stature" (Luke 2:52) with respect to the human nature, since with respect to the divine nature he is already omniscient and omnipotent. Likewise, he both walks from Galilee to Jerusalem and eats a meal with respect to the human nature, since with respect to the divine nature he is both omnipresent (and so already present at Jerusalem) and suffers no hunger (lacking a digestive system).

Such a view provides conceptual space for the idea that, if any suffering is to be had in God, it must be by way of the only nature that could be subject to suffering, and that was presumed to be the human nature alone. Thus, the early church opposed "patripassianism"—the idea that the Father suffers on the cross—precisely because the Father does not have a human nature like the Son, and so cannot be said to suffer. More generally, the Monophysite view (that Christ had only one nature, not two) was opposed on the grounds that Christ's one nature would not be an appropriate place to locate Christ's suf-fering, because it would not preserve divine immutability and impassibility. The assumption, again, was that divinity as such could not suffer. The human nature was needed.

Beyond this ancient (and medieval) opposition to patripassianism and Monophysitism, which seem to presuppose that God does not suffer, early modern Reformed confessions enshrine the view that God is "without body,

---

2.   Philip Schaff, *The Creeds of Christendom,* vol. 2 (New York: Harper & Brothers, 1877), 62.

parts, or passions."³ It is difficult to attribute literal suffering to a God who is without passions.⁴

The Promise of Divine Suffering

Still, it is not hard to find extremely intelligent and very pious Christians arguing that God not only does suffer but *must* suffer, and to see such Christians advertising the apologetic and pastoral benefits of this view as well. For example, this perspective comes to the fore in Christian philosopher Nicholas Wolterstorff's book, *Lament for a Son*.⁵ Wolterstorff wrote this book after the untimely death of his college-aged son in a mountain-climbing accident. I regularly assign it to seminary students in my problem of evil class, and I will return to his pastoral wisdom in part 4 of this book, as Wolterstorff makes many extraordinarily helpful points about coming to grips with suffering. These include exposing us to the full range of the questions of the grieving, coming to appreciate the intrinsic value of grief (as something not to be ashamed of),⁶ the importance of lament as a balanced, biblical response to suffering,⁷ the relevance of Christian hope in helping us realize there is more to life than the loss suffered,⁸ how to deal meaningfully with our regrets,⁹ and the reality of divine inscrutability.¹⁰

But in addition, Wolterstorff introduces the theme of the suffering of God:

> We strain to hear. But instead of hearing an answer we catch sight of God himself scraped and torn. Through our tears we see the tears of God. . . . Why do you permit yourself to suffer, O God?
>
> For a long time I knew that God is not the impassive, unresponsive, unchanging being portrayed by the classical theologians. . . . God is not only the God of the sufferers but the God who suffers. The pain and fallenness of humanity have entered into his heart. Through the prism of my tears I have seen a suffering God. . . . Instead of explaining our suffering God shares it.

---

3. *Westminster Confession of Faith*, chapter 2, section 1; *Second London Baptist Confession of Faith*, chapter 2, section 1.
4. The incompatibility of the divine nature with the experience of *our* characteristic kinds of sufferings will be further argued below, under "A Dilemma for Divine Suffering."
5. Nicholas Wolterstorff, *Lament for a Son* (Grand Rapids: Eerdmans, 1987).
6. Wolterstorff, *Lament for a Son*, 5, 13, 28, 31–32.
7. Wolterstorff, *Lament for a Son*, 6, 22, 70–71.
8. Wolterstorff, *Lament for a Son*, 38, 92–93, 101–2.
9. Wolterstorff, *Lament for a Son*, 64–65.
10. Wolterstorff, *Lament for a Son*, 67–68, 74, 76–77.

Do we also mirror God in suffering? Are we to mirror him ever more closely in suffering? Was it meant that we should be icons in suffering? Is it our glory to suffer?

God is love. That is why he suffers. To love our suffering sinful world is to suffer. God so suffered for the world that he gave up his only Son to suffering. The one who does not see God's suffering does not see his love. God is suffering love. So suffering is down at the center of things, deep down where the meaning is. Suffering is the meaning of our world. For Love is the meaning. And Love suffers. The tears of God are the meaning of history.

We're in it together, God and we, together in the history of our world. The history of our world is the history of our suffering together. Every act of evil extracts a sob from God. But also the history of our world is the history of our deliverance together. God's work to release himself from his suffering is his work to deliver the world from its agony; our struggle for joy and justice is our struggle to relieve God's sorrow.[11]

Wolterstorff is not the only Christian philosopher to find value in the notion that God suffers as God. Alvin Plantinga, one of Wolterstorff's classmates at Calvin College in the 1950s, also endorses this view:

As the Christian sees things, God does not stand idly by, coolly observing the suffering of his creatures. He enters into and shares our suffering. He endures the anguish of seeing his son, the second person of the Trinity, consigned to the bitterly cruel and shameful death of the cross. Some theologians claim that God cannot suffer. I believe they are wrong. God's capacity for suffering, I believe, is proportional to his greatness; it exceeds our capacity for suffering in the same measure as his capacity for knowledge exceeds ours. Christ was prepared to endure the agonies of hell itself; and God, the Lord of the universe, was prepared to endure the suffering consequent upon his son's humiliation and death.[12]

---

11. Wolterstorff, *Lament for a Son*, 80, 81, 83, 90, 91.
12. Alvin Plantinga, "Self-Profile," in *Alvin Plantinga*, eds. James Tomberlin and Peter van Inwagen (Dordrecht: D. Reidel, 1985), 36.

The key idea in both thinkers seems to go beyond Christ's redemptive suffering *as a man* on our behalf. Rather, in all our suffering, God suffers *as God*. And the knowledge that God suffers somehow *helps us* in our own suffering. Whatever the virtues of the traditional view of God, it supposedly comes up short in this respect.

A Dilemma for Divine Suffering

I am sympathetic to the reasons many have for believing that God suffers as God, and that he must do so if he is to comfort us in our griefs. Still, I face two roadblocks in accepting this view, one intellectual and the other practical. Though these are linked, they can be distinguished.

On the intellectual side, there seems to be a dilemma for the very idea of divine suffering, one that poses a challenge to its coherence. Reflect on what is characteristic of our own suffering—what makes it so awful? There is the raw, physical pain. But in addition, a whole host of feelings and passions cloud our judgment and push us to the breaking point:

- *Ignorance:* Will my suffering end? I have no idea. Beyond that, the intensity of it surprises me.
- *Helplessness:* I feel as if there is *nothing* I can do to fix my situation.
- *Frustration:* I *try* again and again to relieve my pain, but nothing works.
- *Hopelessness:* I do not see *any* light at the end of the tunnel. When will this pain end? I have no idea, and I only expect more.
- *Despair:* At times, I simply lack confidence that life is worth living. I struggle to come up with reasons to go on.
- *Anguish and agony:* Forget the future—my pain is so great that it is difficult to think or even function in the present. I cannot do the things I normally do.
- *Anxiety:* All that I ever hoped to do with my life is now under threat. Will I finish my projects? Will I lose my friendships? If I do not make it through my pain, does my life not lack significance?
- *Loneliness and alienation:* Why is God not delivering me from this? Has he abandoned me? Does he not care for me?
- *Limitation:* All the previous feelings put together make me keenly aware of my limitations. I cannot remove my pain, *and* I cannot go on with my pain. I feel small and fragile, continually at the mercy of forces I cannot control.

If we are honest with ourselves, "the suffering in our suffering" is found in the above list. Now, either God's own suffering shares the above characteristics or it does not. Either way lie consequences impossible to accept. If God's suffering genuinely *does* share these characteristics, then he is subject to *limitations as God*, and that seems to undermine our very confession that he *is* God. (Or, at the very least, we have a God who *believes* he is radically limited when he is not, which seems just as bad, since a radically deceived being cannot be God.)

But if God's suffering as God does not share these characteristics, then how does God genuinely enter into *our* suffering? On this view, God "suffers," but he is not ignorant, or helpless, or frustrated, or hopeless, or despairing, or anguished, or agonizing, or anxious, or lonely, or alienated from God, or limited. But if not, then how is his "suffering" at all like our suffering (see Heb. 5:7–8)? He does not *really* suffer as we do. But then what is the significance of his suffering, since he suffers no *real* limitation in it?

Thomas Weinandy seems to make a similar point: unless God suffers *as a man*, his suffering is not really an entering into *our kind of suffering*. Suffering *as divine* would be an experience totally alien to us mere human beings, and so such divine suffering leaves us *alone* in our suffering:

> Even if one did allow the Son of God to suffer in his divine nature, this would negate the very thing one wanted to preserve and cultivate. For if the Son of God experienced suffering in his divine nature, he would no longer be experiencing human suffering in an authentic and genuine human manner, but instead he would be experiencing "human suffering" in a divine manner which would then be neither genuinely nor authentically human. . . . If one wishes to say in truth that the Son of God actually experienced and knew what it was like to be born, eat, sleep, cry, fear, grieve, groan, rejoice, suffer, die, and most of all, love *as a man*, and it seems this is precisely what one does want to say, then the experience and knowledge of being born, eating, sleeping, crying, fearing, grieving, groaning, rejoicing, suffering, dying, and again most of all, loving must be predicated of the Son of God solely and exclusively *as a man*. . . . This is what humankind is crying out to hear, not that God experiences, in a divine manner, our anguish and suffering in the midst of a sinful and depraved world, but that he actually experienced and knew first hand, as one of us—as a man—human anguish and suffering within a sinful and depraved world.[13]

---

13. Weinandy, *Does God Suffer?*, 204 n. 60, 206. Weinandy cites Thomas Aquinas's commentary on the book of Hebrews as supporting his position. On Aquinas's view, God "*understands* our misery" as God, and does so "without any passion." But only in Christ has God "*experienced* our misery."

There is a practical problem as well. Even if I could intellectually reconcile divine suffering with God's status as God, it is wholly unclear what the
pastoral value of God's suffering as God is supposed to be. Wolterstorff clearly
thinks there is such pastoral value:

> Upon entering the company of the suffering, they discern the
> anguish of God. By this anguish they are comforted. Upon
> joining the crowd on the bench of mourning, they hear the
> sobs and see the tears of God. By these they are consoled.[14]

But why? Why would we be consoled to hear the sobbing of God? When I
think of sobbing, I think of someone who does not have things under control,
who cannot guarantee tomorrow, who cannot make things right. Why would
a God in that kind of situation be a *comfort* to me? Why would a God who is
subject to all the characteristics listed above be a help to me? And as it turns
out, Wolterstorff indicates that this "suffering God" motif leaves things mysterious, generating more questions than he had before:

> But mystery remains. Why isn't Love-*without*-suffering the
> meaning of things? Why is *suffering*-Love the meaning? Why
> does God endure his suffering? Why does he not at once re-
> lieve his agony by relieving ours?[15]

When I look for real help in my struggles, I am not looking for someone
who is in the same psychological quicksand in which I am sinking. I need
someone who is standing on solid ground, who from that vantage point can
reach down and rescue me. Or, to switch metaphors, a physician does not
need to feel the pain of the patient to be a good doctor. In fact, if a physician
or psychiatrist were suffering as much as the patient, he would be in no position to treat the patient. If God suffers, is God a manic-depressive? This is not
a frivolous question. Many millions of people suffer every day. If God suffers
along with them, would God not be very depressed, even suicidal?

The Scriptural Witness
This is not to say that there is no *prima facie* scriptural support for the
view that God suffers. There is. But such language needs to be carefully interpreted. The earlier quote from Plantinga does refer to the scriptural narrative
about the cross. But the idea that the Father "endures the anguish of seeing
his son" on the cross, and "was prepared to endure the suffering consequent
upon his son's humiliation and death," does not seem to be anything that the

14. Wolterstorff, *Lament for a Son*, 88.
15. Wolterstorff, *Lament for a Son*, 90.

scriptural writers ever say. In fact, what Scripture we have about God's emotional state toward the cross does not really communicate that God the Father *suffers* in light of it. While Jesus was "a man of sorrows and acquainted with grief" (Isa. 53:3), the divine author of that suffering isn't said to suffer. Rather, "It was the will of the LORD to crush him" (Isa. 53:10).[16]

In *Lament for a Son*, Wolterstorff mentions three Scripture passages that seem to indicate divine suffering. First, "If the death of the devout costs you dear (Psalm 116:15), why do you permit it?"[17] But this text does not say that God suffers, but rather that our death is precious to him: "Precious in the sight of the Lord is the death of his saints." Wolterstorff interprets this in terms of our death being "costly" to God (i.e., God incurs a loss by our death). But why not see it as simply a statement of his great love for us? We are "highly valued" or "prized" by him (see Ps. 72:14). He takes care of us and preserves us. A second passage is Isaiah 53:4.[18] But traditionally, that has been seen as speaking of Christ in his humanity. The third passage is Isaiah 63:9:

> In all their affliction He was afflicted, And the angel of His presence saved them; In His love and in His mercy He redeemed them, And He lifted them and carried them all the days of old. (NASB 1995)[19]

However, as several translations point out, an alternate reading of the Hebrew for "He was afflicted" is "He was not an adversary" or "He did not afflict." And the entire passage is rather poetic: "He *lifted* them and *carried* them." Isaiah is using the language of accommodation (63:5, "arm"; 63:12, "arm"). God does not literally have the qualities *we* have in our anguish: a sense of hopelessness, helplessness, or despair. God does not endure mood swings, going from a state of anguish to not being anguished. With him there is no variableness (James 1:17). However, he does have a powerful disposition of compassion toward his people. Indeed, this is God's *unchanging* disposition toward his people.[20]

---

16. Or as the KJV says: "It pleased the LORD to bruise him."
17. Wolterstorff, *Lament for a Son*, 80.
18. Wolterstorff, *Lament for a Son*, 81–82, 90, 108.
19. Wolterstorff, *Lament for a Son*, 108.
20. See Psalm 103:17: "But the steadfast love of the LORD is from everlasting to everlasting on those who fear him." Calvin comments on Isaiah 63:9: "By speaking like this he declares the incomparable love that God bears toward his people. In order to move us more powerfully and draw us to himself, *the Lord accommodates himself to human understanding* by attributing to himself all the affection, love, and compassion that a father can have. And yet in human affairs it is impossible to conceive of any sort of kindness or benevolence that God does not immeasurably surpass" (emphasis added). See John Calvin, *Isaiah*, vol. 24, The Crossway Classic Commentaries (Wheaton, IL: Crossway, 2000), 375.

Summary

While this Question has introduced the topic of "divine suffering," it has by no means *proven* that defenders of the latter are misguided. But I do think that God's suffering *as God*, if it were to exist, would be far less helpful to us in our suffering than many proponents advertise. There seem to be some inconsistencies in the arguments for divine suffering. Finally, I do not find the scriptural case for divine suffering to be all that compelling. For these reasons, few of my apologetic and pastoral perspectives on suffering and evil (parts 3 and 4 of the book) depend on the idea that God literally suffers. Though I put great stock in the idea that God is loving, merciful, and compassionate—as well as all-wise and all-powerful—the only kind of suffering I will be attributing to God is that which he experiences *as a man*. Advocates of divine suffering are invited to supplement the arguments of parts 3 and 4 with additional perspectives of their own.

REFLECTION QUESTIONS

1. Assuming that God is independent of the creature, immutable, and omnipotent, could he still suffer as God? How would such suffering have to differ from ours?

2. Could God suffer while also remaining "blessed forever" (Rom. 1:25; 9:5; 2 Cor. 11:31)?

3. Wolterstorff says that God "sent his beloved son to suffer *like* us" (*Lament for a Son*, 81). Is that not suffering as a man, since that is the only way *we* suffer?

4. "The suffering in our suffering" was described in nine ways. Could there be a kind of suffering that is not describable in *any* of those ways?

5. What would be a good reason to interpret the "bodily," anthropomorphic language about God nonliterally, but interpret the "feeling," anthropopathic language about God literally?

PART 3

Apologetic Questions About Suffering and Evil

Questions Related to
General Apologetic Strategies
on the Problem of Evil

What Is the Intellectual Problem of Evil Against God's Existence?

The problem of evil is one of the most discussed objections to the existence of God. A quick perusal of the typical philosophy anthologies focusing on objections to God's existence reveals that this objection always seems to be included, regardless of editors or publishers. This is probably because the problem of evil is a top reason many unbelievers give for their unbelief. My primary reason for thinking this is my experience in talking with unbelievers for thirty-eight years and teaching in a seminary context for twenty years. I was brought up in a non-Christian home, my wife and I are the only evangelical Christians in our extended families (with a couple of exceptions), and I went to non-Christian schools (except for seminary). We have lots of conversations with unbelievers, and the problem of evil *is* a top reason for many. In addition, I have lots of students who come to me as an apologetics professor with questions from their unbelieving friends, and again their concern about evil confirms my suspicions.

This evidence is admittedly anecdotal. However, recent research seems to support the idea that the problem of evil is a top reason given for unbelief. A few years ago, Barna Research Group published their research on Generation Z unbelievers, compared with Millennials, Gen X, and Boomers.[1] They found that atheism among Gen Z is double that in the general population, and when you ask them why they are atheists, their number-one answer is: "I have a hard time believing that a good God would allow so much evil or suffering in the world." This is the top answer among seven answers given. This same answer is the second highest one for Millennials, the third highest one for Gen X, and the fifth highest for Boomers. That is, the generational trend is

---

1. Barna Research Group, "Atheism Doubles Among Generation Z" (January 24, 2018; https://www.barna.com/research/atheism-doubles-among–generation-z/).

that *the problem of evil is the increasingly popular answer people give for their unbelief when you go from past to present.* Clearly, ministry focused on the Great Commission (Matt. 28:18–20) would do well to take this issue seriously.

To that end, this Question commences part 3 of the book, "Apologetic Questions About Suffering and Evil." As we learned in Question 1, "apologetics" comes from the Greek word *apologia*, which means "reasoned defense." Christian apologetics is the practice of defending the Christian faith from intellectual objections. The phenomenon of suffering and evil in the world has been used as the basis of an argument against the existence of God, often called "the problem of evil." We seek to develop an effective response to this argument by reviewing *general apologetic strategies* on the problem of evil (Questions 17–20) and *specific apologetic answers* to the problem of evil (Questions 21–28). We do this by building upon and applying the methodological, biblical, and theological foundations laid earlier in parts 1 and 2.

The current Question distinguishes the intellectual problem of evil from the very different emotional problem of evil, identifies two versions of the intellectual problem of evil (logical and evidential), and surveys historical sources for the problem. It closes by offering a simple statement of the intellectual problem, thus providing a clear basis for subsequent discussion in later Questions about how to answer it.

Distinguishing the Intellectual and Emotional Versions of the Problem

Fundamentally, the intellectual problem of evil is a reasoned argument against the existence of God, whereas the emotional problem of evil is a psychological or spiritual condition of alienation from God. They are both problems we face because of the evil in the world, but they pose different challenges and call for different solutions. The intellectual problem of evil argues that the evil in the world gives us a good reason to reject the existence of God. It is an argument for atheism, claiming to start from premises everyone accepts (the fact of evil, and that God is supposed to be perfectly powerful and good) and concluding that God cannot exist (or, alternatively, that God probably does not exist). By way of contrast, the emotional problem of evil is not so much an argument as a *mood*, a kind of perplexing distress that can descend upon us when we personally suffer evil or observe the suffering of others. As Question 1 put it, "suffering and evil are a challenge to living the Christian life" because "experiencing suffering and evil can unsettle our faith in God's promises, distort our perception of God's character, weaken our loyalty to God's purposes, and harden our hearts so that we are bitter toward God and others." The intellectual problem of evil primarily calls for our reasoned response by way of counterargument and will occupy our attention throughout part 3 (apologetic questions). The emotional problem of evil primarily calls for our prayer, presence, and personal counseling for those who suffer it, and will occupy our attention in part 4 (pastoral questions).

The intellectual problem of evil can take different forms: "logical" and "evidential." The logical problem of evil says that evil is *logically incompatible* with the existence of God—the existence of just one speck of evil in the world, no matter how small or trivial, is sufficient to show that God *cannot* exist. For if God is all-powerful, he would be able to prevent any evil, and if he is all-good, then he would want to prevent all evil. So, the existence of *any evil at all* is a decisive disproof of God's existence. Because God's attributes require that there be no evil at all, God and evil could never coexist. One might as well think there could be a world with an irresistible force and an immovable object. Such a world would be contradictory, and the same goes for a world with both God and evil. It is an impossible situation, argues the atheist. It could never exist. Since the existence of evil is obvious, it is belief in the existence of God which must go.

The evidential problem of evil makes a somewhat more modest claim: evil is *evidence against* the existence of God. Strictly speaking, perhaps the existence of God is logically compatible with there being some evil in the world. Maybe God has a good reason for allowing that evil (to preserve free will, to shape our character, and so on). But there is just *so much* evil in the world, and some of it is so absolutely horrific and utterly unnecessary, that it is surely very *unlikely* that God exists (even if that is not impossible). If you walked through Metropolis and saw constant acts of murder, terrorism, rape, and theft, along with plagues and tornadoes, it might be *possible* that Superman lives in Metropolis. But you would regard it as very unlikely. Would there not be a lot less evil if someone with his powers and good intentions were around? How much more unlikely would it be that an *all*-powerful and *all*-good being is around?

Imagine if we could come up with clever replies to the intellectual problem of evil (in both its logical and evidential forms). Perhaps we can show the reasoning is invalid or weak, or there is a key premise somewhere that is insufficiently supported or even false. It might take a lengthy detour through many pages of complicated philosophy, but perhaps it can be done. Such an academic triumph might not help someone who remains numb, grief-stricken, and alienated from God due to their *experience* of evil. That is, answers to the intellectual problem of evil may be ill-equipped to serve what Christian philosopher Alvin Plantinga calls a "pastoral function." As he puts it:

> Confronted with evil in his own life or suddenly coming to realize more clearly than before the *extent* and *magnitude* of evil, a believer in God may undergo a crisis of faith. He may be tempted to follow the advice of Job's "friends"; he may be tempted to "curse God and die." Neither a Free Will Defense

nor a Free Will Theodicy [that is, answers to the *intellectual* problem of evil] is designed to be of much help or comfort to one suffering from such a storm in the soul. . . . Neither is to be thought of first of all as a means of pastoral counseling. Probably neither will enable someone to find peace with himself and with God in the face of the evil the world contains. But then, of course, neither is intended for that purpose.[2]

Plantinga makes this point as a way of defending the "Free Will Defense"—his preferred answer to the logical problem of evil—from the following kind of objection: "Your intellectual answer does not make me *feel* any better about the pain and suffering I see and experience." Plantinga's point is that his philosophical rebuttal to atheists is not *meant* to do that; other, more pastoral resources are needed.

Plantinga's response seems true as far as it goes. But although we can distinguish the intellectual and emotional problems of evil in this way, we should be wary of completely separating them. God has made us "holistic" beings, and our cognitive, affective, and volitional aspects are not easily separated. They form one (very complicated!) whole, such that the single biblical category of the *heart* of man can refer to any one or all of these aspects. The heart is where a person thinks, feels, and chooses. Regardless of what we think about the so-called "five stages of grief"—denial, anger, bargaining, depression, and acceptance[3]—people are at the very least dynamic, not static, in their view of their own suffering over time. When the initial shock of the suffering has subsided, people may quite naturally wonder whether there is any "justification" or "reason" God could have for allowing such an experience, and they may consult their fellow Christians (or other religious friends) on this topic. Such an inquiry, and the answers it generates, would have seemed unthinkably insensitive or misplaced at the outset, but with time clearer habits of thinking settle in. Many people desire to know if they are *right* to feel that God is distant or even nonexistent, and Christians should be prepared to give thoughtful, intellectual reflection when asked. The emotional problem of evil can eventually lead to deep contemplation about the intellectual problem of evil.[4]

---

2.   Alvin Plantinga, *God, Freedom, and Evil* (Grand Rapids: Eerdmans, 1977), 28–29.
3.   See Elisabeth Kübler-Ross, *On Death and Dying* (New York: Scribner, 2014 [1969]), 37–132.
4.   "While for many of us there are times in our lives when 'philosophical twaddle' about God and evil seems nothing more than a bunch of irrelevant nonsense, for most reflective people there will come a time when almost nothing else will be more important" (Daniel Howard-Snyder, "God, Evil, and Suffering," in *Reason for the Hope Within*, ed. Michael J. Murray [Grand Rapids: Eerdmans, 1998], 80–81).

Who Has Raised the Intellectual Problem of Evil?

Agonizing over the perplexing question of why God allows evil is nothing new for believers—this kind of concern is well-represented in Scripture (Job 3:1–26; Ps. 6:3; Jer. 12:1; Hab. 1:1–4, 12–17; Luke 13:1–5; John 9:1–2). But beyond this, at least three groups of unbelievers have raised the intellectual problem of evil for believers in an especially influential way: the ancient Greeks (such as Epicurus), Enlightenment skeptics (such as David Hume), and modern philosophers (such as J. L. Mackie and William Rowe). In one form or another, the basic ideas behind their presentations have filtered down from the academy into the broader culture where Christians live and minister.

Ancient Greeks: The Atomist Epicurus (341–270 BC)

The eighteenth-century Enlightenment skeptic David Hume cites the ancient Greek atomist Epicurus (341–270 BC) as the source of an unusually concise version of the intellectual problem of evil. Saying that "Epicurus' old questions are yet unanswered," Hume cites Epicurus as asking:

> Is he [God] willing to prevent evil, but not able? then is he impotent. Is he able, but not willing? then is he malevolent. Is he both able and willing? whence then is evil?[5]

Epicurus references two attributes of God: his power, by which he should be "able . . . to prevent evil," and his goodness, because of which he should be "willing . . . to prevent evil." Since God is supposed to be both powerful and good—that is, "both able and willing"—then there should be no evil. The implication is that since obviously there *is* evil, God is either "impotent" (lacking power) or "malevolent" (lacking goodness). In short, the intellectual problem of evil is generated by an alleged conflict between the existence of evil and God's attributes.

The philosopher Tim O'Keefe points out that this version of the argument is mediated to us (and, apparently, to David Hume) by way of "the early Christian writer Lactantius," and O'Keefe gives several reasons for thinking that "we should be cautious about reading this precise problem back on to the Epicureans."[6] But there is no doubt that this formulation of the argument has taken on a very influential life of its own, whether or not it can be found verbatim in Epicurus.

---

5. Epicurus, cited in David Hume, *Dialogues Concerning Natural Religion* (Indianapolis: Hackett, 1980 [London, 1779]), 63.
6. Tim O'Keefe, *Epicureanism* (Berkeley: University of California Press, 2010), 47–48. See also Thomas A. Blackson, "Epicureanism" in *The History of Evil in Antiquity: 2000 BCE–450 CE*, eds. Tom Angier, Chad Meister, and Charles Taliaferro (New York: Routledge, 2018).

Enlightenment Skeptics: David Hume (AD 1711–76)

In his posthumously published work, *Dialogues Concerning Natural Religion* (1779), David Hume not only conveys Epicurus's version of the problem of evil (see above), but offers a version of his own:

> For this [pain and suffering in the world] is not, by any means, what we expect from infinite power, infinite wisdom, and infinite goodness. Why is there any misery at all in the world? Not by chance, surely. From some cause then. Is it from the intention of the Deity? But he is perfectly benevolent. Is it contrary to his intention? But he is almighty. Nothing can shake the solidity of this reasoning, so short, so clear, so decisive.[7]

Hume here outlines three possible sources for evil: from uncaused chance, from God's intention, or from a source contrary to God's intention. The first is ruled out immediately, and the next two are ruled out by God's goodness and power, respectively. Hume's argument is therefore quite similar to Epicurus's: the existence of evil contradicts God's attributes, so a being with those attributes does not exist. What is fascinating about Hume's presentation is that not just once but twice he offers the reader a way out of his argument. First, immediately after the ellipsis in the citation of Hume above, when he boasts that his argument from evil is "so short, so clear, so decisive," Hume says:

> . . . except we assert that *these subjects exceed all human capacity*, and that *our common measures of truth and falsehood are not applicable to them*; a topic which I have all along insisted on.[8]

Second, a few pages later Hume speaks of a person confident that God *does* exist, but who is nevertheless puzzled by the evil in the world. According to Hume, such a person

> would never retract his former belief, if founded on any very solid argument; since *such a limited intelligence must be sensible of his own blindness and ignorance*, and must allow, that there may be many solutions of those [evil] phenomena, *which will forever escape his comprehension*.[9]

---

7. Hume, *Dialogues Concerning Natural Religion*, 65–66. This occurs near the end of Section 10 of the work (pp. 58–66), the entirety of which is devoted to discussing the problem of evil.

8. Hume, *Dialogues Concerning Natural Religion*, 66 (emphasis added).

9. Hume, *Dialogues Concerning Natural Religion*, 68 (emphasis added). In an article that came to be a very important contemporary contribution to problem of evil studies, Christian

In both quotations, Hume seems to think that if we humans are finite in our intelligence, then God and his ways may be inscrutable to us, in which case we may not be able to construct a good argument against his existence from evil after all. This strategy of solving the problem of evil, now widely known as "skeptical theism," will be introduced in Question 20 and further discussed in Questions 31 and 35.

Modern Philosophers: J. L. Mackie and William Rowe

The celebrated Oxford atheist J. L. Mackie contended in 1955 that "the problem of evil . . . is a logical problem": religious beliefs "are positively irrational" because "the several parts of the essential theological doctrine are *inconsistent* with one another."[10] In particular, "God is omnipotent," "God is wholly good," and "evil exists" are an inconsistent triad; "if any two of them were true the third would be false."[11] Crucial for Mackie's argument is his definition of two key terms. On his view, "omnipotence" implies that "there are no limits to what an omnipotent thing can do," and "good" implies that "a good thing always eliminates evil as far as it can."[12] So, if God were both omnipotent and good, there would not be any evil. But obviously there is evil. Thus, no omnipotent, good being exists, which means that God does not exist.

The atheist philosopher William Rowe put forth in 1979 an "evidential" problem of evil that was significantly different from Mackie's 1955 "logical" version of the intellectual problem of evil. Rowe's idea was not that evil makes God's existence impossible, but instead makes it very *unlikely*. This is because cases of apparently pointless animal suffering provide substantial evidence (that is, rational support) for rejecting the existence of God, even if they do not disprove his existence altogether. Rowe's argument focuses on allegedly pointless instances of evil in the world, where these are "instances of intense suffering which an omnipotent, omniscient being could have prevented without thereby losing some greater good or permitting some evil equally bad or worse."[13] That is a mouthful, but it can be simplified: a "pointless evil" is an evil that God did not *need* to permit in order to enable a greater good to occur or to block a worse evil from occurring. A good God would prevent

---

philosopher Stephen Wykstra cites this second quote from Hume, arguing that Hume is drawing attention to the possibility that we have "limited cognitive access" to explanations for evil. See Stephen J. Wykstra, "The Humean Objection to Evidential Arguments from Suffering: On Avoiding the Evils of 'Appearance,'" *International Journal for Philosophy of Religion*, 16 (1984): 73–93. Reprinted in Marilyn M. Adams and Robert M. Adams, eds., *The Problem of Evil* (Oxford: Oxford University Press, 1990), 138–60. Wykstra quotes Hume on p. 157 of the reprint.

10. J. L. Mackie, "Evil and Omnipotence," *Mind* 64, no. 254 (April 1955): 200.

11. Mackie, "Evil and Omnipotence," 200.

12. Mackie, "Evil and Omnipotence," 201.

13. William L. Rowe, "The Problem of Evil and Some Varieties of Atheism," *American Philosophical Quarterly* 16, no. 4 (October 1979): 336.

all such pointless evils, only allowing evils that are "greater-good-enablers" or "worse-evil-blockers." He will only allow evils that have a point.

Unfortunately, argues Rowe, there are lots of pointless evils in the world, in the sense he has defined. He points to the case of a fawn that is burned in a forest fire caused by lightning far from human observation. The fawn suffers several days of agony before dying. What purpose could that possibly serve? Given these and similar evils, Rowe's argument can be summarized:

> Factual premise: There exist instances of pointless evil.
> Moral premise: God would prevent pointless evil.
> Conclusion: God does not exist.

Rowe's goal is not to *prove* his conclusion decisively. Rather, he thinks he has immense *evidence* in support of his factual premise. This means he has similarly immense support for his conclusion. So, on his view, it is very unlikely that God exists.

The Intellectual Problem Simply Stated

The intellectual problem of evil can be stated simply and clearly, following Epicurus's concise statement of it.[14]

The Intellectual Problem of Evil	
Epicurus's words	**My paraphrase of Epicurus's words**
"Is he willing to prevent evil, but not able? Then he is not omnipotent."	*Premise 1:* A perfectly powerful being *can* prevent any evil.
"Is he able, but not willing? Then he is malevolent."	*Premise 2:* A perfectly good being *will* prevent evil as far as he can.
"Is he neither able nor willing? Then why call him God?"	*Premise 3:* God is perfectly powerful and good.
"Is he both able and willing? Then whence cometh evil?"	*Conclusion:* Therefore, if a perfectly powerful and good God exists, then there is no evil.

If God's power *can* prevent any evil (claim 1) and God's goodness *will* lead him to prevent any evil that his power can prevent (claim 2), then if God exists (claim 3) *all evils will in fact be prevented.* Since the existence of God *precludes* evil, it follows that the evil in the world requires the nonexistence of

---

14. The following chart is adapted from Greg Welty, *Why Is There Evil in the World (And So Much of It)?* (Fearn, Ross-shire: Christian Focus, 2018), 22.

God. In the next few Questions, we will begin to identify good and bad ways to respond to this argument.

Summary

The intellectual problem of evil is an argument against God's existence that starts from the existence of evil in the world. It concludes that God's existence is either impossible (the logical argument) or unlikely (the evidential argument). The argument can be found in every era of intellectual discourse, giving eloquent expression to concerns already voiced by the biblical authors. Finally, the intellectual problem (an argument against God) should be distinguished from the emotional problem of evil (a condition of alienation from God), though each can lead to the other.

REFLECTION QUESTIONS

1. Would it be acceptable for a Christian to solve the logical problem of evil, but leave the evidential argument untouched? What would be the problem with accepting an argument that concludes God's existence is very unlikely? Is that really a *problem* for our faith, or instead an *opportunity* for our faith (to believe in God despite his unlikelihood)?

2. Have you seen, in your own experience or in those of others, how the emotional problem of evil can lead to the intellectual problem (or vice versa)?

3. The versions of the problem of evil canvassed in this Question refer to God's power and goodness, but not to God's knowledge. Could *that* be a plausible solution to the problem: God allows evil to exist because he does not know about it?

4. Were you surprised to learn that Hume may have (possibly) supplied a way out of the problem of evil? Is this evidence that he was in fact undecided about the problem?

5. Rowe's example of the fawn burning to death seems particularly difficult to explain, given that the usual explanations that Christians offer do not seem to apply to this case (the fawn is being punished for sin, the fawn needs to wake up to its need for God, the fawn needs its character shaped by adversity, and so on). Even at this early stage of reflection, do you have any explanations in response?

What Are Some Bad Answers to the Intellectual Problem of Evil?

How should we respond to the intellectual problem of evil? In future Questions, I will identify some *helpful* ways to respond to this argument, namely, "the way of theodicy" and "the way of inscrutability." While I do not think either of these ways are sufficient all by themselves, when combined they form a powerful method of reply. But there are some *unhelpful* ways to respond to the argument, ways that we need to avoid if we are to develop an effective Christian apologetic. These unhelpful ways include the following: deny the existence of suffering and evil, deny the logic of the argument, deny God's attributes, or redefine God's attributes. By identifying and pushing back against these problematic ways to respond, this Question will help us focus on good ways of response, ways that are consistent with both reason and the Scriptures.

Here again is the simple and clear statement of the intellectual problem of evil (see Question 17):

The Intellectual Problem of Evil	
Epicurus's words	**My paraphrase of Epicurus's words**
"Is he willing to prevent evil, but not able? Then he is not omnipotent."	*Premise 1:* A perfectly powerful being *can* prevent any evil.
"Is he able, but not willing? Then he is malevolent."	*Premise 2:* A perfectly good being *will* prevent evil as far as he can.
"Is he neither able nor willing? Then why call him God?"	*Premise 3:* God is perfectly powerful and good.
"Is he both able and willing? Then whence cometh evil?"	*Conclusion:* Therefore, if a perfectly powerful and good God exists, then there is no evil.

Do Not Deny the Existence of Suffering and Evil

Here is a quick way to "solve" the intellectual problem of evil. First, concede the argument entirely, and agree that God's existence *would* rule out there being any evil. Second, insist that *there is no evil*. At worst, there are just various things that we *think* are "evil." If there is no "genuine evil," there is no challenge to God's existence from evil.

Unfortunately, common sense and Scripture are wholly opposed to this move. First, since we have defined "evil" as "significant cases of pain and suffering"—and then distinguished "moral evil" and "natural evil" by way of their immediate causes—one would have to deny the existence of any significant pain and suffering in the world to deny that "evil exists." But pain and suffering are some of the most evident facts of our experience. Even if the physical world did not exist, and it was all illusion—an idea "in our head"—there would still be significant pain and suffering. It would be all the significant pain and suffering experienced *because of the illusion*. Common sense renders the denial of evil a nonstarter for any thinking person.

Second, this move is clearly inconsistent with biblical teaching, and it would be a Pyrrhic victory at best to deny the Bible to defend the Christian faith. The whole point of Questions 2 and 3 was to analyze the meaning of the biblical words for "evil" (*ra'ah, ponēros, kakia*) by surveying the kinds of evil described *in the Scriptures*. Beyond this, Question 6 surveyed the wide range of suffering and evil that occurs in the Bible. So, the nonexistence of evil seems impossible to reconcile with the Bible. But what about the fact that God may *use* various evils to bring about good? Does that not mean the evils are not "genuine" evils? As a matter of fact, the Bible is entirely opposed to this position. As we saw in Question 7, the betrayal of Joseph by his brothers was an event with two sets of intentions behind it, human and divine. If ever there was a proof text for the idea that evil used by God for good is not "really" evil, it would be Genesis 50:20: "You meant evil against me, but God meant it for good." But it is this very passage which explicitly characterizes the actions of Joseph's brothers as "sin," "transgression" (twice), and "evil" (three times), while *also* recognizing that "God meant it for good." Clearly, the latter does not cancel the former. The brothers' actions are also called "guilty" and "sin" in Genesis 42:21–22. Apparently, an event can be intrinsically evil while good as a means.[1]

---

1. This seems to be the mistake that process theologian David Ray Griffin makes in his critique of Augustine's greater-good theodicy. He simply assumes, but nowhere shows, that an evil is not a "genuine evil" if God uses it for good. As far as I can tell, Griffin's argument would imply that the cross of Christ was not "genuine evil," which seems to take the concept of "Good Friday" a bit too far, to say the least. See David Ray Griffin, "Augustine and the Denial of Genuine Evil," in *The Problem of Evil: Selected Readings*, 2nd ed., ed. Michael Peterson (Notre Dame, IN: University of Notre Dame Press, 2016), 242–61. On Griffin's view, a sin is only "genuinely evil" if "the universe would have been a better place without it" (p. 258).

Do Not Deny the Logic of the Argument

There are only two ways to attack an argument: its matter or its form (that is, its content or its structure). Either one of the premises is false (or at the very least, insufficiently supported), or the inference from premises to conclusion is flawed in some way (that is, the argument commits a fallacy in reasoning). But the above argument seems to be impeccable with respect to its form or reasoning. The argument is valid, which means that if its premises are true, then the conclusion must be true as well. One might say that this is a "truth-preserving inference"—if there is truth in the premises then there is guaranteed to be truth in the conclusion. Even as in a good piece of plumbing, if water flows in from the start of the pipes, then water will flow out at the end, so in a good piece of reasoning, there are no intellectual leaks. If truth "flows in" from the start of the reasoning (the premises), then truth will "flow out" at the end. In a valid argument, the plumbing is good, as it were, and this seems to be the case with the above argument.

After all, if a perfectly good being *will* prevent evil as far as he can (premise 2), and a perfectly powerful being *can* prevent any evil (premise 1), then a being with both attributes will prevent *all* evil whatsoever. If God is such a being (premise 3), then there will be no evil (conclusion). The intellectual problem of evil says that God has two key attributes (perfect power and goodness, premise 3), that each attribute implies something about how God relates to evil (premises 1 and 2), and that when you put these consequences of God's attributes together, you get the nonexistence of evil. Since there *is* evil, the God who would eliminate all evil if he existed must not exist.

It is important not to be intimidated by valid arguments for conclusions which we reject. It fails to follow from the fact that an argument is valid, that therefore the conclusion is true, for maybe we lack any reason to accept the premises. Likewise, it fails to follow from the fact that a piece of plumbing is good, that therefore water is flowing through it. Maybe the pipes, though good, are empty. Here is another valid argument for a conclusion which we would reject:

> *Premise 1:* If anyone believes anything by faith, then he is insane and a danger to society.
>
> *Premise 2:* Christians believe some things by faith.
>
> *Conclusion:* Therefore, Christians are insane and a danger to society.

Again, the *logic* of this argument is impeccable. If the premises were true, then the conclusion would be true. But thankfully, the first premise should strike anyone as obviously false (or at least unsupported). So, the argument is fatally flawed, in its matter if not its form. To successfully push back against an argument, one does not have to say that an argument is a failure in *every* respect. One must only show that the argument is flawed in one way or another. Indeed, it is quite helpful to simply acknowledge that the intellectual problem of evil, as formulated above, is valid. We need not waste time attacking its form or structure. We can instead focus our attention on criticizing its matter or content, that is, challenging the truth of its premises (which we should).

Do Not Deny God's Attributes

Speaking of the premises, which ones should we reject? There are only three, so there is not much room to maneuver. How about "Premise 3: God is perfectly powerful and good"? Is *that* the flawed part of the argument? No doubt some ancient Greek polytheists might have a problem with premise 3. Their gods (and their Roman counterparts) seem less than perfectly powerful and good, given their tendency to be driven by lust and petty revenge, to play tricks on humans out of dubious motivations, and to be sometimes constrained by the Fates.

By way of contrast, the Christians against whom this argument is directed should have no problem with premise 3 at all. Indeed, denying God's perfect power and goodness might make the problem of evil *worse*, since it will have led us to deny an essential of our faith to solve an intellectual problem. We dare not minimize God's attributes, so that God is weak rather than perfectly powerful, or is somewhat malevolent rather than perfectly good.

With respect to God's power, the Bible teaches that it is as perfect as power could possibly be. Addressing himself to the "Lord God," the prophet Jeremiah says, "It is you who have made the heavens and the earth by your great power and by your outstretched arm! Nothing is too hard for you" (Jer. 32:17). A few verses later, God says, "Behold, I am the Lord, the God of all flesh. Is anything too hard for me?" (Jer. 32:27). The obvious, implied answer to this rhetorical question is "no." In order to explain how the virgin Mary will conceive and how Elizabeth will conceive a son in her old age, the angel Gabriel says, "Nothing will be impossible with God" (Luke 1:37). Answering his disciples' question about who can be saved, Jesus replies, "With man this is impossible, but with God all things are possible" (Matt. 19:26).

With respect to God's goodness, again the Bible teaches that it is as perfect as goodness could possibly be. God's very nature is love (1 John 4:8, 16), and his grace, mercy, patience, love, goodness, and kindness extend to his entire creation:

> The Lord is gracious and merciful, slow to anger and abounding in steadfast love. The Lord is good to all, and his mercy is over all that he has made. . . . The Lord is faithful in all his words and kind in all his works. (Ps. 145:8–9, 13)

When Jesus tells his hearers, "You therefore must be perfect, as your heavenly Father is perfect" (Matt. 5:48), the context of this perfection claim is explicitly God's *goodness*: "For he makes his sun rise on the evil and on the good, and sends rain on the just and on the unjust" (Matt. 5:45).

In general, the problem with challenging premise 3 is that we should never reject the heart of the Christian confession about God to solve the problem of evil. God is the all-knowing, all-powerful, perfectly good creator and providential sustainer of the world. It would be futile to say to the skeptic, "Believe in the God of the Bible, despite evil! All you must do is *reject* the God of the Bible!"

Don't Redefine God's Attributes

Perhaps, rather than saying that God is not perfectly powerful and good, we can continue to affirm that he *is* perfect in these respects but then proceed to *redefine the meaning* of these attributes, so that they lack the implications they seem to have. In doing this, we would be denying premise 1 or premise 2 (or both). The idea is that God *is* perfectly powerful, but he *cannot* prevent just any evil. Some evils are beyond his power to prevent (and so premise 1 is false). Or God is perfectly good, but he *will not* prevent evil even if he can prevent it (and so premise 2 is false). This "redefinition" strategy is a bit more subtle than just outright denying divine perfection altogether. What should we say about it?

Redefining Perfect Power

Redefining "perfect power" by denying premise 1 should be a nonstarter for Christians. God can prevent any case of moral evil by simply removing the free will by which it is done. (Free will is a gift of God.) And God can prevent any case of natural evil by suspending the natural processes that cause it. (The laws of nature are created by and subject to God.) While God cannot do the *contradictory* (make square circles, prevent two and two adding up to four, create a universe not created by God), there is nothing contradictory about a being as powerful as God intervening to prevent moral evil (murder, rape, theft) or natural evil (forest fires, cancer). Ordinary humans like you and me aim to do this all the time, and we sometimes succeed. Can bad people, bad weather, or bad genetics be more powerful than God? Surely a perfectly powerful being *can* prevent any evil (whether moral or natural), and so premise 1 looks just as true as premise 3.

In case there is any doubt about this, consider God's power to prevent people from drowning. Apparently, he has this power, preventing the Israelites' drowning in the Red Sea (Exod. 14:21–22), preventing Jonah drowning in the Mediterranean (Jonah 1:17), and preventing the disciples drowning in the Sea of Galilee (Matt. 8:23–27). God can also prevent the exercise of free will, such as when he sends a flood that drowns human beings (Gen. 7:11–24), strikes down Nadab and Abihu to stop their idolatrous worship (Lev. 10:2), drowns an army (Exod. 14:27–28), or keeps Abimelech from sinning against him (Gen. 20:6). God just seems to have the power to prevent both natural processes and the exercise of free will. Not only does he have this power; he has exercised it many times.

Various cults and false religions redefine the person of Jesus Christ. They say they "believe in Jesus," but the Jesus they believe looks nothing like the Jesus revealed in the Scriptures.[2] We should be loath to redefine divine power so that it is similarly unrecognizable from a biblical perspective.

Redefining Perfect Goodness

What about redefining "perfect goodness" by denying premise 2? Maybe perfect goodness does not mean that God will automatically prevent any evil that he could prevent. Here matters seem to be much different than the claim about divine power. In fact, it is hard to see why anyone would think it *automatically* counts against a person's goodness if that person fails to prevent evil he could prevent. What if he has a *good reason* for permitting evil, a reason compatible with his good character?

Consider a dentist who does her job, in the ordinary course of which she often causes (short-term) pain to patients. This is clearly suffering that she could easily prevent, for she could quit her job and not be a dentist. But just as clearly, her goodness does not *require* her to prevent the suffering, even though she *can* prevent it. Or consider a father who disciplines his children, thereby bringing about short-term, moderate pain he could easily prevent (by not exercising discipline at all). Does the father fail to be good because he does this? Is he not instead good *because* he inflicts the pain? In both cases, if there is a good reason that justifies the person in permitting (or even bringing about) the pain, then the person's goodness is not impugned.

So, while premise 1 (about God's power) seems true, premise 2 (about God's goodness) seems false. And far from "redefining" God's attribute of perfect goodness, we are sticking with a concept of "goodness" that we already apply to human beings. And the same goes for God in Scripture: he often causes pain and suffering he could easily prevent, to punish us, or to shape our character through trial, or to get our attention, or to provide redemption through the cross, and so on. It is *not* the case that a good being, even a perfectly good being, will always prevent evil he could prevent.[3]

---

2. For example, see Matthew Aaron Bennett, *40 Questions About Islam* (Grand Rapids: Kregel, 2020), particularly Question 30, "Is 'Isa in the Qur'an the Same Person as Jesus in the Bible?"

3. The previous sentence presents in miniature several "theodicies" that could be God's reason for allowing evil. See Questions 21–26.

"The Claim"

We have in fact finally identified the Achilles' heel of the intellectual problem of evil: premise 2 is entirely questionable. Yes, a perfectly good being will prevent evil as far as he can, *unless* he has a good reason for permitting it. Well, *does* he have a good reason for permitting it? If he does, then premise 2 is false. If he lacks a good reason, then premise 2 is true after all: God would prevent any evil he can prevent, since he does not have any good reason for permitting it.

So, this is *the* question when facing the intellectual problem of evil: Does God have a good reason for permitting the evils in the world? To ensure the truth of premise 2, the skeptic must insist that *there are no good reasons that would justify God in permitting evil*. Let us call this "the claim." We will be focusing on "the claim" in the remainder of part 3 of the book, "Apologetic Questions About Suffering and Evil." Roughly speaking, "the way of theodicy" argues that "the claim" is *false*, by offering good reasons that God could have for permitting evil. By way of contrast, "the way of inscrutability" argues that "the claim" is *unsupported*. God may or may not have good reasons, but skeptics have unsuccessfully argued for the latter claim. For all they can *show*, God does have good reasons for permitting the evils he permits, even if they fail to guess what such reasons might be. But if "the claim" is unsupported, then so is the conclusion that is supposed to follow from it: that God does not exist.[4]

Summary

Good ways to respond to the intellectual problem of evil include "the way of theodicy" and "the way of inscrutability," and the Questions that remain in part 3 of the book will explore the viability of these responses. But there are bad ways to respond to the argument: deny the existence of suffering and evil, deny the logic of the argument, deny God's attributes, or redefine God's attributes. All these ways seem contrary to evident reason and experience, if not the Scriptures themselves, except for one. God's goodness can be *clarified* as implying that God would prevent any evil that he could prevent—unless he has a good reason for permitting the evil. If God has a good reason, then he does not fail to be good simply because he does not prevent an evil he could prevent. This is not a cynical "redefinition" of what goodness requires in order to get out of the intellectual problem of evil. Rather, it respects how we use the term "goodness" in human contexts and is in accord with the Scripture's characterization of divine goodness. But does God have such a good reason? Is the claim that he lacks a good reason a true claim? Is it even a claim that

---

4. The Christian philosopher Daniel Howard-Snyder anticipates and indeed influences my argumentative strategy here. See Daniel Howard-Snyder, "God, Evil, and Suffering," in *Reason for the Hope Within*, ed. Michael J. Murray (Grand Rapids: Eerdmans, 1999), 76–115 (see esp. p. 84).

unbelievers can support by way of decent argument? Investigating these matters is next on the agenda.

REFLECTION QUESTIONS

1. Another way to reply to the argument, related to the "there is no evil" reply, is to say that unbelievers cannot raise the argument because they cannot *define* "evil" (perhaps because they are atheists who have no way to "account for" or "justify" moral standards). Do you think this is a good way to reply?

2. What would be so bad if we "deny the logic of the argument"? Perhaps the argument is valid only in "man's logic" but is invalid in "God's logic." Could you *make a case* for this point of view?

3. Did the fact that we could state the argument in separate, numbered premises help you think through this argument more clearly? When could such numbering hinder communication rather than help it?

4. Maybe premise 1 is false, because God has no hands, arms, or legs, and therefore cannot prevent car accidents, fires, or gun deaths.[5] Is it plausible to think that God cannot do these things, because he is a spiritual being?

5. Do you agree the ways discussed in this Question are "unhelpful ways" out of the argument? Can you think of others?

---

5. Thomas Jay Oord, *God Can't: How to Believe in God and Love after Tragedy, Abuse, or Other Evils* (Grasmere, ID: SacraSage Press, 2019), 33.

Is Theodicy a Good Answer to the Intellectual Problem of Evil?

The previous Question argued that the cogency of the intellectual problem of evil as an argument against God comes down to the critic's ability to argue for "the claim": "There is no reason that justifies God in permitting evil." If the critic is right that this claim is true—if God has no good reason for permitting evil—then God's goodness seems to be compromised, for then God allows enormous amounts of pain and suffering for no reason whatsoever. But if the critic is wrong and this claim is instead false—if God *does* have a good reason for permitting evil—then the fact of evil does not count against God's goodness after all and the intellectual problem of evil is solved. So is "the claim" true, or is it false? Does God lack justifying reasons for permitting evil, or does he have them?

This Question introduces "the way of theodicy," which involves Christians attempting to prove "the claim" false by offering God's reasons for permitting evil. We will define "theodicy," argue for two assumptions behind all successful theodicy, and illustrate how theodicy can fail to satisfy these assumptions. We will then consider whether the Scriptures point us in the direction of theodicy.

What Is a Theodicy?

The Meaning of "Theodicy"

What are the prospects for proving "the claim" to be false? Since "the claim" which the critic is insisting on says that a certain territory is *empty*—the territory of God-justifying reasons for permitting evil—we can prove this claim false by showing the territory is not empty. We can give God's reasons for permitting evil. This is the way of "theodicy." The latter is a technical term in the problem of evil literature that comes from two Greek words, *theos*

(God) and *dikios* (justify). Theodicy is a justification of the ways of God to human beings. It is a story we tell so that we can *see* that God is indeed justified in allowing all evil, or at least a certain type of evil, or perhaps even a particular evil. There might be different stories we tell about different kinds of evils. Perhaps there is no one-size-fits-all reason that God has here. But if there is *a* theodicy for each evil or kind of evil, then "the claim" has been proven false. The territory of God-justifying reasons is not empty after all, and the intellectual problem of evil is a failed argument against God.

The Qualifications for Theodicy
    Not just anything counts as a theodicy. Typically, a theodicy has the following structure: there are goods that God is aiming at in his universe, but because of the kinds of goods God is aiming at, he cannot get them without permitting various evils. Questions 21–26 will consider many such goods, allegedly connected to various evils. One general approach to theodicy, which some call a "greater-good theodicy," has the following structure:

> The pain and suffering in God's world play a necessary role in bringing about (or being a part of) greater goods that could not be brought about (or exist) except for the presence of that pain and suffering. The world would be worse off without that pain and suffering, and so God is justified in pursuing the good by these means.

The words "necessary role," "greater goods," and "worse off" recognize two assumptions behind successful theodicy. First, the goods God is aiming at must *depend on* and therefore require the evils (at least their possibility, if not their actuality). Second, the goods God is aiming at must be goods that are *worth pursuing*. Let us look at these assumptions in more detail.

Two Assumptions Behind All Theodicy

The Dependence of Goods
    Successful theodicy claims that various evils play a "necessary role" in bringing about or being a part of various goods. The goods God is aiming at depend on and therefore require the evils. It must be that God cannot get these various goods he is aiming at *unless* he permits the evils. After all, if God could get these goods *without* permitting the evils, then why would he not do so? Would it not be better to just bypass the evils altogether?
    Here is an example of such dependence of goods on evils: the good is defined as some sort of *response* to the evil, such as an overcoming of the evil. If that is the case, then the good cannot exist unless the evil does as well (otherwise, there would be nothing to respond to or overcome). So, if it is a

good thing for society to cooperate in order to defeat the threat of cancer, then there cannot be such cooperation unless there is the threat of cancer. Or if it is a good thing to be brave in the face of battle, then there cannot be such bravery except in the face of battle (and so there must be battle).

It is no part of this requirement that any evils are necessary *per se*. For God could simply decline to create anything, or he could decide to create but decline to make a universe with *these* goods in them. If so, then there would simply be no evil. That is surely up to God. Rather, the idea is that if God wants a universe with *these* goods in them, then he must allow the evils as well. This dependence assumption is not the Manichaeism that the early Augustine wrestled with and then rightly abandoned, according to which good and evil were equally ultimate principles at the back of the universe, each equally necessary if there was to be any creation at all.

Defective theodicies do not satisfy this dependence assumption. For example, as we saw in Question 3, the atheist William Rowe discusses the example of a fawn who burns to death in a forest fire, suffering terrible agony for several days before expiring. Why would God allow this? What goods could be connected to *that*? I once had a well-meaning student who argued that such fawns *had* to die so that future generations could get oil. (The idea was that the fawn's corpse liquefies in the ground over ages and produces oil deposits for future oil-dependent humans.) Unfortunately, this fails the dependence assumption, since God could just *put* the oil in the ground, no fawns needed. And even if some crazy law of the universe required God to produce oil from fawn corpses, the real evil here is not the mere death of the fawn but the pain and suffering of the fawn over several days. Why was that needed? God could just allow the fawn to die of a painless heart attack, and have still gotten the good of the oil, but without the evil of the suffering. Since the goods aimed at (oil) could have been achieved without the attendant evils (pain and suffering of the fawn), the goods do not depend on the evils at all, and so this is just a bad theodicy.

The Weightiness of Goods

Successful theodicy also claims that the goods God is aiming at must be *worth* pursuing. They must be deep and substantive, not trivial. They must be "greater goods" that outweigh the evils on which they depend: things are better with the goods (even with their attendant evils) than without the goods at all. For example, assume I can overcome a bout of life-threatening cancer only if I submit to a painful but temporary regime of chemotherapy. Eradicating cancer is a great good, so the tradeoff is worth it. Surely "suffered chemotherapy, no more cancer" is a *better* situation than "no chemotherapy, died of cancer." Here, "no more cancer" is an outweighing good—it outweighs the pain of chemotherapy.

Defective theodicies do not satisfy this weightiness assumption. Getting a pathetically trivial good by way of an enormous evil will have made the universe *worse* than it was before. Things would be better off with neither of those things than with them both. Assume someone "justified" God's allowing the Holocaust by saying, "Unless it happened, Rocky Road ice cream would not have been invented" (and then they tell some crazy story that allegedly links these two things). Even if we grant that the invention of this ice cream flavor *did* depend upon the suffering of the Holocaust, this theodicy completely fails the weightiness assumption. Clearly, the tradeoff was not worth it. Far better that the Holocaust *never* occurred than that it occurred so we could get ice cream. The good here is so trivial that no good person (not to mention a *perfectly* good person) would allow the Holocaust in order to aim at that!

The Assumptions Combined
    Both assumptions come together in Augustine's explanation of why God allowed fallen mankind to exist: "For God judged it better to bring good out of evil than not to permit any evil to exist."[1] First, there is the weightiness assumption. According to Augustine, God considers two situations and judges one of them to be "better" than the other. "To bring good out of evil" is better than "not to permit any evil to exist" at all. Second, there is the dependence assumption. One cannot "bring good out of evil" unless there is evil.
    To summarize "the way of theodicy": evils that are to be explained by way of theodicy will always be connected to dependent and weighty goods. They are dependent goods: evils must be permitted to get them. They are weighty goods: things are better with the goods (even with their attendant evils) than without the goods at all. If every evil can be traced to a dependent, weighty good, then the task of theodicy has done its job. Questions 21–26 will look at a variety of specific theodicies for different kinds of evil in the world.

Scriptural Materials for Theodicy
    Does Scripture indicate that Christians should pursue "the way of theodicy"? Not explicitly. Indeed, the intellectual problem of evil is not explicitly raised in Scripture, at least not in the precise way we posed it at the end of Question 17. Nevertheless, 2 Timothy 3:16–17 teaches that God's word was given "that the man of God may be complete, equipped for every good work." Presumably, this includes the good work of defending God's goodness in the face of evil by answering the questions of critics. Surely, *God's response to evil* is a fundamental theme of the Bible. If so, we should not ignore any Bible passages which may shed light on God's relation to evil.
    In addition, perhaps the Bible encourages the view given earlier that "the pain and suffering in God's world play a necessary role in bringing about (or being a part of) greater goods that could not be brought about (or exist) except for the presence of that pain and suffering." Consider

1. Augustine, *Enchiridion* 8.27.

the great wealth of Bible passages which were examined in part 2 of this book ("Biblical and Theological Questions About Suffering and Evil"). Apparently, both natural evil and moral evil can be "of the Lord" (Questions 9 and 10), such that God wills all suffering and evil (Question 11). Human responsibility is preserved because God relates to moral evil only through "dual-agency" (Questions 13 and 14). In addition, God's *modus operandi* when it comes to diverse kinds of evil is to combine the goodness of his purpose (he is a God who aims at great goods) with the sovereignty of his providence (he often intends these great goods to come about by way of various evils) (Question 7). This biblical material certainly *seems* relevant to helping Christians develop an overall perspective on evil that is not only biblically faithful, but forms a foundation for answering the apologetic question that is now before us.

God aims at *great* goods: in Job's case, the vindication of God's name; in Joseph's case, the preservation of Israel amid famine; in Jesus's case, the salvation of the world. And God intends these great goods to come about *by way of* various evils: Job's sufferings, Joseph's betrayal, and Jesus's cross. In some of this, the weightiness assumption is obviously satisfied—what could be a greater good than the redemption of the world and the exaltation of God in all his attributes (through the cross)? At other points, the dependence assumption is obviously satisfied—Job cannot "display great perseverance in the midst of great suffering" *without* there being great suffering.

But in other respects, the biblical narratives do not *obviously* satisfy the high standard for theodicy we have been considering in this Question. Does the Joseph story satisfy the dependence assumption? Is the betrayal of Joseph the *only* way open to God to preserve his people from famine? Can God not just provide them food? Does the Job story satisfy the weightiness assumption? Is it clearly *better* to refute Satan's lies about Job by way of Job's suffering than to simply leave Satan's lies unrefuted and spare Job the suffering? Why is putting Satan in his place so important?

So Christians should be cautious about whether they can *show*, even on the basis of the Bible's wisdom, that all evils are connected with goods that are both weighty and dependent. The scriptural narratives gesture in this direction but are not as decisive as we would like. Perhaps a better route for Christians to take is not to attempt to prove "the claim" is false but instead to argue that it is *unsupported*. That is, critics of God's existence are in no position to claim that the evils in the world are not connected to weighty, dependent goods. This would be "the way of inscrutability," and we will consider it in the next Question.

Summary

"Theodicy" combines two Greek words (*theos* and *dikios*) and means "a justification of the ways of God to human beings." Theodicy is directly relevant to proving that "the claim" in the intellectual problem of evil is a false claim. Rather than it being the case that "there is no reason that would justify God in permitting evil," *there is* such reason available to God, and theodicy tells us what it is. Not just any reason counts as a successful theodicy—the goods God is aiming at by way of evils must *depend* on the evils (or at least depend on their possibility) and must *outweigh* the evils. The Scriptures might provide us with ample material in order to construct theodicy, but Christians should be cautious here: the dependence and the weightiness of the goods is not always obvious. Perhaps divine inscrutability is an equally important theme to consider.

REFLECTION QUESTIONS

1. In arguing about the "territory" of God-justifying reasons for permitting evil, critics claim that this territory is empty, whereas Christians claim that it is not empty. In your view, who has the harder task, and why?

2. Does real forgiveness depend on the existence of real sin? If so, does it follow that God *must* allow sin? Or does it only follow that God must allow sin *if* he wants a world with forgiveness in it?

3. Do you think it is likely that Christians and non-Christians will disagree about which goods are "weighty" enough for God to pursue? How might you go about resolving that difference?

4. Second Timothy 3:16–17 was mentioned as indirectly implying that the Scriptures are relevant to the task of theodicy. Can you think of any other Scriptures that similarly imply this?

5. If God pursues goods *by way of* evils, is God then "do[ing] evil that good may come" (Rom. 3:8)? If not, then what is he doing?

Is Divine Inscrutability a Good Answer to the Intellectual Problem of Evil?

In Question 18 we saw that the intellectual problem of evil is only cogent as an argument against God's existence if "the claim" turns out to be true rather than false: "There is no reason that justifies God in permitting evil." So, *does* God have a good reason for permitting evil, or not? This seems to be a central question that unifies a lot of writing on the problem of evil. In the last chapter (Question 19), we saw that the first main strategy for responding to the intellectual problem of evil is to argue that "the claim" is *false*, because we can offer good reasons God would have to justify evil. If there are such theodicies, then "the claim" is false. But we also saw that it might be difficult to find theodicies, in the Bible or elsewhere, that clearly satisfy the dependence and weightiness assumptions. How do we know that the goods God is aiming at *require* the evils? And how do we know that they *outweigh* the evils?

But there is a second main strategy for responding to the intellectual problem of evil: argue that "the claim" is *unsupported*. We might not be able to come up with a reason that justifies God in permitting evil. But it does not follow from our inability to do this that therefore there is no reason that justifies God. As Christian philosopher Alvin Plantinga puts it, suppose God has a reason for permitting evil

> . . . and suppose we try to figure out what that reason might be: is it likely that we would come up with the right answer? Is it even likely that we would wind up with plausible candidates for God's reason? . . . [There is an] epistemic distance between us and God: given that God *does* have a reason for permitting these evils, why think we would be the first to know? Given that he is omniscient and given our very substantial epistemic limitations, it isn't at all surprising that his

reasons for some of what he does or permits completely escape us.[1]

Notice that this strategy is more modest than the first one. Rather than
going out on a limb and asserting—perhaps in a way that smacks of arrogance
and dogmatism—that *we know* what God's reasons are, we can instead point
out that no one can make a reasonable case that God *does not* have a reason.
But in the absence of such a case, "the claim" is unsupported. There is literally no reason to believe it. And that means the conclusion of the intellectual
problem of evil is similarly unsupported since that conclusion depends on
"the claim."

This chapter will consider the extent to which this second strategy, often
called "skeptical theism" or an appeal to "divine inscrutability," is supported
by human reason and the Bible. It will also identify four potential problems
that are raised by this approach.

Does Human Reason Indicate "the Claim" Is Without Support?

Most atheist writers support "the claim"—the assertion that God has
no good reason to permit evil—by appealing to how things *seem* to them.
Because it does not *seem* that there could be a good reason for allowing the
fawn to suffer in the forest fire, or for allowing the little girl to be attacked, or
for allowing someone to get cancer, and so on, therefore most likely there is
not a good reason. This is even more persuasive when one has thought about
these hard cases not just for a few minutes, but for months and years. Surely
if I cannot come up with a good reason, after all that reflection, then there is
not a good reason![2]

But despite appearances, there is something deeply flawed about this reasoning, and one need not appeal to the Bible to see the flaw. To be clear, the
problem is not that the atheist is appealing to his "seemings." That seems like a
perfectly good basis for acquiring rational belief. It *seems* to me that there is a
computer monitor in front of me; that is as good a reason as any for thinking
that there *is* a computer monitor in front of me. The problem is not even that
the atheist is appealing to "negative seemings," to what *does not* appear to him
to be the case. Again, that seems perfectly in order: it *seems* to me there is no

---

1. Alvin Plantinga, *Warranted Christian Belief* (Oxford: Oxford University Press, 2000),
   466–67.
2. Again, the now-classic presentation of this kind of reasoning is found in William L. Rowe,
   "The Problem of Evil and Some Varieties of Atheism," *American Philosophical Quarterly*
   16, no. 4 (October 1979): 335–41. Rowe repeatedly appeals to what *seems* to him to be
   the case: "so far as we can see," "there does not appear to be," "nor does there seem to be,"
   "doesn't it appear," "the fawn's apparently pointless suffering," "we cannot see how," "does
   not appear," "seemingly pointless," and "it seems quite unlikely" (337).

elephant in the room, therefore most likely there *is no* elephant in the room. What could be more intuitive?

Rather, the problem with inferring "there is no good reason" from "it seems to me there is no good reason" is much more specific. The atheist is gratuitously assuming that he has what it takes to tell the difference between a situation in which God has a good reason for permitting evil, and a situation in which God does not. But why think that is the kind of thing we would be able to detect? As it turns out, we can only reliably infer "there is no X" from "it seems to me there is no X" if the following is true of us: I would have seen an X if one were there. *Sometimes* that is true, and if so, then the inference is a good one. But there are plenty of circumstances in which the inference is a bad one. Consider the following six inferences, in which our *cognitive limitations*, or *lack of expertise or familiarity* in a certain area, means that the inference is flawed:

- *Perceptual inference:* It does not seem to me that there is a ladybug on that tree a mile away; therefore, most likely there is no ladybug on that tree.
- *Scientific inference:* It does not seem to me that this latest book on quantum mechanics makes sense; therefore, most likely it makes no sense.
- *Moral inference:* It did not seem to earlier generations that freedom from racial oppression was a fundamental human right; therefore, most likely it is not a fundamental human right.
- *Linguistic inference:* It does not seem to me (a person who knows no philosophy or ancient Greek) that this sentence from Plato's *Apology* has any meaning; therefore, most likely it lacks a meaning.
- *Aesthetic inference:* It does not seem to me that Beethoven projected the sonata form onto his symphonies as a whole; therefore, most likely Beethoven did not do this.
- *Parental inference:* It does not seem to my one-year-old son that his parents have a good reason for subjecting him to painful inoculations under the British healthcare system; therefore, most likely his parents lack a good reason.[3]

The point here is not to contend that we *cannot* reason from appearances in the areas of perception, science, morality, linguistics, aesthetics, and parental motivation. Clearly, we do this all the time, and do so successfully.

---

3. This strategy of identifying bad "noseeum" inferences can now be found in many writers. See Daniel Howard-Snyder, "God, Evil, and Suffering," in *Reason for the Hope Within*, ed. Michael J. Murray (Grand Rapids: Eerdmans, 1999), 76–115 (esp. pp. 103–12); and Daniel Howard-Snyder and Michael Bergmann, "Evil Does Not Make Atheism More Reasonable Than Theism," in *The Problem of Evil: Selected Readings*, 2nd ed., ed. Michael Peterson (Notre Dame, IN: University of Notre Dame Press, 2016), 143–65 (esp. pp. 145–53).

Rather, the point is that these kinds of inferences are worthless *if we lack the relevant expertise, familiarity, or cognitive powers needed to discern the things we are looking for.* The last inference on the list is especially telling. God is omniscient and his providential plan is very complex. As Christian philosopher Stephen Wykstra puts it, that we should discern *on our own* the goods that God is aiming at in our suffering "seems about as likely as that a one-month old should discern most of his parents' purposes for those pains they allow him to suffer—which is to say, it is not likely at all."[4]

One need not appeal to an "epistemic gap" between God and us, to God's omniscience, or to the complexity of God's providential plan, to make this point. Rather, we can simply note that we have no reason to think that the range of goods we know of are representative of all the goods there are and that we have no reason to think that the dependence relations we know of (how goods might depend on evils) are representative of all the dependence relations there are. Yes, I might not be able to *see* a good that justifies permitting the evil or *see* how that good might depend on some bad things occurring. But that gives me little reason to think there *is not* such a good, or that there *is not* such a dependence.[5]

As we saw in Question 17, even the Enlightenment skeptic David Hume recognized that one could dodge his version of the intellectual problem of evil if one became "sensible of his own blindness and ignorance," and recognized that "human capacity," "intelligence," and "comprehension" were "limited" in various respects. The Christian philosophers cited earlier are simply developing the strategy Hume handed them.

Does the Bible Indicate "the Claim" Is Without Support?

What about the Bible? Does God's Word reveal that this second strategy against the intellectual problem of evil has something going for it? As a matter of fact, in part 2 of this book, "Biblical and Theological Questions About Suffering and Evil," we already investigated this issue at length in Question 8, "Does God Hide His Reasons for Why He Permits Suffering and Evil?" There, we saw that divine inscrutability was a prominent theme in the Job, Joseph, and Jesus narratives. Yes, God's purposes are good and his providence is sovereign. (That was the import of Question 7.) But in addition, it is *typically* the case that God's reasons for allowing suffering are "unguessable" by us. Neither Job's friends, nor Joseph's brothers, nor Jesus's tormentors, would have guessed correctly as to why God allowed or brought about Job's, Joseph's,

---

4. Stephen Wykstra, "The Humean Objection to Evidential Arguments from Suffering: On Avoiding the Evils of 'Appearance,'" *International Journal for Philosophy of Religion* 16 (1984): 88.
5. Michael Bergmann makes this point throughout his "Skeptical Theism and Rowe's New Evidential Argument from Evil," in *God and Evil*, ed. Michael Peterson, 505–29.

and Jesus's sufferings. How could Job's friends (or Job himself) have known about God's prior dialogue with Satan? How could Joseph's brothers have known about God's purpose to deliver the Israelites from famine by way of Joseph's betrayal? How could pagan Romans have known what God was up to redemptively in Jesus's cross? But clearly their ignorance of these goods, and their ignorance of how the goods depended on the evils, was no reason to think there *were not* these goods or dependences.

Beyond this, God *tells* us quite explicitly that his judgments are "unsearchable," and his ways are "inscrutable." No one has "known the mind of the Lord" or "been his counselor" (Rom. 11:33–36). And when people in the Bible try to guess what God is up to with respect to suffering, they invariably get it wrong (Job 42:7; Luke 13:1–5; John 9:1–3; Acts 28:3–6). While it is clear to readers of these narratives that God knew what he was doing, many of the participants *in* the narratives did not know what that was. One gets the impression that the very "hiddenness" of God in this respect could itself be by divine design. When God spoke to Job out of the whirlwind in Job 38–41, he had the perfect opportunity to reveal to Job the reason for his suffering, perhaps recounting the dialogue in Job 1–2 between God and Satan. But he does no such thing, preferring instead to reinforce the theme of divine inscrutability.

So, biblical testimony seems to match up quite well with what reason suggests (in the previous section of this chapter). If "the way of inscrutability" is just good common sense, then it is common sense with a biblical precedent. Just because we cannot guess God's reason does not mean God is without a reason.

Potential Problems with the "Divine Inscrutability" Strategy

Despite the apologetic promise afforded by this second strategy against "the claim," there are at least four problems that divine inscrutability potentially raises for Christians. Here I simply highlight each difficulty. It remains for future Questions to address them.

First, is this appeal to divine inscrutability a cosmic "cop-out" when it comes to apologetics? People want answers, and we give them our ignorance. What kind of a "reasoned defense" is that? We are supposed to be people of the Book, and God has given us sixty-six books that compose that Book, and all we can say is, "I do not know"? Does it not stand to reason that if *Christians* cannot give God's reason, then one does not exist? We will consider this concern in Question 27.

Second, if in fact God *has* a reason, should I not at least try to find out what it is? Would it not honor God if I try to study or discover his providence in this way? Would it not give me reason to glorify him for his wisdom? To be left in the dark seems counterproductive to Christian sanctification. Surely it would exalt God for us to know what he is doing. We will consider this concern in Question 31.

Third, it seems that the appeal to divine inscrutability proves too much. If we are *that* limited in coming up with justifying reasons, then maybe we do not know enough to convict *human beings* of wrongdoing. After all, even if someone *seems* to be an unjustified mass murderer, what do I know? Maybe he has some secret motivation or reason that justifies him. Who am I to rule that out? So the price I pay for taking this way out of the intellectual problem of evil is the dismantling of our systems of earthly justice. I could never convict someone of a crime in a court of law, due to my apparent "cognitive finitude." How can we make *any* moral evaluation if God is beyond moral evaluation? We will consider this concern in Question 34.

Fourth, does a focus on this divine inscrutability theme make God distant and hidden? If we understand so little about him, maybe I cannot trust him to be present to me in my suffering. What is the difference between an "inscrutable" God, and no God at all? We will consider this concern in Question 35.

Summary

"Skeptical theism" is not skepticism about *whether* God exists. Rather, it is skepticism that we can *reliably discover* God's reasons for permitting suffering. But if we cannot do that, then the fact that we cannot come up with God's reasons is no cause to think he does not have reasons. Rather than being a clever bit of subterfuge, this appeal to divine inscrutability is a potentially powerful strategy against "the claim" that God has no such reasons. Whereas the way of theodicy seeks to prove "the claim" false (by providing God's reasons), the way of inscrutability seeks to show that "the claim" is without support. It seems that both human reason and the Bible indicate that this second strategy against "the claim" has some merit: eminently sensible common sense dovetails with what the Scriptures teach anyway. There is need, however, to address several problems raised by this approach—something that will be done in later Questions.

REFLECTION QUESTIONS

1. We saw six inferences, in six different areas, which are bad inferences in virtue of our lacking relevant expertise, familiarity, or cognitive powers. Give some examples of *good* inferences in these six areas. In each case, what made the difference between the bad inference and the good inference?

2. Repeated reference was made to "the claim" as central to the atheist's case against God's existence by way of the intellectual problem of evil. Have we rightly identified what this claim is? Do you think there is a better candidate for what is central to the argument?

3. Do you find it ironic that David Hume might have supplied contemporary Christians with a strategy that solves the problem of evil? Or does it make sense that unbelievers might hit upon the truth, in spite of themselves and their goals?

4. This Question's section on the biblical material was shorter than the section on human reason. This is because we were able to draw upon our earlier "biblical foundations" material, rather than reinventing the wheel. Does that suggest a priority to you in how Christians should go about investigating difficult apologetic matters?

5. The final section of this Question wondered whether this second strategy asks us to pay too high a price, biblically, theologically, and practically speaking. Why is it important to face such issues head-on?

Questions Related to
Specific Apologetic Answers
to the Problem of Evil

Could Suffering and Evil Be God's Way of Punishing Us?

Part 3 of this book, "Apologetic Questions About Suffering and Evil," began by looking at *general apologetic strategies* on the problem of evil: what the problem is (Question 17), some bad answers to it (Question 18), and some potentially good strategies against it (theodicy—Question 19, and divine inscrutability—Question 20).

Part 3 now continues by applying this earlier material, looking at *specific apologetic answers* to the problem of evil (Questions 21–28). Most of these are *defensive* answers, utilizing either theodicy (Questions 21–26) or divine inscrutability (Question 27). Part 3 ends with an answer that "goes on the offensive": perhaps the problem of evil is a reason to *believe* in God's existence (Question 28), rather than a reason to doubt it. As before, part 3 builds upon the methodological, biblical, and theological foundations laid earlier in parts 1 and 2 of the book.

The current Question considers *the punishment theodicy* as an explanation for the suffering and evil in the world. We will see that this theodicy has an extensive biblical basis and might help explain the existence of both natural evil and moral evil in the world. However, it faces substantial limitations as well. We will close by looking at how the punishment theodicy can nevertheless play an important role in answering the intellectual problem of evil.

Defining the Punishment Theodicy

The punishment theodicy says that suffering is a result of God's just punishment of evildoers. This idea has considerable scriptural support. In Genesis 3:14–19, God curses the earth, increasing pain and difficulty for both Adam and Eve because of their disobedience to God. They are even made liable to death itself, so that they will "return to the ground . . . and to dust you shall return" (v. 19). Reflecting on this Genesis narrative, Paul teaches in Romans

5:12 that "sin came into the world through one man, and death through sin, and so death spread to all men because all sinned." Apparently, Adam's sin in the garden of Eden is universally applied, and so the consequence is that death spreads to all. So, it makes sense that later Paul says that "the wages of sin is death" (Rom. 6:23). Death is what sin *deserves* and therefore "earns" for us, because sin is rebellion against a perfectly good and holy God who deserves our fealty, love, and obedience.

Finally, God's curse affects the whole world: "the creation was subjected to futility" and suffers a "bondage to corruption" (Rom. 8:20–21). It seems to follow from all this that the world is liable to produce quite a bit of awful suffering for the sinners who inhabit it. In fact, the most prominent divine judgments in Scripture have a kind of "global scope" that makes sense considering the curse that was originally brought on *all* creation. These include God's sending the flood over all the earth (Gen. 6–8), his relentless sending of ten plagues that destroyed an entire country (Exod. 7–12), and the final day of judgment itself (Rev. 15–20).

Notice that this theodicy seems to satisfy the "dependence" and "weightiness" assumptions, which were identified in Question 19 as the two assumptions behind all successful theodicies. The dependence assumption says that the goods God is aiming at depend in some important sense upon the sufferings that God permits or brings about. Here, if the good is "God's just punishment of evildoers," then there is no way to get that good *without* punishment. The weightiness assumption says that God must be aiming at very *valuable* goods rather than trivial goods, such that they outweigh the evils that come in their wake. But God's judgment of sin seems like a very good thing: it upholds God's justice and reveals it to the world. The world would be worse off with God's justice unrevealed, or with sin unpunished, than if God punished sin. So the latter is a *better* situation than the former. Or so claims the advocate of the punishment theodicy.

Natural Evil and Moral Evil as Forms of Divine Punishment

It is important to see that *any* pain and suffering can potentially be explained by the punishment theodicy, whether it is natural evil or moral evil.[1] First, natural evil can be God's punishment of evildoers. If death itself—the paradigmatic "natural evil"—is God's just judgment for sin, then anything short of death can also be that judgment. In Question 9 ("Is Natural Evil Ever 'of the Lord'?"), we saw that a whole range of natural evils are (ultimately) brought about by God, quite often for the sake of punishment: famine, drought, rampaging wild animals, disease, birth defects, plague, stormy weather, as well as death itself. For example, earthquakes, whirlwinds, and tempests can occur as divine judgment (Isa. 29:5–6; Ezek. 38:19; Rev. 6:12;

---

1. Recall our earlier definition of "natural evil" and "moral evil" as two different kinds of pain and suffering, distinguished by their immediate cause being "nature" or "free will" (respectively). See Questions 2 and 3.

11:13; 16:18). As we saw in that Question, God seems to use natural disasters and painful effects of nature as a way of rebuking or punishing humans for their sin. There is no way around this, and if God is judge of all, it seems fitting that he is in control of how he brings about his judgment.[2]

Second, moral evil can be God's punishment of evildoers as well. It is a startling fact that in Romans 1:24–32 Paul says that God can give people over to further sin (that is, to their moral evil) *as* punishment on them for their earlier sin. There is a threefold repetition of the phrase "God gave them up" in the wide-ranging list of sins that Paul notes in this passage. The existence of moral evil can apparently be both the reason for God's punishment and a form of the punishment itself. This perspective is confirmed when we consider the examples surveyed in Question 10 ("Is Moral Evil Ever 'of the Lord'?"). Several cases of moral evil—Rehoboam and Amaziah rejecting wise counsel, the assassination of Jeroboam's house, Absalom's adultery, and Saul's suicide—were the means of God's judgment on the individuals involved. Again, the idea is that God's judgment on sin is a *good* thing, even when that judgment proceeds by way of these (obviously) *bad* things.

Given its potential application to both natural evil and moral evil, the punishment theodicy is an extremely wide-ranging theodicy. Could it be that we can end our survey of theodicies as quickly as we began it? Maybe the punishment theodicy is a "one-size-fits-all" theodicy that needs no supplementation. God's "good reason" for permitting evil *just is* punishment, and so "the claim" in the intellectual problem of evil has been proven false, for all evil whatsoever. As we will see in the next section, we should be cautious about drawing such a far-ranging conclusion.

Limitations of the Punishment Theodicy

The same Bible that teaches that punishment is *often* God's reason for permitting or bringing about suffering also teaches that punishment is not *always* God's reason for this. Here are five examples.

The Bible Teaches This Is Not a Total Explanation of Evil

First, Job's suffering was not punishment for his own evildoing. Rather, Job was selected because of his *faithfulness*. It was because Job "was blameless and upright, one who feared God and turned away from evil" (Job 1:1), that "the LORD said to Satan, 'Have you considered my servant Job, that there is none like him on the earth, a blameless and upright man, who fears God and turns away from evil?'" (Job 1:8; cf. Job 2:3). Apparently, in the face of Satan's

---

2. To be clear, the right to punishment is a right God has that we do not possess—that is, unless God specifically delegates it to us. He is the creator and author of life, and the just judge of all the earth. See Question 12, particularly its section "The Reality of the Divine Right to Take Life."

accusation against Job and slander against God—that God is only worthy to be served for what he gives rather than for who he is—God's good purpose was to turn back the accusation and vindicate his name by giving Job the opportunity to display great faithfulness in the face of great suffering. In the book of Job, the punishment theodicy is continually on the lips of Job's "friends" (Job 4:7–11; 8:1–4; 11:6, 14–20; 15:20–35; 18:5–21; 20:4–29; 22:5–30; 33:8–28; 34:5–37). But God specifically rebukes them for *not* speaking of God what is right (Job 42:7–8). Apparently God's purposes for suffering in the world can go beyond punishment for sin. This is highly significant, since the book of Job is one of the most extended treatments of God's relation to suffering and evil in the entire Bible.

Second, Joseph's suffering was not punishment for his own sin. To be sure, Joseph "brought a bad report" of his brothers to his father (Gen. 37:2), and he was perhaps unwise to share with his family the God-given dreams that indicated his future prominence (Gen. 37:5–11). But the narrative gives no indication that either of these things were *sin* on Joseph's part, such that he deserved to be betrayed by his brothers and sold into slavery. Rather, the brothers' actions were due to their jealousy (Gen. 37:11). And Joseph's imprisonment certainly was not punishment for Joseph's sin; on the contrary, he was a paragon of virtue in his interactions with Potiphar's wife (Gen. 39:6–12) and was imprisoned because of a false accusation. Rather, Joseph suffered because it was God's means of "sending" Joseph into Egypt "to preserve life" and "to preserve for you a remnant on earth" (Gen. 45:5, 7), "to bring it about that many people should be kept alive" (Gen. 50:19–21; cf. Ps. 105:16–17).

Third, the blind man was not born blind because of his sin or the sin of his parents (John 9:1–3). Jesus's disciples seem to presuppose that this sort of punishment theodicy explains the man's blindness, but Jesus flatly denies that explanation. Rather, the man was born blind "that the works of God might be displayed in him" (v. 3), and this higher divine purpose is fulfilled when Jesus immediately goes on to heal the man of his blindness.

Fourth, Jesus's suffering was not punishment for his own sin, because he was without sin (Heb. 4:15; 7:26; 1 John 3:5). Of course, Jesus's suffering *was* punishment for the sins of mankind. So, in a way, the cross vindicates the central idea of the punishment theodicy—all sin must be punished—while highlighting that the *distribution* of that punishment can occur in a way that is unanticipated. It can fall on those who do not deserve it.

Fifth, Paul experienced suffering that was not punishment for his own sin. The narrative in the book of Acts indicates that it was typically Paul's *faithfulness* to gospel norms that generated the persecutions he suffered. Indeed, both Jesus (John 15:18–21; 16:1–4, 33) and the apostles (2 Cor. 4:7–12; 6:4–10; 1 Peter 2:19–21; 3:13–17; 4:12–19; 5:8–10) prepare ordinary believers for persecution that occurs for righteousness rather than for sin. Beyond this, the pagans on the island of Malta used the punishment theodicy to explain why

Paul was bitten by a poisonous viper. He was allegedly being punished by the gods for his sin. But the narrative reveals this was a wholly mistaken inference on their part (Acts 28:3–6).

Logic Shows This Cannot Be a Total Explanation of Evil

Assume, for the sake of argument, that punishment is God's just response to prior human sin. But then it cannot explain God's permission of the very first sin (Adam's sin). It cannot be that the first case of moral evil is permitted as God's punishment on the first case of moral evil. Rather, there must be *another* reason for why God permitted the first sin. Adam's sin cannot itself be punishment on Adam's sin. Satan's rebellion cannot be punishment on Satan's rebellion. Therefore, the punishment theodicy cannot explain *all* evil as God's punishment on prior sin. This is probably why many people who think that there is something right about the punishment theodicy nevertheless appeal to a different theodicy—perhaps the "free will theodicy"—to explain the first sin.[3]

What About Nonhuman (Animal) Suffering?

Finally, while the punishment theodicy can explain quite a bit of the suffering visited on human beings (and other moral agents, such as fallen angels), it seems to stand mute before animal suffering. No doubt if God has cursed the world because of human sin, then animals live in a world that is liable to produce suffering for them. But the fawn in the forest fire cannot be suffering for its sins because it was sinless. It seems strange to think that a just response to human sin involves punishing those who did not sin. Imagine you enter my house and deliberately break my precious vase. By way of punishment on you, I kick my dog. What did the dog do, exactly? Perhaps a different theodicy, such as the "natural law theodicy," might explain animal suffering.[4]

What Role Can the Punishment Theodicy Play?

There are other theodicies we will discuss in this book (soul-building, megaphone, natural law, free will, greater-good). But looking at the punishment theodicy gives us an opportunity to appreciate a point that applies to all the later theodicies as well. That point is about *the burden of proof.* Clearly it would be theologically presumptuous and spiritually disastrous to "rule in" the punishment theodicy as the explanation for any particular case of evil. Given the limitations we have just surveyed, punishment cannot be God's reason for permitting or bringing about *every* case of suffering in the world. Christians just should not attempt to use this theodicy comprehensively.

But he who affirms must prove, and it is the critic of God's existence who is asserting "the claim" that "there is no reason that justifies God in

---

3. The free will theodicy is examined in Question 24.
4. The natural law theodicy is examined in Question 25.

permitting evil." But then the critic needs a way of *showing* that this is true. So the problem here is not that Christians cannot rule in the punishment theodicy for all cases of evil. The problem is that it is not very clear that unbelievers know enough to *rule it out*. This seems like a sensible thing to say considering our earlier material on divine inscrutability (in Question 20). But if they cannot rule it out, then why believe "the claim" is true? We will revisit this question of burden of proof when we return to divine inscrutability (in Question 27).

Summary

There is no doubt that punishment *can* be a reason that God is justified in permitting or bringing about various kinds of suffering. This includes the suffering characteristic of both natural evil and moral evil. If it is good that sin is punished, one cannot get that good without punishment. It is not that punishment is a *means* to a greater good. Punishment would *be* the good, according to this theodicy. However, there are quite a few reasons, both biblical and logical, for thinking that this theodicy cannot explain all suffering and evil in the world. Whether or not that leaves any meaningful role for the punishment theodicy in answering the intellectual problem of evil might depend on how we assess the burden of proof. This is an issue we will return to in Question 27, which will ultimately combine these two themes of theodicy and divine inscrutability into a single comprehensive strategy against the intellectual problem of evil.

REFLECTION QUESTIONS

1. We are at the halfway point in the book, and already there is quite a bit of reference back to earlier Questions, and anticipation of later Questions. Can Christian apologetics be practiced in a vacuum? Or does it essentially rely on methodological, biblical, theological, and pastoral reflection for its success?

2. Some have thought that God's curse on Adam's sin brought death *for human beings only*. (The idea, typically associated with "old earth creationism," is that death was already a reality for animals prior to Adam's sin.) Others think God's curse brought death for the first time *for any creature*, human or nonhuman. Who has the best view, and why?

3. A footnote said that the right to punishment is a right God has which we do not have—that is, unless God specifically delegates it to us. To what extent is the idea of "God's right" an important one to think about when it comes to formulating and evaluating theodicies?

4. Some limitations to theodicy are intrinsic: they face conceptual limits which show they *cannot* apply to all evil, logically speaking. Other limitations are extrinsic: regardless of what logic may show, God simply *tells us* the theodicy does not explain all evils. Which kinds of limitations does the punishment theodicy face?

5. Why do so many people find it entirely natural to apply the punishment theodicy to someone's suffering? (See Job's friends, the disciples about the blind man, the Maltese natives about Paul, all of whom were mistaken.) Is it because of our fallenness that we tend to do this, or because of our (correct) sense of justice, or what?

Could Suffering and Evil Be God's Way of Shaping Our Character?

Theodicies are good reasons God could have in permitting or bringing about suffering. Like the punishment theodicy examined in the previous Question, the *soul-building theodicy* seems to have an extensive biblical basis and could explain both natural evil and moral evil. As with all theodicies surveyed in this book, the soul-building theodicy faces limitations as a one-size-fits-all theodicy, but these do not preclude it playing a useful role as an answer to the intellectual problem of evil. The current Question develops all these points.

Defining the Soul-Building Theodicy

The soul-building theodicy says that suffering is providentially ordered pain that shapes our character and leads us from self-centeredness to other-centeredness. If God displays his justice in the punishment theodicy, he displays his *goodness* in the soul-building theodicy. By promoting character development, suffering can lead us to be more loving, more patient, and more merciful to others. Suffering is a kind of regimen for our souls that is analogous to a physical regimen one would go through in a gymnasium. Even as physical discipline promotes our physical success, so God's fatherly spiritual discipline promotes our spiritual success:

> And have you forgotten the exhortation that addresses you as sons? "My son, do not regard lightly the discipline of the Lord, nor be weary when reproved by him. For the Lord disciplines the one he loves, and chastises every son whom he receives." It is for discipline that you have to endure. God is treating you as sons. For what son is there whom his father does not discipline? If you are left without discipline, in which all have participated, then you are illegitimate children and not sons.

Besides this, we have had earthly fathers who disciplined us and we respected them. Shall we not much more be subject to the Father of spirits and live? For they disciplined us for a short time as it seemed best to them, but he disciplines us for our good, that we may share his holiness. For the moment all discipline seems painful rather than pleasant, but later it yields the peaceful fruit of righteousness to those who have been trained by it. (Heb. 12:5–11)

As in all theodicies, here we see a "good" (v. 10) that God is aiming at: a painful trial "yields the peaceful fruit of righteousness to those who have been trained by it" (v. 11). In this way we come to imitate God himself, which is surely a great good (whether we recognize it as such). So the "weightiness assumption" is satisfied. As for the "dependence assumption," let us distinguish two kinds of dependence, constitutive versus causal. *Constitutive* dependence is part/whole dependence—a whole depends on its parts to be the whole it is. That is the kind of dependence in the punishment theodicy: God justly punishing sinners is an overall good situation, but it would not *be* the situation it is without having the punishment as a part. *Causal* dependence is means/end dependence—something can be a means to bringing about something else that is distinct from it. That is the kind of dependence in the soul-building theodicy: painful providences are means to cultivate virtues like humility and love. These virtues are distinct from the suffering that produces them, whereas just punishment *just is* the suffering God brings. But either way the goods depend on the evils, either constitutively or causally.[1]

Biblical Support for the Soul-Building Theodicy

It is precisely because such weighty goods of character can depend upon suffering in this way that God repeatedly exhorts us to submit to the painful trials he often brings, for God intends to do us spiritual good by them:

Before I was afflicted I went astray, *but now I keep your word.* (Ps. 119:67)

It is good for me that I was afflicted, *that I might learn your statutes.* (Ps. 119:71)

Not only that, but we rejoice in our sufferings, knowing that *suffering produces endurance,* and endurance produces

---

1. See Question 19 for the explanation of the "two assumptions behind all theodicy"—the dependence of goods and the weightiness of goods—apart from which we would not have a theodicy in the first place.

character, and character produces hope, and hope does not put us to shame, because God's love has been poured into our hearts through the Holy Spirit who has been given to us. (Rom. 5:3–5)

For we do not want you to be unaware, brothers, of the affliction we experienced in Asia. For *we were so utterly burdened beyond our strength* that we despaired of life itself. Indeed, we felt that we had received the sentence of death. *But that was to make us rely not on ourselves but on God who raises the dead.* He delivered us from such a deadly peril, and he will deliver us. On him we have set our hope that he will deliver us again. (2 Cor. 1:8–10)

So we do not lose heart. Though our outer self is wasting away, our inner self is being renewed day by day. *For this light momentary affliction is preparing for us an eternal weight of glory beyond all comparison,* as we look not to the things that are seen but to the things that are unseen. For the things that are seen are transient, but the things that are unseen are eternal. (2 Cor. 4:16–18)

Count it all joy, my brothers, when you meet trials of various kinds, for you know that *the testing of your faith produces steadfastness.* And let steadfastness have its full effect, that you may be perfect and complete, lacking in nothing. (James 1:2–4)

In this you rejoice, though now for a little while, if necessary, you have been grieved by various trials, so that *the tested genuineness of your faith*—more precious than gold that perishes though it is tested by fire—*may be found to result in praise and glory and honor* at the revelation of Jesus Christ. (1 Peter 1:6–7)

So suffering is a means that leads us to endurance and steadfastness, to a hope for future glory, and away from self-reliance. Remarkably, in this last passage the apostle Peter asserts that it may be "necessary" for us to be "grieved by various trials." The perseverance of Christian believers is so important for the praise and glory of God, and the faith by which they persevere is so valuable, that God may deem it *necessary* that they suffer, so that their faith is tested and thereby strengthened.

While Jesus's trials did not lead him from sinful self-centeredness to virtuous other-centeredness, they did fit him to be an intercessor sympathetic to our weaknesses. "For it was fitting that he, for whom and by whom all things exist, in bringing many sons to glory, should make the founder of their salvation perfect through suffering" (Heb. 2:10; see 4:15). Each stage of Jesus's earthly life gave him ample opportunity to trust and obey his heavenly Father and rely upon God's Word during trial (Matt. 4:1–11), in a way that was appropriate for that stage, and so he grew to maturity as the perfect man (Luke 2:52).

Trials that remove our health, prosperity, or social standing can bring us to the end of ourselves, leading us to reflect more deeply on what is valuable, and on what is worth living for. Not without reason does the preacher in Ecclesiastes advise: "It is better to go to the house of mourning than to go to the house of feasting, for this is the end of all mankind, and the living will lay it to heart. . . . The heart of the wise is in the house of mourning, but the heart of fools is in the house of mirth" (Eccl. 7:2, 4). There are deep spiritual lessons for us when we meditate on death and on things that can bring us close to death (*memento mori*). Painful trials help us realize that life is transitory and may be briefer than we realize. Finally, when God comforts us in our afflictions, we are thereby trained to comfort those in similar affliction, with the comfort we received from God (2 Cor. 1:3–7). In all these ways, suffering can be just as much a gift of God as faith is (Phil. 1:29).

Finally, advocates of the soul-building theodicy are quick to emphasize that God can have the right to expose his creatures to substantial sufferings, even if *we* do not have the right to do this to each other. This is not just because God is the potter, and we are the clay (Rom. 9:20–21). It is also because God is the greatest benefactor we could possibly imagine. "In him we live and move and have our being" (Acts 17:28), "he himself gives to all mankind life and breath and everything" (Acts 17:25), and "every good gift and every perfect gift is from above" (James 1:17). We are far more dependent on God for every good thing than children are on their parents. And if parents have a very limited right to impose short-term suffering on their children for their good (Prov. 13:24), while having no such right with respect to other people's children, how much more does God have that right with respect to all his creatures! This is precisely the inference the inspired author is making in Hebrews 12:9–10 from the rights of earthly fathers to the rights of God when it comes to discipline.[2]

Beyond this, God has sufficient wisdom and power to do us good by our sufferings, a degree of wisdom and power which we lack. Given our ignorance and impotence, we would be irresponsible bumblers at best—trying to effect brain surgery with a hammer, as it were—if *we* tried to bring about long-term good through suffering. It makes sense that this right is God's alone. God is an expert in bringing good out of suffering, whereas we are not. As philosopher of religion Eleonore Stump puts it:

---

2. For a stimulating discussion of this topic, see "God's Right" in Richard Swinburne, *Providence and the Problem of Evil* (Oxford: Oxford University Press, 1998), 223–36.

In the case of suffering and its role in redemption, it seems clear that at least in the great majority of cases we don't know enough to turn suffering into a help toward spiritual health. We have to rely, therefore, on God's expertise instead.[3]

Limitations of the Soul-Building Theodicy

Soul-building Does Not Always Occur

Imagine God is engaged in some sort of "soul-building endeavor" through the sufferings his creatures experience. If so, does it not seem that that endeavor is often an utter *failure*? Sometimes suffering seems to make people worse off than they were before, rather than better. The businessman is not humbled by his failures but grows more bitter. The cancer patient does not learn to depend on God more and count her blessings; she takes up Buddhism and renounces any personal conception of God instead. The mugging victim becomes fearful and paranoid rather than independent and self-reliant. What should we say about these cases?

Some advocates of the soul-building theodicy hold to "risky providence." They do not believe that God can ensure outcomes amid human freedom. Rather, God does the best he can with the means at his disposal. These Christians would say, with respect to these cases of failure, that perhaps the suffering was nevertheless the best that God could do in the circumstances, consistent with human libertarian free will. God will not *coerce* us into making better choices in our lives, and so if his choice is between bringing suffering that might fall short in its intended effect and bringing suffering that is so intense that it removes all freedom of choice, God will always opt for the former, not the latter.

Of course, Calvinists, Molinists, and other Christians who hold to a "risk-free providence" cannot use this explanation (see Question 15). They believe that God *does* ensure outcomes, either through determinism or middle knowledge. But they could say one of two things here. First, perhaps the suffering was the best that God could do given *other* things God is aiming at. For example, God knows the person will not cultivate virtue in response to suffering, but he nevertheless brings it because it is an eloquent witness to God's commitment to use even harsh means to rescue us from ourselves. God does not give up on us, even if our hearts are hard.

Second, perhaps we do not *know enough* to conclude that the suffering was a "failure." If the person is still alive, then for all we know the intended effect will come in the future, even if it is not present now. And if the person is no longer with us, what do *we* know about how the suffering shaped a person's soul—beneath the surface, as it were—and perhaps in their last moments, in

---

3. Eleonore Stump, "Aquinas on the Sufferings of Job," in *The Evidential Argument from Evil*, ed. Daniel Howard-Snyder (Bloomington: Indiana University Press, 1996), 59.

their private thoughts and choices before God? Perhaps their selfishness was known only to them and God, such that their painful circumstances were perfectly suited above all others to help them improve. As theologian Sinclair Ferguson puts it, "Spiritual growth is like an iceberg—only part of it can ever be seen above the surface."[4] At least 90 percent is below sea level, outside the awareness of the people around them. Using outer appearances as a guide to what is going on beneath the surface is a woefully unreliable indicator of people's needs, struggles, victories, and failures.

The Biblical Promises Seem to Be Limited to Believers and to Exclude Unbelievers

The biblical passages cited earlier indicate God has specially promised that the suffering of *believers* will do them good. But these same passages say next to nothing about the trials of *unbelievers*. Does the soul-building theodicy apply to them? If not, then this theodicy seems irrelevant to the vast amount of suffering in the world.

Here we could go in one of two directions. First, we could try to extend the soul-building theodicy to unbelievers, that is, to everyone in the world. As it turns out, philosopher of religion John Hick almost single-handedly revived philosophical discussion of the soul-building theodicy in the twentieth century through his highly influential volume *Evil and the God of Love*. Hick speaks of the entire world as a school of hard knocks intended by God to cultivate opportunity for developing virtue, so that humanity would progress from immaturity to maturity:

> But nevertheless our sinful nature in a sinful world is the matrix within which God is gradually creating children for himself out of human animals. For it is as men and women freely respond to the claim of God upon their lives, transmuting their animality into the structure of divine worship, that the creation of humanity is taking place. And in its concrete character this response consists in every form of moral goodness, from unselfish love in individual personal relationships to the dedicated and selfless striving to end exploitation and to create justice within and between societies.[5]

---

4. Sinclair Ferguson, *Grow in Grace* (Colorado Springs: NavPress, 1984), 148.
5. John Hick, "Soul-Making Theodicy," in *The Problem of Evil: Selected Readings*, 2nd ed., ed. Michael Peterson (Notre Dame, IN: University of Notre Dame Press, 2016), 270. Hick's more developed presentation of his theodicy is found in John Hick, *Evil and the God of Love* (New York: Palgrave Macmillan, 2010 [1st ed. 1966, 2nd ed. 2007]).

Unfortunately, Hick's theodicy not only fails to include reference to Christ; it seems to *preclude* Christ as the author of our salvation. Rather, humanity in general—apart from Christ—works out its salvation on its own. Salvation is the development of civilization, no Christ and his sacrifice needed.

Because Hick's more universal soul-building theodicy blurs the believer/unbeliever distinction in a way that is unrecognizable by the orthodox Christian tradition, a second direction is open for us to take. Simply admit that the soul-building theodicy is primarily oriented toward believers, and then use a *different* theodicy to explain the suffering of unbelievers. If, as Eleonore Stump argues (following Thomas Aquinas), the greatest need of any human being is to be united to God and to flourish in that union, then God might use pain as a "megaphone" to get *unbelievers into* that union (see next Question), while also using pain as a kind of "soul-building" to help *believers grow* in that union (see this Question).[6]

Summary

The soul-building theodicy explains suffering and evil as a means to shaping our souls for good. Many biblical promises express God's intention to use trials in this way, presenting God as having the authority, knowledge, and power needed to be both good and successful in this endeavor. We should not confuse the appearance of failure with actual failure, though perhaps other theodicies are better suited to explain the suffering of unbelievers.

REFLECTION QUESTIONS

1. What kind of virtues or character development can occur through suffering? (Be specific in your examples.)

2. The Scriptures often connect suffering with effective evangelism (see 2 Tim. 2:10; 2 Cor. 4:15; 12:15; Eph. 3:13). What are some examples of this, in the Bible or in your experience?

3. Suffering that quickly ends one's life (Nadab and Abihu, Lev. 10:1–3; Korah and his household, Num. 16:31–35; Herod, Acts 12:20–23) seems unable to shape one's character. Do you agree?

---

6. According to Eleonore Stump, "The benefit defeating a person's suffering has to do either with enabling a person to have the best thing for human beings [flourishing in union with God] or with enabling him to ward off the worst thing for human beings [lacking union with God]" (*Wandering in Darkness: Narrative and the Problem of Suffering* [Oxford: Oxford University Press, 2010], 455).

4. Does this theodicy leave animal (nonhuman) suffering unexplained? Surely the fawn in the forest fire does not need to undergo "character development." Is there a way to adapt this theodicy to cover this kind of case?

5. Some cases of suffering involve not only victims (those who suffer), but perpetrators (those who bring the suffering) and onlookers (those who see others suffering). Could the soul-building theodicy speak to each of these groups?[7]

7. These three categories are adapted from Marilyn Adams, "Redemptive Suffering: A Christian Solution to the Problem of Evil," in *Rationality, Religious Belief, and Moral Commitment*, eds. Robert Audi and William J. Wainwright (Ithaca, NY: Cornell University Press, 1986).

Could Suffering and Evil Be God's Way of Getting Our Attention?

According to twentieth-century Oxford don and Christian apologist C. S. Lewis:

> We can rest contentedly in our sins and in our stupidities ... we can ignore even pleasure. But pain insists upon being attended to. God whispers to us in our pleasures, speaks in our conscience, but shouts in our pain: it is His megaphone to rouse a deaf world.[1]

But what is God *rousing* us to, by way of the pain we experience? Lewis continues:

> If the first and lowest operation of pain shatters the illusion that all is well, the second shatters the illusion that what we have, whether good or bad in itself, is our own and enough for us. Everyone has noticed how hard it is to turn our thoughts to God when everything is going well with us. We "have all we want" is a terrible saying when "all" does not include God.[2]

On Lewis's view, God may use pain as a "megaphone" to get us "to turn our thoughts to God," to get us to realize that we do not have everything worth wanting if we do not have God. If the soul-building theodicy (last Question) explains pain as that which helps believers grow in their union with God,

---

1. C. S. Lewis, *The Problem of Pain* (New York: HarperOne, 2001 [1940]), 90–91.
2. Lewis, *The Problem of Pain*, 94.

the pain-as-God's-megaphone theodicy (this Question) explains pain as that which helps unbelievers choose to be united with God in the first place.

Defining the Pain-as-God's-Megaphone Theodicy

The megaphone theodicy says that suffering is permitted and even brought about by God to get our attention, so that we would give up the worldly goods and purposes to which we are wedded and unite ourselves to God instead. Providentially ordered pain aims at a great good: our deliverance from the wrath to come. God is willing for us to experience a bit of the horror of that future judgment so that we would be delivered from it entirely as we take refuge in him. Very difficult circumstances, which can result from natural evil and moral evil, can accomplish much in our lives. They can wake us up from our devotion to the world, leading us to reflect upon and consider the life to come, our dependence on God, and our obligation to seek him in our trials.

These painful providences are an alternative to God *coercing* us to come to him. Such coercion would bypass our capacities for rational reflection and deliberation, leaving us unfree and non-responsible for whatever "choice" we have been coerced into making. Rather, God works indirectly through our environment so that we would clearly see that money, fame, success, and pleasure are fleeting. If we remain devoted to these baubles of the world, then we will never be delivered from the wrath to come. So God removes them, often painfully.

Biblical Basis for the Megaphone Theodicy

The Old Testament Prophets

Lewis has given an evocative label to a very old idea, one that appears throughout the Bible. First, consider the ministry of God's prophets in the Old Testament. Interpreters have long noticed that two streams come together in the prophetic ministry: coming judgment and coming salvation. On the one hand, the prophets are like God's "lawyers," prosecuting a wayward people for flouting their covenant obligations. Because of idolatry, immorality, and injustice, the Israelites deserve to have the sanctions of the covenant fall upon them:

> And the haughtiness of man shall be humbled, and the lofty pride of men shall be brought low, and the LORD alone will be exalted in that day. And the idols shall utterly pass away. And people shall enter the caves of the rocks and the holes of the ground, from before the terror of the LORD, and from the splendor of his majesty, when he rises to terrify the earth. (Isa. 2:17–19)

Or again:

> For behold, the LORD will come in fire, and his chariots like the whirlwind, to render his anger in fury, and his rebuke with flames of fire. For by fire will the LORD enter into judgment, and by his sword, with all flesh; and those slain by the LORD shall be many. (Isa. 66:15–16)

But on the other hand, the prophets foresee a day in which the Israelites will be delivered from the very judgment they deserve:

> The LORD saw it, and it displeased him that there was no justice. He saw that there was no man, and wondered that there was no one to intercede; then his own arm brought him salvation, and his righteousness upheld him. (Isa. 59:15–16)

God even promises to bring this salvation through "a man of sorrows," "despised and rejected by men," one who "poured out his soul to death and was numbered with the transgressors; yet he bore the sin of many, and makes intercession for the transgressors" (Isa. 53:3, 12).

In short, God's threat of coming judgment is a means to produce faith and confidence in the one who would take that judgment for them. But such Israelite faith and confidence in God the Redeemer requires *repentance* from their present ways, and the latter might not happen unless God brings real pain, to show he is serious about that coming judgment.

This is why, in the Old Testament, God does not just threaten final judgment; he sometimes brings a foretaste of it. The curses of Deuteronomy 28:15–68 are no idle threat. These pains, largely (though not exclusively) the sufferings associated with natural evils of various sorts, come upon Israel throughout her history (see Question 9). For example, there is a long compendium of "punishments for disobedience" that God lists out in Leviticus 26:14–45. But these are not *mere* punishments. God reveals a more ultimate purpose behind these pains, a purpose repeatedly interspersed among these increasingly uncomfortable judgments:

> And if in spite of this you will not listen to me . . . (v. 18)

> Then if you walk contrary to me and will not listen to me . . . (v. 21)

> And if by this discipline you are not turned to me but walk contrary to me . . . (v. 23)

But if in spite of this you will not listen to me, but walk contrary to me . . . (v. 27)

But if they confess their iniquity . . . (v. 40)

Clearly, these temporal judgments are *redemptive* in purpose, in that God wants this pain to lead wayward human beings to "listen" to him, "turn" to him, and "confess their iniquity." *Any* pain suffered by the unrepentant prior to the final judgment could be placed in this category. They are not being punished *for* their sins. They are being pursued by a God who wants to deliver them *from* their sins. If the punishment theodicy displays God's justice and the soul-building theodicy displays God's goodness, the megaphone theodicy displays God's mercy.

The Tower of Siloam (Luke 13:1–5)
Second, consider how Jesus responds to his hearers' questions in Luke 13:1–5:

> There were some present at that very time who told him about the Galileans whose blood Pilate had mingled with their sacrifices. And he answered them, "Do you think that these Galileans were worse sinners than all the other Galileans, because they suffered in this way? No, I tell you; but unless you repent, you will all likewise perish. Or those eighteen on whom the tower in Siloam fell and killed them: do you think that they were worse offenders than all the others who lived in Jerusalem? No, I tell you; but unless you repent, you will all likewise perish."

Here, Jesus considers and then rules out the punishment theodicy in the case of "the Galileans" (murdered by Herod) and the "eighteen" (killed by the falling tower). The idea that they died *because* they "were worse sinners" than others is rejected. But then Jesus hints at an alternative theodicy: Yes, those individuals have died, and there is nothing we can do about them now. But what about you? Are *you* ready to die? God can end life at any moment. For Jesus, these sobering events are a warning to his hearers that the whole world will be judged on the final day. The megaphone has sounded. The message is the same as that of the Old Testament prophets: unless you repent now, you will perish in the future.

In Romans 2:4, Paul speaks of those who "presume on the riches of his [i.e., God's] kindness and forbearance and patience, not knowing that God's kindness is meant to lead you to repentance." The very fact that God has kindly and patiently preserved their life for another day is evidence that God is not done with them yet, that the day of salvation is yet open. What the mega-phone theodicy says is that God's *severity* is meant to lead us to repentance as well. We are addicted to God's blessings, and we take no thought of the giver. But pain teaches us that our life is relatively short, that it has been filled with good things and opportunities, and that we did not earn these things and do not really deserve them. We are led to ask, "Whom should we thank?" "Whom should we serve?" and "What about my guilt over having lived for myself all this time? How do I get rid of that?" The vanities of earth have been drowning out God's voice, but the megaphone of God's pain is finally heard above the din.

Limitations of the Megaphone Theodicy

Since the megaphone theodicy is similar to the soul-building theodicy (except that its focus is unbelievers rather than believers), it inherits some of the same limitations. These include its efficacy and scope.

Why Would "Christians" Need Pain to Start a Relationship with God? They Already Have One!

Those who have already been converted, who are united to God by faith, do not need pain to get them into such a union. So the megaphone theodicy cannot really explain *their* pain.

This seems right, but then that would be a reason to think that some *other* theodicy might explain why they are suffering. As was pointed out in the last Question, if our greatest good is to flourish in our union with God and our greatest evil is not to be united to God at all, then the pain justified by way of the megaphone theodicy is aimed at helping unbelievers avoid the latter, rather than being aimed at helping believers secure the former.

What About Pain That Seems to Go "Far Beyond" What Is Needed to Get Someone's Attention?

Maybe the first year of cancer led us to consider God. It definitely got our attention! But then what were the next three years for? So much suffering of unbelievers seems excessive, given this theodicy.

Here we should be careful. What is the state of the soul of the person who is experiencing the pain? God does not just want to "get our attention." He wants *us*. If the person who has suffered is still not united to God by faith, then (for all we know) the subsequent years of difficulty might be aimed at bringing that about. Alternatively, if the person *is* united to God by faith (after the first year of cancer, let's say), then there is no need for the megaphone theodicy to explain the subsequent pain. Perhaps the soul-building theodicy explains that.

In thinking through the prospects for theodicy in solving the intellectual problem of evil, there is simply no need for a one-size-fits-all theodicy that explains all pain whatsoever. As long as every pain is explained by some theodicy or other, there is no need for one theodicy to explain all of it.

What About Animal (Nonhuman) Suffering?

This question has come up when evaluating all three of the theodicies. As far as we know, animals do experience pain (at least animals with a sufficiently developed brain structure that can support the production of such mental states). Why else would a dog howl when cut by a sharp stick, or a deer moan when hit by a car? Are these not then precisely the kinds of responses we make when we are in pain? But the punishment, soul-building, and megaphone theodicies seem to be total nonstarters when it comes to explaining the animal suffering we see all around us. Animals do not commit sins that need punishing, are not subject to character development, and do not need conversion!

One way to respond is to admit that animal suffering cannot be explained by the megaphone theodicy, and so we must look for a theodicy that is more plausible in that context. (For example, the natural law theodicy to be considered in Question 25.) But another way to respond to the suffering of animals is to say that perhaps we need to see *their* suffering as well, in order to turn to God. The suffering of these innocents is an eloquent testimony to us that we live in a deeply flawed world, perhaps one that is cursed. How awful is that curse, how awful is the human sin that called it forth, if even the animals suffer, these sentient creatures capable of pain but who do not know right from wrong! But at the same time something in us cries out that it *ought not* to be this way. Recognizing this as evidence that we do live in a fallen world, and wondering how it can be set right, how our own lives can be set right, may be just the means God uses to awaken us to a spiritual perspective on our real needs.

At this point a new limitation of the megaphone theodicy appears: Why *so much* animal suffering? Would we not still know the world was cursed if there were just half the animal suffering there is now? What this means is that we do not know enough to rule in the megaphone theodicy as *the* explanation in a great many cases—indeed, perhaps we cannot rule it in for *any* case. But unbelievers do not know enough to rule out this theodicy, and so they cannot reliably conclude that God does not have a good reason for permitting evil. We will return to this question of burden of proof when we return to divine inscrutability again (in Question 27).

Summary

The pain-as-God's-megaphone theodicy seems uniquely suited to explaining the suffering of unbelievers as redemptive. Not that such suffering atones for sin—only Christ's suffering does that. But God might use painful circumstances to lead someone to seriously consider their need for Christ, perhaps by way of reflecting on the brevity of life and on God as the giver of every good and perfect gift. The Old and New Testaments seem to share this perspective, and there are reasonable replies to those who think this theodicy is limited in its efficacy or scope.

REFLECTION QUESTIONS

1. It seems to be a common theme in many conversion stories that God used a period of great lack and even suffering to lead someone to deeper spiritual reflection. Can you testify to this in your own life, or in the life of anyone you know?

2. Could it be that *all* suffering experienced by unbelievers prior to the final judgment is *redemptive* suffering rather than punitive suffering (in the sense of "redemptive" as explained in the summary above)? Is there anything in the Bible that would preclude this? What are the advantages of this view, if any?

3. According to the Old Testament prophets, the threat of future judgment is real, but so is the promise of salvation. How can present pain lead us to appreciate both of these facts?

4. Do the words of Jesus, "Unless you repent, you will all likewise perish," seem to lack compassion? After all, Jesus has just been told about the brutal deaths of many people. Or are his words instead an instance of divine compassion?

5. Why prioritize the megaphone theodicy over the soul-building theodicy, when explaining the suffering of unbelievers? Would this have something to do with what is the greatest good for an unbeliever?

Could Moral Evil Be Due to Our Abuse of Free Will?

Perhaps moral evil is due to abuse of free will (this Question), and natural evil is due to the laws of nature (next Question). If so, then these next two theodicies complement one another, each explaining what the other does not. And taken together, they might be a way of explaining all suffering whatsoever, no matter its immediate cause. In addition, these two theodicies might have the advantage of removing divine intention out of the picture entirely when it comes to pain and suffering. On the free will and natural law theodicies, suffering and evil are ever and always the unintended and unneeded side effect of what God *does* intend: our enjoying the gift of free will, and our exercising it in a stable environment. Making evil something that is unintended (by God) and unneeded (as a means to divine ends) would be a considerable advantage for these theodicies in answering the intellectual problem of evil.[1]

Defining the Free Will Theodicy

C. S. Lewis provides an elegant statement of the FWT:

> Free will is what has made evil possible. Why, then, did God give them free will? Because free will, though it makes evil possible, is also the only thing that makes possible any love or goodness or joy worth having. A world of automata—of creatures that worked like machines—would hardly be worth creating. The happiness which God designs for His higher creatures is the

---

1. According to the theodicies examined in the preceding three Questions, suffering and evil are divinely intended either as ends in themselves (punishment) or as a means to divine ends (soul-building, megaphone). None of this is the case in the free will and natural law theodicies.

happiness of being freely, voluntarily united to Him and to each
other. . . . And for that they must be free. Of course God knew
what would happen if they used their freedom the wrong way:
apparently He thought it worth the risk.[2]

Here Lewis highlights the dependence and weightiness assumptions,
which we argued were the two assumptions behind all successful theodicy
(Question 19). According to Lewis, the dependence assumption is satisfied
because the great good of free will depends on the possibility of evil—"it
makes evil possible." You simply cannot have free will without the possibility
of evil, and so the former depends on the latter. And the weightiness assumption
is satisfied because free will is a *great* good, for it is "the only thing that
makes possible any love or goodness or joy worth having." At the heart of the
FWT, God is making a value judgment: any world with free will, even if that
free will gets abused, is greater, more valuable, than a world without free will.
That is why Lewis says, "He thought it worth the risk." God's judging that free
will was *worth* the risk is what led him to give the gift of free will in the first
place. It is that valuable a gift.

The introduction of the category of "risk" is very significant. The FWT
does not say that moral evil is inevitable or guaranteed to happen just because
God gives someone the gift of free will. Rather, the gift of free will carries with
it the *risk* of moral evil. Moral evil may or may not occur—that is up to us.
We could receive the gift of free will and never abuse it, always choosing what
is morally right on every occasion. Choosing evil is not required in order to
have free will. In fact, advocates of the FWT would say that if choosing evil
were required in order to have free will—if you had to use your free will for
evil—then you simply did not have *free* will in the first place!

It is important to see that the kind of free will in the FWT is libertarian
free will, which was defined and contrasted with "compatibilist" free will in
Question 15. As was said there, people with libertarian free will "can do otherwise
in the same exact circumstances because what they do in those circumstances
is up to them." It is a kind of free will that is incompatible with
determinism, for if God ensured that we would use our free will in a particular
way, then our choices would not really be "up to us."

Notice the extraordinarily broad range of moral evils in the world,
surveyed earlier in Question 6. These involve the breaking of all Ten
Commandments by both men and women in every age group, by members of
religious communities, and by whole nations (whether through their leaders
or the common people), with resulting widespread physical pain, psychological
scarring, and social isolation among individuals, families, laborers, the

---

2. C. S. Lewis, *Mere Christianity* (New York: HarperOne, 2001 [1952]), 48. Lewis's definition
of the megaphone theodicy was cited in the last Question.

poor, and so on. The FWT says that *all* of that is due to creatures abusing their libertarian free will. Would the world be better if God just swooped in and kept people from abusing their free will in these ways? Certainly the world would be better *with respect to* not having all this moral evil! But advocates of the FWT contend that a world in which God constantly intervened to prevent moral evil would not be better *overall*, because such a world would be without free will. That is, a world with free will and all this moral evil is better than a world lacking both things. That is the value judgment at the heart of the FWT. Likewise, God cannot pry apart free will and the possibility of evil. That is the dependence claim at the heart of the FWT.

Here is another statement of the FWT, this time from biblical scholar Brian Han Gregg:

> These evil choices and their consequences are the cost paid by God and his creation for his unwillingness to compromise our free will. God, who is just, allows injustice to take place, and suffering multiplies. It may seem cruel, but for God there is much at stake. If he were to compel righteousness, our freedom would be an illusion. Therefore, he lets us sin and be sinned against, so that we might also freely love and worship and serve.[3]

Here again we see the dependence assumption ("the cost paid by God") and the weightiness assumption ("there is much at stake").

Biblical Basis for the Free Will Theodicy

Philosophers have come up with some interesting arguments for the FWT. In fact, the preceding section clearly lays out the central argument implicit in Lewis's and Gregg's statements. But is there a *biblical basis* for affirming the FWT, as revealing to us "the real reason" why God gave us free will, and why he allows moral evil that he could easily prevent? In the previous three Questions we did find some kind of positive biblical support for each of those theodicies. God seems to just *tell us* that pain and suffering can be punishment from him or can be trials used by him to shape our character or can be ways of waking us up to our need for him. But the FWT is different. The Bible nowhere suggests that God permits suffering and evil *because of* the value of free will.[4]

---

3. Brian Han Gregg, *What Does the Bible Say about Suffering?* (Downers Grove, IL: InterVarsity Press, 2016), 46. Notably, Gregg goes on to list several "serious difficulties" for "free will" as a "means of understanding why God allows suffering" (p. 46).

4. Obviously, being fallible, prone to error, and incompletely sanctified, I may have over-looked something in the biblical materials on this point. But that is how things look to me, after examining those materials for several decades. I would be pleasantly surprised to learn that I am wrong here, however.

In fact, there also is lacking any *indirect* argument from the Bible for the FWT. The main reason for this is that God does not ever tell us that he places value on the kind of free will that is needed for the FWT: libertarian free will. Of course, it is consistent with this biblical silence that God nevertheless *does* value libertarian free will, that we *have* libertarian free will, and that God allows moral evil *because* he values libertarian free will. All that could be true. But again, the Bible does not say any of these three things. So it is hard to say there is a biblical case for the FWT, though that does not prevent the FWT from being *consistent* with the Bible. And maybe the latter is all we need for an answer to the intellectual problem of evil. Who says the Bible must support a theodicy for that theodicy to be useable by Christians as an answer to the intellectual problem of evil?

Perhaps the following is one way to make a biblical case for the FWT:

1. *God* has libertarian free will. After all, God is free to create or not to create.
2. God gave *us* libertarian free will (1 Cor. 10:13 implies this).[5]
3. Libertarian free will is *extraordinarily valuable* because by it we resemble our Creator (the most valuable being of all), who created us in his image.
4. God created us *knowing* that we could abuse our free will.
5. Therefore, God must have known that the worth of free will *outweighs* all the evils that could flow from its abuse. For if free will *was not* that valuable, surely God would not have given it to us.
6. Therefore, the value of free will outweighs all the moral evils that flow from its abuse.

Readers will likely differ on the extent to which the claims above are in fact derived from Scripture. While claim 4 seems right (given that God is all-knowing), one could wonder about the case for claims 1–3.

Limitations of the Free Will Theodicy

What Is the Question?

Regardless of whether there is biblical support for the FWT, philosophers and Christian apologists have given various arguments from reason for the theodicy. Do these arguments show that the theodicy is a good one?

It is important to be clear regarding the question we are asking. We are not wondering if abuse of free will *explains* the existence of moral evil. Pretty clearly, it does. After all, that is how "moral evil" is defined: significant pain

5. See William Lane Craig, "The Middle-Knowledge View," in *Divine Foreknowledge: Four Views*, eds. James K. Beilby and Paul R. Eddy (Downers Grove, IL: IVP Academic, 2001), 202.

and suffering that is immediately caused by abuse of free will (see Questions 2 and 3). Rather, we are wondering whether abuse of free will is a *good theodicy* for moral evil. While every theodicy is an explanation, not every explanation is a theodicy. A theodicy is a special kind of explanation. It not only explains where suffering and evil come from; it also supplies a *good reason* for God's allowing it to happen. Compare: an earthquake might explain why a building collapsed, but that would not (by itself) give us a good reason for why God allowed it to happen. Likewise, free will might explain why there is moral evil, but that would not (by itself) give us a good reason for why God allowed the evil to happen.

Free will is supposed to be a weighty, dependent good. It is weighty (valuable) because it provides the only possibility of moral good and of our imaging God. It is dependent in the sense that we cannot have it without creating the real possibility of moral evil. It therefore explains why God is justified in permitting moral evil. But here we can ask two questions. Does moral good really *depend* on libertarian free will? And is libertarian free will truly *valuable*? Consider the following pushback against these claims.

The Possibility of Restricted Free Will

Christian philosopher Michael Murray (utilizing an idea in Peter Geach) describes a creative possibility for God:

> God could have simply given us free choice among only good alternatives . . . it is surely plausible that God could have wired us so that thoughts of evil acts never occurred to us, while thoughts of diverse good courses of action always would, thus leaving us plenty of genuine alternatives in choice.[6]

Notice that in such a world, it is *up to us* what we choose on any occasion—walk the dog, or research chemistry, or go out to dinner with a friend, or paint a picture—and we would be free from divine determinism in each case. Such a world would have lots of moral good, but no moral evil. So what is the value of *unrestricted* free will, since we can choose moral good without it? And why think free will *depends* on the possibility of moral evil?

The Actuality of God's Free Will

According to Scripture, God cannot do evil or even be tempted to do evil (James 1:13). But God is the most valuable being it is possible for there to be. It is counterintuitive to think that we humans have a great-making property (unrestricted libertarian free will) which God lacks. So, once again, either

---

6. Michael Murray, Review of "Geach, Peter, *Truth and Hope*. University of Notre Dame Press, 2001," *Notre Dame Philosophical Reviews*, February 4, 2002.

libertarian free will is not as valuable as claimed (God, the most valuable being, doesn't have it) or free will does not depend on the possibility of doing evil (God is free, but can't do evil). The value judgment at the heart of the FWT seems contradicted by the nature of the Being it seeks to defend.

The Hope of Heavenly Free Will

It is at least a traditional Christian belief that heaven's inhabitants cannot choose evil, such that redemptive history must start all over again. The "heavenly Jerusalem" is "the assembly of the firstborn who are enrolled in heaven" and the abode of "the spirits of the righteous made perfect" (Heb. 12:22–23). Perfected saints *cannot* be sinners, for their Savior "is able to keep you from stumbling and to present you blameless before the presence of his glory with great joy" (Jude 24). This makes sense, because the three great sources of temptation—the world, the flesh, and the devil—will be gone in heaven, and so there would be no temptation to sin, and so no opportunity for sinning.

If this is right, then heaven is a place where we lack a kind of freedom: the freedom to do evil. But is heaven not the most valuable place it is possible for there to be? Once again, it is counterintuitive to think that our earthly life has a great-making property (unrestricted libertarian free will) that heaven lacks. So the value judgment at the heart of the FWT seems contradicted by the most valuable kind of life possible: worship and eternal happiness in the presence of God himself. Either libertarian free will is not as valuable as claimed (heaven, the most valuable environment of all, does not have it), or free will does not depend on the possibility of doing evil (we are free agents in heaven, but cannot do evil).[7]

Summary

The FWT argues that a world with free will, even if that free will is abused, is more valuable than a world without free will. So, God is justified in allowing moral evil, because it is the price he pays (the risk he takes) in giving us the great good of free will. While the Bible does not suggest this theodicy, the idea has seemed intuitive and appealing to many who wrestle with the intellectual problem of evil. In this short space, only a few potential limitations of the FWT have been considered.

---

7. Advocates of the FWT have interesting replies to the issues addressed in this chapter. Rich discussions of this topic can be found in *Free Will and Theism: Connections, Contingencies, and Concerns*, eds. Kevin Timpe and Daniel Speak (Oxford: Oxford University Press, 2016); Laura W. Ekstrom, *God, Suffering, and the Value of Free Will* (Oxford: Oxford University Press, 2021); and Heath White, *Fate and Free Will* (Notre Dame, IN: University of Notre Dame Press, 2020).

REFLECTION QUESTIONS

1. Free will does not seem to be an absolute good, since sometimes God intervenes and *prevents* its exercise (e.g., the flood, the exodus from Egypt, holy war in Canaan). But if it is "up to God" whether instances of moral evil occur, then is it really "up to free will"?

2. According to Molinism (see Question 15), God did not "take a risk" when he gave us free will, for God knew in advance exactly what we would do with it. Does this give us a better version of the FWT, or does it create a new problem for it?

3. Maybe it is better to have the real opportunity to do evil, *and decline it*, than not to have the real opportunity to do evil at all. Could *that* be what is truly valuable about free will?

4. What did you think of the "biblical case for the FWT" presented earlier? Could you defend its premises? Is there a better case to be made?

5. Do you agree that while every theodicy is an explanation, not every explanation is a theodicy?

Could Natural Evil Be Due to the Laws of Nature?

According to the "natural law theodicy" (NLT), natural evil is the unintended side effect of the existence of the laws of nature. But the laws of nature are a great good—they provide a stable environment in which we can exercise free will. So God is justified in permitting natural evils like earthquakes, tornados, and genetic defects. These are the price God pays for getting us an overall stable environment. To what extent is this theodicy suggested by Scripture? Or is it instead inconsistent with Scripture?

Defining the Natural Law Theodicy

In Questions 2 and 3 we defined "natural evil" as "any evil caused by impersonal objects and forces, rather than by people's defect of will," where "evil" is "any significant case of pain and suffering." Natural evil comes from "how nature goes on," quite independently of human choices. Examples include pain and suffering caused by disease, earthquakes, falling trees, famine, forest fires, genetic defects, hurricanes, plague, poisonous food and water, predatory beasts, rolling boulders, tornados, and tsunamis.[1]

To explain God's permission of natural evil, the NLT is interestingly similar in structure to the free will theodicy (FWT), which is supposed to explain God's permission of moral evil (see Question 24). In the FWT, God aims at a great good: the gift of free will itself. But this great good can only exist if there is the possibility of moral evil. Free will turns out to be a weighty, dependent good—the possibility of moral evil is the price God pays to get us the great good of free will. Similarly, in the NLT, God aims at a great good: a stable

---

1. Of course, if any of these things were to be caused by scheming humans—such as corrupt governments inflicting famine, disease, or plague on their people—then these would be cases of moral evil, not natural evil.

environment in which we can reliably predict the immediate consequences of our choices:

> To live happily and productively requires a universe of reg-
> ular law, so that we can make plans and fulfill them. If, when
> I reached for my comb in the morning, it randomly turned
> into a tortoise, I would not be able to develop a dependable
> plan and practice of combing my hair.[2]

Imagine there was a serious chance of my comb randomly turning into a poisonous snake when I grabbed it in the morning. I would probably stop making that particular choice. Ditto if turning doorknobs randomly caused doors to sometimes dissolve into clouds of poisonous gas. We would stop making free will choices in a chaotic world that lacks any discernible and dependable regularities. But if God is going to get us the great good of a world with laws of nature, then there must be the possibility of natural evil, of nature causing us pain and suffering in various ways when we "bump up" against those firm and inflexible laws of nature. If God gave us a world in which "a wooden beam became soft as grass when it was used as a weapon," or "the air refused to obey me if I attempted to set up in it the soundwaves that carry lies or insults," then "freedom of the will would be void." Rather, the world needs "fixed laws, consequences unfolding by causal necessity, the whole natural order."[3]

So, God will not suspend the laws of nature simply because their operation might on occasion prove inconvenient to us, as that would undermine the stability of the environment they provide. If we decide to dance on a cliff edge and then stumble, God is not going to temporarily repeal the law of gravity so that we float harmlessly to the ground. If we foolishly step in the path of an oncoming car, God will not suddenly suspend laws about the inertia of large metal objects. The same law of conservation of momentum that enables you to shake someone's hand without punching him is the same law that guarantees you will be crushed by a boulder speeding toward you if you do not jump out of the way. There can be quite a bit of pain when we live in an environment subject to these regularities. That is the price you pay when you live in a stable environment that enables you to engage in meaningful choice-making. You cannot benefit from that aspect of the laws and then wish there were no such laws.

So, like free will, the laws of nature turn out to be a weighty, dependent good—the possibility of natural evil is the price God pays to get us the great

---

2. John M. Frame, *Apologetics: A Justification of Christian Belief* (Phillipsburg, NJ: P&R Publishing, 2015), 168. Frame goes on to raise criticisms of the NLT that are similar to those I raise later in this Question.
3. C. S. Lewis, *The Problem of Pain* (New York: HarperOne, 2001 [1940]), 24–25.

good of laws of nature. Indeed, the FWT and NLT do not just parallel each other in their structure. They are intimately connected to each other. Laws of nature provide a kind of needed environmental "scaffolding" in which free will can be exercised. Therefore, free will is at the heart of explaining both moral evil and natural evil. Moral evil happens when we abuse free will, and natural evil happens when we bump up against the very laws of nature that are needed to meaningfully exercise free will.

Although it is *libertarian* free will that is at stake in the FWT, it is *any* kind of free will—libertarian or compatibilist—that is at stake in the NLT. Even if compatibilist free will is the right view of free will, such that we do not need to be able to do otherwise in the same exact circumstances to have genuine freedom, we would still need to be able *to do what we want to do.* And that requires laws of nature just as much as libertarian free will requires it. *Any* kind of meaningful freedom in choice gets destroyed if we live in a chaotic environment devoid of the laws of nature.[4]

Biblical Basis for the Natural Law Theodicy

The previous Question noted that there is no argument in the Bible, direct or indirect, for the FWT. Things seem almost as dismal for the NLT. To be sure, the Bible everywhere indicates that the physical world *is* subject to the various regularities that scientists study, discover, and more precisely publish to the world as "the laws of nature." It would be impossible to make sense of the biblical category of miracle, of "signs and wonders," except in contrast to there being a way nature usually behaves. It is because there is a way things usually go—dead people stay dead—that the existence of extraordinary events that *do not* go that way are used by God to draw attention to his presence and power, to get us to believe that someone greater than nature is here. Since God is the creator and providential sustainer of the world, doubtless it is up to him what the laws of nature are.

In addition, it seems otiose to look to the Bible for some kind of positive confirmation that the laws of nature are needed for the exercise of free will. One might as well look for a "biblical case" that "food is nutritious." Is it not obvious that our everyday choice-making depends on our living in a stable environment? Insofar as the first main assumption of the NLT is that the laws of nature are a weighty good, we hardly need to search the Bible for *that*.

Rather, what is missing in the Bible is some kind of positive support for the second main assumption of the NLT: that the laws of nature are a dependent good. Do the Scriptures ever indicate that for there to be laws of nature, there must be the real possibility of natural evil? Advocates of the FWT claim that genuine free will and the possibility of moral evil cannot be pried apart. If you have the first, you must have the second. Likewise, advocates of the NLT

---

4. Again, libertarian free will was contrasted with compatibilist free will in Question 15.

claim that the laws of nature and the possibility of natural evil cannot be pried apart. If you have the first, you must have the second. But it is unclear if the Bible teaches either of these dependence claims.

Indeed, what we seemed to learn in our lengthy survey of Bible passages in Question 9 is that various pains and sufferings having nature as their immediate cause seems compatible with having God as their ultimate cause. God using nature (and its laws) for the good purpose of providing a stable environment does not necessarily *require* that God put up with the possibility of natural evil. Rather, it is ultimately up to God whether natural evil occurs. These observations pave the way for an even sharper critique of the NLT in the next section.

Limitations of the Natural Law Theodicy

The last Question revealed three potential counterexamples to the FWT's claim that free will and the possibility of moral evil could not be pried apart. These were the possibility of restricted free will, the actuality of God's free will, and the hope of heavenly free will. As it turns out, something similar goes for the NLT—the Bible provides some counterexamples to the claim that the laws of nature and the possibility of natural evil cannot be pried apart.

The Garden of Eden—A Stable Environment Without Natural Evil

Imagine if Adam and Eve had not sinned. Are we really to imagine that their paradise would nevertheless have been subject to endless disease, famine, genetic defects, and so on, because of "the laws of nature"? The Scriptures tell a different story: these things entered the creation because of God's curse, in response to the fall of man. That is not to say that any *specific* case of disease should be seen as God's punishment on the one who has it. Rather, creation itself became liable to these pains and sufferings because it was God's will that it be in bondage to that sort of decay:

> For the creation was subjected to futility, not willingly, but because of him who subjected it, in hope that the creation itself will be set free from its bondage to corruption and obtain the freedom of the glory of the children of God. For we know that the whole creation has been groaning together in the pains of childbirth until now. (Rom. 8:20–22)

The possibility of natural evil seems to be a feature of *fallen* worlds, not something inevitable for worlds *per se*.

The New Heavens and the New Earth—A Stable Environment Without Natural Evil

Natural evil seems even less likely in the new heavens and the new earth that God will create for his people (Rev. 21:1). Rather:

He will wipe away every tear from their eyes, and death shall be no more, neither shall there be mourning, nor crying, nor pain anymore, for the former things have passed away. . . . No longer will there be anything accursed, but the throne of God and of the Lamb will be in it, and his servants will worship him. (Rev. 21:4; 22:3)

Could natural evil intrude into this eternal, immutable, and perfect fellowship with God, bringing "death," "mourning," and "pain"? Certainly not.

Notice that the reason Eden and heaven have no natural evil is that *God makes them perfect environments.* Apparently God is well able to do that. Notice also that each environment involves lots of meaningful choice-making. The inhabitants are not robots, but human beings exercising free will. In Eden, humans "work and keep" the garden (Gen. 2:15). They are to seek responsible dominion and stewardship over the earth, in response to God's command (Gen. 1:26, 28). Likewise, in the new heavens and the new earth, humans *fellowship* with God and with each other. They practice both social community and cultural production (Rev. 21:24–26). Again, that involves lots of meaningful choice-making.

All that to say, two of the most important environments described in the Bible seem to refute the dependence claim that is central to the NLT, that stable environments with meaningful exercise of free will require the possibility of natural evil. But if that claim is false, then we should not be appealing to it in order to answer the intellectual problem of evil.

Summary

Even as the free will theodicy (FWT) is supposed to explain God's permission of moral evil, so the natural law theodicy (NLT) is supposed to explain God's permission of natural evil. Assuming that free will is valuable, natural laws must be in place to ensure the kind of environmental stability that is needed for the meaningful exercise of free will. But once natural laws are in place, the possibility of natural evil is automatically generated. God could only preclude natural evil by precluding laws of nature. If we wished that God would get rid of natural evil by getting rid of laws of nature, then we are wishing for a world without free will (whether libertarian or compatibilist). It seems clear that a world without free will would be drained of its value. So we need laws of nature, and apparently the price God pays for that is the real possibility of natural evil.

The reasoning behind the NLT seems plausible. But it seems to run headlong into specific claims Christians are already committed to on the basis of the Bible. Far from God paying a price for laws of nature, *Christians* would be paying far too high a price to urge the NLT as an answer to the intellectual problem of evil.

REFLECTION QUESTIONS

1. The FWT and the NLT, put together, promise to explain all evil whatsoever, whether moral or natural. The simplicity of this package has been compelling to many. How important is it that we have a *simple* answer to the intellectual problem of evil?

2. Do you agree that a stable environment is required in order to exercise compatibilist free will, as well as libertarian free will?

3. Maybe earthquakes, hurricanes, tornados, and the like *can* occur in Eden and the new earth, but due to their fellowship with God, people in these environments would have such enhanced cognitive capacities that they would be able to *avoid* these regularly occurring events. So natural evil *would* exist in these environments; it just would not be able to cause us pain. How plausible is this defense of the NLT?[5]

4. There are more sophisticated versions of the NLT than what is presented in this Question. For example, Richard Swinburne argues that there must be lots of natural evil if we are to *know* that we have a real, free will choice between using nature to harm people and using it to help them. What do you think of this idea?[6]

5. What exactly is the problem with God *intending* natural evil? Do we not already know that God intends to punish people, or shape their souls, or get their attention, by way of the pains of nature?

---

5. Here I follow a suggestion made by Christian philosopher Daniel Howard-Snyder in "God, Evil, and Suffering," in *Reason for the Hope Within*, ed. Michael Murray (Grand Rapids: Eerdmans, 1999), 93.
6. See Richard Swinburne, *Providence and the Problem of Evil* (Oxford: Oxford University Press, 1998), especially chs. 9–10.

Could All Suffering and Evil Be a Means to a Greater Good?

When the topic of theodicy was first introduced in Question 19, it was claimed that "greater-good theodicy" (GGT) was a "general approach to theodicy" that "has the following structure":

> The pain and suffering in God's world play a necessary role in bringing about (or being a part of) greater goods that could not be brought about (or exist) except for the presence of that pain and suffering. The world would be worse off without that pain and suffering, and so God is justified in pursuing the good by these means.

Several specific theodicies were then introduced and discussed (Questions 21–25). To what degree do these specific theodicies support and vindicate the general approach just mentioned? On the one hand, each specific theodicy says that God aims at a great good (displaying his justice, shaping our souls, getting our attention, giving us free will and the laws of nature), but he cannot get that good without allowing actual evils (or at least their possibility). On the other hand, any appeal to these specific theodicies must be tempered with a good dose of divine inscrutability (Question 20), for the existence of these goods, their greatness, and their necessary relation to various evils, are not always or even usually discernible by us.

This chapter completes the case for the GGT by drawing upon this earlier theodicy material, and by combining it with our (even earlier) examination of biblical narratives (Questions 7–8) and universal Scripture texts about God's relation to all calamity, all human decision-making, and all events (Question 11). We will see that the GGT is a kind of faith stance we can take up with respect to the sufferings and evils in the world, but a faith stance that has a biblical and rational foundation.

What Is the Greater-Good Theodicy?

As seen in the introduction above, the GGT makes a very general claim: the pain and suffering in God's world (wherever and whenever it exists) is required for the existence of greater goods, and these greater goods could not (in any other way) be brought about except for the presence of that pain and suffering. This claim is very general and far-reaching. By itself it says nothing about the kinds of goods God is aiming at or the kinds of dependence that the goods have on the evils.

There is a very good reason for this. The GGT is not so much a theodicy as an umbrella under which the more specific theodicies exist. The GGT incorporates important insights to be found in the narrower, more specific theodicies, utilizing them to offer a general perspective on all evils.

Here is one way the GGT builds on the more specific theodicies: it can organize their insights into relatively simple anthropocentric *and* theocentric perspectives on all the pain and suffering in the world. According to an anthropocentric (human-centered) approach to theodicy, God allows evils for *our* good. All evils are for the sake of believers or unbelievers, for believers as soul-building (to help them flourish in their relationship with God) or for unbelievers as a megaphone (to get their attention so that they would begin a relationship with God). Indeed, even punishment is good for us if it is *redemptive* (prior to the final day of judgment).[1]

Alternatively, according to a theocentric (God-centered) approach to theodicy, God allows evils for *his* good. All evils enable the display of God's justice or the display of God's redemptive love. Either way, they are means to his glory. On this view, all natural evils display God's justice (because they are divine punishment for sin), and all moral evils either enable the display of God's justice (because he punishes those who commit them) or enable the display of divine forgiveness (because he forgives those who commit them, if they repent of their sins and place their faith in Christ).

For all we know, these anthropocentric and theocentric perspectives are entirely compatible, such that they cover all evils twice over. Why is it impossible for the goods that God is aiming at be goods for us *and* goods for God? Why must one of these categories exclude the other? If they are compatible, then this complex coherence of divine providence would further reveal "the manifold wisdom of God" (Eph. 3:10). It would also be unwise to talk about

---

1. See Question 21 for an argument that all punishment prior to the final day of judgment can have redemptive aspects, and that the Old Testament prophets seem to indicate this.

the reason why God permits a case of pain and suffering. Why assume there is just one reason?[2]

Biblical Basis for the Greater-Good Theodicy: Specific Biblical Narratives

But just because we *can* make the very general claim that the GGT makes, and even state it in a way that is understandable, does not automatically mean we *should* do this. Why should we think that God is aiming at goods that outweigh evils—goods that make the world better than it would otherwise be—in *all* pain and suffering? Why think he governs his universe in that way? There is a twofold biblical basis for accepting the generality of the GGT: an induction from specific biblical narratives, and a deduction from general biblical texts. Let us consider these in turn.

Questions 7 and 8 argued that multiple biblical narratives repeatedly weave together three themes that reveal the goodness of God amid the world's evils:

- The goodness of God's purpose—God aims at great goods.
- The sovereignty of God's providence—God often intends these great goods to come about by way of various evils.
- The inscrutability of God's ways—God typically leaves created persons in the dark (either about *which* goods he is aiming at, or about *how* these goods depend on the evils which occur, or both).

As we saw in those earlier Questions, these three themes come together in the Job, Joseph, and Jesus narratives, revealing a kind of divine *modus operandi* when it comes to diverse kinds of evil in the world. These narratives, not hidden in a corner but covering large stretches of the Bible, say to us: *This is who God is. This is how he works.*

In Job's case, God aims at the refutation of Satan's charges, the frustration of Satan's predictions, and the vindication of God's own worthiness to be served for who he is rather than for the earthly goods he supplies. But this triple good is only realized by way of a combination of moral evils and natural evils, amid which Job displays great perseverance.

In Joseph's case, God aims at preserving his people in a time of famine so they would become a great nation in the land of Canaan and so that the Savior of the world would come from their descendants. But this humanitarian and redemptive purpose is only realized through brotherly betrayal, enslavement, false accusations, imprisonment, and lonely years of isolation.

---

2. Alvin Plantinga stresses a theocentric perspective on theodicy that can also include anthropocentric goods. See Alvin Plantinga, "Supralapsarianism, or 'O Felix Culpa,'" in *Christian Faith and the Problem of Evil*, ed. Peter van Inwagen (Grand Rapids: Eerdmans, 2004), 1–25.

In Jesus's case, God aims at the redemption of the world and at the display of his glorious attributes: his justice (for judging our sin in Jesus), love, grace, and mercy (for providing an atonement for undeserving sinners), wisdom (for devising this perfect plan of redemption), and power (for orchestrating historical events over millennia to fulfill this plan). But this greatest good (for both humans and God) is realized through a perplexing chain of perverse moral evil, including murderous plots, satanically inspired betrayal, unjust show trials, cowardly condemnation of an innocent man, and the brutality of crucifixion.

In these narratives, God is not a merely passive observer and permitter of events, beholden to wishful thinking and hoping for the best. Rather, he is active in providence, in ways the participants themselves often could not discern, to realize divine purposes that we can trust are good. Whether Gentile kings or Jewish leaders, whether soldiers or the mob, they "do whatever your hand and your plan had predestined to take place" (Acts 4:28). "The claim" in the intellectual problem of evil—"There is no reason that justifies God in permitting evil"—simply assumes that *things cannot be this way*, that God cannot be like this.

Biblical Basis for the Greater-Good Theodicy: General Biblical Texts

The generality of the GGT is of course not secured simply by pointing to three narratives. That would be an overreading of those texts. Nor is it proven if we add in the further biblical testimony considered in Questions 9 and 10, that there are quite a few cases of natural evil and moral evil, beyond those in the three narratives, that can be traced back (ultimately) to the divine will. But, as was argued in Question 11, there are more general texts of Scripture which *do* seem to extend divine providence to all calamities, all human decision-making, and all events, giving us a broader vision that we can integrate with the particulars of Questions 7–10. And perhaps these particular and general passages illuminate each other: the particular passages reveal instances of the more general view taught elsewhere, while the general passages provide a perspective in which the otherwise surprising particular passages make more sense. Of the fifteen general passages considered in Question 11, let's return to two of them.

Romans 8:28

At first glance, the following affirmation appears to be a clear endorsement of the GGT:

> And we know that for those who love God all things work together for good, for those who are called according to his purpose. (Rom. 8:28)

Four observations seem appropriate. First, the phrase "all things" is quite sweeping in its implications. Not a few things, not most things, but all things are worked by God for good, at least for the good of Christians ("for those who love God," "for those who are called according to his purpose").

Second, the "all things" surely include the very negative things Paul mentions just prior to and after this verse:

- "we suffer with him" (8:17)
- "the sufferings of this present time" (8:18)
- "futility" (8:20)
- "bondage to corruption" (8:21)
- "groaning together in the pains of childbirth" (8:22)
- "our weakness" (8:26)
- "tribulation, or distress, or persecution, or famine, or nakedness, or danger, or sword" (8:35).

"All things," therefore, seems to include just about every conceivable suffering a Christian could face.

Third, "all things" *actually* work together for good. There is a confidence expressed here by the apostle Paul, a divinely inspired guarantee of success in divine providence. There is an action ("works together"), an implied subject for that action (God), an object for that action ("all things"), and a result of that action ("for good"). The idea is not that God is working *in* all things, to get some good out of them, without any guarantee that he will *get* any good for us by his well-intentioned efforts. After all, the preposition "in" (indicating that God merely works *in* all things for good, rather than actually *working* all things together for good) is absent from the text. Rather, all things do work together for good. That is what happens.

The verses that immediately follow embed this wildly optimistic promise of Romans 8:28 within the realization of a divine plan that stretches from eternity to eternity (Rom. 8:29–30), securing a clear providential basis for that promise. This makes sense. Christians who are suffering in the ways indicated throughout Romans chapter 8 could hardly be comforted by the thought that God has good but *ineffectual* intentions on their behalf. Who would be encouraged by knowing that God sympathizes with their plight but cannot really do anything about it except attempt the best and hope it succeeds?

Paul's confidence here is like that expressed in 2 Corinthians 4:8–11, 17, where being "afflicted," "persecuted," "struck down," and "being given over to death" is *doing* something, not just for Paul but for all believers who similarly suffer: it "is preparing for us an eternal weight of glory beyond all comparison." This is no mere hope, speculation, or feeling. It is a factual claim about what all such sufferings *will* produce.

Fourth, though the scope of this promise is restricted to Christians, that is its only restriction. However, consider the converse: if God can work *every* suffering of *every* Christian for good—and he in fact does so—doesn't that at least make it reasonable to believe that he can do so with the rest? Many sufferings of Christians come from non-Christians, and yet that is no bar to God working all of it for good. Why think the sufferings of non-Christians are somehow outside his good, wise, and powerful providence? Here is where the categories of redemptive punishment and megaphone-sized attention-getting, outlined in Questions 21 and 23, indicate some of the good providential purposes God can have with respect to the suffering of unbelievers.

Romans 11:36

In Romans 9–11, Paul develops an extensive argument intended to vindicate God from the charge of being unfaithful to his promises (Rom. 9:6) and unjust in his ways (Rom. 9:14). Paul's presentation combines the two kinds of material that have been brought together in this Question: specific biblical narrative and general claims. His main idea appears to be that the evil of Jewish apostasy—the widespread failure of first-century Jews to place their faith in Jesus their promised Messiah—is an evil that God intends to work for a greater good, one that would have been unknown even by Paul except for God's revealing it to him (Rom. 11:33–35). Space does not permit extended exegesis of these chapters, but a few points seem prominent.

First, God *aims at a great good*: the salvation of the Gentiles and ultimately the salvation of the Jews.

Second, God intends this great good to come about *by way of* the evil of Jewish apostasy: it will open the way to the Gentiles flooding into the church, and this in turn will stir up the Jews to jealousy so that they will repent as well (Rom. 11:11–32).

Third, God leaves various humans *in the dark* that this is indeed his reason for the evils. (Surely the unbelieving Jews who refused to accept Jesus as their Messiah had no inkling of how God would turn their evil to good.) By stressing the inscrutability of God's plan (Rom. 11:33–35), it is as if Paul were saying, "I would know nothing of the divine plan I just revealed over these past three chapters unless God had personally revealed to me, and he has."

Fourth, God's *modus operandi*—revealed in Romans 9–11 and summarized in the preceding three points—can be extended to all events whatsoever:

> For from him and through him and to him are all things. To
> him be glory forever. Amen. (Rom. 11:36)

All things being "from him" speaks of his plan: nothing happens unless God wills it to happen. All things being "through him" speaks of his providence: nothing occurs apart from his sustaining power. All things being "to him" speaks of his good purpose: nothing fails to (ultimately) redound to his glory, even if it initially appears God is unfaithful or unjust.

The verse fails to say just about anything else. Most importantly, the verse says absolutely nothing about the *how*, perhaps because God's judgments are "unsearchable" and his ways are "inscrutable" (Rom. 11:33). Could it be that the grand, sweeping scope of divine providence is what guarantees its inscrutability to us, apart from divine revelation? Does it not then make sense that Paul would weave these two themes together in his doxology?

Summary

The "greater-good theodicy" (GGT) is a very general claim about the goods God is aiming at in providence, and the relation of these goods to cases of suffering and evil. It incorporates the insights of the narrower theodicies discussed earlier (Questions 21–25), and there is a biblical basis for at least three of those theodicies (punishment, soul-building, megaphone). In addition, the generality of the GGT is itself a good induction from specific biblical narratives and a good deduction from general biblical texts. Given all this, the Bible at least *points* in the direction of the GGT. As an apologetic approach to the intellectual problem of evil that has scriptural backing, the way of theodicy offers anthropocentric and theocentric perspectives on the pain and suffering of both believers and unbelievers.

This chapter ended by stressing the connection between the sovereignty of divine providence and its inscrutability. As seen earlier in Questions 8 and 20, divine inscrutability is indeed a major theme in the Bible. Our ignorance limits the kinds of ways we can apply the GGT to any case of suffering and evil as a response to the intellectual problem of evil. Of course, it also limits the ways one can *object to* the GGT. But are Christians abdicating their apologetic responsibilities by relying on this theme of divine inscrutability as an answer to the problem of evil? The next Question takes up this concern.

REFLECTION QUESTIONS

1. Would you include the FWT and the NLT (see Questions 24–25) in the GGT, even if they had no explicit biblical basis? How well do those theodicies *fit* with the biblical material presented in this Question?

2. How important is it that the way of theodicy include "anthropocentric" goods and not just "theocentric" goods?

3. How wise is it to get "general truths" from specific biblical narratives? What are some pitfalls to this approach? Does it have any advantages?

4. Could a perfectly good God permit something for absolutely no reason at all? If not, then would his reason (whatever it is) not be the good he is aiming at?

5. Concerning Romans 8:28 it was argued that the promise would hold little encouragement for the readers unless the good was guaranteed. Do you agree?

Can We Defend Christianity Without Offering God's Reasons for Suffering and Evil?

As noted at the end of Question 18, "the claim" in the intellectual problem of evil says: "There is no reason that justifies God in permitting evil." Whereas the way of theodicy (Question 19) gives reasons for thinking "the claim" is false (by supplying God's reasons for permitting evil), the way of inscrutability (Question 20) gives reasons for thinking "the claim" is unsupported (by pointing out that our inability to supply God's reason is no reason to think God does not *have* a reason).

However, Question 20 also raised several potential problems for this apologetic appeal to divine inscrutability, including the following:

> Is this appeal to divine inscrutability not just a cosmic "cop-out" when it comes to apologetics? People want answers, and we give them our ignorance. What kind of a "reasoned defense" is that? We are supposed to be people of the Book, and God has given us sixty-books that compose that Book, and all we can say is, "I do not know"? Does it not stand to reason that if *Christians* cannot give God's reason, then one does not exist? We will consider this concern in Question 27.

Having now arrived at Question 27, let us reply directly to this important concern.

Which Arguments from Silence Have Force?

There is something reasonable about the above complaint from the critic of the inscrutability strategy. It correctly surmises that Christianity is a knowledge tradition and should be held to that standard. Whereas certain Eastern religious traditions seem to highly prize the recognition of profound ignorance and paradox when speaking of transcendent matters, Christianity is based on verbal revelation from a rational, all-knowing, personal God. The text of the Bible runs to almost 800,000 words. God has taken the time to speak on almost every topic of conceivable concern to us: God, Christ, the Holy Spirit, creation, angels, humanity, animals, providence, miracles, human history, sin, redemption, spiritual growth, baptism, spiritual gifts, prayer, church community, ethics, practical wisdom, final judgment, and the new heavens and the new earth.

The world has been continually devastated by suffering and evil from almost the very beginning, in all the ways canvassed in Questions 6 and 29. "The problem of evil" is consistently one of the top reasons many unbelievers give for their unbelief. And yet amid all the revelation just summarized, God could not be bothered to state, clearly and on the record, why he allows so much suffering and evil that he could easily prevent? Some biblical books seem to include minutiae, such as the precise number of fish caught by the disciples (John 21:11), or that winged insects without jointed legs are unclean to eat but those with jointed legs are clean to eat (Lev. 11:21). We get lengthy genealogies and census counts of populations. But on a topic that could easily assist Christians in defending the faith to a watching world, God does not give us a comprehensive theodicy that can clearly be said to *work* in all cases. Why would he fail to do that?

Admittedly, there is a lot here in this complaint to unpack. It is tempting to dismiss it as a failed argument from silence. God does not tell us why he called Abraham out of Ur of the Chaldeans either, rather than some similar person down the road (Gen. 11:31–12:3). But it is hard to convert that failure to divulge a bit of knowledge into some disproof of Christianity. Not much follows from our ignorance! Why did King David rule for forty years rather than forty-one? I have no idea because God has not told me. Is that evidence against the Christian faith? Why?

Still, not all arguments from silence are without force. Some should be taken seriously. When? Well, the absence of something is significant only if I should rightly *expect* it to be there, and that always depends on the larger context. If a page in a recipe book contains a recipe title at the top but no recipe, that is evidence that something has gone wrong. It is a recipe book, after all. The recipe should be there. But why think things are relevantly similar when it comes to God revealing convincing theodicies in the Bible? Does that not depend on the *purpose* of the Bible? And does that not depend in turn on *God's* purposes in giving it? Well, what are those? Christians typically characterize the purpose of the Bible in the following ways:

It is "the rule of faith and life," containing "the whole counsel of God, concerning all things necessary for His own glory, man's salvation, faith, and life."[1]

"Holy Scripture containeth all things necessary to salvation."[2]

"God makes himself known to us more clearly by his holy and divine Word, as much as we need in this life, for God's glory and for our salvation."[3]

"Everything one must believe to be saved is sufficiently taught in it."[4]

It is a commonplace among Christians to confess that Scripture has a redemptive purpose, to communicate to us how to be saved and how to live to God's glory. Could it be possible that God has decided that leaving us in (relative) darkness on the topic of theodicy best serves those ends? More to the point, what is the critic's argument *against* this being the sober truth of the matter? Is it some self-evident truth that God, if he were to exist and communicate with us, would answer all the questions *we* deem most important? Presumably, given his omniscience and our own finitude, he would have a more accurate opinion about the most important questions than we would.

Why Would God Hold His Knowledge in Reserve?

As it turns out, God has a track record in Scripture of holding his knowledge in reserve. Christians interested in defending the faith from the problem of evil do not have to speculate about this in some *ad hoc* fashion. It is an evident scriptural datum. Here are five examples.

First, after Job's terrible sufferings from natural and moral evils, when God finally speaks to Job out of the whirlwind (Job 38–41), he had the perfect opportunity to reveal to Job the reason for his suffering, perhaps recounting the dialogue in Job 1–2 between God and Satan. But God does no such thing, preferring instead to reinforce the theme of Job's ignorance of God's ways. Why would God hold his knowledge in reserve in this way? God's love for Job is evident at the end of the book, when he blesses Job, vindicates Job's speech about God while condemning the speech of Job's friends (Job 42:7) and "gave Job twice as much as he had before" (Job 42:10). God seems to be making a

---

1. *Westminster Confession of Faith* I.1, I.6; see also the 1689 *Second London Baptist Confession of Faith* I.1, I.6.
2. Article 6, *Thirty-nine Articles of Religion.*
3. Article 2, *Belgic Confession.*
4. Article 7, *Belgic Confession.*

judgment here: Job doesn't need to know the answers to theodicy questions to flourish as a human being.

Second, after Adam and Eve rebel against God by eating the forbidden fruit in the garden of Eden, God comes to them and asks a series of questions: "Where are you?" (Gen. 3:9), "Who told you that you were naked?" (Gen. 3:11), "What is this you have done?" (Gen. 3:13). God perfectly well knows the answers to all these questions. In asking them, God seems to have a kind of pastoral purpose in mind. It is better for Adam and Eve to wrestle with these questions in their own thinking, for them to consciously reflect on what they have done, than for God to recite out the answers he obviously knows. Some things are more important for us than God displaying his knowledge.

Third, just prior to miraculously providing bread and fish for the five thousand, Jesus asks a question:

> Lifting up his eyes, then, and seeing that a large crowd was coming toward him, Jesus said to Philip, "Where are we to buy bread, so that these people may eat?" He said this to test him, for he himself knew what he would do. (John 6:5–6)

Jesus *knew* where the bread would come from. The text tells us this. But Jesus does not, at that point, tell Philip what he will do and why. Rather, he asks a question "to test him," to refine and purify his thinking toward spiritual ends. As a test, the question is a means of getting Philip to discover and reflect upon the distinctive divine solution to the present dilemma.

Fourth, it was precisely because Jesus was one "knowing their thoughts" that he asked the scribes, "Why do you think evil in your hearts?" (Matt. 9:4). Jesus, "knowing their thoughts," was not ignorant of the answer to his own question. He had knowledge to offer here. But rather than divulging his knowledge, Jesus asks a question intended as a means of bringing home to the scribes' consciences the evil of their false accusation against him. There was a pastoral purpose in Jesus withholding the knowledge he could easily state.

Fifth, Jesus asks the disciples on the road to Emmaus, "What is this conversation that you are holding with each other as you walk?" (Luke 24:17). Surely Jesus knew what they had been talking about, for Jesus knew the inward thoughts of man (Matt. 9:3–4; Mark 12:15; Luke 11:17). This question (and its follow-up, "What things?"; v. 19) was for the disciples' benefit, not Jesus's. It was to draw out of them their foolishness and slowness of heart so that Jesus could correct it (vv. 25–27).

Beyond these potentially pastoral reasons for God not always giving to us the knowledge he could give, there is a potential *intellectual* reason. Perhaps God's reason for permitting suffering and evil (including the especially horrendous instances of it) is just so complicated that we would not understand it even if it were stated to us. Does the critic have any argument that things are not this way? As Christian philosopher Alvin Plantinga puts it:

> And when God replies to Job, he doesn't tell him what his reason is for permitting these sufferings (*perhaps Job couldn't so much as grasp or comprehend it*). Instead, he attacks the implicit inference from Job's not being able to see what God's reason is to the notion that probably he has none; and he does this by pointing out how vast is the gulf between Job's knowledge and God's.[5]

There is a kind of resilience to the inscrutability strategy against the intellectual problem of evil. Not only might God have good reasons for permitting suffering and evil in the first place (even if we cannot guess what those reasons are), he might have good reasons for not sharing with us these reasons. As Christian philosopher William Alston puts it:

> There is, to be sure, a question as to why . . . God doesn't fill us in on His reasons for permitting suffering. Wouldn't a perfectly benevolent creator see to it that we realize why we are called upon to suffer? I acknowledge this difficulty; in fact it is just another form taken by the problem of evil. And I will respond to it in the same way. Even if we can't see why God would keep us in the dark on this matter, we cannot be justified in supposing that God does not have sufficient reason for doing so.[6]

What Are the Conditions for a "Cop-Out"?

Finally, what of the accusation that the inscrutability defense is a "cosmic 'cop-out'" of apologetic responsibility? Well, does that not depend on what our responsibilities and opportunities are? If you ask me whether the number of stars in the universe is odd or even, and I say, "I do not know," have I copped out? Only if I am *supposed* to know such things.

Who bears the burden of proof in this discussion, Christian or non-Christian? It is a maxim in legal argument that he who affirms must prove.[7] The

---

5.   Alvin Plantinga, *Warranted Christian Belief* (Oxford: Oxford University Press, 2000), 496 (emphasis added).

6.   William Alston, "The Inductive Argument from Evil and the Human Cognitive Condition," *Philosophical Perspectives* (1991), vol. 5, Philosophy of Religion, 29–67. The quote is from 64 n. 22.

7.   "Affirmanti (non neganti) incumbit probatio," in Aaron X. Fellmeth and Maurice Horwitz, *Guide to Latin in International Law*, 2nd ed. (Oxford: Oxford University Press, 2021), 25.

intellectual problem of evil is an argument posed by the *critic* of Christianity. That argument contains premises affirmed by the critic, including "the claim" that we have returned to again and again to guide our discussion in Questions 18–26: "There is no good reason that would justify God in permitting evil." What is the argument for "the claim," and is it a good one? The critic cannot rest content with asking puzzling questions. Although we as humans may not know enough to *rule in* a theodicy as explaining a particular evil on a particular occasion, the burden of proof is on the critic of Christianity to show that we know enough to *rule out* the applicability of any theodicies. As Question 20 sought to argue, this burden has not been met, and the biblical material in Question 8 suggests that it cannot be met. If this is right, then the intellectual problem of evil cannot be an *intellectually rational* reason to reject the existence of God.

Beyond this, the Christian position as represented in this book has not remained *silent* on the topic of theodicy. It is not the case that *all* we have said is, "I do not know"! Have we not considered five different theodicies that (taken together) could explain God's permission of all evil for the sake of anthropocentric and theocentric goods? (see Questions 21–25). Granted, it is hard to see how some (or any) of these theodicies could apply to particularly difficult cases of evil. But that is different from offering pure ignorance to the world.

Summary

It is understandable that some think the inscrutability defense against the intellectual problem of evil is in considerable tension with Christianity being a knowledge tradition that prizes God's verbal revelation as a source of knowledge on a whole host of very important topics. But the tension disappears once we consider the pastoral purposes God might have in withholding the revelation of at least some of his knowledge. The context of the divine silence might be to fulfill the redemptive purposes God has for the Bible. Finally, the inscrutability defense is a reminder that the burden of proof in the problem of evil is on those who are raising that problem. As it turns out, the way of theodicy and the way of inscrutability work in tandem: theodicy can neither be ruled in (by the Christian) nor ruled out (by the unbeliever). This approach seems to provide a balanced, robust response to the problem of evil, putting both believers and unbelievers in their place. Such humbling can promote intellectual caution and spiritual health.

REFLECTION QUESTIONS

1. This Question noted that "there is something reasonable" about the "cop-out" objection to the inscrutability strategy. How important is it for

Christian apologetics to note where a critic is being reasonable? Why are we often afraid to make this observation?

2. An argument from silence says: a source did not mention X; therefore, most likely, the source endorses not-X instead. Can you give an example where context might reveal that this kind of inference is a good one after all?

3. Can you think of other problems that could be generated if we misunderstand the purpose(s) for which the Bible was given?

4. Advocates of the "divine hiddenness" argument against God's existence often say that since God is like a perfect parent, of course he would always explain to us why we suffer if he knew the answer (and he would know the answer).[8] How would you push back against this claim?

5. "Evil means that God does not exist." "No, because God has a reason for permitting it." "Why does he not tell us what it is?" "Well, see here, in the Bible it says . . ." "You are appealing to the Bible to defend God, but the Bible is worthless as a source unless there is a God. So you are assuming God to get around my argument against God." Is this exchange an accurate representation of what is going on, or not?

---

8. See, among his many other writings, J. L. Schellenberg, "Divine Hiddenness Justifies Atheism," in *Contemporary Debates in Philosophy of Religion*, 2nd ed., eds. Michael L. Peterson and Raymond J. Vanarragon (Hoboken, NJ: Wiley-Blackwell, 2019), 165–76.

Is the Problem of Evil a Reason to Believe in God's Existence?

The previous Questions in this part of the book, "Apologetic Questions About Suffering and Evil," illustrated apologetics as "defense." This way of defending the faith focuses on answering the questions of unbelief. The intellectual problem of evil (Question 17) is an argument against the existence of God, and the appeals to theodicy (Questions 19, 21–26) and divine inscrutability (Questions 20, 27) are ways of showing that that argument against God is unsound. One of its central premises—which we have been calling "the claim"—is either false or unsupported.

But there are at least two other ways of doing Christian apologetics, which we can call apologetics as "proof" and apologetics as "offense."[1] In apologetics as proof, the Christian tries to make a positive case for distinctive theistic or Christian claims, appealing to assumptions that Christians and non-Christians have in common, such as reason, sense experience, and moral intuition. (For instance, there might be a good historical argument for the resurrection of Christ, once we get rid of double standards in historical inquiry and consider the best explanation of the historical evidence.) In apologetics as offense, the Christian goes on the offensive against non-Christian worldviews (such as atheism, pantheism, pluralism, and the traditional non-Christian religions), seeking to show that the assumptions made in these worldviews are destructive of reasoning, knowledge, science, ethics, and so on. (For instance, the naturalistic evolutionary claim that our cognitive capacities were produced by way of a blind, purposeless process that was sensitive only to the conditions for survival might, if true, undermine our claim to know anything at all.)

---

1. These three ways of doing apologetics, and my way of explaining them, come from John Frame, *Apologetics: A Justification of Christian Belief* (Phillipsburg, NJ: P&R Publishing, 2015), 1–3. The entire book is structured around this tripartite division of apologetic labor.

This Question uses the topic of suffering and evil to briefly pursue apologetics as proof and apologetics as offense. Rather than defending God from the alleged implications of suffering and evil (i.e., apologetics as defense), we can attempt to argue *for* God by way of our recognition of evil in the world, particularly moral evil. That is apologetics as proof. And we can maintain that unbelieving worldviews undermine the rationality of recognizing moral evil as moral evil. That is apologetics as offense.

Apologetics as Proof: The Case for God from Moral Evil

Different Kinds of Moral Argument
There is a large body of work on the so-called "moral argument for God's existence".[2] There are several ways to sketch out this argument:

1. Objective moral obligations exist, and it is implausible to suppose they exist in the absence of God.
2. We make judgments about some actions being morally right, and other actions being morally wrong, and our capacity to make such discriminations is best explained by God's giving us that capacity.
3. The horror we feel when we observe or otherwise consider a particularly perverse case of evil is in some way tied to the fact that such an evil constitutes defiance of God.

Statement (1) is primarily a *metaphysical* argument: the existence of objective moral obligations requires God's existence, perhaps because their absolute bindingness can only be grounded in a necessarily existing being like God. Statement (2) is primarily an *epistemological* argument: our knowledge of objective obligations requires God's existence, perhaps because unless God produced (or guided the development of) our knowledge capacities, we would have little reason to think our judgments about moral obligation are true judgments (rather than being merely useful beliefs that help our species survive). Statement (3) is primarily, for lack of a better term, an *existential*

---

2. See David Baggett and Jerry L. Walls, *Good God: The Theistic Foundation of Morality* (New York: Oxford University Press, 2011); David Baggett and Jerry L. Walls, *God and Cosmos: Moral Truth and Human Meaning* (New York: Oxford University Press, 2016); David Baggett and Marybeth Baggett, *The Morals of the Story: Good News about A Good God* (Downers Grove, IL: InterVarsity Press, 2018); and David Baggett and Jerry L. Walls, *The Moral Argument: A History* (New York: Oxford University Press, 2019). See also Mark Murphy, *God & Moral Law: On the Theistic Explanation of Morality* (New York: Oxford University Press, 2011); Angus Ritchie, *From Morality to Metaphysics: The Theistic Implications of Our Ethical Commitments* (Oxford: Oxford University Press, 2012); Gregory E. Ganssle, "Evil as Evidence for Christianity," in *God and Evil: The Case for God in a World Filled with Pain*, eds. Chad Meister and James K. Dew Jr. (Downers Grove, IL: InterVarsity Press, 2013), 214–24; and C. Stephen Evans, *God and Moral Obligation* (New York: Oxford University Press, 2013).

argument for God's existence. In seeing that horrifying evil is exceedingly appalling and wicked, we are seeing what is (ultimately) the defiance of an infinitely good and righteous Being (i.e., God); even worse, it is defiance perpetrated by (and often against) those created in the image of such an infinite Being, and that is a further reason for its appalling nature.

C. S. Lewis in Mere Christianity

In his popular level, highly influential presentation of the moral argument for God's existence—"Right and Wrong as a Clue to the Meaning of the Universe"—C. S. Lewis argues for three fundamental claims:

1. The *objective existence* of the moral law
2. The *unique nature* of the moral law
3. The *religious interpretation* of the moral law

First, we know the moral law *objectively exists* because we presuppose it in our daily life:

> Human beings, all over the earth, have this curious idea that they ought to behave in a certain way, and they cannot really get rid of it. . . . They know the Law of Nature.[3]

We appeal to it when we make moral accusations against others ("You should have kept your promise"), and when we defend ourselves from the moral accusations of others ("I agree people should keep their promises, but there were extenuating circumstances"). Both responses presuppose that a moral standard is already in place. As for allegedly differing moralities among different civilizations in history, these differences are often exaggerated. (In an appendix to *The Abolition of Man*, Lewis demonstrates the fundamental unity of moral codes throughout history, across religions and cultures.) In addition, these differences are not always differences over moral principle, but about what the facts are. (Our ancestors killed witches not because our ancestors had fundamentally different moral principles from us, but because they believed there were such things as witches.)

Second, the nature of the moral law is *unique* because it cannot be reduced to a description of how we in *fact* behave. It is not like laws of nature pertaining to gravity or genetics. Rather, in the moral law there is

> something above and beyond the actual facts of human behavior. In this case, besides the actual facts, you have

---

3. C. S. Lewis, *Mere Christianity* (New York: HarperOne, 2001 [1952]), 8.

something else—a real law which we did not invent and which we know we ought to obey.[4]

In short, the moral law is a consciousness of how we *ought* to behave, regardless of how we do in fact behave.

Third, given these two points, the best interpretation of the moral law is the *religious* one: it is nothing less than God speaking to us. In figuring out what is the best interpretation of the phenomenon of conscience, we are guided in part by the previous two theses. Since the moral law has objective existence, there is something there to explain. And since the moral law has a unique nature, science cannot explain it. Science can only explain what is the case (what Lewis calls "third-person facts"), not what ought to be the case (what Lewis calls "first-person facts").

On Lewis's view, the moral law is best understood as the influence or command of a superior being who is trying to get us to behave in a certain way. Two things are being claimed here: the moral law is the voice of a person, and it is the voice of a moral superior. It is the voice of a *person* (and so grounded in mind, not matter):

> I think we have to assume it is more like a mind than it is like anything else we know—because after all the only other thing we know is matter and you can hardly imagine a bit of matter giving instructions.[5]

It is the voice of a *moral superior*, to whom we are called to submit:

> We know that men find themselves under a moral law, which they did not make, and cannot quite forget even when they try, and which they know they ought to obey.[6]

But if the voice of conscience is not the voice of a mindless universe, nor the voice of a moral equal (such as fellow humans), then whose voice is it? We have run out of nontheistic options, as it were. These considerations point in the direction of God.[7]

---

4. Lewis, *Mere Christianity*, 21.
5. Lewis, *Mere Christianity*, 25.
6. Lewis, *Mere Christianity*, 23.
7. No doubt Christian philosopher David Baggett is correct that, while Lewis's presentation "may serve the purposes of popular apologetics . . . it is much too hasty to serve the purpose of subjecting secular ethical theory to robust critical scrutiny" ("An Abductive Moral Argument for God," in *The Plantinga Project: Two Dozen (or so) Arguments for God*, eds. Jerry L. Walls and Trent Dougherty [New York: Oxford University Press, 2018], 271). Still,

Apologetics as Offense: No Absolute Norms If There Is No Personal Absolute

What about apologetics as offense? Can we go on the offensive against unbelieving worldviews, showing that they have no good explanation of the phenomenon of conscience? At one level, this is an exceedingly difficult task. Different Christian philosophers say different things in their theistic accounts of morality:

> Efforts by theistic ethicists to account for moral obligations range from natural law accounts to divine motivation theories; from divine will theories to divine command theories; from divine desire theories to divine attitude theories; and more besides.[8]

Likewise, there is

> a range of secular ethical and meta-ethical approaches, both naturalistic and non-naturalistic, ranging from Philippa Foot's natural law view, to Shafer-Landau's non-naturalism, to supervenience accounts like Erik Wielenberg's, to naturalistic ethical accounts like those of the Cornell realists, to various evolutionary approaches, to Korsgaardian constructivism, and more besides.[9]

Space permits interaction with just one of these approaches: the evolutionary one. On evolutionary "subjectivism," there is no moral law, but evolution has fooled us into thinking that there is one, because such belief was useful to survival. An initial problem is that this means all our moral beliefs are *false* (though useful). But then why not think the same for all the other outputs of our cognitive faculties, also developed by evolution? Why does the availability of evolutionary explanation undermine conscience, but not perception or reasoning?

On evolutionary "objectivism," there is a moral law, because evolution has taught us that we *should* promote the survival of our species. But if this is a truth we all know, is it not an incredible coincidence that a blind, purposeless process gave us the correct moral beliefs?[10] Beyond that, this is an inadequate an explanation of what I *believe*. I do not believe rape is wrong because it

---

one must start somewhere, and Baggett's own work is a fine place to build on and extend Lewis's argument. See the resources listed in footnote 2 above.

8. Baggett, "An Abductive Moral Argument for God," 274.
9. Baggett, "An Abductive Moral Argument for God," 272.
10. J. P. Moreland and William Lane Craig, *Philosophical Foundations for a Christian Worldview*, 2nd. ed. (Downers Grove, IL: InterVarsity Press, 2017), 503.

undermines the stability of the family unit and therefore species survival. I believe it is wrong because it violates the intrinsic dignity of a person. So this is not explaining the truth I think I know, but something else entirely. Finally, "promoting survival" is not the only thing involved in the evolutionary process. In fact, what is *more* characteristic of that process is the production of lots of senseless death. So why is *that* (I should produce senseless death) not the moral lesson I should learn from evolution? Why arbitrarily single out *survival* as the morally relevant thing?

Christian theologian John Frame offers a general account of what is going wrong here. He points out that many non-Christian accounts of moral obligations either offer an absolute being who is impersonal (Platonic forms, cosmic fate), or offer a personal being who is not absolute (pagan Greek and Roman gods). The former cannot explain why there are any obligations at all, since obligations arise in the context of personal relationships, whereas the latter fails to explain why our obligations are absolutely binding upon us. What is needed is the "personal Absolute" of Christianity.[11]

No Replacement for Apologetics as Defense!

It is important to see that neither apologetics as proof nor apologetics as offense, briefly pursued above, is a *replacement* for the apologetics as defense that has been pursued in all the earlier Questions of part 3. Even if we are right that moral evil is an indirect argument for God's existence (apologetics as proof) and that unbelievers face a more difficult challenge than Christians in accounting for that moral evil as moral evil (apologetics as offense), the intellectual problem of evil still stands as a potential challenge that Christians must address on its own terms. It matters not if the critics of our faith are moral relativists or nihilists and cannot account for moral norms. What matters is whether the *argument* they present against God is a good one. The cogency of that argument does not rise or fall based on their personal beliefs. If they are right that God would prevent any evil he could prevent and that God can prevent any evil, then they have raised a problem *for us*, and we must challenge either the premises or logic of the argument. Changing the subject to whether *they* (as unbelievers) can account for evil does not by itself get around the argument raised against us. So, all three kinds of apologetics are needed on this topic.[12]

---

11. John Frame, *Apologetics*, 101–7.
12. One way to put this point is to say that the intellectual problem of evil is a "*reductio ad absurdum*" against a Christian worldview. It attempts to "reduce to absurdity" Christian claims, by showing that what we believe about God's goodness (he would prevent evil if he could) and God's power (he can prevent any evil) should lead us to deny an evident fact (that there is evil). A *reductio ad absurdum* does not start from one's own premises, but from an *opponent's* premises. That's why the personal beliefs of the critic are irrelevant to the cogency of the intellectual problem of evil.

Summary

"Apologetics as proof" seeks to argue for God's existence from the existence of moral obligations, from our capacity to judge between right and wrong actions, and even from our recognition of horrendous evil. C. S. Lewis's moral argument for God's existence offers the religious interpretation of the moral law as the best interpretation of the phenomenon of conscience. "Apologetics as offense" seeks to argue not that unbelievers *lack* sincere moral beliefs, but that their other unbelieving assumptions make it very difficult to *maintain* or *explain* moral truth.

REFLECTION QUESTIONS

1. What do you think of the threefold distinction between apologetics as defense, proof, and offense? Which aspect of Christian apologetics do you think is most neglected in our own day? Which is most effective?

2. Which version of the moral argument for God strikes you as the most promising: metaphysical, epistemological, or existential?

3. "But atheists can be moral without believing in God." Why is this an irrelevant reply to the moral argument for God's existence?

4. "You should not murder human beings." "What is growing in the womb is not a human being." Which best represents the *difference* of belief between pro-choice and pro-life advocates, the first (moral) claim or the second (factual) claim?

5. Alvin Plantinga argues that even if apologetics as defense is a failure (maybe the problem of evil is a good argument against God), maybe apologetics as proof could come to the rescue (maybe the arguments *for* God outweigh any arguments *against* God).[13] Do you agree?

---

13. Plantinga pursues this approach in Alvin Plantinga, "The Probabilistic Argument from Evil," *Philosophical Studies* 35, no. 1 (1979): 1–53, esp. 2–4; Alvin Plantinga, "Reason and Belief in God," in *Faith and Rationality: Reason and Belief in God*, eds. Alvin Plantinga and Nicholas Wolterstorff (Notre Dame, IN: University of Notre Dame Press, 1983), 16–93 (esp. pp. 21–23); and Alvin Plantinga, "Advice to Christian Philosophers," *Faith and Philosophy* 1, no. 3 (July 1984): 253–71 (esp. pp. 259–60). Plantinga also thinks there are pathways to rational belief in God apart from argument, such as through what John Calvin calls the *sensus divinitatis*, or 'sense of the divine,' that God has given us. See Plantinga, "Reason and Belief in God."

PART 4

Practical Questions About Suffering and Evil

SECTION A

Questions Related to How
Suffering and Evil Impact Our Lives

What Kinds of Suffering and Evil Occur in the World Today?

This Question begins part 4 of the book ("Practical Questions About Suffering and Evil"), which considers how we can respond to suffering and evil in our own lives (Questions 29–35), and how we can counsel others who are affected by it (Questions 36–40). Of course, part 4 is deeply related to the earlier parts of the book. If we are to have a proper basis for answering the kinds of practical questions posed in part 4, we need to be clear about our definitions (part 1), about what the Bible and mature theological reflection have to say about suffering and evil (part 2), and about how we can defend the Christian faith from those who would use suffering and evil as an argument against our faith (part 3).

Even if we need to be informed about what the Bible teaches on the topic of suffering and evil (perhaps because of widespread biblical illiteracy), why go on and detail the suffering and evil in the modern world? Would readers of this book not already know about that, since they live in the modern world? Yes, but there may be something very salutary about reviewing what we know about our own era *and reflecting on it*, noting explicitly how the world has changed since biblical times. We may not be aware of all the ways that biblical principles can be applied to understanding and responding to the modern-day suffering and evil we know all too well.

Since Questions 29–35 are "related to how suffering and evil impact our lives," we need to have a clear view of how *our* lives are impacted. We live in the present, not the past. Renowned evangelical theologian John Stott argued that the contemporary preacher lives "between two worlds," with one foot firmly planted in the world of the Bible and the other foot planted in the world of modern people. Any such preacher, to be effective, must be able to travel between both worlds, speaking ancient truth in new contexts.[1] Something similar applies when it comes to the topic of this book.

This effort to travel between both worlds faces two dangers. On the one hand, if we overstate the differences between past and present suffering, we threaten to make the Bible irrelevant to what we are *really* suffering in the here and now. If the present is so unique that the Bible cannot possibly speak to it, then why consult the Bible at all? On the other hand, if we pursue a reductive approach that reflexively assimilates contemporary suffering and evil to "how it has always been," we may overlook distinctive ways that moderns suffer, lessening the impact of our message.

In the following, we will look at three ways the modern era adds to the suffering and evil we have already considered in this book: it adds more sufferers of evil, more kinds of evil, and more awareness of evil. But as we will see, it also adds more opportunities to minister in the presence of evil.

More Sufferers of Evil

It is an obvious fact that the sheer *amount* of suffering and evil in the world will multiply as the world population rises. More people means more perpetrators of evil, more victims of evil, and more sufferers. Currently the world population is eight billion persons, as opposed to 200 million in the first century AD, an increase by a factor of 40x.[2]

Some have argued that the amount of suffering in the world can be exaggerated if we overlook its subjective nature. No one person suffers all the suffering in the world. C. S. Lewis makes this point at length:

> We must never make the problem of pain worse than it is by vague talk about the "unimaginable sum of human misery." Suppose that I have a toothache of intensity x: and suppose that you, who are seated beside me, also begin to have a toothache of intensity x. You may, if you choose, say the total amount of pain in the room is now $2x$. But you must remember that no one is suffering $2x$: search all time and all space and you will not find that composite pain in anyone's consciousness. There is no such thing as a sum of suffering, for no one suffers it. When we have reached the maximum that a single person can suffer, we have, no doubt, reached something very horrible, but we have reached all the

1.   John R. W. Stott, *Between Two Worlds: The Art of Preaching in the Twentieth Century* (Grand Rapids: Eerdmans, 1982).
2.   See "Current World Population" (https://www.worldometers.info/); Carl Haub, "How many people have ever lived on earth?," *Population Today* (Feb. 1995) 23(2): 4–5.

suffering there ever can be in the universe. The addition of a million fellow-sufferers adds no more pain.[3]

Lewis's argument is well-intentioned. He is trying to make "the problem of pain" more tractable for Christians to solve. But the argument is entirely invalid. It is true that "no one is suffering *2x*," and that the "composite pain" is not "in anyone's consciousness." But it does not follow that "there is no such thing as a sum of suffering." Surely there is. One might as well say that "there is no sum" of all the food that is eaten in the world, on the grounds that no one person eats it. Lewis's observations seem true but irrelevant in supporting his conclusion. I would not expose my entire family to suffering, when I alone could suffer it, on the grounds that *no one* is experiencing everything when my whole family suffers. Surely it makes a *moral* difference whether I permit more pain than is justified. I cannot get around this by arguing that there is no such thing as "more pain" in the aggregate.

Alternatively, some could argue that this quantitative increase in the amount of suffering due to population growth is more than offset by the development of multiple technologies that alleviate that suffering: modern medicine, anesthetics, water purification, and enhanced food production techniques. But this calculation is not obvious. It is true that technology helps achieve all these ends. But once technologies have been developed that exploit, extend, or redirect natural processes toward beneficial ends, there is always the possibility for those technologies to be abused or have unintended consequences. People can develop technology that deliberately (or unintentionally) causes or spreads disease, extends or magnifies pain, or poisons a population, doing so on a scale hitherto undreamed of. Technological development is a double-edged sword that can vastly increase the *kinds* of evil in the world.

More Kinds of Evil

Kinds of moral evil have multiplied since biblical times, as humanity develops in its knowledge of the world, of which causes bring about which effects, and of how to produce bad effects with the greatest efficiency and scope. By studying nature, we learn more and more about its fundamental processes, that is, if this happens then that happens. We can then develop technology that brings about the effects we want when we want. We can utilize ever more complex causes to reliably bring about more complex effects.

We are then faced with a choice: develop technology that will alleviate suffering and help people flourish or develop technology that will increase suffering and undermine human flourishing. In addition, there is always the possibility of unintended side effects of the technology we develop, so that we

---

3.   C. S. Lewis, *The Problem of Pain* (New York: HarperOne, 2001 [1940]), 116–17.

Question 29 What Kinds of Suffering and Evil Occur in the World Today?

aim at human flourishing but bring about lots of suffering instead (or in addition to the flourishing that the technology does bring).

This two-edged nature of technological progress exists no matter what area of science gets applied: biology, chemistry, genetics, physics (kinetic or nuclear), or computers. Through these we have developed more ways to kill, more ways to damage the environment (or the environment of a people group), and more ways to exploit or be exploited by others—in short, more ways to suffer.

More Ways to Kill

Civilization has developed weapons of mass destruction—including biological, chemical, and nuclear weapons—that can be used against populations on a large scale by nation-states, or on a smaller but still lethal scale by terrorist organizations. Likewise, conventional weapons that can kill many people in a short amount of time (so-called automatic and semiautomatic weapons) are more widely available, making possible mass shootings in schools, businesses, and hospitals.

The ability to kill human life in the womb has advanced to the point that, even with the overturning of *Roe v. Wade*, most abortions can be (and now are) performed via chemicals in the privacy of one's home. Also, genetic editing of the human genome via CRISPR technology, if deployed without vigilant surveillance, would seem to be a threat to whole populations.

More Ways to Damage the Environment

According to the "2022 World Air Quality Report" prepared by IQAir (an air-quality technology company), only 10 percent of the world's citizens "are breathing air that does not pose a risk to their health."[4] The Energy Policy Institute at the University of Chicago makes a lengthy case that "particulate air pollution is the single greatest threat to human health globally."[5] The industrial revolution enabled the generation of such pollution on a large scale, and the sharp rise in global population since then only exacerbates the degree of suffering.

Beyond this, the case for anthropogenic (i.e., human-caused) climate change on a global scale seems strong. NASA's Jet Propulsion Laboratory at the California Institute of Technology summarizes the evidence from "multiple peer-reviewed studies from research groups across the world," arguing "that climate-warming trends over the past century are extremely likely due

4. "2022 World Air Quality Report," IQAir website (https://www.iqair.com/us/world-air-quality-report). See also Emma Newburger and Gabriel Cortes, "Here Are the Most Polluted Cities in the U.S. and World," CNBC website, March 17, 2023 (https://www.cnbc.com/2023/03/17/most-polluted-cities-and-countries-in-the-world-according-to-iqair.html).
5. "Pollution Facts," AQLI website (https://aqli.epic.uchicago.edu/pollution-facts).

to human activities."[6] Of course, the fact (if it is a fact) that climate warming is human-caused would not automatically reveal the best way to combat it (e.g., government intervention, economic incentives, technological innovation, or a combination of these). It is easier to recognize problems than agree on strategies to solve them. No doubt if climate change *is* occurring on a global scale, then it will produce untold human suffering unless reversed, including longer wildfire seasons, increasing drought, rising sea levels with attendant flooding, more severe heat waves, and so on. That would be true even if it is part of a natural cycle that proceeds independent of human activities. So regardless of ultimate cause, climate change is a very significant case of "suffering and evil" that forms our modern environment, whether it is moral evil or natural evil.

More Ways to Exploit or to Be Exploited by Others
The rise of mass media technologies, combined with the power of totalitarian states to control the flow of information, gives unprecedented ability to such states not only to manipulate their populations in ways that exploit and oppress them, but to protect the oppressors from severe reprisals. The (relatively recent) rise of social media reveals the ease with which populations can be polarized, so that pathways to helpful political consensus are obstructed if not obliterated. The link between social media use and various forms of psychological depression is currently the subject of vigorous academic study. The internet distribution of child sex abuse material and videos depicting real-life gratuitous violence continues at a horrific pace, so much so that it takes an army of moderators to detect and remove it, often at the cost of their own well-being.[7] And a case can be made that modern techniques of mass incarceration, cynically and unfairly applied to specific racial groups, can worsen outcomes for those groups and tear the larger social fabric.[8]

There is nothing new in principle about drug addiction and alcoholism. The Bible repeatedly warns against drunkenness (Prov. 20:1; 23:19–21; 23:29–35; Isa. 5:22; Eph. 5:18). But in modern times, chemical techniques enable the synthesis of a very wide range of highly addictive drugs that go far beyond what was naturally available in biblical times. The damage such addiction can wreak at an individual, family, and societal level is tremendous.

This list only scratches the surface. No doubt some of my examples are controversial. But all these evils are *new* kinds of evils, since their means for

---

6. "Scientific Consensus: Earth's Climate Is Warming," Earth Science Communications Team, NASA's Jet Propulsion Laboratory, June 9, 2023 (https://climate.nasa.gov/scientific-consensus).
7. Casey Newton, "The Trauma Floor: The Secret Lives of Facebook Moderators in America," *The Verge*, February 25, 2019 (https://www.theverge.com/2019/2/25/18229714/cognizant-facebook-content-moderator-interviews-trauma-working-conditions-arizona).
8. Michelle Alexander, *The New Jim Crow: Mass Incarceration in the Age of Colorblindness*, 10th anniversary ed. (New York: The New Press, 2020).

production did not exist in biblical times. Kinds of moral evil have multiplied because the intrinsic good of scientific discovery offers humanity the opportunity of using that knowledge for evil rather than for good, and on a scale only enabled by that technology. By way of contrast, natural evil continues as in biblical times, because nature is roughly the same (e.g., earthquakes, tsunami, hurricanes, tornadoes, famine). Of course, one possible exception here is the climate change discussed earlier.

More Awareness of Evil

Finally, beyond there being more sufferers of evil and kinds of evil, modern media and travel technologies combine to make humanity far more *aware* of global suffering and evil than ever before. We are far less isolated because "the world is flat" in the era of globalization.[9] Though this increased awareness is distinctive of our hyperconnected, wireless internet modern times, there is no need to label it as a further evil. Still, such awareness brings challenges both to Christian apologetics and counseling, the main themes of the last two parts of this book. Defending the faith against the intellectual problem of evil becomes harder, practically speaking, when there are so many ongoing examples of widespread suffering and evil in the modern world that critics can cite with ease. And the constant threat of nuclear or biological catastrophe, combined with the knowledge that nearly a billion people are undernourished *right now* or that nearly the same number have no access to a safe drinking water source, can induce a state of anxiety that is hard to counsel oneself out of.[10]

All that to say, Christians should not be deaf to the cries and questions modern people have about contemporary kinds of suffering and evil. We should do our homework about the world our generation is in by God's providence. We should remind ourselves that the greater variety and awareness of evil today gives us an expanded evangelistic context and opportunity. There are *more* reasons to reflect on how things "ought to be" and on which worldview makes the most sense of that. We should be motivated to consider more deeply the practical and counseling Questions that form the remainder of this book.

We must also remember that some things *do not* change: the Bible as the essential and supreme source of insight about the role of suffering and evil in the world (Question 4); the fact that God's providence is good, sovereign, and inscrutable (Questions 7–8); the fact that both natural evils and even moral evils (through dual-agency) can serve his good, wise, though mysterious purposes (Questions 9–11, 14); the fundamental points made by the punishment,

---

9. Thomas Friedman, *The World Is Flat: A Brief History of the Twenty-First Century*, 3rd ed. (New York: Picador, 2007).
10. For these last two statistics, see (again) the front page of Worldometer (https://www. worldometers.info/).

soul-building, and megaphone theodicies (Questions 21–23); and the need to ground moral norms in God (Question 28). There is no reason to put the Bible back on the shelf just because we live in the modern world.

Summary

Though we and those to whom we minister live in the modern world and are aware of its suffering and evil, there is reason to review what we know in this area and reflect on it. Only with such knowledge can we adequately apply the biblical and reasoned principles we have worked out in earlier parts of this book. To the suffering and evil we have already considered in this book, the modern era adds more sufferers of evil, more kinds of evil, and more awareness of evil. But it also adds more opportunities to minister in the presence of evil.

REFLECTION QUESTIONS

1. Review the nature, sources, victims, and consequences of the evils we surveyed back in Question 6, where we restricted our focus to the biblical narrative. How do these compare with the kinds of evils surveyed in this Question? Are modern evils represented *in principle* in the biblical materials, or not?

2. Could I have misunderstood C. S. Lewis's point in the passage cited earlier? Try to restate his point in a way that would be helpful to understand today.

3. This chapter did not seek to adjudicate whether technology has made the world better overall or worse overall. Do you think making such a judgment is important for responding to the suffering and evil in the world? Why or why not?

4. Do you agree that "it is easier to recognize problems than agree on strategies to solve them"? Where have you seen that on display in your own life or community?

5. Is there a significant kind of evil distinctive to our modern era that you think should be added to the list given?

How Do Suffering and Evil Challenge Our Living the Christian Life?

It is inevitable that human beings around the globe are deeply affected by suffering and evil, which has persisted in our world from almost the very beginning (Question 6), and which is multiplied in ways distinctive to our modern era (Question 29). And Christians are certainly not immune to its challenge. As pointed out earlier in Question 1:

> The Scriptures are full of faithful believers who are genuinely perplexed by the evils that they or their community suffer. The psalmist cries out, "How long, O Lord?" (Ps. 13:1), the prophet is bewildered that God sets iniquity before him and fails to judge the wicked (Hab. 1), and the righteous man faces unexpected counsel to "curse God and die" because of the evil he has suffered (Job 2:9).

Most of part 3 addressed "the intellectual problem of evil," and the impression can be given that that material was primarily directed to atheists and unbelievers. They are the primary historical source of that argument against God, and so we need to refute *them*. But while unbelievers do claim that suffering and evil in the world gives them good reason to reject God's existence (and so it is important to develop a reasoned defense against their arguments), that same suffering and evil gives many *Christians* great temptation to doubt God's existence and give up serving him. So "the problem of evil" is a question which has intra-faith application, which means that Christian answers must be directed not only to the world but to the church.

To motivate taking this task seriously, this Question aims to develop a "realism" about the ways suffering and evil genuinely tempt Christians to unbelief (about what God has promised and about who he is) and tempt them to anger and resentment (about how God has governed the world). But it is important to be not only realistic about suffering and evil but *hopeful* about the prospects for good in its midst. This hopefulness is grounded in the biblical and theological material we have already considered in the earlier parts of the book.[1]

Suffering and Evil Can Unsettle Our Faith in God's Promises

As we have seen earlier (Questions 2–3, 6), "evil" is any significant case of pain and suffering, including physical pain, psychological scarring, and social isolation. It involves the deprivation of anything that would have intrinsic value for the victim. Moral evil and natural evil are then distinguished by whether the immediate cause of the pain and suffering is human beings or nature, respectively.

There are two sorts of divine promises that can be challenged by our experience of such evils: God promises good to us in the present, and God promises good to us in the future. But suffering and evil seem to teach us the opposite: God *is not* doing good to us in the present, and present evils *block* or otherwise *prevent* the good that God says he will do in the future. So both kinds of promise, about the present and about the future, are seemingly falsified by our experience of suffering and evil. Of course, it is not clear we know enough to determine whether either of those things is true. In each case, suffering could be a means to bring about great good in the present or in the future, even if we do not see it. We (at best) have access to the human intentions behind the moral evil—what the person was hoping to accomplish by inflicting pain upon us—but this affords us no insight as to why God permitted them to act that way. Likewise, we might have access to the short-term effects of natural evil but be completely unaware of long-term goods God might be realizing via the tapestry of providence.

It seems to be part of (fallen) human nature to simply assume the worst about the suffering that befalls us—it *must* have power to cut us off from God's intended blessing. We really do think that things like tribulation, distress, persecution, famine, nakedness, danger, and sword can cut us off from God's love, even when they have no power to do so at all (Rom. 8:35–39). It is instead *through* such things that "we are more than conquerors through him who loved us" (Rom. 8:37).

Here are ten examples of suffering and evil (whether actual or merely anticipated) disposing God's people to suppress, forget, or doubt God's promises.

---

1. Future Questions will further chart the impact of suffering and evil on our lives: I can become anxious trying to figure out God's reasons for why I suffer (Question 31), aloof or dehumanized as I feel like a pawn on God's chessboard (Question 32), indifferent about fighting evil in the world (Question 33), skeptical about the possibility of distinguishing good from evil (Question 34), and distant from a God who seems increasingly hidden (Question 35).

This is no small thing, since it can distort our perception of God's character and weaken our loyalty to God's purposes.

First, when the patriarch Jacob receives news of his son Joseph's (apparent) death, "he refused to be comforted" (Gen. 37:35), and when Simeon is detained in Egypt and Benjamin must be taken next, Jacob says, "Everything is against me!" (Gen. 42:36 NIV). As a matter of fact, everything was for him: Joseph was alive, none of his sons were under threat, and God was continuing to fulfill his covenant promises to Jacob.

Second, when God's promise to deliver the enslaved Israelites (Exod. 4:29–31) was followed by even harsher Egyptian oppression (Exod. 5:1–18), the slaves subsequently lost their faith in God's promise, saying to Moses and Aaron, "The Lord look on you and judge, because you have made us stink in the sight of Pharaoh and his servants, and have put a sword in their hand to kill us" (Exod. 5:21). As a matter of fact, God's purpose to deliver them was now getting underway.

Third, while under threat from Pharaoh's army, the Israelites stand before the Red Sea and abandon all hope of their deliverance, saying to Moses,

> Is it because there are no graves in Egypt that you have taken us away to die in the wilderness? What have you done to us in bringing us out of Egypt? Is not this what we said to you in Egypt: "Leave us alone that we may serve the Egyptians"? For it would have been better for us to serve the Egyptians than to die in the wilderness. (Exod. 14:11–12)

As a matter of fact, the Red Sea was about to be parted, and God's promise of deliverance would be fulfilled.

Fourth, the Israelites doubt they will have water to drink (Exod. 15:24; 17:1–2; Num. 20:2–5) or food to eat (Exod. 16:2–3). In each case, their doubt was prompted by their genuine suffering, but God was about to provide the very thing they lacked.

Fifth, God had earlier promised the Israelites: "But if you carefully obey his [the angel's] voice and do all that I say, then I will be an enemy to your enemies and an adversary to your adversaries" (Exod. 23:22). He promises to "give the inhabitants of the land into your hand" (Exod. 23:31). Despite all this, when the Israelites hear from the spies about the threat of the Canaanites, they lose faith in these earlier promises, and instead say, "We are not able to go up against the people, for they are stronger than we are" (Num. 13:31). They wish they had died in the wilderness and wish to go back to Egypt (Num. 14:1–4). Here it is clear that just the *threat* of suffering can unsettle our faith in God's promises.

Sixth, the Israelites ask for a king to rule over them (1 Sam. 8:19–20), losing faith in God's commitment to be king over them (1 Sam. 8:7; 10:19). In his farewell address, the prophet and judge Samuel reveals that their request for a king was due to anticipated suffering, because of fear "when you [the Israelites] saw that Nahash the king of the Ammonites came against you" (1 Sam. 12:12).

Seventh, when waiting for Samuel to arrive, Saul took matters into his own hands and made a burnt offering, something it was not the king's prerogative to do. Why did Saul lose faith in Samuel's promise to return and make a burnt offering on his behalf? Because of anticipated suffering—he was afraid that "the Philistines will come down against me at Gilgal" (1 Sam. 13:8–12).

Eighth, when did Saul seek out a medium rather than trust in God's revelation to him about his situation? "When Saul saw the army of the Philistines, he was afraid, and his heart trembled greatly," and so his faith in God's revelation was unsettled (1 Sam. 28:3–7).

Ninth, Elijah's persecution by Jezebel leads him to despair of God's provision, and even of life itself (1 Kings 19:1–18).

Tenth, in the Psalms, it is particularly when David faces opposition from his enemies and receives real suffering from their persecutions, that he is tempted to despair of the fulfillment of God's promises. At times he thinks that God has hidden himself (Ps. 10:1) or has even forsaken him (Ps. 22:1–2).

Suffering and Evil Can Harden Our Hearts into Bitterness Toward God and Others

In addition to tempting us to unbelief (in God's promises and good character), the experience of suffering and evil can tempt us to anger and resentment about God's providence so that we are bitter about how he has governed the world. It can redirect our emotions and affections, so that we are no longer disposed to rejoice in God, love God, and love other people. Again, here are ten examples.

First, Job's (quite considerable) suffering prompts a faithless admonition from his wife: "Do you still hold fast your integrity? Curse God and die" (Job 2:9). This is not a mere call to unbelief but to blasphemy. Job does not go that far, but he does end up despising the day of his birth (Job 3:1–26; see Jer. 15:10).

Second, in the wake of her bereavement in a time of famine, Naomi wants to be called "Mara" ("bitter"),

> for the Almighty has dealt very bitterly with me. I went away full, and the LORD has brought me back empty. Why call me Naomi, when the LORD has testified against me and the Almighty has brought calamity upon me? (Ruth 1:20–21)

Third, the mocking of others can provoke us bitterly, particularly when we are perceived as not living up to society's standards. Hannah's rival (Peninnah) used to provoke Hannah grievously because of Hannah's barrenness, to the point that "Hannah wept and would not eat" (1 Sam. 1:6–7). "She was deeply distressed and prayed to the LORD and wept bitterly" (1 Sam. 1:10) and spoke to the Lord out of "great anxiety and vexation" (1 Sam. 1:16).

Fourth, seeing the suffering of others can remind us that we are not immune from it and that we could very well be next, which can bring anxiety into our own hearts. God's striking down Uzzah for touching the ark made David both angry and afraid (2 Sam. 6:8–9).

Fifth, the psalmist wonders how God's people can possibly "sing the LORD's song in a foreign land" when asked to do so by their "captors" and "tormentors" (Ps. 137:1–6). There can be no rejoicing there; they are too grieved by their losses and their change of fortune.

Sixth, Jeremiah is repeatedly filled with grief for the people of Israel (Jer. 8:18–9:1; Lam. 1:16; 2:11). Their sufferings are his sufferings, and his solidarity with them brings tears to his eyes.

Seventh, it is quite possible to have a worldly grief that produces death, rather than a godly grief that "produces a repentance that leads to salvation without regret" (2 Cor. 7:10). Such worldly grief burns us out from the inside, leaving us hopeless, inwardly turned, and without strength.

Eighth, the Christians addressed in the book of Hebrews, due to their many persecutions, were on their way to "growing weary or fainthearted" (Heb. 12:3). Spiritually speaking, they had "drooping hands" and "weak knees" (Heb. 12:12) and were in danger of becoming "defiled" by a "root of bitterness" springing up and causing trouble (Heb. 12:15).

Ninth, the apostle James seems to discern that it is precisely in times of suffering that God's people can be prone to "grumble against one another" (James 5:9), which is why he warns against it.

Tenth, it is when suffering comes that God's people must be encouraged to "not repay evil for evil or reviling for reviling" (1 Peter 3:9). In general, the New Testament authors would not warn against bitterness amid suffering unless the latter were a pathway to the former.

From Realism to Hopefulness

By challenging our belief and trust, and by manipulating our affections, suffering and evil can tempt us to apostasy, and thus to abandon the faith. That is the ultimate way that suffering and evil can challenge our living the Christian life. But there are at least two great reasons for hope, even after considering the material in this chapter: God prepares us for the time that we face these exact temptations, and God offers us a choice (to receive suffering as a pathway to blessing).

First, as we have seen throughout this chapter, God tells us that suffering can pose a deadly threat to our faith and faithfulness, and he gives us specific examples, so that we will not be alarmed when we begin to perceive similar effects of suffering and evil in our own lives. Learning from the past in this way can give us hope in the present and the future:

> For whatever was written in former days was written for our
> instruction, that through endurance and through the en-
> couragement of the Scriptures we might have hope. May the
> God of endurance and encouragement grant you to live in
> such harmony with one another, in accord with Christ Jesus,
> that together you may with one voice glorify the God and
> Father of our Lord Jesus Christ. (Rom. 15:4–6)

Christians can endure and be encouraged, both individually and in community, when they recognize the instruction written for them "in former
days." God gives us more than just lists of commands. He clothes his principles in the vividness of historical narrative, so that we can *see* the consequences of trusting God (or not) amid suffering.

Second, the experience of suffering and evil offers us a choice, to "choose
this day whom you will serve" (Josh. 24:15). Yes, we need to be realistic, and
so be aware of how suffering and evil can discourage and harden our hearts,
tempting us to respond badly under its influence. But suffering also holds out
real hope, since God can use suffering, even unjust suffering, in our lives for
good, and there can even be blessing in it. This was the import of the many
Bible passages cited earlier in support of the soul-building theodicy (Question
22). The mourners and the persecuted can be blessed, both comforted and heirs
of the kingdom (Matt. 5:4, 10–12). It can be good for us to be afflicted, so that
we keep God's word and learn his statutes (Ps. 119:67, 71). Indeed, the psalmist
was often in a different place spiritually at the end of his psalm than at the beginning. Suffering can produce endurance (Rom. 5:3), dependence on God
(2 Cor. 1:8–10), steadfastness (James 1:2–4), and tested faith that proves genuine, something "more precious than gold" (1 Peter 1:6–7). Jesus is the perfect
example here. In the face of persecution and suffering he did not stop praying,
stop trusting, or stop serving. He did not sin, deceive, revile, or threaten, "but
continued entrusting himself to him who judges justly" (1 Peter 2:23).

To help us be better equipped to make the right choice here, Questions
31–35 are meant to warn us away from wrong inferences about the suffering
and evil in our lives. Instead, we should remind one another of the character
of God (Question 37), his works in history (Questions 38–39), and the gospel
itself (Question 40).

Summary

Experiencing suffering and evil can unsettle our faith in God's promises,
distort our perception of God's character, weaken our loyalty to God's purposes, and harden our hearts to make us bitter toward God and others. The
Scriptures amply testify to this danger so that we will be prepared ahead of
time against this possibility. And there is nothing inevitable about suffering
leading us into apostasy. The Scriptures give us many reasons and strategies

for the working of suffering and evil for good in our lives, and these will be considered in the remaining Questions of this book.

REFLECTION QUESTIONS

1. Are there any other apologetic questions that have "intra-faith application," besides the intellectual problem of evil?

2. The repeated apostolic counsel that we should forgive each other (2 Cor. 2:7; Eph. 4:32; Col. 3:13) presupposes that Christians can be the source of suffering and evil for other Christians. Why would that phenomenon be an especially severe source of bitterness?

3. Jesus warned his would-be disciples to "count the cost" before deciding to follow him (Luke 14:28–33). How would the material in this chapter relate to that?

4. This Question (and the previous one) focused on the reality and effects of suffering and evil. Are there any dangers in studying the problem more than the solution?

5. Suffering is not the only pathway to apostasy. Sometimes pleasure, contentment, and absence of conflict can lead us in that direction as well. How?

Should Christians Attempt to Figure Out Why They Face Suffering and Evil?

The remaining Questions in this part of the book defend and apply the overall perspective on suffering and evil that has been argued so far. Whether we are defending a position from objections or applying it to individual and community life, the best first step is to clearly understand what the position says and does not say. To that end, this Question briefly summarizes the overall perspective argued so far, and then addresses an initial objection: because God aims at "greater goods" in cases of suffering and evil, we are therefore consigned to a lifetime of (perhaps fruitless) searching as to what that greater good might be.

Future Questions will consider additional objections to the book's perspective and make application to individual and community life. In effect, the remainder of this book emulates the apostle Paul's "put off / put on" dynamic for sanctification in the Christian life (e.g., Eph. 4:22–24; Col. 3:5–14). Questions 31–35 will direct us to "put off" false inferences from our suffering, whereas Questions 36–40 will direct us to "put on" true thinking that would help us in times of suffering.

What Biblical, Theological, and Apologetic Claims Have We Argued?

This book can be summarized by way of four main claims:

1. *God's providence is both good and sovereign.* As the sovereign creator and providential sustainer of the world, God permits natural and moral evils as necessary means for bringing about great goods that outweigh the evils. (Questions 7, 9–11)
2. *God's providence is also inscrutable.* Humans typically go wrong when they try to guess at God's reasons for permitting evil and bringing about suffering. This applies to both advocates and critics of the Christian faith. (Questions 8, 20, 27)

3. Though the existence of natural and moral evils can be (ultimately) traced back to divine purposes, *the existence of moral evils involves a "dual-agency"* that preserves human freedom and divine goodness. God is not a sinner who commits acts of sin. (Questions 13–14)

4. *Three theodicies that appear to have some biblical support are the punishment, soul-building, and megaphone theodicies*, and these can be fitted into a larger, "greater-good" perspective on suffering and evil. (Questions 21–23, 26)

Several subsidiary claims have been made as well, including:

5. The moral evil/natural evil distinction is important and biblically derivable. (Questions 2–3, 6)

6. The Bible is our main source of insight on this topic, though reason is needed to interpret the Bible and to evaluate and further confirm our interpretation of the Bible. (Questions 4–5)

7. The Job, Joseph, and Jesus narratives reveal a consistent divine *modus operandi* when it comes to suffering and evil. (Questions 7–8)

8. Three principles for interpreting divine commands can help us make sense of biblical passages about capital punishment, holy war, and the sacrifice of Isaac (reality of divine right, permissibility of divine delegation, and irrelevance of human fallibility). (Question 12)

9. The biblical data is best accommodated by the Calvinist or Molinist models of providence, rather than the Arminian or Open Theist models. (Question 15)

10. The nonexistence of God would bring about an even worse "problem of evil": the problem of grounding moral norms and our knowledge of them. (Question 28)

The position summarized above is subject to various objections. While each individual Question has sought to interact with objections that could be made to the argument of that chapter, there are remaining objections to the project as a whole. Typically, these objections express theological, pastoral, or ethical concerns, such that the position defended in this book either challenges God's goodness, makes it harder to live the Christian life, or undermines our moral motivation to fight evil or even believe in the difference between good and evil. Let us consider one of these objections now and leave the others for later (Questions 32–35).

Does This Perspective Motivate Fruitless Searching?

If God aims at greater goods in cases of suffering and evil, are we not therefore consigned to a lifetime of fruitless searching for this "greater good"?

The idea behind this objection is simple. There is a *lot* of suffering and evil in the world (Questions 6, 29). It can lead to some very bad consequences in our lives (Question 30). So if God is working it all out to some greater good—such that the world is better with that good, even with the attendant suffering and evil, than without the good and the evil—then that good must be *extraordinarily* valuable! For the sake of getting it, God allows *a lot*. Surely it would be extremely important to find out what that greater good is, for the sake of which God permits the evil. Knowing that would provide insight into what is of most consequence for us. In a world so often devoted to trivial pursuits, learning about this great good would be a goal worth having, illuminating depths of meaning it would be tragic to miss.

The desire to figure out why we have suffered in the ways we have, by perpetrators either mindless or malevolent, can be as immediate and visceral as the pain itself. Perhaps our whole life has changed in a single day, and that means we cannot rest until we find out *why*. To be ignorant of this when there *is* an answer, is to be content with a surface understanding of who we are and what we were meant for. To be kept in the dark is to trivialize the suffering, to avoid the lesson the suffering was meant to teach us. So we must know, and leave no stone unturned in the search.

This line of thinking is both deep and understandable. No one could be blamed for responding to the problem of suffering, and to their own experience of suffering, in this way. And yet the reasoning is a *non sequitur* from all that has gone before. It simply does not follow from the fact of a greater good that we have any kind of obligation, duty, or need to find out what that greater good is. It is no part of the biblical teaching on divine providence, and it is not implied by any advocacy of a "greater-good theodicy," to claim that *we can know* or that *we ought to know*, in any particular instance of suffering, *what is* the greater good aimed at by God in that suffering (what it looks like, who it applies to, when it will be realized, and so on).

This book's attempt to fruitfully respond to the problem of suffering and evil, whether in its intellectual or pastoral dimensions, fundamentally depends on taking two doctrines together rather than isolating them from each other. Divine *sovereignty* in providence speaks to how reality is, whereas divine *inscrutability* in providence speaks to our limited perspective on how reality is. Each doctrine on its own might generate insoluble conundrums for the Christian believer, but together they provide a stable path around multiple dangers. Perhaps this explains why the doctrines appear together in the Job, Joseph, and Jesus narratives (Questions 7–8), and side by side in Paul's doxology (Rom. 11:33–36). As pointed out earlier, "the grand, sweeping scope of divine providence is what guarantees its inscrutability to us, apart from divine revelation" (Question 26). Sovereignty and inscrutability are friends, not enemies.

As argued in Question 27, God has a track record in Scripture of holding his knowledge in reserve, and this includes divulging his reasons for suffering and evil. He has seemingly made the judgment that we do not need to know the answer to specific theodicy questions to flourish as human beings. Given that he designed us, he should know. However, there can be indirect knowledge that can give us the comfort and assurance which we thought only direct knowledge of "the reason" would get us. Assurance *that* God has a reason, even if we do not know *what* that reason is, already communicates that God is on the side of good, that God knows what he is doing, and that he has our sufferings and our plight well in hand. That does not deliver everything we would want, but it gives us a great deal of it, and perhaps the most important part. There is a substantial biblical case for the view that this indirect knowledge is most certainly a kind of knowledge we can have (Questions 7–11, 26).

So, return to the objection: "If God aims at greater goods in cases of suffering and evil, are we not therefore consigned to a lifetime of (perhaps fruitless) searching for this 'greater good'?" As we have just seen, there are different levels at which to ask this question. To search for what God has never promised to give (*what* the reason is) would be fruitless. Repeatedly in the Bible, people guess at this and get it completely wrong (Question 8). But to humbly receive what God has already revealed (*that* he has a reason) is to find knowledge that gives us most of what we want and that we can obtain without a lifetime of shaky speculation and frantic guessing. Pointing out that we can and ought to have the latter kind of knowledge would not be some kind of objection to the greater-good theodicy, but an application of it.

What Is the Wisest Course?

The Bible regularly encourages us to trust God even when we cannot figure him out. So, leaving these particular matters with God is the wisest course. Every biblical truth must be handled with great thoughtfulness and compassion, including this one: that the God who failed to prevent suffering and evil that he *could* have easily prevented is not only good and wise, but was motivated *by* that goodness and wisdom when he allowed the suffering and evil. The writers of the Bible did not shrink back from encouraging this perspective, and neither should Christians in their counsels to each other (Rom. 8:28; 2 Cor. 4:17; 1 Peter 1:6). We should respect inscrutability because the Bible respects it, while leading sufferers to the God who knows what he is doing.

The English Puritan Thomas Watson wrote a treatise in 1653 on Philippians 4:11, "I have learned, in whatsoever state I am, therewith to be content" (KJV). Entitled *The Art of Divine Contentment*, the book contains a line later quoted by Charles Spurgeon and which repeatedly shows up in popular Christian preaching and song lyrics: "Trust God where you cannot trace him."[1] Trust—not panicky, desperate searching—is the proper response to our epistemological darkness about God's specific purposes for our suffering. Watson had a "high" view of divine providence that seems to endorse the "greater-good theodicy":

> All God's providences, how cross or bloody soever, shall do a believer good; "And we know that all things work together for good to them that love God." Not only all good things, but all evil things work for good; and shall we be discontented at that which works for our good?[2]

But this conviction that God *has* a reason did not lead Watson to infer that we should *search* for it, to obtain knowledge of what God has not revealed. But neither does it mean that faith amid suffering should be blind and despairing. In a remarkable section of *The Art of Divine Contentment*, Watson gives separate and detailed responses to each of the following complaints. (He calls his responses "apologies," because they are reasoned defenses against the claim that God is unkind or cruel to allow us to suffer in these ways.) Apparently we already know enough to adequately counsel ourselves in each of the following kinds of suffering and evil, even if we do not know "the reason" why we suffer it:

- "I have lost a child." (48)[3]
- "It was my only child." (52)
- "I have a great part of my estate strangely melted away, and trading begins to fail." (54)
- "My child goes on in rebellion; I fear I have brought forth a child for the devil." (59)
- "But, my husband takes ill courses; where I looked for honey, behold a sting." (62)
- "But my friends have dealt very unkindly with me, and proved false." (64)

---

1. The full quote is: "True faith will trust God where it cannot trace him, and will adventure upon God's bond [his promise], though it has nothing in view." Thomas Watson, *The Art of Divine Contentment* (London: L. B. Seeley and Sons, 1829), 140. In a series of posthumously published sermons on the *Catechism* of the Westminster Assembly, Watson says something similar when speaking of the wisdom of God: "Trust him where you cannot trace him. God is most in his way, when we think he is most out of the way." See Thomas Watson, *A Body of Divinity* (Carlisle, PA: Banner of Truth, 1962 [1692]), 76.
2. Watson explores this providential perspective at length in a different book. See Thomas Watson, *All Things for Good*, 2nd ed. (Carlisle, PA: Banner of Truth, 2021), 127.
3. All numbers in parentheses are page numbers in *The Art of Divine Contentment*.

- "I am under great reproaches." (70)
- "I have not that esteem from men, as is suitable to my quality and graces." (74)
- "I meet with very great sufferings for the truth." (77)
- "The prosperity of the wicked." (80)
- "The times are full of heresy." (82)
- "I live and converse among the profane." (87)
- "I cannot discourse with that fluency, nor pray with that elegancy as others." (89–90)
- "The troubles of the Church." (91–92)
- "It is not my trouble that troubles me, but it is my Sins that do disquiet and discontent." (95)

Watson's separate answers to these cases led him to subsequently formulate a kind of "Christian Directory, or Rules about Contentment" (197), with which he closes the book:

- "Advance faith." (197)
- "Labor for assurance." (199)
- "Get an humble spirit." (201)
- "Keep a clear conscience." (202)
- "Learn to deny yourselves." (205)
- "Get much of heaven into your heart." (207)
- "Look not so much on the dark side of your condition, as on the light." (208)
- "Consider in what a posture we stand here in the world." (210)
- "Let not your hopes depend upon these outward things." (212)
- "Let us often compare our condition." (214)
- "Try not to bring your condition to your mind, but bring your mind to your condition." (221)
- "Study the vanity of the creature." (222)
- "Get fancy [i.e., imagination, speculation, desire] regulated." (223)
- "Consider how little will suffice nature." (224)
- "Believe the present condition is best for us." (225)
- "Do not too much indulge the flesh." (226)
- "Meditate much on the glory which shall be revealed." (228)
- "Be much in prayer." (230)

We might wonder whether Watson has rightly identified all the principles worth considering. Perhaps some have been left out, or some that he has included are not as important as he thinks. But it seems unmistakable that this is an area worth exploring, precisely because it seeks to apply what we *do* know.

Summary

Not all darkness is created equal. Being ignorant of some things—such as "the reason" why God allows us to suffer in the specific ways we have suffered—does not mean we are ignorant of *all* things, or even the most important things. The perspective on suffering and evil articulated and defended in this book can be summarized in four main claims and six subsidiary claims. But the idea that God permits suffering and evil for greater goods does not carry with it the implication that we should spend the rest of our lives in a fruitless search to find out what those greater goods are. Rather, we know enough to adequately counsel ourselves amid suffering and evil, even if we do not know "the reason" why we suffer it. Even as we do not know enough to *rule in* any of God's possible reasons as applying to us, we do not know enough to *rule out* these reasons either. Christians must learn to trust God where they cannot trace him, where they cannot figure him out.

REFLECTION QUESTIONS

1. This Question distinguished "four main claims" from "six subsidiary claims" that were argued in this book. Which of the claims do you think leads most directly to the objection considered in this chapter?

2. This Question categorized typical objections as expressing "theological, pastoral, or ethical concerns." Are there any other categories of objections that would be important to consider?

3. "To be ignorant of *why* God allowed us to suffer is to be content with a surface understanding of who we are and what we were meant for." How would you respond to someone who thought this?

4. Imagine you believed in divine sovereignty *or* divine inscrutability (pick one), but not both. How would that affect the impact suffering and evil have on your life?

5. Review Watson's list of fifteen kinds of suffering and evil and pick one. How might you counsel yourself (from the Bible) if you experienced it?

Does Divine Providence Turn Us into Pawns on God's Chessboard?

If God works all things together for good, including things like tribulation, distress, persecution, famine, nakedness, danger, and sword (Rom. 8:28, 35), then where does that leave humanity? Are we not dehumanized in God's providential plan, pawns on his chessboard, our suffering simply a means to his ends? And if God *is* treating persons as means to an end rather than as ends in themselves, does that not mean the greater-good theodicy defended in Question 26 is no better than failed ethical theories like utilitarianism, according to which any action is right if it has the best consequences? In the end, for God to have *any* purpose that led him to expose us to suffering both dethrones God and unmakes man: God is no longer good, and we are no longer people, but objects. On this view, the greater-good theodicy is not a reply to the intellectual problem of evil; rather, it *generates* multiple problems of evil.

This chapter untangles and then reweaves the various threads of this objection. It is no doubt right to say that a perspective on suffering and evil that is incompatible with divine goodness and human personhood is not a perspective worth having. But it is not obvious that God's "working all things for good" has these consequences. This chapter will investigate these concerns.

What Is Utilitarianism?

Utilitarianism is a consequentialist theory of moral rightness. It says: always act such that you secure the greatest good for the greatest number of people. Applied to the morality of individual actions (whether by God or human beings), it says that "the rightness or wrongness of an action depends only on the total goodness or badness of its consequences, i.e., on the effect of the action on the welfare of all human beings (or perhaps all sentient beings)."[1] Consequentialist theories of moral rightness have a complex history impossible to summarize here. But they all embody "the basic intuition that what is best or right is whatever makes the world best in the future."[2]

As many critics point out, utilitarianism strongly suggests that it is morally right to make one person benefit at the expense of another. All that would matter, morally speaking, is that the badness suffered by the second person leads to the greatest amount of goods for the others (compared with other actions that could be taken). So it might be "moral" to eliminate minorities violently and ruthlessly from a society if that would lead to social peace overall. Or it might be "moral" to unequivocally murder an innocent person in cold blood if someone else has said they will kill even more people if I do not do this.[3] In both cases, people are killed simply as a means to an end, which offends our moral sensibilities that persons are relevantly different from objects or tools to be used as we wish. Could it ever be right that someone be coerced, or tortured, or deprived of life, or humiliated, or otherwise have his or her dignity and intrinsic value trampled, so that *someone else* can benefit?

But if that is objectionable, then what are we to say about a system of divine providence that "aims at goods" by way of the evils on which they depend? (see Questions 7–11, 26). If sufferers exist for the "greater good" of others getting to show them sympathy, or the needy exist for the "greater good" of others getting to show them compassion, or the sick exist for the "greater good" of others getting to display patience toward them, then it is regularly the case that some people benefit at the expense of other people, that these other people are *means* to ensuring goods for others. Surely the question must be asked: Is *any* evil permissible so long as it ensures a greater good? How am I to view myself, and God, if this is how providence is?

In the remaining sections of this chapter, four points will be made in response to these concerns. First, it is obvious that, in the Bible, God *does* use people as means to his ends, but in a way that does not seem to dehumanize them. Second, God has rights over us in providence that we do not have over each other in everyday life. Third, God has knowledge of us (and of our situation) which we do not have, knowledge that is relevant for determining

---

1. J. J. C. Smart, "An Outline of a System of Utilitarian Ethics," in J. J. C. Smart and Bernard Williams, *Utilitarianism: For and Against* (Cambridge: Cambridge University Press, 1973), 4.

2. Walter Sinnott-Armstrong, "Consequentialism," *The Stanford Encyclopedia of Philosophy* (Winter 2022 ed.), eds. Edward N. Zalta and Uri Nodelman (https://plato.stanford.edu/archives/win2022/entries/consequentialism/).

3. These examples are adapted from Bernard Williams, "A Critique of Utilitarianism," in Smart and Williams, *Utilitarianism*, 98–99, 105. There are nonmoral criticisms of utilitarianism as well, for example, epistemological ones. Are we ever in a condition where *we can know or calculate* what would be "the greatest good for the greatest number of people"? How could we know a thing like that, for any particular action?

whether or not God's providential planning is ethical. Fourth, for all we know, God does not *merely* use us as means, and if not, then the ethical concerns raised in this chapter do not offer much of a challenge to God's goodness.

God's Using People as Means in the Bible

It is obvious that God uses people as means to his ends. There is no way to eliminate or explain away this aspect of the biblical testimony. Here are six examples, though many more could be given.

First, Pharaoh is a means to an end. When God announces his seventh plague on Egypt, he says the following to Pharaoh:

> Let my people go, that they may serve me. For this time I will send all my plagues on you yourself, and on your servants and your people, *so that you may know that there is none like me in all the earth.* For by now I could have put out my hand and struck you and your people with pestilence, and you would have been cut off from the earth. *But for this purpose I have raised you up, to show you my power, so that my name may be proclaimed in all the earth.* (Exod. 9:13–16)

Here, God aims at patient-centered and other-centered goods. A "patient-centered" good is a good gained by the sufferer. Apparently, the plague is for *Pharaoh's* benefit. God sends it "so that you [i.e., Pharaoh] may know that there is none like me in all the earth," that is, "to show you my power." The plague gives Pharaoh a certain sort of knowledge of God he would not otherwise have had. But right alongside this, there is an "other-centered" good, in which someone *other* than Pharaoh benefits (namely, God): "so that my name may be proclaimed in all the earth." So Pharaoh is a means to a good for God, but that is not the only thing God is aiming at.[4]

Second, the Assyrian army is a means to an end. The language used to describe these warriors is the language of tools that are used by a person to get a job done. They are an "axe" that God "hews" with, a "saw" that he "wields," and a "rod" and a "staff" that he "lifts." Their warmongering is "the rod of my anger" against the disobedient Israelites, so that "the staff in their hands is my fury" (Isa. 10:5, 15). What is fascinating is that, despite being wielded for God's purposes, God treats them as responsible agents, for when their warfare is ended God turns around and judges the very rod he raised up (Isa. 10:12). Apparently God can use them as means without destroying their humanity. In Question 14, we saw how human intentionality can be preserved through "dual-agency." In these and similar passages there is no hint of divine

---

4. The apostle Paul cites this passage in Romans 9:17, though there his focus seems to be on these goods as God-centered.

coercion, brainwashing, zapping, or physical pushing, pulling, dragging, or slapping. Because two sets of intentions (divine and human) can be distinguished with respect to the same set of events, the human intentions can be evil (and foolish, and ignorant, and risky), while the divine intentions are good (and wise, and knowledgeable, and without risk-taking).

Third, Judas is a means to an end. "For the Son of Man goes as it has been determined, but woe to that man by whom he is betrayed!" (Luke 22:22). Apparently the betrayal of Jesus was "determined" by God, but it did not occur in a vacuum. Rather, Judas was the *means* of the betrayal, "that man *by whom* he is betrayed." Indeed, just about every participant in the passion narrative was a means to the cross. This was the view of the early Christians in their prayers:

> For truly in this city there were gathered together against
> your holy servant Jesus, whom you anointed, both Herod
> and Pontius Pilate, along with the Gentiles and the peoples
> of Israel, *to do whatever your hand and your plan had predes-*
> *tined to take place.* (Acts 4:27–28)[5]

Again, the portrait of Judas is of a responsible individual, despite his being a determined means. Yes, "Satan entered into Judas," but this failed to dehumanize him, for at the same time, Judas "conferred" with the chief priests and officers about how to betray Jesus, then "consented" to their purposes, then "sought" an opportunity to betray him (Luke 22:3–6). There is no ignorance, coercion, or passivity here. Rather, we see what one would expect of responsible choice-making.

Fourth, both Paul and Paul's afflicters are a means to an end. Paul's suffering is considerable—he is "afflicted in every way," "perplexed," "persecuted," "struck down," "carrying in the body the death of Jesus," "given over to death for Jesus' sake" (2 Cor. 4:8–11). But all this suffering is but "light momentary affliction," for it "is preparing for us an eternal weight of glory beyond all comparison" (2 Cor. 4:17). The interesting question here is: *who* is being used as a means to an end? The passage reveals two answers. On the one hand, God is using the affliction, and therefore the *afflicters*, to sanctify and fit Paul for heaven. That is the role they play, though doubtless they are unaware of this. On the other hand, one could say that "present Paul" (and his sufferings) is a means to bring about "future Paul" (and his glory). Present Paul suffers so that future Paul can be fit for heaven. God's using people as means in this way is something we often overlook, but it seems to be a pervasive aspect of divine providence.

---

5. We discussed this passage in Question 7, when considering the sovereignty of God's providence in the Jesus narrative.

Fifth, the wicked are means to an end. "The LORD has made everything for its purpose, even the wicked for the day of trouble" (Prov. 16:4). It is important not to read into the text more than it says. Is "the day of trouble" the coming day of judgment, so that this text teaches some sort of doctrine of reprobation? Not necessarily. This could instead refer to everyday "trouble" coming from the wicked to sanctify God's people. Either way, the main idea is to unite the concept of creation ("the LORD has made everything") with a divine plan of some sort ("for its purpose"), and the wicked are just as much means in this plan as anyone or anything else.

Sixth, all things are a means to God's end. "For from him and through him and to him are all things. To him be glory forever. Amen" (Rom. 11:36). Since all things are not only from God and through God, but also *to* God, then each thing in God's universe is already a means: a means to God's glory. Paul's doxology abstracts away a lot of detail—surely there is *more* to divine providence than this! But God's providence involves *at least* this.

So despite the "strong" view of providence that seems to be taught in the various biblical passages cited throughout this book, and even in the passages just considered, not a single passage indicates that God's providence in using persons as means erases or suppresses our capacity for deliberation, reasoning, and choosing between alternatives we consider and reflect on. No one is coerced to make choices against their will. Rather, outcomes seem to crucially depend on what *they* choose in the situations in which they find themselves. On the biblical portrait, human beings are not *obviously* dehumanized just because God's providence is meticulous and purposeful. Puppets do not deliberate, or choose for reasons, or seek to realize goals they envision for themselves. But human beings are continually doing those things, and Scripture is often at pains to point this out.

God's Right over Us and Knowledge of Us

But regardless of whether people remain *free* when God uses them as means, do human beings not have the fundamental right not to be used for another person's purposes? Can we not be dehumanized in *that* way, such that we lose our intrinsic dignity, even if we do not lose our freedom? God never *asked us* if we would like to play various roles in his providential plan. Rather, he orchestrates outcomes without so much as a "May I?" to Pharaoh, the Assyrians, or Judas.

But the Creator/creature distinction seems relevant here. Reflecting on the divine prerogatives at work in the Exodus passage about Pharaoh, the apostle Paul likens God to a potter and his creatures to clay (Rom. 9:17, 20–23). Every creature is God's possession, first existing by God's creative power, and then sustained moment by moment by God's providential power. This applies to all human beings: "He himself gives to all mankind life and breath and everything. . . . In him we live and move and have our being" (Acts 17:25,

28). If all this is true, and if "from him and through him and to him are all things" (Rom. 11:36), then God will have prerogatives that no one else has.[6]

It is precisely because the fundamental and pervasive relationship God sustains to his creatures is thoroughly *unique* that he can have rights over us in providence that we do not have over each other in everyday life. We have not created anyone *ex nihilo*, but God has. We do not give any creature— much less all creatures—life, breath, and everything else, moment by moment throughout their lives, but God does. We do not give every good and perfect gift from above, no matter how great or small, but God does.

As for obtaining our consent, what if God *had* asked us if we would like to be used as means to his ends? What would we have said? Do we know? What if God had revealed to us what we do not presently know: exactly which goods he would be aiming at in the history of the universe, and how those goods depend on various evils? Would that secure our cooperation? And what if God had put the question to a better version of us, with our thoughts unclouded by selfishness and a heart devoted to perfect love of God and others? What answer would we have given? Is it possible we *would* have freely consented, and God simply knows this about us?[7]

These questions are admittedly speculative, and their answers are admittedly not easily discernible. But combining God's prerogatives with his perfect knowledge of us should at least give us pause before concluding that God *must* be doing something wrong when he uses creatures as means to his ends, and that we would object to it, if asked. That is no small thing. Sometimes what is crucial for living the Christian life is not merely making the applications we should make, but avoiding the applications we should not make. Quite a few wrong inferences from our suffering need to be identified and rejected. In the last Question, we blocked an inference: if God *has* a reason for permitting suffering, then we should *seek to find out* what that reason is. There is no good reason for thinking this. Likewise, the current Question blocks an inference: if *we* do not have the right to treat persons as means, then neither does *God*.

God Doesn't *Merely* Use Us as Means

Here is a final thought, powered by the kind of "divine inscrutability" perspective defended in Questions 8, 20, 27, and 31: we have no reason at all to think that God *merely* uses us as means to an end. Why think that, either with respect to us or anyone else in the world? For all we *know*, in every case of suffering which we experience, God always aims at—and obtains—goods

6. We earlier broached this subject in Question 12 (when discussing the basis of the divine right to take life), and in Question 22 (when arguing for the soul-building theodicy).

7. Here I adapt a line of reasoning pursued by Alvin Plantinga in "Supralapsarianism, or 'O Felix Culpa,'" in *Christian Faith and the Problem of Evil*, ed. Peter van Inwagen (Grand Rapids: Eerdmans, 2004), 1–25 (see esp. the last section).

for us as well as goods that are not for us. Perhaps there is even a threshold of goods for us that he meets in each and every case of our experience of suffering. As Question 26 argued, why can God not aim at both anthropocentric and theocentric goods, such that one does not exclude the other? Do we know enough to know this is not the case?[8]

Perhaps God would be blameworthy for using us as means if he were merely hoping and wishing that things would turn out a certain way, and then signing us up for his risky, probabilistic experiment. But that does not seem to be what he is doing. Rather, God's providence is sovereign as well as good (Questions 7, 9–11, 14, 26), and so he can secure the outcomes he is aiming at. If so, then just about everything we know about God—his being creator and providential sustainer, the goodness of his purpose, and his perfect knowledge of us and of his plan—speaks to God's exercising his prerogatives as compatible with moral rightness.

Summary

If God uses persons as means to his ends, then this possibly undermines God's goodness (turning him into a utilitarian) and dehumanizes the persons he uses (violating their freedom or bypassing their consent). Though it is tempting to simply deny that God uses persons as means, the biblical testimony is too clear on this topic to ignore. Rather, we should recognize that God is able to preserve human personhood while exercising rights over us that we do not have over each other. Getting clearer on the extent of God's knowledge and the range of goods he may be aiming at (including goods for us) will also help undermine this objection.

REFLECTION QUESTIONS

1. To conclude that we are "dehumanized" requires that we have a clear conception of what it takes to be "human" in the first place. What would go on your list of "essentials for human personhood"?

2. To what extent did you derive your list from Scripture (see previous question)? Does it matter if you didn't do this?

---

8. In the "theodicy" section of this book, special attention was paid to identifying various "anthropocentric goods *for us* that God might be aiming at in providence (see especially Questions 21–23). One extremely thought-provoking consideration involves the great good of "being of use" to other people (and to God). See Richard Swinburne, *Providence and the Problem of Evil* (Oxford: Oxford University Press, 1998), 101–5, 241–46.

3. Some writers on the problem of evil insist that the problem cannot be solved unless we guarantee "patient-centered goods" in *every* case of suffering. Do you agree? Why would someone think this is important?

4. Saying that God has prerogatives that we do not have seems to imply that *God* can be a "utilitarian" even if we cannot. Is that the right way to see it, or are there better ways to describe the Creator/creature relationship?

5. What is the difference between God using persons as means and *merely* using them as means? In what other controversies about Christian theology or practice is the word "merely" a very important word?

Does Divine Providence Undermine Our Resolve to Eliminate Suffering?

The preceding parts of this book argued for a strong thesis: God works all evils for good (Question 26). It is characteristic of divine providence to aim at great goods, and to do so sovereignly—often achieving those great goods by way of evils—while leaving creatures in the dark as to what the goods are or how they depend on the evils (Questions 7–8). God certainly aims at theocentric goods in all things: "From him and through him and to him are all things" (Rom. 11:36). And for all we know, God also aims at anthropocentric goods in all things, including soul-building for believers and attention-getting for unbelievers (Questions 22–23).

In earlier Questions, we considered the biblical and theological basis for this view of providence (parts 1 and 2) and used it to make an apologetic defense against the intellectual problem of evil (part 3). But it seems there is a very high *practical* price to be paid for such a high view of providence. Does the "all things for good" idea not paralyze our moral decision-making? If God will work even my evil for good, then what reason do I have to *avoid* evil? If God's sovereignty has the shape just described, then *it matters not* what I choose. Not only can God turn the worst evils toward great goods; he does in fact do this. So why fight the worst evils, or try to avoid them, or even seek to eliminate worldly suffering at all? On this view, the greater-good theodicy in Question 26 is a temptation to be resisted, not a view to be endorsed. If I embrace it, then I trivialize what is most distinctive to my human nature: the motivation to deliberate and make significant decisions in life.

This reasoning *looks* sound. But it contains hidden assumptions we have no reason to accept, and good reason to reject. This Question exposes those assumptions to critical scrutiny, and further explores the relationship between divine providence and our moral decision-making. We will learn that what powers this conundrum is a misguided commitment to a utilitarian ethic that reduces morality to consequences.

Why Think Divine Providence Destroys Moral Motivation?

As we saw in Question 13, the view known as "deism"—the view that God created the world but subsequently never intervenes in it—hardly seems reconcilable with the specifics of Scripture. Rather, God often intervenes in human history to *prevent* evils, evils that *would* have happened if he had allowed either free will or impersonal nature to take its course. For example, God intervened to prevent the Israelites from drowning in the Red Sea (Exod. 14:21–22), intervened again to prevent Jonah from drowning in the Mediterranean (Jonah 1:17), and intervened yet again to prevent the disciples from drowning in the Sea of Galilee (Matt. 8:23–27). But God does not always exercise his providential power and prerogatives in this way. There are, after all, lots of cases of people who do drown. For them, God did not exercise on their behalf the power he exercised on behalf of the Israelites, Jonah, and Jesus's disciples. Indeed, for any case of evil that does occur, God permits what he could have prevented.[1]

This Question is not about whether God is *justified* in exercising his power in that selective way. That issue in Christian apologetics was already addressed in part 3 of this book, by way of combining "the way of theodicy" with "the way of inscrutability." God always has a good reason for permitting an evil he could have prevented, and even if we cannot come up with that reason—at best we can come up with some possible candidate reasons—it fails to follow from our ignorance that God does not have a good reason. Critics who reject God's existence because of evil have not sustained (and cannot sustain) the relevant burden of proof needed to make that argument.

Rather, this Question is about the *practical impact* such a view of divine providence might have upon our everyday deliberations and choice-making. Imagine that the "greater-good theodicy" is correct, as a general approach to theodicy:

> The pain and suffering in God's world play a necessary role in bringing about (or being a part of) greater goods that could

---

1. Thus, I accept premise one of the intellectual problem of evil: "A perfectly powerful being *can* prevent any evil." For argument for why Christians should accept this premise, and dispute premise two of the problem instead, see Question 18. Notice that God is not only able to use his power to stop nature from causing natural evil. He can also use his power to stop persons from using their free will to cause moral evil. He sends the flood on sinful mankind (Gen. 7:11–24), strikes down Nadab and Abihu to stop their idolatrous worship (Lev. 10:2), sends plagues to end the moral evil of Egyptian slavery (Exod. 7–14), drowns an army to prevent the reacquisition of those slaves (Exod. 14:27–28), and keeps Abimelech from sinning against him (Gen. 20:6). All of this is well within God's power.

not be brought about (or exist) except for the presence of that pain and suffering. The world would be worse off without that pain and suffering, and so God is justified in pursuing the good by these means. (Questions 19 and 26)

Does this "for the best" approach to divine providence over evil not paralyze my moral decision-making? At the very least, God's goodness, knowledge, and power are a kind of filter that impacts what God allows and what God prevents. The buck stops with God, as it were. On many occasions, God decides to prevent evil, because he judges that it would be better to prevent it than to allow it. But on many other occasions, God decides to permit evil that he could have prevented because he judges it would be better to permit it than to prevent it. Both kinds of cases involve a divine decision to prevent or permit evil, based on his judgment as to what would be best overall.

Imagine I am contemplating whether I should go ahead and harm a person. (Perhaps he is my boss and has treated me or my friends unjustly at work.) Should I do the evil thing and retaliate (Matt. 5:44; Luke 6:27–28)? Or should I do the right thing and bear up under unjust suffering (Luke 6:29–30; 1 Peter 2:18–23; 3:9; 4:12–19), and seek nonviolent, legitimate ways to address the situation? That being said, if I go ahead and do the evil thing that I am contemplating doing, *and God allows it to happen*, then this reveals that this evil will be worked to a greater good. (If not, then God would not have allowed it.) Therefore, I lack any reason *not* to choose the evil option. Whether I do good *or* evil, God will always work it out "for the best." Therefore, it does not matter what I choose.

Where Does the Argument Go Wrong?

That seems like a powerful argument against a "for the best" view of providence.[2] But it only seems persuasive because there is an act of misdirection taking place. The argument rightly draws our attention to something that a "for the best" view of providence typically accepts, which is:

1. "If I were to *harm* person P, then God will work it to a greater good."

The idea behind (1) is that God only allows what is for the best. So, if he allows me to go ahead and make a bad decision, it must be because he knew he would work it to a greater good, a situation that would be better than if he

---

2. If it *is* a powerful argument, it would count not only against a *Calvinist* view of providence that says God ordains or determines all things, but also against an *Arminian* view of providence that says God only permits bad things and never plans them. For on either view, God always decides whether to prevent or permit an evil. It is always *up to God* whether he allows what he could prevent. And if he allows it, he must have had a good reason for doing so.

had intervened and kept me from making that bad decision. Maybe it was better to permit me to do a bad thing because my exercise of free will is just that valuable (at least in that instance), or because witnessing my bad decision was needed for me to see other things that are very important (such as my bad character), or because the suffering I caused would be worked for the conversion or the sanctification of the one who suffered. In reality, it matters not if we choose one of these hypotheticals. The idea behind (1) is that God does not permit evils *for no reason at all*. So if he does permit an evil (e.g., my unethically harming someone), something like (1) above explains in very general terms why he allowed it. But then that gives the harm I inflicted, if I *do* end up inflicting it, a kind of status: it will be worked out by God to make things better than if he had prevented it. (If it was better for God to prevent it than to allow it, then why in the world did God allow it when he could have prevented it?)

But while the argument rightly draws our attention to (1), it completely ignores something else that is true at the same time:

2. "If I were to *help* person P, then God will work it to a greater good."

Notice that (2) is also true according to a "for the best" view of divine providence. If my harming P really *is not* for the best, then God is not going to allow that. The thesis that God only allows what is for the best does not tell us ahead of time, for any situation, *what* would be for the best. Only God knows something like that. That is above our pay grade as mere human deliberators. Since *both* (1) and (2) would be true according to a "for the best" view of divine providence, that view gives us no reason at all to choose the bad thing rather than the good thing. Whatever effect we thought that (1) might have on our moral motivation gets canceled out by way of (2).

What the argument has overlooked is that, according to the view of providence in question, God does not only work all evil things for good; that is, (1). He also works all *good* things for good; that is, (2). He works *all* things together for good (Rom. 8:28). Since (1) and (2) are both true, then I have no reason to harm P *rather than* help him. In fact, it is obvious that I do not know ahead of time what will end up being true: (1)'s antecedent or (2)'s antecedent. I certainly do not know, ahead of time, what God has willed to permit. I never know a thing like that. It follows that a "for the best" view of providence does not lead me in *either* direction. I am in the dark as to which of the things I am contemplating doing is the thing God will work out toward a greater good. The fact that God *does* work things out to a greater good is therefore irrelevant as a practical motivator (or demotivator).

Relating God's knowledge and power to our everyday decision-making is an old problem, and it crops up in many areas of theological inquiry. These problems all admit of similar solutions because the arguments behind them go astray in similar ways. For example, if God chooses ahead of time who will be saved (Eph. 1:3–14), then maybe I should refrain from evangelizing altogether. For all I know, this person sitting next to me on the plane is not elect, in which case she does not need my witness. And if she is elect, then she is guaranteed to end up being saved anyway. So it does not matter what I do. But this is a fallacious way of thinking. It overlooks the possibility that the person *is* elect and that she will be called to faith *through* my witness and not apart from it. So election is not a demotivator against personal witness.[3] Likewise for God's foreknowledge. God either foreknows that the person will not exercise faith or that she will. Correct. But how does that affect *my* decision to bear witness? If God does foreknow the person will come to faith, surely he also foreknows what means would be used toward that end, and for all I know, those means involve *me*. The fact of God's foreknowledge does not excuse me from the call to witness to others. That would be a *non sequitur* of the highest order.

What Grounds Our Moral Motivation?

But then if "God is sovereign" does not point me in the "do a bad thing" direction instead of the "do the right thing" direction, then what *is* my motivation to do the right thing? Consider the following:

- God has told me in the Ten Commandments not to harm people (Exod. 20:1–17).
- God has told me in the Sermon on the Mount not to harm people (Matt. 5–7).
- My parents have reinforced this in my upbringing.
- I can just *see* by moral intuition that harming persons for no good reason is wrong.

All these motivations (divine command, parental example, moral intuition) point in one direction: do not harm people. And none of these motivations is undermined by convictions about divine providence. The reason is not hard to see—they are all nonconsequentialist in nature. These motivations do not say, "Make sure you choose what would lead to the greatest overall good for the world. Try very, very hard to base your moral decisions on the sum total of their predicted consequences over time." And a good thing too, since I have no way of calculating this anyway. *God* might be in a position to plan the world such that goods are maximized by way of his providential choices, but *we* certainly are not. Imagine I save a person from starving, and then he grows up to be the next Hitler. What follows from this? That I failed to

---

3. The apostle Paul seemed to agree, since he engaged in vigorous activity to fulfill God's predestinating purposes. "Therefore I endure everything for the sake of the elect" (2 Tim. 2:10).

do a genuinely good thing? Or that consequentialism is not the right standard for goodness? Surely it is the latter.[4]

We live to obey God and image his character in the world, not to calculate consequences. Therefore, God's providential planning does not paralyze our decision-making. In fact, far from undermining our moral commitments, a good case can be made that a "greater-good theodicy" strengthens them. Augustine, arguably an advocate of such a theodicy, once explained that God allowed fallen mankind to exist because he "judged it better to bring good out of evil than not to permit any evil to exist."[5] Lo and behold, that is the same ethic which God commands us: "Do not be overcome by evil, but overcome evil with good" (Rom. 12:21). But here is the difference. In contrast to God, we rarely (if ever) have the right or competence to impose suffering on others for good. So our focus should be on what *is* within our right and competence: overcoming evil with good. So we should devote our lives to this, and leave the results to God.

Finally, notice that when Paul considers the question of whether we should "do evil that good may come" (Rom. 3:5–8), he does not deny the doctrine of divine providence that led to the question. He does not deny that our unrighteousness *is* a means of showing God's righteousness, or deny that our lying *is* a means for God's truth to abound to his glory. God's providence may ensure both things. Rather, Paul strongly denies that consequentialism gives us moral motivation at all. Even though God does use our evil in these ways, for us to "do evil that good may come" is worthy of just condemnation and slanderous to suggest (Rom. 3:8).[6]

Summary

If by divine providence "all things work together for good," that does not give us any reason to do evil rather than good. For the source of our ethical motivation is not our having a preview of what God will permit or prevent. Nor is it our having an ability to calculate the long-term consequences of our choices. Rather, our motivation comes from what God has commanded and from our status as divine image-bearers in the world.

---

4.   For an accessible, practical introduction to a non-consequentialist, "virtue theory" of ethics, with an argument that such a view best aligns with Scripture, see N. T. Wright, *After You Believe: Why Christian Character Matters* (New York: HarperCollins, 2010).

5.   Augustine, *Enchiridion* 8.27.

6.   The argument of this chapter is further developed in Greg Welty, "Open Theism, Risk-Taking, and the Problem of Evil," in *Philosophical Essays Against Open Theism*, Routledge Studies in Philosophy of Religion, ed. Ben Arbour (Routledge, 2018), 140–58. The "moral motivation" objection to meticulous providence is presented in William Hasker, *The Triumph of God over Evil* (Downers Grove, IL: InterVarsity Press, 2008), 190–98.

REFLECTION QUESTIONS

1. Could there be evils that God just *cannot* prevent? Imagine you accepted this view. Would it affect your decision-making in any way?

2. This Question wonders whether an apologetic answer we gave in part 3 generates a practical problem for everyday life. Should we care about potential conflicts like these? Why or why not?

3. "The idea behind (1) is that God does not permit evils *for no reason at all.*" But what if he did? Would that impact your concept of God's goodness?

4. We do not know ahead of time what God will permit or prevent, who God has elected, or what God foreknows. How does our ignorance in each case preserve the importance of our choices?

5. Unlike God, we rarely know the long-term consequences of our choices. How does that make the Creator/creature distinction central to the argument of this Question?

Can We Make Any Moral Evaluation If God Is Beyond Moral Evaluation?

Questions 7 and 8 argued that God's providence is good, sovereign, and inscrutable. Presumably, no practical problems for our lives are raised by the *goodness* of God's providence. It is a great comfort to know that God works for our good even in our sufferings (Rom. 8:32; 2 Cor. 4:16–17). However, Questions 32 and 33 examined whether the *sovereignty* of divine providence would negatively impact our daily lives in some way. Does God's sovereignty turn us into pawns on his chessboard (Question 32) or undermine our resolve to eliminate worldly suffering (Question 33)? Having answered those concerns, this Question and the next examine whether the *inscrutability* of divine providence would negatively impact our daily lives. Does divine inscrutability turn us into moral skeptics (this Question) or lead us to regard God as distant and hidden from us (Question 35)?[1]

At first glance it might seem odd to think that God's ways and thoughts being "higher" than our ways and thoughts (Isa. 55:8–9) would mean that we cannot engage in moral evaluation or reasoning. This chapter gives the argument for that connection, recognizes the kernel of truth behind it, but then argues that moral skepticism is not something we should be worried about even if God's providence is inscrutable. Despite the theology commended in the earlier parts of this book, we can continue in our daily lives to make the kind of moral judgments about our fellow humans that our moral conscience would lead us to make.

---

1. For God's providence to be "inscrutable" is for the reasons behind God's decisions to be unknowable by us (unless he specifically reveals them). This is how Paul uses the word in Romans 11:33. The idea of God's providence being inscrutable was explored in Questions 8, 20, and 27.

What Is the (Alleged) Connection Between Divine Inscrutability and Moral Skepticism?

The intellectual problem of evil can be seen as an attempt to show that a God who permits evil (or permits a certain amount of evil or permits certain kinds of horrible evil) should not be regarded as good, where the goodness in question is *moral* goodness. Premise 2 of the argument claims that "a perfectly good being *will* prevent evil as far as he can" (Question 17). Since it is obvious that much (if not all) of the evil in the world is something that God could have prevented, it follows that God is not perfectly good. Therefore, the intellectual problem of evil can be seen as an attempt to *morally evaluate* God, concluding that God violates proper moral standards by allowing evil that he could prevent. Notice that the argument presupposes that we can make such a moral evaluation, that our moral beliefs can be applied to God.

We have given the intellectual problem of evil a thorough hearing in part 3 of this book and found it wanting. Taking our cue from "the way of theodicy," we learned that if there is a theodicy—a good reason God has for permitting evil—then premise 2 above is false. And taking a further cue from "the way of inscrutability," we learned that, at the very least, no one can show that there *is not* a theodicy (or theodicies) available to justify God's permission of evil. Just because we cannot come up with God's reason does not mean there is no reason. So, at the very least, no one can show that premise 2 above is true. We lack a compelling reason to *accept* the claim that "a perfectly good being will prevent evil as far as he can." For if he has good reason to permit the evil, then he does not have to prevent it to remain perfectly good. But then we lack any compelling reason to accept the conclusion based on that claim: that God does not exist.

No doubt this summary will strike some as a bit simplistic. Readers are invited to review part 3 (Questions 17–28) to see the details, including defenses from various criticisms. This Question is about what happens if we *accept* that response to the intellectual problem of evil. Imagine we have vindicated God, morally speaking, and have "saved" him from negative moral evaluation. What price did we pay to do this, practically speaking? As in previous Questions, so here: it is always important to see whether the intellectual answers we accept raise insoluble practical problems for our daily lives. For if they do, that might be an indication that we were naïve to accept the intellectual answer in the first place, and that perhaps we should revisit the issue. God's truth is not supposed to undermine but *help* our living a life that is pleasing to him.

Here is the practical problem. Imagine an awful case of suffering in the world: an innocent animal burns to death, a child is abused, an entire people-group is subject to genocide. God's permission of these things looks like a stain on his moral character. "But no," we say, armed with the arguments of part 3. "Appearances are deceiving. It might *look* like God is unjustified in allowing this awful stuff. But who are we to say that God lacks a good reason for allowing it? *Maybe* there is a greater good that God is aiming at through this (even though we have no idea what that good might be). *Maybe* there is a dependence of that good on this evil (even though we have no idea what that dependence might be either). We cannot rule out either of these things. So we do not *know* that God is unjustified, that he is violating proper moral standards, and that his providential decisions should be condemned. As Thomas Watson puts it, 'True faith will trust God where it cannot trace him.'"[2]

This is a nice speech. But notice the move we are making: we refuse to morally condemn God for his decision-making, because *for all we know* he has a good reason for making that decision. To absolve God of the charge of moral turpitude, I am not appealing to my knowledge of his justifying reason. Rather, I am appealing to my *lack* of knowledge, to my finitude, my smallness. He could have motives, reasons, justifications undiscerned by me. Given my intellectual limitations, I am not in a *place* to condemn him. I do not know enough to do that. His providence, after all, is inscrutable.

But if this is so, then maybe I should refrain from morally condemning *anyone*, even my fellow human beings. For maybe they have, unbeknownst to me, a good reason for doing what they did (even though they look guilty to me). My inability to come up with that reason on their behalf is no reason to think they do not have a reason. Who am I to say they *do not* have a justification? But if I cannot morally condemn anyone, due to my finitude, then that spells the end of all trials in criminal court—no one will ever be found guilty again! Worse, it spells the end of all personal relationships. "I do not know why you are punching me in the face right now, but for all I know you have a good reason for doing it, so by all means go ahead!" So, the price we pay for this way around the intellectual problem of evil is a very steep one, practically speaking. I must become a moral skeptic, and then live that out. Neither God *nor man* is rightly condemnable by me. Christians often criticize non-Christian religions and philosophies as "unlivable." But how could anyone live consistently with moral skepticism?[3]

---

2. Thomas Watson, *The Art of Divine Contentment* (London: L. B. Seeley and Sons, 1829), 140 (see Question 31, n. 1).
3. The idea that the inscrutability of divine providence would lead to moral skepticism is raised by many philosophers. Indeed, the last fourth of a recent book on the problem of evil is devoted to this question. See "Part IV: Skeptical Theism's Implications for Morality," in *Skeptical Theism: New Essays*, eds. Trent Dougherty and Justin P. McBrayer (Oxford: Oxford University Press, 2014). See also Bruce Russell, who argues that "Moral skepticism about God's omissions entails moral skepticism about our own omissions" ("Defenseless," in *The Evidential Argument from Evil*, ed. Daniel Howard-Snyder [Bloomington: Indiana University Press, 1996], 198).

Why Doesn't Moral Skepticism Follow?

The Kernel of Truth
There is a kernel of truth behind this argument for moral skepticism: our cognitive limitations *are* relevant to whether we can rightly make various inferences. If we lack the relevant expertise, familiarity, or cognitive powers needed to discern the things we are looking for, then our reasoning from "it seems to me there is no X" to "there is no X" will be an unreliable piece of reasoning. This is precisely the point that was amply illustrated by the series of analogies given in Question 20. These were analogies to the problem of evil, in which the critic reasons from "it seems to me that God has no good reason for X" to "therefore, God has no good reason for X." But like that inference in the problem of evil, in each of the cases below, the inference from appearance to reality is not a good one because of our cognitive limitations:

- *Perceptual inference:* It does not seem to me that there is a ladybug on that tree a mile away; therefore, most likely there is no ladybug on that tree.
- *Scientific inference:* It does not seem to me that this latest book on quantum mechanics makes sense; therefore, most likely it makes no sense.
- *Moral inference:* It did not seem to earlier generations that freedom from racial oppression was a fundamental human right; therefore, most likely it is not a fundamental human right.
- *Linguistic inference:* It does not seem to me (a person who knows no philosophy or ancient Greek) that this sentence from Plato's *Apology* has a meaning; therefore, most likely it lacks a meaning.
- *Aesthetic inference:* It does not seem to me that Beethoven projected the sonata form onto his symphonies as a whole; therefore, most likely Beethoven did not do this.
- *Parental inference:* It does not seem to my one-year-old son that his parents have a good reason for subjecting him to painful inoculations under the British healthcare system; therefore, most likely his parents lack a good reason.[4]

This is the kernel of truth revealed in the above inferences: sometimes we can go wrong in our inference-making because we do not *know* enough about the thing we are reasoning about. Each of the above inferences goes wrong in that way. But none of these inferences gives us a reason for *universal* skepticism when it comes to moral reasoning or any of the topics above. The kernel of truth illustrated in the above examples cannot sprout into full-blown skepticism about our ability to *ever* conclude that *anyone* is morally unjustified in his

---

4.   See Question 20, footnotes 3 and 4 for comment on the source of these analogies.

or her actions. And the reason is not hard to see. In each case above, we lack expertise or familiarity *in a certain area*, not in all areas. While I cannot see ladybugs on trees a mile away, that does not mean that I am physically unable to see *anything*, at *any* distance. Surely I can see my computer monitor in front of me. Although I cannot discern the cogency in a quantum mechanics text, that does not mean I am unable to discern the cogency in *any* piece of writing. I can understand my wife's note to me about what to get at the store or the general narrative conveyed in the average newspaper article. Local skepticism about a certain intellectual territory does not support global skepticism about all inference-making whatsoever. We accept the idea that the above inferences are flawed, but surely that is not enough to make us total skeptics about all perception, science, morality, linguistics, aesthetics, and parental motivation.

We Are Familiar with Human Motivation

And now we are in a place to see why the inscrutability of divine providence is not a reason to embrace moral skepticism when it comes to morally evaluating human beings. The territory that the critic is reasoning about in the problem of evil is God's motivations for permitting evils that God can easily prevent. It seems God couldn't have good motivation to do what he does; so, God doesn't have good motivation to do what he does (says the critic). But that is not a territory with which the critic (or any human being) is familiar. It is not like we have completed a bachelor's degree, or even a shorter six-week seminar, in providentially planning universes down to the very small details (like sparrows or human hairs; Matt. 10:29–30). Our reasoning from appearances to reality *in this territory* is bound to go awry. But that is not how it is when it comes to morally evaluating *human beings*. This is a territory with which we are deeply and intimately familiar. We are fellow humans, and we are familiar with the range of motivations accessible to human beings.

Christian philosopher Michael Bergmann puts it well. Imagine that a human onlooker (who we will call "Stan") doesn't act to prevent the death of a fawn in a forest fire or to prevent a case of child abuse when he easily could. Influenced by the inscrutability of divine providence, should we "be agnostic about whether Stan's inaction is wrong"? No, because the territory of human motivation is a territory with which we are familiar. If *we* cannot see what outweighing good is involved in Stan's inaction (and we cannot!), then "we *can* be sure that it isn't what is motivating him since it is reasonable to think that he, like us, can't see what that good might be." Since Stan is a fellow human being, "we can be reasonably sure that Stan's inaction is unjustified," for "we know Stan lacks appropriate motivation for permitting such evil when he could easily prevent it."[5]

5. Michael Bergmann, "Skeptical Theism and Rowe's New Evidential Argument from Evil," in *The Problem of Evil: Selected Readings*, 2nd ed., ed. Michael Peterson (Notre Dame, IN:

Bergmann's analysis lines up with the Genesis 37–50 narrative we already examined in Question 8. Joseph's brothers first did something they ought not to have done: sell their brother into slavery. Then they failed to do something they ought to have done: deliver their brother from slavery. Let's focus on this latter sin, their inaction, since that is the kind of case that Bergmann is talking about. The inaction of *Joseph's brothers* (in delivering Joseph from abandonment and slavery) was wrong, even if *God's* inaction was not wrong. They had no good motivation for not intervening, and much bad motivation for not intervening! But it does not follow from the brothers' bad motivation that there were not goods known and aimed at by God in that situation, goods which would rightly motivate *God* in this situation. The model of dual-agency, outlined and defended in Question 14, shows us that there can be two different sets of motivations (divine and human) with respect to the same set of events.

Summary

Stressing the inscrutability of divine providence in our response to the intellectual problem of evil does not saddle us with a general skepticism about all moral judgments whatsoever. We are not God, and so it is entirely expectable that *some* of the reasons God has for the things he does (or permits) would be hidden from us. This divine inscrutability involves a local, not global, skepticism, a local skepticism about a particular territory in which we lack expertise: the full range of complex, deep goods discernible by God, and the necessary connections between present evils and these deep goods. But you do not have to be God to be familiar with the kinds of justifications and motivations accessible to (and employable by) human beings. You just have to be a human being. So there seems little reason to think that the transcendence of God should turn us into moral skeptics. God's being inscrutable does not mean *everything* is inscrutable.

REFLECTION QUESTIONS

1. Do you agree that if an interpretation of Scripture leads to insoluble practical difficulties, that might be a reason to at least reexamine that interpretation of Scripture? Why would someone think this?

University of Notre Dame Press, 2016), 522–23. Bergmann goes on to defend his point from objections. Christian philosopher William Alston makes a similar point at the end of "The Inductive Argument from Evil and the Human Cognitive Condition," *Philosophical Perspectives*, vol. 5, Philosophy of Religion (1991), 60–61.

2. Why is it important to recognize "the kernel of truth" in an objection to our views? How can doing that ultimately help the person giving the objection? How can it help *us*?

3. Would it ever be right to conclude that we know nothing about a topic because we do not know some things about it?

4. Is the cross of Christ an example of God aiming at a good that the human participants (Judas, Pilate, the Sanhedrin, the Roman soldiers) could not possibly have been aiming at?

5. Many times, this book has relied on a point made by a "Christian philosopher." How important is it that there are Christians who specialize in examining the cogency of pieces of reasoning directed against the Christian faith?

Is God Distant and Hidden If His Ways Are Inscrutable to Us?

Because God's providence is inscrutable, humans typically go wrong when they try to guess at God's reasons for permitting evil and bringing about suffering (Questions 8, 20, and 27). But does the inscrutability of divine providence not make God distant and hidden? If I understand so little about God and his ways, then maybe I cannot trust him to be present to me in my suffering. What is the difference between an "inscrutable" God and no God at all?

Initially, the answer to the question posed by this chapter's title seems utterly obvious. Certainly God is "distant and hidden" if his ways are "inscrutable" to us. Is that not what "inscrutable" *means*? But as it turns out, such a conclusion goes far beyond what "inscrutable" means. God's providence being inscrutable means, at worst, that the reasons behind God's decisions in providence are unknown and unknowable by us unless he specifically reveals them. But lack of knowledge about *that* is compatible with God being both near to us and revealed to us in highly significant ways. In fact, God is closer and more present to us, in every moment of life, than any human being could ever be. And God has spoken to us of his plans and purposes to a degree that is unmatched in worth and value by even the best of our human friends. God is revealed and present to us in creation, in daily providence, and in redemptive history. The rest of this Question examines these points in turn.

God Is Revealed to Us in Creation

Even as a work of art testifies to the wisdom and capabilities of the artist, so "the creation of the world"—all "the things that have been made"—reveals God's "invisible attributes, namely, his eternal power and divine nature" (Rom. 1:20). Some theologians—notably, Thomas Aquinas—suggest that the knowledge Paul speaks of here is mediated by way of a *reasoned inference* from the data of nature to the existence of God. These arguments for God that we are supposed to reason out can get quite complicated.[1] But it seems better to take this revelation of God in nature as something that *immediately* produces in us knowledge of God's existence and nature, where "immediately" means "without the medium of reasoning."[2]

For one thing, Paul's metaphor of perception ("have been clearly perceived," v. 20) seems to indicate non-inferential apprehension of divine reality, not a complicated reasoning *to* divine reality. That is why, in the passage earlier cited, Calvin describes this knowledge as produced by a quasi-perceptual "sense of the divine," a *sensus divinitatis*. In addition, if the knowledge of God through nature depended on our reasoning out a complicated inference of some sort, it is difficult to see how this knowledge "gets through" to those who lack either the ability or opportunity to follow such reasoning. But Paul's argument in Romans 1 for the universal guilt of mankind requires that this knowledge of God also be universal, extending to everyone, since it forms the basis for our guilt in rejecting and suppressing it.

If this is right, then we are continuously immersed in a global theater of divine revelation of God's attributes every day and night. As Psalm 19 puts it, creation is a kind of *speech* about God that constantly occurs, speech that reaches *everyone*:

> The heavens declare the glory of God, and the sky above proclaims his handiwork. Day to day pours out speech, and night to night reveals knowledge. There is no speech, nor are there words, whose voice is not heard. Their voice goes out through all the earth, and their words to the end of the world. (Ps. 19:1–4)

As God's testimony to himself, all of creation declares "the glory of God" and proclaims that it is indeed "his handiwork."

Beyond the fact that our very being, and the being of the whole world, testifies to God's wisdom and power, our conscience testifies to his moral voice. In all mankind "the work of the law is written on their hearts, while their conscience also bears witness" to whether God's moral standard will "accuse" or "excuse" them on the day of judgment (Rom. 2:15–16). Again, on Paul's view we have God's moral voice within us. It is part of our very being. The voice of conscience is the voice of God, saying to us: "This is the way, walk in it" (Isa. 30:21).[3] It is a form of moral knowledge granted to all human

---

1. See Aquinas's *Summa Theologica*, part 1, question 2 for details.
2. This is John Calvin's view in his *Institutes of the Christian Religion* (1.3.1).
3. To be clear, Isaiah is talking about the specific corrective guidance God will give to his children in the future kingdom, not about the general phenomenon of conscience. But our conscience is *like* this: authoritative revelation from God about how we are to live. See

beings in virtue of their being created by God in his image. In fact, Gentiles who have never seen God's written law have considerable moral knowledge, and therefore knowledge of God's character. They not only know the stipulations of God's law—"they know God's righteous decree"—but the sanctions of God's law as well, "that those who practice such things [against God's law] deserve to die" (Rom. 1:32).

All that to say, the mere fact of creation gives us knowledge of God's existence, of his nature, and of his basic moral will for our lives. To a considerable extent God is not hidden at all.

God Is Near to Us in Providence

But we can go further. According to Paul's sermon on Mars Hill in Athens, God is not just the creator, making "from one man every nation of mankind to live on all the face of the earth," so that "we are indeed his offspring" (Acts 17:26, 28). In addition, God *sustains* everything he has made and does so continuously. Rather than taking a "hands off" approach to his creation, he constantly "gives to all mankind life and breath and everything" (v. 25), so that "in him we live and move and have our being" (v. 28). Here we learn something about every moment of our existence: God is present, not passively but actively. And his presence has a depth and breadth that we rarely appreciate, involving God's threefold work of conservation, concurrence, and benevolence.

First, there is divine conservation: "In him we live and . . . have our being" (v. 28). The very reason we endure moment by moment is because of God's work conserving us in existence. Since he is "sustaining all things by his powerful word" (Heb. 1:3 NIV) and "in him all things hold together" (Col. 1:17), if God were to cease to sustain us for even a moment, we would flicker out of existence like a candle in the wind. We live and have our being in God precisely because "life and breath and everything" come from him (Acts 17:25). This is why, when God takes away the breath of creatures, "they die and return to their dust" (Ps. 104:29).[4]

Second, there is divine concurrence: "In him we . . . *move*" (Acts 17:28). Not only do we have a bare existence by God's activity, we also *do things* with the powers God has given us. We cannot even take a step across the room unless God's power concurs with our decision, so that we do take a step. Apart from such divine activity—this guarantee that every time we move, we move "in him" and not apart from him—we would not exercise any of our powers. We would be as inert as ball bearings, as causally impotent and irrelevant as dust

---

Question 28 for C. S. Lewis's argument that the voice of conscience is best understood as the voice of God.

4. "It is characteristic of all that is creature, that it cannot continue to exist in virtue of its own inherent power. It has the ground of its being and continuance in the will of its Creator" (Louis Berkhof, *Systematic Theology*, 4th ed. [Grand Rapids: Eerdmans, 1949], 170).

in the wind. Such concurrence carries us through the Christian life: with our gifting "there are varieties of activities, but it is the same God who empowers them all in everyone" (1 Cor. 12:6). We are to work out our own salvation because "it is God who works in you, both to will and to work for his good pleasure" (Phil. 2:13). Apart from him we could *do* nothing (John 15:5).

Third, there is divine benevolence: God "gives to all mankind . . . *everything*" (Acts 17:25). Thus, "every good gift and every perfect gift is from above, coming down from the Father of lights" (James 1:17). There is a kindly purpose to providence: "that they should seek God, and perhaps feel their way toward him and find him" (Acts 17:27). God wants us to discover him, to be led to him and know him. Every moment of our lives is meant to forward that good purpose.

The teaching we have been considering is often called "general providence," since it contrasts with God's "special" or "extraordinary" providence, such as when he works occasional miracles. But "general providence" can be a misleading term, since it applies not just in general but extends to the smallest details of our daily lives. God does not just provide for "things in general." He provides *for us*, sustaining us, empowering us, and directing us to our greatest good: himself.

It follows that God is the greatest benefactor we could possibly have. Our every good comes from him, and we are more dependent on him than on anyone else, including our parents and the best doctors and nurses. (The latter would be no help to us unless *they* were sustained and empowered by God.) It also follows that divine creation, conservation, concurrence, and benevolence give us an immense wealth of knowledge about who God is, what he wants from us, and what he is doing for us. No wonder Paul says of God that "he is actually not far from each one of us" (Acts 17:27).

God Is Revealed and Draws Near to Us in Redemptive History

In addition to creation and providence, God is revealed in redemptive history. In the incarnation of his Son, Jesus Christ, in Jesus's perfect life, and in his death on the cross, God comes even nearer to us than he does in general providence. The sum and substance of the Bible is God's *will* to redeem the world through Christ, his *work* of redemption through Christ, and his *revealing* that this redemption is in fact his will and work. From the announcement of God's redemptive plan in Genesis 3:15 (in which God declares he will crush the head of the serpent by way of the seed of the woman), all the way to the final fulfillment of that plan in Revelation 22:17 (in which the Spirit and the Bride say "come" to those who are thirsty, that they may now "take the water of life without price"), the Bible is a progressive unveiling of the heart of God for humanity.

While our traveling through these "40 Questions About Suffering and Evil" is meant to be conducted in the light of this grand revelation, it must be admitted that even the biblical narrative of redemptive history does not tell each of us why *we* are suffering *now*, in *these* specific ways, and for *this* long. Such knowledge has not been given to us, even as it was not given to Job. In that respect, God remains inscrutable, despite all we have said. But there is a connection between redemptive history and our own personal suffering that we dare not miss, one that offers us hope amid our darkness.

Theologian John Frame speaks of a "problem of evil" generated for the Old Testament saints, because at their location in redemptive history they experienced "a kind of dialectic between justice and mercy":

> The prophets proclaim justice: Israel will certainly be judged for her disobedience. But they also proclaim grace: God is coming to redeem his people. Judgment is coming, but the promises to Adam and Abraham will nevertheless be fulfilled. Yet how can this be? Israel's sins are worse than those of the pagan nations of Canaan, even of Sodom and Gomorrah, which God destroyed. How can a just God do anything less than wipe the nation out entirely? Yet the promise of grace comes again. God will surely redeem his people. But how can he wipe them out and redeem them at the same time? It seems as though God's justice violates his mercy and vice versa. God, it seems, is in a bind. If he redeems, he must wink at sin; if he judges, he must renege on his promise.[5]

Frame goes on to show how, as redemptive history moved on to fulfillment, Jesus "solves the problem of evil in its particularly virulent Old Testament form. Christ is the theodicy of Romans 3:26":

> Notice that the atonement vindicates both God's justice and his mercy. It is just and it justifies the ungodly. In Christ, the just penalty for sin is paid once for all. And because Christ endures that penalty in the place of his people, they receive lavish mercy beyond our power to imagine. God demonstrates both his justice and his love (Rom. 5:8); neither is compromised, but each is demonstrated in virtually infinite degree.[6]

What does God being both "just and the justifier of the one who has faith in Jesus" (Rom. 3:26) have to do with us, with our suffering in the here and now? Frame explains:

---

5. John Frame, *Apologetics: A Justification of Christian Belief* (Phillipsburg, NJ: P&R, 2015), 181–82.
6. Frame, *Apologetics*, 182.

Now, I grant that this redemptive history does not solve the problem of evil in every sense. It does not explain genocide or the suffering of little children, nor does it explain our present waiting as we look forward to God's final vindication. But here is the lesson for us: If God could vindicate his justice and mercy in a situation in which such vindication seemed impossible, if he could vindicate them in a way that went far beyond our expectations and understanding, can we not trust him to vindicate himself again? If God is able to provide an answer to the exceptionally difficult Old Testament form of the problem of evil, does it not make sense to assume that he can and will answer our remaining difficulties? Does it not make sense to trust and obey, even in the midst of suffering?[7]

Summary

Is God distant and hidden from us? Imagine constructing a pie chart that represents all the ways that God is revealed to us and near to us. By creation, God's existence and invisible attributes are known. Our very being testifies to his wisdom, and our conscience testifies to his voice. By providence, God continuously draws near in conservation, concurrence, and benevolence. All of creation testifies to his care. In redemptive history, his saving will and work for the world are revealed. In fact, God's redemptive plan is itself a basis to trust that he has our daily suffering well in hand. Only a relatively small slice of this pie chart is hidden from us, though admittedly it is the slice we are most interested in: Why do we suffer?

But even here, the inscrutability of divine providence does not undermine our assurance that God's providence is *good*. It only restricts the form that such assurance can take. As argued in Question 31, assurance *that* God has a reason, even if we fail to know *what* that reason is, already communicates that God is on the side of good, that God knows what he is doing, and that he has our sufferings and our plight well in hand. The "inscrutability" of divine providence, as it has been explained and defended in this book, is compatible with knowing a *lot* about God's character, decision-making, and closeness to us.

REFLECTION QUESTIONS

1. If all human beings know God "by nature," then why are there so many people who identify themselves as atheists or agnostics? Is it possible to

---

7. Frame, *Apologetics*, 183.

know of God's existence and nature, but deny (to oneself and others) that one knows this?

2. Having defended Christianity on college campuses for several decades, Christian apologist William Lane Craig says that the moral argument for God's existence typically ends up being more attractive and persuasive to his hearers than the "kalam cosmological argument" for a first cause, which he has spent so much time developing. Why do you think that might be?

3. Do you think a combination of "conservation" and "concurrence," as explained in this chapter, is the best way to make sense of Paul's specific claims in Acts 17:25, 28? If not, what would be a plausible alternative?

4. Reflect on "every good gift" that you have ever received in life. Spend some time making a list. Were you surprised at just *how many* things fall into this category? What does this say about the nearness and goodness of God?

5. What did you think of the lesson Frame draws from how God solved "the Old Testament problem of evil"? How could the many "heroes of faith" (Heb. 11) have persevered without knowing precisely *how* God would reconcile his justice with his mercy?

Questions Related to
Counseling Those Who Suffer

What Is the Best Response to Those Asking Why They Are Suffering?

Starting with this Question, our "Practical Questions About Suffering and Evil" in part 4 turn from "How Suffering and Evil Impact Our Lives" (part 4A, Questions 29–35) to how we should approach "Counseling Those Who Suffer" (part 4B, Questions 36–40). While our fundamental perspective in counseling should be informed by the definitional, biblical, and theological material in Questions 1–35, we need guidance in how to *use* this material in ways that help sufferers rather than make things worse for them.

Perplexity and bewilderment in the face of suffering and evil is normal and to be expected. It is experienced by both psalmist and prophet (Ps. 13:1; Hab. 1). Jesus himself felt sorrowful to the point of death (Matt. 26:38) and expressed his "cry of derelicition" on the cross: "My God, my God, why have you forsaken me?" (Matt. 27:46, quoting the psalmist's own experience of spiritual desertion in Ps. 22:1). The apostle Paul openly shared with the Corinthian church the deep psychological and spiritual distress produced by his suffering and affliction. He was burdened beyond his strength and despaired of life itself (2 Cor. 1:8), feeling he had received the sentence of death (2 Cor. 1:9). He was perplexed at his affliction and persecution (2 Cor. 4:8), groaned and was burdened by his earthly life (2 Cor. 5:4), was sorrowful in his sufferings (2 Cor. 6:10), was afraid (2 Cor. 7:5), and lived through many a sleepless night (2 Cor. 11:27).

One of the worst aspects of suffering is how experiencing it may alienate us from those who should love us (Job 2:9). But even as community with others is threatened by suffering and evil, those same communal bonds may provide the best help amid suffering and evil. If we are to "imitate" and "put into practice" what we have seen in the apostle Paul (Phil. 3:17; 4:9; 1 Cor. 11:1), then there should be no shame in expressing to others our deep distress, just as he did. And those who do so are to be received by us with all sympathy and eagerness to help, not shunned (Gal. 6:2). We are to "have mercy on those who doubt" (Jude 22). Toward that end, this Question covers what we should and should not do when those who suffer come to us for answers.

How to Make Things Worse

In trying to come up with the *best* response to the questions of sufferers, we can unwittingly make things worse for them, and be a source of further suffering rather than help. Here are four ways we can do that.

Assume the Worst About Their Spiritual State

First, we can assume the worst about their spiritual state, perhaps due to the intensity of their grief. But questions are not arguments, and not everyone who asks why is challenging God's existence. Think of a husband who does something inexplicable, such as gamble away the family savings. Upon discovering this, an incredulous wife screams, "Why?" She is not questioning the existence of her husband. Her faith is being severely tested, but it is not absent. (If faith were completely gone, there would be no communication, as she would already have packed her bags, or kicked the husband out.) The words, "My God, my God, why have you forsaken me?" are an expression of faith twice over: the speaker is praying to God, and recognizing that God is *his* God.

Why does this matter? When we place sufferers into the category of "the worst," inferring from their extreme behavioral or emotional responses that they must no longer be among the faithful, we trivialize their suffering *and* the strength of God's grip on them. Suffering can be so awful that it can warp the feelings and perspectives even of the genuinely faithful. And God can be enabling them to persevere in ways that are not discernible by us. Amid their harsh words and terrible pronouncements, what do we *really* know about their inner struggles, the faith that remains but lies unexpressed? "For who knows a person's thoughts except the spirit of that person, which is in him?" (1 Cor. 2:11).

Here is an opportunity for the Psalms to impose a kind of biblical realism on us, to prepare us for the full range of the emotions of the grieving. Of special importance is the sense of *desertion by God* that God's people can feel. Many psalms start with the psalmist in a bleak state, and he has to actively toil toward a state of hopefulness by remembering and meditating on the promises and works of God. Let us not assume that the greatness of someone's struggles means that God has given up on him or her. That is the punishment theodicy in disguise.[1]

---

1. An extraordinarily helpful book on the phenomenon of spiritual desertion, and how select Psalms reveal its reality and its solution, is Sinclair B. Ferguson, *Deserted by God?* (Grand

Assume We Know How Theodicy Applies to Their Situation

Second, we can make things worse for sufferers by arrogantly assuming that we know why they are suffering. On the one hand, their suffering *may* be due to obvious choices they have made in the past or in the present. The book of Proverbs is a sustained look at how the bad choices of both the foolish and the simple-minded cause them needless suffering. That is how God has structured the world, morally speaking, and is why Paul warns, "Do not be deceived: God is not mocked, for whatever one sows, that will he also reap" (Gal 6:7).

But on the other hand, enormous amounts of suffering cannot be reliably traced by any observers to the specific choices of the sufferer. This includes most natural evil and most moral evil committed by others against the sufferer. We simply do not know the details here and are left largely in the dark. Is this not why Job's friends needed to be rebuked (Job 42:7) and why Jesus's disciples were subject to correction (Luke 13:1–5; John 9:1–3)? They each converted the bare possibility of divine punishment into a probability, if not a certainty. But it is God's prerogative to judge, not ours: "Beloved, never avenge yourselves, but leave it to the wrath of God, for it is written, 'Vengeance is mine, I will repay, says the Lord'" (Rom. 12:19). Likewise, it is also God's prerogative to *know* whether or not he is judging someone, not ours.[2]

This observation applies to the other theodicies we have considered. Even if God *does* permit suffering and evil to "shape our character" or "get our attention" (Questions 22–23), we cannot *know* that either of these (or some other reason altogether) is "the reason" why the person is suffering. If it is folly and shame to give an answer before one hears (Prov. 18:13), how much more to give an answer based on no information at all!

Minimize the Emotional Impact of Their Suffering

Third, we can make things worse by minimizing the emotional impact of their suffering, pretending that "true Christians" will stoically bear up against whatever God throws at them, and will deny real hurt and pain so they can be an example of strong faith. But to assume that passive resignation ought to be the "normal" response to suffering is to forget we are human, not superhuman. God shows compassion to his children precisely because "he knows our frame; he remembers that we are dust" (Ps. 103:13–14). To "superhumanize" others is to dehumanize them. In the Bible, when people get bad news, they have heart attacks (1 Sam. 25:37) or fall backward and break their neck (1 Sam. 4:18). They

---

Rapids: Baker, 1993). Ferguson gives an extended exposition of Psalms 13, 22, 23, 42–43, 51, 55, 73, 102, 119, and 131.

2. See Question 21 for argument that the sufferings of Job, Joseph, the blind man (John 9:1–3), Jesus, and Paul were not God's judgment on their sin, despite what others may have thought.

weep uncontrollably (Jer. 9:1; Lam. 2:11) and lament (Ps. 102:1–11). They groan and cry (Ps. 5:1–2), they languish until their bones and soul are troubled (Ps. 6:2–3). A mighty warrior of God can be reduced to this:

> I am weary with my moaning;
>> every night I flood my bed with tears;
>> I drench my couch with my weeping.
> My eye wastes away because of grief;
>> it grows weak because of all my foes. (Ps. 6:6–7)

Helpfully counseling others with compassion starts with receiving them *in* their brokenness. That is who they really are, even if we rightly hope (with them) that that is not where they will always be.

Impose a Timeline and Deadline on Their Grief

Fourth, and related to the previous point, we can make things worse by imposing a timeline on their grief, and a deadline for it to end, and then scold, shame, or isolate them when such deadlines have been exceeded. But to do this is to fail to recognize the intrinsic value of grief, to wrongly turn it into a reason for shame. Oftentimes those who grieve think there is something wrong with their grieving. They might be ashamed that they grieve, alarmed that their grief, especially in its initial stages, dominates their entire life and their every thought, such that they feel like a helpless rag doll that has been taken by a dog in its jaws and cast about. "Surely there is something *wrong* with me if I grieve deeply. Should I not have this under control by now?"

Christian philosopher Nicholas Wolterstorff, whose son died in a mountain-climbing accident, addresses the issue:

> The wound is no longer raw. But it has not disappeared. That is as it should be. If he was worth loving, he is worth grieving over. Grief is existential testimony to the worth of the one loved. That worth abides.[3]

Grief affirms the goodness of what God has given and then taken away. We are not Gnostics; we do not believe creation is inherently evil. We believe that everything God has created is good, and when that is taken away from us—marriage, children, friends, health—we suffer a *loss*. Not a phantom loss, a fake loss, but a real loss. It might be ultimately outweighed by that of which we have yet no inkling (2 Cor. 4:7–12, 16–18), but nevertheless it is a loss. To think otherwise is to think that the things we love, the people we love, the gifts of God we receive, are of no worth. And we dare not think that. To lament and

---

3. Nicholas Wolterstorff, *Lament for a Son* (Grand Rapids: Eerdmans, 1987), 5.

grieve is not to abandon faith but to express one's faith in the value of God's great gifts and in the goodness of the giver.[4]

How to Make Things Better

Here are four things we *should* do on behalf of those suffering who come to us for answers: offer our physical presence, our listening ear (including our silence), our counsel, and our commitment to discipleship as preparation.

Offer Our Physical Presence

First, we should offer our physical presence, especially in our modern age when disembodied communication has increasingly become the norm. Those who grieve can be lonely, for many different reasons. Their uncontrolled response to suffering and evil may have driven away many friends. Or the perplexing nature of their loss has baffled would-be counselors into keeping their distance, lest their lack of wisdom and thoughtfulness be exposed. Or the magnitude of the suffering leads counselors to judge it would be too painful *for them* to get any closer to the awful reality. Nevertheless, our willingness to simply be with them, with or without wise words, or any words at all, can be a source of solace.

We are physical beings, not packets of information on the internet. So much of our suffering is sourced in physical proximity. We think next to nothing of thousands of children starving in a far-off land; the daily emotional impact of knowing this fact is minimal at best. But if we were to see a single infant, though a stranger, die on our very doorstep, we would be deeply affected for months, if not years. How much more if our own child? So it makes sense that *comfort* amid suffering is also sourced in physical proximity. It makes an extraordinary difference for someone to actually visit rather than send a text. Again, Wolterstorff comments:

> What do you say to someone who is suffering? Some people are gifted with words of wisdom. For such, one is profoundly grateful. There were many such for us. But not all are gifted in that way. Some blurted out strange, inept things. That's OK too. Your words don't have to be wise. The heart that speaks is heard more than the words spoken. And if you can't think of anything at all to say, just say, "I can't think of anything to say. But I want you to know we are with you in your grief."

---

4. Notice that even when Joseph is explaining to his brothers how God worked their evil (*ra'ah*) for good, he does not cease to call it "evil," for Joseph's suffering was real, his lost years in prison were real, and the brothers and others did cause it (Gen. 50:20).

Or even, just embrace. Not even the best of words can take away the pain. What words can do is testify that there is more than pain in our journey on earth to a new day. Of those things that are more, the greatest is love. Express your love. How appallingly grim must be the death of a child in the absence of love. . . .

What I need to hear from you is that you recognize how painful it is. I need to hear from you that you are with me in my desperation. To comfort me, you have to come close. Come sit beside me on my mourning bench.[5]

Offer Our Listening Ears, and Even Our Silence

Second, beyond our physical presence, we should offer our listening ears. Many people process their trauma by describing it to others and hearing their own descriptions of it. Talking about it is a way of taming it. That is a first step for many people, and our listening provides them with this opportunity. And, of course, willingness to be *silent* is a prerequisite for listening to others. We can become so focused on having (and then communicating) a right theological view of the sufferings of others that we forget the value of silence, of putting our arm around someone, of weeping with those who weep as much as we rejoice with those who rejoice (Rom. 12:15). There is a time and place for everything under the sun: a time to speak, but also a time to keep silence (Eccl. 3:7).

Initially, Job's three friends "sat with him on the ground seven days and seven nights, and no one spoke a word to him, for they saw that his suffering was very great" (Job 2:13). Such a powerful scene! Some suffering is so awful it *should* take our breath away, and therefore our words. Trying to fill every gap in the conversation with our own words may wrongly communicate that our (admittedly tentative) reflections are more important than recognizing the impact of their (very real) suffering.

Offer Our Counsel

Third, we must be willing to offer words of wisdom, insofar as we think we have some, and speak largely in response to the questions of the sufferer (rather than on our own initiative, when nobody asks). I will be brief here, and expand further in Questions 37–40, when we reflect on the relevance of God's attributes and works, of Christian community, and of the gospel itself, to counseling those who suffer. Hovering in the background is the central truth of parts 1–3 of this book: God's providence is good, sovereign, and inscrutable. Questions 1–28 sought to articulate, develop, and defend that

---

5. Wolterstorff, *Lament for a Son*, 34.

overall perspective. Then part 4A (Questions 29–35) helped us apply that material to our own lives. All of this in turn, insofar as it rests on good biblical and theological foundations, should shape the wisdom we share with others.

But timing is everything. Like human beings in general, sufferers are dynamic over time, not static. Those who experience the shock of suffering most likely want our listening ear, our silence, our works of love, and our prayers for God's sustaining grace, rather than a theological lecture. At some point when the initial shock recedes, they are usually (though not always) interested in our answers to difficult questions. Because we are holistic beings, such that the emotional cannot be separated from the intellectual, those who suffer will *eventually* be interested in intellectual and theological perspectives on their suffering. Our continuing to respect inscrutability because the Bible respects it, while leading them to the God who knows what he is doing, is exactly what the Bible would counsel.

Rather than preaching a premade sermon, a helpful approach at this stage is to simply ask good questions. Both God and Jesus ask questions in the Bible, for pastoral reasons.[6] What does the sufferer think of his or her situation? Then comment on and interact with the answers. As argued in Question 17, many conversations that may have seemed unthinkably insensitive or misplaced at the outset are more natural to have when clearer habits of thinking settle in with time. Many people really do want to know if they are *right* to feel that God is distant or even nonexistent, and Christians should be prepared for thoughtful intellectual reflection when asked.

Envision Discipleship as Preparation

Fourth, we should envision Christian discipleship as preparation. By its very nature, this final guideline is not implemented in our conversations with those who suffer but rather is an ideal we pursue as a Christian community *prior* to that time, if possible. The armor of God is put on in preparation for the day of battle (Eph. 6:11), not while the battle is in progress. The reason is not hard to see. The best time to be intellectually prepared to face suffering and evil is before the day of evil comes. As creatures made in the image of God who are nevertheless fallen, we are not only susceptible to intellectual attacks upon our faith (what was called "the intellectual problem of evil" in part 3), but also to *emotional* or *existential* attacks upon our faith as well. For any one of us, it is possible for the emotional needs of the moment to dictate to us our theology, so that we come through difficult experiences with our faith intact but having settled for a view of God and his ways that is less than orthodox. At a time of great shock, when the rug is pulled out from underneath us,

---

6.   Question 27 gave several examples of God asking questions of Adam and Eve, and Jesus asking questions of his disciples, where the purpose was clearly *pastoral*: to lead the person to a better place by helping them think through where they are now.

whatever our *theology* happens to be (right or wrong), that is what we are going to grab on to, for stability. And if our theology is wrong, we may end up in a worse place than we were before, because truth matters for life.

So it is much easier, and safer, to develop deeply rooted convictions through careful meditation on the word of God in Christian community ahead of time. The time to think through possible theological answers from a biblical point of view—whether we ourselves are grieving or we are trying to comfort the grieving—is not on the fly, in real time, while the shock is there, but *ahead of time*, when we are in a frame of mind to develop clear-headed convictions away from the point of danger. Such preparation seems to be the theme of Psalm 119:9, 11:

> How can a young man keep his way pure? By guarding it according to your word. . . . I have stored up your word in my heart, that I might not sin against you.

It is no wonder that the first piece of armor Paul mentions is "the belt of truth" (Eph. 6:14), for if you lose truth, you lose all else: righteousness, peace, faith, and salvation. So this guideline calls for the church to revisit and perhaps develop new strategies for Christian discipleship and witness. Everyone benefits if the Christian community has as a goal the training of even its newest members in what the Bible says about suffering and evil. Jesus did not shrink back from warning his followers to "count the cost" (Luke 14:25–33), and the letters of the New Testament are filled with instruction about how to live amid suffering and evil. This kind of instruction is in the foundational documents of our faith, rather than being peripheral.

Summary

How we speak the truth is just about as important as knowing the truth (Eph. 4:15). Otherwise, even good doctrine can die in our hands. When counseling those who suffer, we can make things worse for them if we assume the worst about their spiritual state, assume we know how theodicy applies to their situation, minimize the emotional impact of their suffering, or impose a timeline on their grief. Rather, we should be committed to offering our physical presence, our listening ear (and our silence), our wise counsel, and a commitment to discipleship as preparation. Community is threatened by suffering and evil, but it can provide real help during it.

REFLECTION QUESTIONS

1. Were you surprised by how openly both Jesus and Paul shared their grief and sorrows with others? What are some reasons that such sharing is often the last thing we want to do?

2. Question 6 quoted Calvin's claim that the Psalms are "an anatomy of all the parts of the soul," and this Question put that on display. What are practical steps the church can take to get the wisdom and realism of the Psalms into our daily lives?

3. Wolterstorff's book offers an extended look into the mindset of the grieving by speaking about his own experience of loss. List some ways that reading such books can be a help to us in counseling. Are there any ways we could misapply such books?

4. Jesus trained his disciples by physically being with them, not by sending them a book. The Bible is a book *sent* to us by God, but it is to be read in the gathered churches (Col. 4:16). How does the physical presence of others make a difference to our Christian discipleship?

5. If "the emotional cannot be separated from the intellectual," does that mean we should focus on the emotional? If not, then what is the significance of this holistic view of human nature?

How Are the Attributes of God Relevant to Counseling Those Who Suffer?

The previous Question offered some guidelines, both negative and positive, about how we are to counsel those who suffer in a way that helps them rather than makes things worse. One of those guidelines involved "offering our counsel." But *what* are we to say, when that time comes? What is the content of our counsel? These final four Questions in the book argue that God's attributes, his works of creation and providence, and the gospel itself, should all profoundly impact the content of what we say.

Knowing God's attributes focuses our attention, so that we can more easily apply diverse biblical narratives to our daily lives. After all, *our* daily lives are not narrated in Scripture. So what do all these narratives have to do with us? Amid all of God's diverse works in history—his work of creation, providence, redemption, and judgment (to be examined in the next two Questions)—is this truth: "Jesus Christ is the same yesterday and today and forever" (Heb. 13:8). It is our *personal relationship with God through Christ* that will get us through hard times. Knowing many fundamental truths about God's character, truths which characterize God in all circumstances, will give us someone to rely on in all circumstances. During turmoil and temptation, "the people who know their God shall stand firm and take action" (Dan. 11:32). We will even learn that it is precisely what is *incommunicable* about God that can speak to us real hope and consolation. There are treasures here waiting to be discovered, if only we have eyes to see.

The Pauline "Therefore" Grounds Life in Doctrine

What we know about God should profoundly affect how we live our lives. We know this because this is how the apostle Paul often structured his pastoral communications to the churches. In his letters, Paul seeks to shepherd the flock of God in various locations through his inspired teaching and exhortation. In these letters, the word "therefore" (*oun*) is often the hinge around which an entire book turns, explicitly grounding ethics in doctrine, the imperative in the indicative. So, for instance, Paul says:

> I appeal to you therefore, brothers, by the mercies of God, to
> present your bodies as a living sacrifice, holy and acceptable
> to God, which is your spiritual worship. (Rom. 12:1)

What are these "mercies of God"? Nothing less than the gospel theology of chapters 1–11, which includes a universally condemned mankind receiving justification by faith alone (chs. 1–4), peace with God through the second Adam (ch. 5), death, burial, and resurrection in our union with Christ (ch. 6), death to the law (ch. 7), life in the Spirit and promise of future glory (ch. 8), and God's faithfulness to his promises to Israel (chs. 9–11). These glorious facts disclose to us "the mercies of God" referred to in Romans 12:1, and Paul's use of "therefore" in Romans 12:1 signals that all these mercies are a profound *reason* to "present your bodies as a living sacrifice, holy and acceptable to God." From here on out, Paul's focus in the letter shifts largely to moral exhortation, to instructing the Roman Christians how to live in light of the doctrine he has expounded. The gospel theology of chapters 1–11 provides grounds for the moral exhortations in chapters 12–16. Doctrine *matters* for life.[1]

Something similar occurs in the book of Ephesians:

> I therefore, a prisoner for the Lord, urge you to walk in a
> manner worthy of the calling to which you have been called,
> with all humility and gentleness, with patience, bearing with
> one another in love, eager to maintain the unity of the Spirit
> in the bond of peace. (Eph. 4:1–3)

These verses are the transition between the doctrines of salvation and church (chs. 1–3) and the exhortations for daily living according to our individual callings (chs. 4–6). The key word is again "therefore." It is what connects "the calling to which you have been called" (again, expounded in chs. 1–3) with the apostolic urging that we "walk in a manner worthy" of that calling (a walk that is explained in detail in chs. 4–6).

So Pauline pastoral wisdom is structured by the conviction that doctrine informs life, that knowledge about God—including who he is and what he

---

1. Notice that Paul's exhortation to live a holy life has nothing less than the impeccable authority of *logic* behind it. Paul is asking us to accept a particular *argument*, that the indicative gives us good reason to embrace a whole host of imperatives. This is yet another way reason is a tool that magnifies rather than mutes the voice of God in Scripture. See Question 5.

has done—guides and fuels obedience to God. The ethical exhortations of the New Testament do not have their feet firmly planted in midair. They follow naturally from supernatural realities revealed from on high.

Knowing God's Communicable Attributes

This puts us in a better position to appreciate the importance of communicating the attributes of God in counseling. This too is divine truth that gives us reason to hope, to pray, and to persevere. The New Testament writers directly command us to be "increasing in the knowledge of God" (Col. 1:10) and to "grow in the grace and knowledge of our Lord and Savior Jesus Christ" (2 Peter 3:18). Theologian J. I. Packer's book on the divine attributes famously starts with an extended quotation from an early sermon by Charles Spurgeon, in which Spurgeon argues for the deep practical effects of the study of God:

> And, whilst humbling and expanding, this subject is eminently *consolatory*. Oh, there is, in contemplating Christ, a balm for every wound; in musing on the Father, there is a quietus for every grief; and in the influence of the Holy Ghost, there is a balsam for every sore. Would you lose your sorrow? Would you drown your cares? Then go, plunge yourself in the Godhead's deepest sea; be lost in his immensity; and you shall come forth as from a couch of rest, refreshed and invigorated. I know nothing which can so comfort the soul; so calm the swelling billows of sorrow and grief; so speak peace to the winds of trial, as a devout musing upon the subject of the Godhead. It is to that subject that I invite you this morning.[2]

There are countless catalogues of the divine attributes as revealed in Scripture. One of the most influential is that found in the *Westminster Shorter Catechism*, question 4:

> Question: What is God? Answer: God is a Spirit, infinite, eternal, and unchangeable, in his being, wisdom, power, holiness, justice, goodness, and truth.

As Spurgeon himself says elsewhere, creeds and catechisms are not fetters to our conscience but aids to our faith, conveniently summarizing inspired

---

2.   Charles Haddon Spurgeon, morning sermon, January 7, 1855, New Park Street Chapel. Quoted in J. I. Packer, *Knowing God* (Downers Grove, IL: InterVarsity Press, 1973), 14.

truth in ways that are memorable and useful.[3] Here, several of the qualities listed have come to be known as God's *communicable* attributes, since
we human beings can have them to a degree: "being, wisdom, power, holiness, justice, goodness, and truth." It would be a profitable exercise for any
Christian to not only memorize these attributes but write down their *implications* for our life amid suffering. Here is just a start:

- If God is *wise*, then he has chosen the best means to the best ends, and
  he can shrewdly bring to nought the foolish plans of those who are opposed to us.
- If God is *powerful*, then he can accomplish all his purposes toward us.
- If God is *holy*, then he is set apart from us and not subject to negative
  evaluation.
- If God is *just*, then all wrongdoing will be punished, and all injustices
  will be set right.
- If God is *good*, then he is deeply interested in promoting our flourishing, not undermining it.
- If God is *true*, then there is a correspondence between what he says and
  how things are. So, he speaks accurately. There is a further correspondence between what he promises and how he acts. So, he is faithful.

Just meditating on the above implications can do us a world of good when
we consider our own circumstances and God's governance of them. The above
claims are pitifully meager as an account of who God is and what he is like.
Eternity will not exhaust for us the riches of our discovery of God's greatness.
But a list like this is a start on the kind of thinking we must do if the attributes
of God are to be relevant to us and then communicated by us as relevant to
those we counsel. Have we realized what it means for *this* being to be the one
who made, sustains, and rules the universe?

Here is a final thought on the communicable attributes: they all characterize the *same* being. Perhaps we know humans who are holy but foolish, or
powerful but evil. It would be a cold comfort to know that someone, somewhere in the world is "just" or "good," if we have no reason to think that such
an individual can *make a difference* in our lives, or even knows who we are.
Why would that offer us encouragement in our sufferings? The grand truth
about God is that the same one who is just or good is also powerful and wise.
How much needless grief would we invite, and how much comfort would we
forgo, if we separate these attributes, accepting some but not the others? We
must keep them all before our mind's eye.

---

3. Charles Haddon Spurgeon, *C. H. Spurgeon's Autobiography: Compiled From His Diary,
   Letters, and Records, by His Wife, and His Private Secretary* (London: Passmore and
   Alabaster, 1898), 2:160.

Finding Further Consolation in God's Incommunicable Attributes

Still, we have not plumbed the depths. What of God's being "infinite, eternal, and unchangeable"? The genius of the catechism's statement is that these are presented not so much as divine "attributes" but as the *modes* of all the divine attributes. They describe for us *how* God has his attributes. We human beings, to a greater or lesser degree, may have "being, wisdom, power, holiness, justice, goodness, and truth." God also has those attributes, but unlike us, he has them to an infinite degree, unlike us, he has them from eternity, and unlike us, he has them unchangeably. The three ways in which God has each of his communicable attributes are wholly incommunicable to us, and to anyone else.

So, God is not some cosmic superman in the sky with a big "G" emblazoned on his chest. He is not like us, only bigger. He is not human nature writ large. He is profoundly transcendent through and through. As noted earlier, it would be extraordinary to meet a human who has all the communicable attributes. But a personal being who has them all in a way that is "infinite, eternal, and unchangeable" would be utterly unique. And that is who God is. More importantly, in our suffering, God's essential difference *from* us makes the difference *for* us. It is a key source of our trust in God that he is "infinite, eternal, and unchangeable" in *every* attribute. Someone limited in wisdom could be outwitted by bad people opposed to us. Someone mutable in power could suddenly lack strength to deliver us when the moment arrives. Someone whose grasp of truth is less than eternal must be dependent on another to know the truth. God is nothing like this. God *could not* be like this. This God is the same, in all the ways that matter to us, throughout all the vicissitudes of our lives. His divinity does not ebb and flow, wax and wane, invite us and then disappoint us. Almighty power allied with infinite goodness secures for us the promise: "Nothing in all creation can separate us from God's love for us in Christ Jesus our Lord!" (Rom. 8:39 CEV). The things unable to separate us from God's love include disappointment, death, and anything else in between. As J. I. Packer puts it:

> Wisdom without power would be pathetic, a broken reed; power without wisdom would be merely frightening; but in God boundless wisdom and endless power are united, and this makes him utterly worthy of our fullest trust.[4]

God's Attributes: A Foundation for Rejoicing in Hope

As we have seen, it is truth about God—who he is and what he has done—that forms the foundation for Paul's exhortations to us. Romans 12 offers a

---

4. Packer, *Knowing God*, 81.

portrait of the Christian life that is filled with love, honor, zeal, service, joy, hope, patience, prayer, and giving:

> Let love be genuine. Abhor what is evil; hold fast to what is good. Love one another with brotherly affection. Outdo one another in showing honor. Do not be slothful in zeal, be fervent in spirit, serve the Lord. Rejoice in hope, be patient in tribulation, be constant in prayer. Contribute to the needs of the saints and seek to show hospitality. (Rom. 12:9–13)

In context, this is a life lived amid suffering, as Paul goes on to say we should "weep with those who weep" (v. 15), "never avenge [ourselves]" (v. 19), and be those who "overcome evil with good" (v. 21), all of which presupposes quite a bit of adversity. But then how could we possibly "rejoice in hope" (v. 12)? Apparently, such rejoicing is compatible with weeping, sorrow, challenge, and suffering.

Central to all hope, and therefore central to what promotes rejoicing, is truth about God. "Rejoicing in hope" means you have a focus on the future as transcending the present. Hope is the great leveler; it grasps that the present is not the entirety of life. If you are satisfied with the present then you do not hope for anything; hope is a kind of judgment on and dissatisfaction with the present, putting it in its place. The present is important because it is an often-mysterious means of bringing about the future. But it is the future, the full fulfillment of God's promises, that we hope for most earnestly, rather than the mere perpetuation of the present.

There is a further dynamic in verse 12. The three things named—rejoicing, patience, prayer—lead to each other. If you are "rejoicing in hope," that will lead you to "be patient in tribulation," and your awareness of your tribulations will lead you to "be constant in prayer." Prayer then leads you to consider your own needs and the needs of others, and so you "contribute to the needs of the saints" (v. 13). Your dissatisfaction with the present, including your suffering, leads you to obey the greatest commandment God ever gave: to love. But it all starts with hope; it can hardly be managed without it. And hope starts with knowing who God is, that the God whose attributes are "infinite, eternal, and unchangeable" is the God who is for us.

Summary

The content of wise counsel to those who are suffering should include the truth about God's attributes. The New Testament is clear that doctrine matters for life. Though the narrative of our lives is not one of the narratives in Scripture, the God whose attributes are revealed in the biblical narratives is the same God who governs our lives today. So his attributes of being, wisdom, power, holiness, justice, goodness, and truth inform our relationship with him as we confront and contend with suffering and evil in the world. God's attributes tell us about the one upon whom we can rely in all circumstances. Since the way God possesses all his attributes is infinite, eternal, and unchangeable, he transcends us and whatever (and whoever) is the immediate source of our suffering. This means (among other things) that all his promises will come to pass, that nothing will separate us from him, and that we can have hope for the future.

REFLECTION QUESTIONS

1. This chapter explained one way the distinction between God's communicable and incommunicable attributes could have practical significance for us. Can you think of any other ways?

2. The Pauline "therefore" not only structures many of Paul's writings, but also is used to make more "local" inferences on particular matters throughout his writing. Does this have any implications for whether you should use logical reasoning in your own teaching ministry?

3. A single practical implication for each of God's attributes was listed above. Is it possible to add a few more implications for each attribute?

4. Is it even possible that God's attributes can be separated, especially if they are infinite? If God were ignorant, could he really be *all*-powerful?

5. Do you agree it is essential to hope to "grasp that the present is not the entirety of life"? Is anything else essential to hope?

How Is God's Work of Creation Relevant to Counseling Those Who Suffer?

This Question and the next will explore how three biblical writers (Isaiah, Peter, and Paul) counsel their readers through suffering by connecting that suffering to God's works in history. This in turn will guide us in counseling sufferers today.[1] God is not a mere passive observer of human history, but an actor, a doer, an agent who wisely exercises his power on behalf of good purposes in every circumstance. He does not merely have a good character—he *does* good. The Scriptures continually declare the great works of the Lord, in creation and in providence. They also draw our attention to two very important works of divine providence: judgment and redemption.

The New Testament makes plain that the early Christians suffered quite a bit in their daily life, either because of their own sin or foolishness, or because unbelieving Jews and Gentiles opposed their way of life, or because Satan opposed them, or because natural processes exposed them (as well as the rest of humanity) to various dangers. But Jesus and the apostles sought to prepare Christians for life in such a world, often by pointing them to the God of creation, providence, judgment, and redemption, which reveal God's goodness, sovereignty, holiness, and grace (respectively). These great works of God do not *directly* tell us why we are suffering. What they do is offer us guidelines to help us interpret our suffering, to keep things in perspective rather than to overreact, and to assist us in bearing up under it.

---

1. Question 35 appealed to the works of God in creation, providence, and redemption to argue that God is not "distant and hidden" from us. This Question and the next have a much broader scope, examining all the ways God's works are relevant to counseling those who suffer.

The Logic of Creatorhood (Isa. 40:28)

The context of Isaiah 40 is suffering, namely, the suffering of God's people in exile under the chastising hand of God. In a foreign land, away from the many blessings of the Promised Land, Israel is tempted to think that their plight is hidden from God, and that the justice God assures for his people is disregarded by him (v. 27). It is precisely to address this suffering, both real and anticipated, that God lists for them his works as creator. It is a reminder they desperately need. No matter where the exiles reside, it is a fundamental truth that the heavens, earth, waters, mountains, and hills exist by God's power and wisdom (vv. 12–14). He sits above the earth, stretches out the heavens, and counts the stars (vv. 22, 26). His wind and tempest easily defeat princes and rulers (vv. 23–24). This narrative of God's creative work, and subsequent control over creation, reaches a crescendo:

> Have you not known? Have you not heard? The LORD is the
> everlasting God, the Creator of the ends of the earth. He does
> not faint or grow weary; his understanding is unsearchable.
> (Isa. 40:28)

Amid suffering, God's people are reminded of God's transcendence, power, and perseverance as creator. This is a truth they can cling to through all the vicissitudes of life. Their trials may exhaust them, but God's divine resources are never depleted. He is always available to strengthen the faint-hearted and make his people soar in every circumstance (vv. 29–31). For him to create from nothing means that nothing is too difficult for him when it comes to accomplishing good for those he loves. This logic of creatorhood is important for sufferers to grasp if they are to have hope. Those who oppose his people are, to God, "a drop from a bucket," "dust on the scales," "less than nothing and emptiness" (vv. 15, 17).

The Imitation of the Creator (1 Peter 4:19)

As mentioned earlier in Question 1, Peter's first epistle is largely devoted to developing a theology of suffering and trial for Christians dispersed among hostile regions (1 Peter 1:6–7; 2:18–25; 3:8–22; 4:1–2, 12–19; 5:1, 9–11). While Peter repeatedly relates the suffering of believers to God's works of providence, judgment, and redemption (see Question 39), there is a reference to God as creator that should not be overlooked:

> Therefore let those who suffer according to God's will entrust
> their souls to a faithful Creator while doing good. (1 Peter 4:19)

In context, Peter is speaking of a very broad range of suffering: "fiery trial" (v. 12), a sharing in "Christ's sufferings" (death) (v. 13), and "insults" (social marginalization) (v. 14). Why does Peter exhort them to entrust themselves to God as a faithful *creator* (v. 19)? The answer goes back to the book of Genesis. Even as God's work as creator was his repeatedly producing works that were "good" and "very good" (Gen. 1:4, 10, 12, 18, 21, 25, 31), so we who suffer should aim to imitate him in "doing good" (1 Peter 4:19). It is as if there is something of great value here that Peter does not want his readers to lose sight of amid their pain. The opportunity to continue to "do good" is an enormous privilege, involving our identity as image-bearers of our Creator, and our sufferings should not distract us from carrying it out. The suffering is "according to God's will," and so God has that well in hand. That is why we "entrust" our souls to him. But it is to the *Creator* we entrust ourselves. We were *made* for good works, and nothing should dissuade us from that task.

At first glance there seems to be an important difference between God and us, which spoils the relevance of God as creator to our suffering. Unlike us, God did not embark on his creative acts of "doing good" *while* he suffered; his creative resources and powers are infinite, and he exercised them entirely unimpeded by outside forces. This is why the Genesis narrative is to be contrasted with the various pagan creation narratives—God faces no opposition from anyone or anything else when he creates all things from nothing. But opposition or not, *what* God created is extraordinarily valuable. After all, it is the work of God and therefore testifies to the most valuable being in the universe, God himself. And in agreement with this, our own persisting in "doing good"—that is, our imitation of God's work of creation—is *so* valuable an activity that it is to be pursued even amid fiery trial, death, and insults. The will of God, supreme in creation (Rev. 4:11) and now also in our suffering (1 Peter 4:19), is honored by us when we submit to suffering while we continue to imitate God in creating.

Witnessing to the Value of Creation

All this talk of the value of creation helps us relate suffering to creation even more profoundly. All suffering as such presupposes that God's work of creation is valuable, and any divine providential purpose *in* suffering further confirms that value. Why do I say this? First, earlier in the book we understood "suffering" as the deprivation of anything that is of intrinsic value to the sufferer (Questions 6 and 30). Consider a man locked away in a featureless, windowless prison cell. Why does this constitute significant suffering for him? It is because he is cut off from what is of great value to him as a human being. He can no longer experience the colors, sounds, smells, beauties, and majesties of nature. Here there is no good food and drink, no family, little friendship, little useful labor. Such imprisonment is an awful reality because these are all features of *creation*, and the suffering involves the deprivation of them all. (How much worse if good health and psychological hope are also removed!) The badness of suffering presupposes the goodness of what is taken away.[2] All right thinking about the nature of suffering must start here. Suffering is not bad simply because we believe it to be bad, or because society deludes us into thinking it is bad. Suffering is bad no matter what we or society think of it, simply because it dislocates us from created good. Our losses are the compliment providence pays to creation. At the bottom of suffering there is a real foundation: the goodness of human flourishing as created and intended by God.

Second, any providential purpose *in* suffering further confirms the value of God's creative work, precisely because that purpose is there. For there to be no providential purpose in suffering is to imply that God treats creation as meaningless. Since there is nothing there of value to be restored or set right through suffering, there is no need for any divine purpose in suffering. But if there *is* providential purpose in suffering—and this is what the many verses discussed in the next Question strongly imply—then such purpose is an indirect confirmation of the value of creation. Suffering is repeatedly traced to God's works of providence, judgment, and redemption *because* God cares about creation—cares about it so much that he is willing to subject it to further pain to restore it to a state even better than its original flourishing.

There are several counseling guidelines offered to us in these thoughts. First, the existence of suffering and the assurance of God's purpose in suffering both point us back to the goodness of God's creation. They should therefore reinforce our commitment to "doing good" amid suffering. Second, suffering can indeed be a time for us to remember our blessings (both what we had, and what remains), to "forget not all his benefits" (Ps. 103:2). Third, suffering is an opportunity for faith that God must be up to something exceptional and astonishing if he is willing to permit *this* in his creation. Our sufferings do not wear their interpretation on their sleeve. We are poor judges of this, especially when we walk by sight and not by faith. The fact that some Galileans were murdered by Pilate did not mean that they were worse sinners than the other Galileans (Luke 13:2–3). Likewise, the fact that God has allowed suffering in our lives does not mean that he has given up on our lives and their value. There is good reason to believe the opposite.

The Glory of Future Creation Outweighs the Badness of Present Suffering (Rom. 8:18–23)

There is a place in the New Testament that explicitly raises the topic of suffering, only to mention "creation" five times in the next five verses:

---

2. As we learned in Question 36, this is why grief has intrinsic value: it is testimony to the worth of what was lost, and therefore grieving is no reason for shame on the part of the griever.

For I consider that the sufferings of this present time are not worth comparing with the glory that is to be revealed to us. For the *creation* waits with eager longing for the revealing of the sons of God. For the *creation* was subjected to futility, not willingly, but because of him who subjected it, in hope that the *creation* itself will be set free from its bondage to corruption and obtain the freedom of the glory of the children of God. For we know that the whole *creation* has been groaning together in the pains of childbirth until now. And not only the *creation*, but we ourselves, who have the firstfruits of the Spirit, groan inwardly as we wait eagerly for adoption as sons, the redemption of our bodies. (Rom. 8:18–23)

For the Roman Christians to understand their sufferings rightly, they must see them as part of a larger reality: "the sufferings of this present time" (v. 18). In Paul's view, "the glory that is to be revealed to us" characterizes a creation that is continuous with the creation that now suffers. There is a cosmic history that goes through multiple phases, but these are all phases of one creation. Currently, there is a kind of "futility" that characterizes creation that did not characterize it in the beginning and certainly will not characterize it in the age to come. This futility is "the sufferings of this present time" (v. 18). But where did it come from? Human sin is surely the proximate cause, but that cannot be the full answer since it was up to the freedom of God how to respond to our sin. Rather, "creation was *subjected* to futility," and this subjection implies the willing choice "of him who subjected it" (v. 20). Creation is "not willingly" in this state of suffering (v. 20), but divine prerogatives in judgment have been exercised. The result is that there is a kind of "bondage to corruption" that now characterizes creation (v. 21).

But alongside all this, there is an overarching divine plan at work, because creation was subjected "in hope," that the creation itself will be set free. The hope is for the obtaining of something: "the freedom of the glory of the children of God" (v. 21), and "the revealing of the sons of God" (v. 19)—a new humanity for a renewed creation. What is most striking here is the presence of divine hope, hope exercised by God himself. Normally, people get up and follow Jesus; Jesus does not get up and follow them. But, sometimes, it happens (Matt. 9:19). Likewise, people normally are motivated by their hope in God; God is not motivated by his hope in them. But, sometimes, it happens, and Romans 8:20 is one of the only references in the Bible to *God's* hope. Of course, God's hope is not ultimately in our unaided abilities. All of Romans 8 is about the necessary assistance that God provides us, by way of Spirit, decree, promise, and love. Nevertheless, God has hope in a plan that *involves* us. He has a hope for all creation, and it explains the regime of suffering he imposed upon it.

The metaphor of "the pains of childbirth" is instructive (v. 22). The old creation *begets* the new, and it does so through much pain. The process itself is a kind of creation, the bringing to birth of a new being that is organically related to the old, but very different as well. It has its own identity. Yes, sin is unnatural, suffering is unnatural, and none of it ought to be. But by likening the pains of "the whole creation" to childbirth, God is saying, "Even sin and suffering cannot thwart my creative plan. I may have added pain to child-bearing, but I did not replace childbearing. The ends of creation will still be fulfilled, even in this altered state."

Admittedly, this is a complex series of thoughts, but apparently Paul thought that the gathered Roman Christians to whom he wrote needed to see their daily "life in the Spirit" in the context of this broader plan if they were to live lives pleasing to God amid suffering. For the point is that their suf-ferings—indeed, *all* the sufferings of the present time—"are not worth com-paring" with the glory of the future creation (v. 18). So their hope should be aligned with God's hope, despite what they experience. Those whom we counsel should be reminded of this, even as Paul reminded the Roman Christians: the whole creation *is in a state of hope*, governed by a God who can bring his hope to pass.

Furthermore, there is a kind of hope for us in simply seeing that *this* was God's response to human sin. Not to annihilate the creation and start over, or abandon creation projects altogether, but to impose a (justly deserved) re-gime of suffering that *will be worked* to a new birth. We have already seen many ways God can use suffering for good in our individual lives, the so-called "ways of theodicy" (Questions 21–26). But the process Paul is talking about in Romans 8:18–23 is larger than us as individuals (though it surely involves us). The work of creation did not end in Genesis 1–2. The work of the *old* creation did, but ever since Genesis 3, God has been setting things up for the new creation, and that crucially involves the cosmos-wide circumstances that give rise to our suffering. God is redirecting all of this to a creative end. And so, in our suffering, "we wait for it with patience" (Rom. 8:25).

Summary

To counsel sufferers helpfully, we should point them to the God of cre-ation, as Isaiah, Peter, and Paul did. For Isaiah, God's people suffering in exile needed to hear that their plight was not hidden and that God would secure justice for them, because as Creator his divine resources can never be de-pleted or even challenged. For him to create from nothing means nothing is too difficult for him. For Peter, suffering Christians should entrust themselves to a Creator who has their plight well in hand. And as image-bearers of the Creator, they have the enormous privilege of continuing to "do good," and so to imitate God himself in creation. In fact, suffering presupposes the value of creation, and divine providential purpose in suffering further confirms that value, and this should lead to thankfulness and faith. Finally, for Paul, we can only understand our sufferings rightly if we see them as not only far outweighed by future glory, but part of a larger, cosmos-wide process of childbirth that will issue in that new creation, just as God hopes.

REFLECTION QUESTIONS

1. No doubt you got a sense that the depths of these passages are hard to exhaust. Go back to Isaiah 40:28, 1 Peter 4:19, and Romans 8:18–23, and their surrounding context. Are there additional points to be made about how suffering can be related to God's work of creation?

2. The exiles to whom Isaiah wrote must have been subject to enormous social, cultural, and geographic dislocation. What are some things that could have increased their suffering?

3. Is there something irreligious in thinking of ourselves as "imitating" our Creator in our efforts to do good? After all, only God can create from nothing.

4. Childbirth was natural in the original state of creation—"be fruitful and multiply" (Gen. 1:28)—but pain in childbirth was not (Gen. 3:16). So if the creation is in "the pains of childbirth," is that a natural state or an unnatural one?

5. Is it theologically naïve or dangerous to think that God has hopes? Is there an alternative interpretation of Romans 8:20 that is more credible?

How Are God's Works of Providence Relevant to Counseling Those Who Suffer?

This Question continues the topic begun in the previous Question: how the biblical writers counseled sufferers by connecting that suffering to the great works of God in history. Even as marriage is dignified by the fact that it is *God* who joins together (and therefore, let no man separate), so our suffering gains a kind of depth and meaning when connected to a divine way of working. Such significance is not invented by us but revealed by God, and therefore provides a sure foundation for hope when we are bewildered, disoriented, and numbed by the painful circumstances that come our way.

There is a fundamental distinction between creation and providence: in creation, God brings about what did not previously exist (Gen. 1:1; John 1:3; Acts 17:24, 26, 29; Rom. 1:20; Col. 1:16; Rev. 4:11), whereas in providence, God upholds and directs creation toward his purposes (Acts 17:25, 28; Col. 1:17; Heb. 1:3). God's creation of all things from nothing was extraordinarily powerful and is the ultimate instance of "doing good." The implications of the divine work of creation for suffering were examined in the previous Question.

But God's work of providence is equally powerful and multifaceted, and thus worth exploring. As Question 35 argued, in providence God actively *conserves* us (so that we continue to exist), *concurs* with our exercise of our powers (so that we can move and choose and be causal agents in the world), and furthers his *benevolent purpose* (so that we receive every good and perfect gift from above, including the discovery and knowledge of God himself). This Question connects our suffering to this robust doctrine of providence, paying special attention to two distinct kinds of divine providential work repeatedly mentioned in the Scripture: his works of judgment and redemption.

Suffering and God's Works of Providence

What is of most interest to us in these sections—on God's works of providence, judgment, and redemption—is not to construct a philosophical theory that could be deployed to counter the intellectual argument against God from evil. That is an important project and has a role to play in Christian apologetics, and it was pursued in part 3 (Questions 17–28). Rather, we are seeking to learn how the biblical writers addressed suffering in practical contexts. This project is complementary to the previous one; there is no reason we cannot pursue both.

The biblical writers repeatedly emphasize God's *purpose* in our trials, and God acting to fulfill his purposes is the great end of providence. Sometimes in Scripture, that purpose is identified (e.g., judgment, or redemption, or both). But most of the time, it is not. Rather, believers are assured *that* God has a purpose in their trials. Far from being an abstract, transcendent truth that torments them, a kind of divine hiddenness that communicates God's lack of care or concern, the divine intent behind all trials is a truth that the scriptural writers repeat for the practical benefit of their readers. The providential nature of all trials is not an embarrassment for the Christian religion. It is front and center in the apostles' pastoral communications with the churches, whose members faced real suffering on a daily basis. Both Paul and Peter make this connection on multiple occasions.

Providence in Paul

When considering the scriptural support for the greater-good theodicy in Question 26, we reflected on Romans 8:28 at length: "And we know that for those who love God all things work together for good, for those who are called according to his purpose." Coming within the scope of the "all things" that God works for good is the fact that "we suffer with him" (v. 17) in "the sufferings of this present time" (v. 18). These sufferings include "our weakness" (v. 26), as well as "tribulation, or distress, or persecution, or famine, or nakedness, or danger, or sword" (8:35). As we saw earlier, "all things" encompasses just about every conceivable suffering a Christian could face.

Three times in 2 Corinthians, Paul openly shares the afflictions which came with his ministry and explains them in light of God's providential purpose. In 2 Corinthians 1:8–10, he speaks of the "affliction" that he and his companions experienced: their being "utterly burdened beyond [their strength]," their "despair[ing] of life itself," their feeling they "had received the sentence of death." But all this had a clear providential purpose: "to make us rely not on ourselves but on God who raises the dead." And indeed, such reliance is on display in the very next verse: God "will deliver us" and "on him we have set our hope" (v. 10).

In 2 Corinthians 4:7–12, Paul and his companions in ministry were "afflicted," "perplexed," "persecuted," "struck down," and "always carrying in the body the death of Jesus" (vv. 8–10). But all this was, again, for a purpose: "so that the life of Jesus may also be manifested in our bodies . . . so that the life of Jesus also may be manifested in our mortal flesh" (vv. 10–11). The death that is at work in them is used by God so that life is at work in the Corinthians (v. 12). Paul freely uses purpose clauses in the Greek to denote the divine purpose behind the affliction: "to show that" (v. 7), "so that" (v. 10), "so that" (v. 11).

Lest we think Paul is being excessively vague in referring to his "affliction" in the previous passages, in 2 Corinthians 11 Paul lists his many sufferings in great detail (vv. 23–29):

- imprisonments
- countless beatings
- near-death experiences
- five lashings
- three beatings with rods
- a stoning
- three shipwrecks
- adrift at sea
- frequent journeys
- danger from rivers
- danger from robbers
- danger from the Jews
- danger from Gentiles
- danger in the city
- danger in the wilderness
- danger at sea
- danger from false brothers
- toil and hardship
- many sleepless nights
- hunger and thirst
- cold weather and exposure
- anxiety for all the churches

These are the things that occurred "so that" the life of Jesus would be manifested in the world through the ministry of Paul and his companions—not suffering in general but suffering day by day. Paul was even able to "boast of the things that show my weakness" (v. 30), for God revealed to him that these things were a way "that the power of Christ may rest on me" (12:9).

A very strong statement of God's providence in suffering is found in Paul's first letter to the Thessalonians. That church had already encountered much affliction, suffering from Gentile persecutors just as the Jewish churches suffered from Jewish persecutors (1 Thess. 2:14). Paul then sent Timothy as a kind of apostolic legate or representative to establish them in the faith, "that

328   Question 39 How Are God's Works of Providence Relevant to Counseling . . . ?

no one be moved by these afflictions" (3:3). Central to that pastoral support was the clear communication to them "that we are destined for this" (3:3), that is, destined for suffering as Christians. In fact, when Paul and his companions were among the Thessalonians in person, they repeatedly taught them "that we were to suffer affliction, just as it has come to pass, and just as you know" (3:4). To be destined for something implies one who so destines, and Paul was confident that such a message would not alienate the Thessalonians from God but establish them in his care. We have every motivation not to "be moved" by our afflictions, if we see them as (ultimately) coming from a powerful God with good purpose.

Providence in Peter

In his first epistle, Peter explicitly characterizes our suffering as "necessary" (1:6), as something to which we were "called" by God (2:21; 3:9), as "God's will" (3:17) and "according to God's will" (4:19). Since it is "necessary" that we suffer, these sufferings must proceed according to providence. Such language is similar to the sayings of Jesus and Paul, that Jesus "must" suffer many things (Luke 9:22; 17:25; 24:26; Matt. 16:21; 17:12; Mark 8:31; Acts 17:3; 26:23). The suffering of Christ was planned suffering—the future cross was revealed in Old Testament times (Ps. 22:1; Isa. 53:1–12). Likewise, the suffering of *Christians* is planned suffering—Christ left us an example of suffering for doing good, "so that" we would follow in his steps (1 Peter 2:21).[1]

Peter is quick to communicate the *blessing* that comes through suffering; its being "planned" is not its only or even its best feature. It is part of his pastoral purpose to communicate to us that goodness. Faith that survives trial results in "praise and glory and honor" on the final day (1 Peter 1:7). Our blessing those who persecute us is a way of *obtaining* a blessing (3:9, 14). God's sovereignty in suffering is not so God can flex his power; it is exercised *for us*.

Suffering and God's Work of Judgment

Beyond these passages about how God's work of providence relates to our suffering, there are times when the biblical writers single out particular *kinds* of providential work amid suffering, namely, his works of judgment and redemption. Both Paul and Peter speak to how God's judgment relates to our suffering. They are not endorsing the punishment theodicy (see Question 21), which says people suffer because God is punishing them. Remarkably, what Paul and Peter say is that the suffering of believers can occasion the

---

1. The "necessity" of the suffering, both in Christ's case and in ours, is a conditional necessity, not an absolute one. It was not inevitable that Christ suffer; that depended on God's purpose to provide redemption. Likewise, it is not inevitable that we suffer; that depends on God's purpose to call us into his kingdom. But *given* these divine purposes, freely pursued by him, the suffering must occur, and this explains Peter's language.

declaration of divine judgment on *someone else*: the unbeliever who brings the suffering.

God's Work of Judgment, According to Paul

So, for instance, Paul observes that the Philippians had "opponents" who generated "conflict" for them (Phil. 1:28, 30). But the Philippians' perseverance amid such suffering (1:27–28) was a kind of double sign. It was a sign to their opponents "of their destruction," and a sign to the Philippians "of your salvation" (1:28). The idea seems to be that the opponents threw at the Philippians all the persecution they could muster, and the Philippians *still* persevered. So something greater than the Philippians must be here; God must be present with them. But if God is for them, he must be against these persecutors. And if God is against them, then woe be to them, for God's purposes must come to pass; the Philippians' perseverance is clear evidence of that. Paul is saying that this implication will not be lost on their opponents; it is a *clear* sign, *to them*, of their destruction (1:28).[2]

Paul says something similar to the Thessalonians in their sufferings. Their displaying "steadfastness and faith in all your persecutions and in the afflictions that you are enduring . . . is evidence of the righteous judgment of God" (2 Thess. 1:4–5). How so? While the afflicters seek to marginalize Christians and remove them altogether from society, the suffering of the Thessalonians shows that God has a different view altogether: they are "considered worthy of the kingdom of God, for which you are also suffering" (1:5). Their perseverance in suffering reverses the harsh verdict their tormentors declare against them . . . and places it on the tormentors instead. It is *they* whom "God considers it just to repay with affliction" (1:6), and he will inflict such vengeance "when the Lord Jesus is revealed from heaven with his mighty angels" (1:7). Once again, we see how the sufferings of Christians evidence the judgment of God against those who bring the suffering.[3]

God's Work of Judgment, According to Peter

Peter also appeals to this theme in his writings, providing a striking confirmation that the apostles were united in the practical advice they gave to Christians gathered in various locations and scattered abroad. Peter exhorts Christians to have "a good conscience, so that, when you are slandered, those who revile your good behavior in Christ may be put to shame" (1 Peter 3:16).

---

2. Since this perseverance amid suffering is a kind of double sign, it was granted in divine providence for *two* ends: judgment and redemption.
3. Sometimes God will use the suffering of Christians as an occasion to *repay* the wicked, and to punish them. Thus, Paul writes: "Alexander the coppersmith did me great harm; the Lord will repay him according to his deeds" (2 Tim. 4:14). Of course, we can never know in any particular case that God is doing this. But we can know that he is *well able* to do this, and that can be a source of comfort in some particularly difficult circumstances.

When we bless those who persecute us, God can use us as a means to pronounce a kind of judgment on the persecutors. Of course, this "shaming" of them does not have to work toward their *ultimate* judgment. God may in turn use this shame toward their salvation if they repent. This is why we pray for our persecutors, rather than just pronounce judgment on them.

Finally, Peter teaches that our perseverance amid suffering instances a more general pattern in history, in which God can rescue us *and* judge our persecutors, simultaneously:

> The Lord knows how to rescue the godly from trials, and to keep the unrighteous under punishment until the day of judgment, and especially those who indulge in the lust of defiling passion and despise authority. (2 Peter 2:9–10)

Peter's argument here is *a fortiori*, from the greater to the lesser. In the past, God's judgment did not spare angels (from *Tartarus*, or hell, v. 4), spare the ancient world (from the flood, v. 5), or spare Sodom and Gomorrah (from ashes and extinction, v. 6). At the same time, God preserved his people (such as Noah and Lot, vv. 5, 7–8) from these terrifying works of judgment. If God did this in the past, then surely in the present day God can judge immoral and authority-despising false teachers while rescuing his godly children from the many trials such people bring about. If he rescued Noah and Lot, he can rescue any Christians today.

All this teaching from Paul and Peter has a general application for us in whatever circumstances we find ourselves: if we suffer unjust suffering, we should remember God's judgment. Our perseverance amid suffering transforms our lives into a kind of imprecatory psalm against unbelievers. God is on his throne, and he can and does redirect our suffering to this end.

Suffering and God's Work of Redemption

Most prominently, the biblical writers tie our sufferings to God's *redemptive* purpose. God's purpose to redeem the world by Christ's suffering gets forwarded, historically speaking, by the suffering of God's people. Any reader of the book of Acts can see that the scattering of the church by persecution is what spread the gospel beyond the confines of the Jewish nation. This is how God works, and God wants his people to know that he is *always* at work for the salvation of suffering's victims (those who suffer), perpetrators (those who bring the suffering), and onlookers (those who see others suffering).[4] Only a sampling of this theme can be presented.

---

4. As pointed out at the end of Question 22, these three categories are adapted from Marilyn Adams, "Redemptive Suffering: A Christian Solution to the Problem of Evil," in *Rationality, Religious Belief, and Moral Commitment*, eds. Robert Audi and William J. Wainwright

The Sanhedrin "called in" the apostles and beat them for preaching the gospel (Acts 5:40), unaware that these men were only there because someone else had called them first. The apostles saw their persecution—a dishonor in the eyes of the world—as an *honor* for which "they were counted worthy" (Acts 5:41). That is because their suffering had a higher meaning; it was "for the name," that is, the name of Jesus. It forwarded his message, put the divine work of perseverance on display, and shamed the perpetrators.

Paul taught his readers that they can rejoice in suffering because of what it produces: endurance, character, and hope, and therefore a kind of testimony that the love of God is in our hearts by way of the Holy Spirit (Rom. 5:3–5). It is a token of our salvation. Paul links our present suffering to our future glory. We suffer with Christ "in order that" we may be glorified with him (Rom. 8:16–17), and these sufferings "are not worth comparing" with that future glory (Rom. 8:18). Indeed, reproach for the sake of Christ is "greater wealth than the treasures of Egypt" (Heb. 11:25–26).

Because Christ "suffered when tempted, he is able to help those who are being tempted" (Heb. 2:18). Likewise, because Christians follow in Christ's steps, the sufferings of the Corinthians equip them to help and comfort others. This is a work of God's providence; he "comforts us in all our affliction, *so that* we may be able to comfort those who are in any affliction" (2 Cor. 1:4).

Though Paul calls his sufferings "light momentary affliction," according to the actual descriptions Paul provides throughout his letter, his afflictions were neither "light" nor "momentary." But *compared to future glory*, they are to be regarded as such. They are servants in the hands of God, subordinate to God's purpose, preparing saints for the life to come (2 Cor. 4:17). The Ephesians were not to lose heart over Paul's sufferings, because those sufferings were for the Ephesians' own "glory" (Eph. 3:13), involved in "the stewardship of God's grace" for them (Eph. 3:2). By suffering in this way for the sake of their redemption, Paul was filling up in his flesh what was lacking in Christ's affliction (Col. 1:24). Not that Paul's suffering was redemptive, paying for the sins of the world. Rather, Paul's sufferings were getting the gospel to the nations (including to the Ephesians and the Colossians), something that Christ's sufferings—by themselves—do not do.

Paul's Roman imprisonment, which was certainly a form of suffering for him, "served to advance the gospel" and made fellow believers "much more bold to speak the word without fear." His imprisonment was because of Christ, and therefore "for Christ," helping fulfill God's redemptive purposes (Phil. 1:12–14). Simply becoming a Christian involved Paul losing all status in the Jewish community and thus "suffering the loss of all things," though of course

---

(Ithaca, NY: Cornell University Press, 1986). Adams is concerned to analyze the range of God's redemptive purposes in cases of Christian martyrdom.

this was great gain for Paul, making it now possible to "attain the resurrection from the dead" (Phil. 3:8, 11).

Though Paul suffered for the gospel, "bound with chains as a criminal," there is a purpose for his enduring of everything—it is "for the sake of the elect, that they also may obtain salvation" (2 Tim. 2:10). His "persecutions and sufferings . . . at Antioch, at Iconium, and at Lystra" occurred because "all who desire to live a godly life in Christ Jesus will be persecuted" (3:11–12). And Timothy is to "share in suffering for the gospel by the power of God" (1:8), "share in suffering as a good soldier of Christ Jesus" (2:3), and "endure suffering" (4:5). This is what all pastors in training need to hear. When a soldier suffers because he encounters the enemy, he needs to know it is suffering for a good purpose.

Joyfulness in trials results from a kind of knowledge: that the steadfastness produced by tested faith makes us "perfect and complete, lacking in nothing" (James 1:2–4), so that we receive the promised "crown of life" in the life to come (James 1:12). Steadfastness in trials also results from a kind of knowledge: that though Satan seeks to "devour" Christians, this is a kind of suffering "experienced by your brotherhood throughout the world" (1 Peter 5:8–9). Apparently it is important for Christians to be aware of their *solidarity* in suffering, that they are not alone in experiencing painful losses and reversals in life. If we have a common faith, it stands to reason we would have a common enemy. In God's providence, this suffering is temporary, unlike the eternal judgment from which we have been delivered. It is only for "a little while," and then what follows is our "eternal glory in Christ," when we are restored, confirmed, strengthened, and established by God (1 Peter 5:10). Keeping this assured future completion of our salvation before us can help us endure suffering in the present.

Summary

Connecting God's great works of creation, providence, judgment, and redemption to our suffering helps us bear up under that suffering. These great themes, to which the New Testament goes back again and again, are four anchors for our soul in the winds of trial. The biblical authors do not shrink from using language like "so that," "in order that," "we were destined for this," "if necessary," and so on, to describe the relationship between the sufferings of believers and the providential purpose of God. God's future work, the fulfillment of all his providential purposes, is especially motivating. "The crown of life" is God's reward for those who are "faithful unto death" amid "prison," "testing," and "tribulation" (Rev. 2:10).

REFLECTION QUESTIONS

1. Is there anything *else* God does in providence, besides judgment and redemption?

2. It seems almost impossible that anyone who individually suffered all the things Paul lists for his readers could remain convinced that God was *good*. What do you think is the best explanation of this?

3. What did you think of the argument that Christ's sufferings, and our own, become "necessary" when seen in light of a divine plan? Is there a better interpretation of the language of "must" and "necessary"?

4. The suffering of believers can be a sign of God's judgment, not against believers, but against the unbelievers who perpetrate it. How does this turn the punishment theodicy on its head?

5. Did you agree with the explanation of how Paul fills up "what is lacking in Christ's afflictions" (Col. 1:24)? How can Christ's suffering be "lacking" if it is the perfect payment for sins?

How Is the Gospel Relevant to Counseling Those Who Suffer?

Question 1 pointed out that the gospel is the good news of God's decisive victory over suffering and evil. Jesus suffers to overcome our evil, and to deliver us from our deserved future suffering on the judgment day. God sent Jesus to live the life we ought to have lived, and to die the death we ought to have died (Rom. 3:24–25; 5:6–11, 18–19; 1 Peter 2:24). Because of Jesus's death, God is just to forgive us our sins, as the payment for our sins has been graciously made in our place by our Redeemer. Because of Jesus's life, we can have his righteousness and be declared righteous—that is, be justified—even though our own righteousness is as filthy rags (Isa. 64:6). Forgiveness, justification, and so many more blessings come by faith in Christ, by which faith we are united to Christ in his death, burial, and resurrection. In him our sins are paid because he paid for them. In him we are righteous because he is righteous. And the gospel has consequences that go far beyond us as individuals. God is bringing about a renewed humanity for a renewed creation, in which cosmic bondage to corruption is no more, all death, mourning, crying, and pain have passed away, and every tear is wiped away (Rom. 8:18–25; Rev. 21:1–4).

In Question 7 we saw how God aimed at great goods in the cross of Christ, goods for both God and man. We saw a divine *modus operandi* on display, a "way of working" that involved God using the evil decisions of Satan, Judas, the Jewish leaders, Pilate, and the Roman soldiers (Acts 2:23; 4:27–28) to secure the greatest good available to us: eternal life in Christ. Because God uses the evil of the world (the cross) to overcome the evil of our hearts (our sin), evil gets put in its place twice over. And since God's plan to redeem the world through Jesus has deep roots in the Bible's entire storyline, it is unsurprising that the three aspects of divine providence on display in the cross (its goodness, sovereignty, and inscrutability) are on display nearly everywhere else: in the Old Testament and New Testament, with respect to all natural evil and moral evil affecting individuals and nations, Jews and Gentiles, believers and unbelievers. Much of this book has been taken up with explaining these points.

God's gospel purposes are clearly foundational for how God relates to the world. They are also foundational for how any believer in that gospel relates to God. This chapter further reflects on the themes of gospel faith, love, and community, to see how the gospel should further shape how we contend with, bear up under, and overcome suffering in our lives.

Overcoming Suffering Through Gospel Faith

Faith in Christ through the gospel is a curious thing, through and through. The parables of the kingdom seem to stress paradox, reversal, and the overturning of expectations. Nothing is as it seems, at least not initially. Those who find their life will lose it, and those who lose their life will find it (Matt. 10:39). Those who have will get more, while those who do not have will find that even what they have will be taken away (Matt. 13:12; Mark 4:25). Unbelievers see but do not see, and hear but do not hear (Matt. 13:13). The smallest of seeds becomes the largest of garden plants (Matt. 13:31–32; Mark 4:31–32). What goes into the mouth does not defile, but what comes out of it does (Matt. 15:11; Mark 7:15). Having one eye can be better than having two (Matt. 18:9). A shepherd leaves ninety-nine sheep to pursue just one (Matt. 18:12). The abandonment of all earthly treasure ensures a far greater treasure (Matt. 19:21). Those who work one hour are paid the same as those who work the whole day (Matt. 20:12), so that the last are first and the first last (Matt. 20:16). A rejected stone becomes the cornerstone (Matt. 21:42; Mark 12:10). Samaritans are more righteous than priests and Levites (Luke 10:29–37). The exalted are humbled, and the humbled are exalted (Luke 14:11). Alleged traitors (tax collectors) are justified before God, but religious experts (the Pharisees) are not (Luke 18:9–14).

None of these are *actual* contradictions that God calls his people to believe. Rather, they are apparent contradictions resolvable upon further scrutiny, as we reason out what God is saying in light of other things he has said. Nevertheless, a standard has been set: paradoxically, we can *expect* the demands of faith to defy our expectations. The fall has made the world topsy-turvy, and God's way of setting it right can unsettle our norms and thoroughly surprise us. Gospel faith can lead us to places where people think we are crazy (Acts 12:15; 17:32; 26:24), where our enemies are the members of our own household (Matt. 10:34–36), and where those who kill us will think they are doing a service to God (John 16:2). More to the point of this chapter, this kind of gospel faith can also lead us to experience suffering and evil, as it did for Peter and Paul and the other early Christians, even though they and we are rightly related to God. And if we walk by sight and not by faith, our experiences of suffering and evil are bound to strike us as utterly meaningless, as cruel to receive at the hands of God. It is quite natural to think of a grain of wheat as needing to die in the ground if it is to bear much fruit. It is quite unnatural to apply that metaphor to human life and make it the standard for Christian discipleship (John 12:24).

What illuminates all this for us is further reflection on the nature of faith. Gospel faith sees what is invisible (Heb. 11:1, 27). Such faith would be literally incredible—unbelievable and nonsensical—if it were in anyone other than God himself. What is impossible with men is possible with God (Matt. 19:26). The paradigm example of gospel faith is Abraham leaving the only country he ever knew while not knowing where he was going (Heb. 11:8–10), then trusting that his barren wife would bear a promised son (Rom. 4:16–25), and then agreeing to sacrifice that very son even though future nations were supposed to come through him (Heb. 11:17–19). Central to Abraham's faith was his conviction that God creates from nothing and raises the dead (Rom. 4:17; Heb. 11:19). Apart from that belief his faith makes no sense. It was a faith in God's goodness, for creation and life are very good things. It was a faith in God's power, for creation and resurrection are extraordinarily powerful acts. It was a faith in the inscrutable, in what cannot be understood in all the ways we would like, for we have no inkling of *how* to create from absolutely nothing, or of *how* to reverse death.

This chapter will not repeat all the arguments previously given for the goodness, sovereignty, and inscrutability of providence. But gospel faith unites us to a God who works like *that*. That is why faith as small as a mustard seed will save us, even weak and faltering faith, because God is strong and sure and not weak and faltering like us. It is not the greatness of our faith but the greatness of our Savior that saves us. But this gospel faith can grow and mature, laying hold not only of a God who *is* like that, but who is *understood* to be like that. And whatever we can do to counsel ourselves and fellow sufferers in the direction of such maturity will be time well spent. Gospel faith perseveres through dark providences, not because religion is "the sigh of the oppressed creature" and "the heart of a heartless world" (as Marx would have it[1]), but because "the people who know their God shall stand firm and take action" (Dan. 11:32).

Overcoming Suffering Through Gospel Love

Consideration of three facts—that Christ's disciples must "suffer with him" (Rom. 8:17), that we face "the sufferings of this present time" (Rom. 8:18), and that we struggle with "our weakness" (Rom. 8:26)—prompts Paul to teach the Christians in Rome about life in the Spirit, about God's plan to

---

1. Karl Marx, "Introduction," *Critique of Hegel's 'Philosophy of Right,'* translated from the German by Annette Jolin and Joseph O'Malley (Cambridge: Cambridge University Press, 1970), 131.

renew the cosmos, and about God's unshakeable love for his own. This last teaching takes the form of an argument, one that has provided comfort to countless Christians over the years when they suffer. Here it is in full:

> What then shall we say to these things? If God is for us, who can be against us? He who did not spare his own Son but gave him up for us all, how will he not also with him graciously give us all things? Who shall bring any charge against God's elect? It is God who justifies. Who is to condemn? Christ Jesus is the one who died—more than that, who was raised—who is at the right hand of God, who indeed is interceding for us. Who shall separate us from the love of Christ? Shall tribulation, or distress, or persecution, or famine, or nakedness, or danger, or sword? As it is written, "For your sake we are being killed all the day long; we are regarded as sheep to be slaughtered." No, in all these things we are more than conquerors through him who loved us. For I am sure that neither death nor life, nor angels nor rulers, nor things present nor things to come, nor powers, nor height nor depth, nor anything else in all creation, will be able to separate us from the love of God in Christ Jesus our Lord. (Rom. 8:31–39)

Paul's conclusion is that nothing we can experience in creation, from now through the rest of our lives, no matter how awful in itself, or ill-intended by perpetrators, can separate us from God's love. The argument for that stupendous conclusion is *a fortiori*, from the greater to the lesser. If God has done the greater thing (and he has!), then surely God can and will do the lesser thing as well.

What is the greater thing he has done? In his infinite mercy he pledged to be "for us," and then his infinite goodness and power went to work, meeting our greatest need: our need for salvation. Sin is the worst problem we could possibly have, because it rightly and justly separates us from God, our greatest good, and has the power to do that for eternity. But God's being "for us" means even our worst problem is no problem for him. So, the Father gave his Son "for us" and justified us. His Son, Jesus, died, rose again, and now intercedes, all "for us."

Because God is fundamentally "for us" in these ways—in the deepest ways *anyone* could be for us—it is unthinkable that this same God would ever be "against us" in any situation, that he would "bring any charge" against us or would "condemn" us (Rom. 8:31, 33–34). God will not reverse or contradict the salvation he accomplished for us. Paul's argument is not from appearances in the present but from facts already accomplished. All charges against us have already been handled, and the only one who *could* condemn us is the one who already took that condemnation upon himself. So the basis for any condemnation is removed for all time.

Still, even if God has accomplished salvation and given it to us (the greater thing), and even if God will not take it away, perhaps something *other* than God can take it away. Maybe we and our circumstances, the suffering and evil we experience, can mess it up. What the Creator has accomplished, perhaps some part of creation can undo. And here Paul is clear that that is equally unthinkable: if God can do the greater thing (get us salvation), he can do the lesser thing as well (keep us in salvation). Love begun is love inseparable, following us through life, guaranteeing that no one "can be against us" and that God will "give us all things" (Rom. 8:31–32).

At first glance, this seems nonsensical, obviously false. What could be more evident than that people and circumstances not only *can* be against Christians but are *often* against Christians? Paul even names many of these things: tribulation, distress, persecution, famine, nakedness, danger, and sword (Rom. 8:35). If no one "can be against us" (v. 31), then what in the world are these things doing? The answer, I think, is that by God's powerful love, expressed in providence, even these things are "worked for good" for us (Rom. 8:28). To the extent that any perpetrators *are* against us, God sees to it that they are not *ultimately* against us. The greater gift of God's Son guarantees the lesser gift of being kept in God's Son.

So this is something else by which we counsel ourselves and fellow sufferers. Gospel faith not only sees the invisible God but receives the love of God as unconquerable, and therefore able to make us "more than conquerors through him who loved us" (Rom. 8:37). If the worst thing in the universe (our sinfulness) could not keep God from loving us and saving us, then surely nothing else in the universe (created circumstances) could separate us from that love and salvation. Any suffering and evil we could possibly experience will have to fall under "things present" or "things to come," and nothing in those categories "will be able to separate us from the love of God in Christ Jesus our Lord" (Rom. 8:38–39).

Overcoming Suffering Through Gospel Community

We can tend to interpret gospel statements individualistically. God loves *me*. Jesus gave himself up for *me*. Nothing can separate *me* from God's love. There is nothing wrong in principle with this kind of application. But a second glance might convince us that something larger and more wonderful for us is afoot. Paul's characteristic mode of expression is that *we* suffer with Christ that *we* may be glorified with him (Rom. 8:17), that future glory will be revealed to *us* (Rom. 8:18), that God is for *us* and will graciously give *us* all things (Rom. 8:32). These plurals are best explained, of course, by the simple fact that Paul is writing to *churches* in his letters. But that only leads us to rediscover a fundamental fact: the gospel does not just save us as individuals but *creates community*.

Most of the metaphors for Christian identity imply plurality: temple (made of stones), body (composed of parts), family/household (with sons and daughters, brothers and sisters), priesthood (with many priests), vine with branches (with many branches), flock (with many animals). In each case there is unity within diversity, a kind of holy redundancy that ensures spiritual needs can be genuinely met by the many when there is a breakdown of the one. God is training his people to view their lives as interconnected with others, running the race together side by side (Heb. 12:1), able and available to lift others up when they fall (Gal 6:1). Even relatively worldly wisdom grasps this simple point:

> Two are better than one, because they have a good reward for their toil. For if they fall, one will lift up his fellow. But woe to him who is alone when he falls and has not another to lift him up! (Eccl. 4:9–10)

Indeed, the New Testament writers seem to assume that our perseverance is typically *through* gospel community and rarely occurs without it. The author of Hebrews prefaces his warning against apostasy (Heb. 10:26–31) with a strong exhortation against "neglecting to meet together," because he sees such regular meetings as the place where "encouraging one another" happens (Heb. 10:25). "Brothers" gathered together should "exhort one another every day" so that no one has "an evil, unbelieving heart" and falls away (Heb. 3:12–13). But it is hard to practice the "one anothers" if there are no others around. Lacking the companionship of Titus, Paul's "spirit was not at rest," and he declined an otherwise viable ministry opportunity (2 Cor. 2:12–13). If apostles need companions in the faith to continue ministry, how much more people like you and me.

It follows from all this that probably one of the worst things for us is to allow our experience of suffering and evil to isolate us from Christian community. We need extra eyes on our lives, so that any temporary but understandable alienation from Christian disciplines does not lead to our giving up the Christian life altogether. We need extra ears to hear our complaints and put them in perspective for us. We need extra arms to carry our burdens when grief and anger paralyze and disable us, extra legs to help us stand or take us where we need to go, extra mouths to pray for and counsel us. Suffering can shut down individuals from functioning as they ought. We are only dust, after all (Ps. 103:14). But a community can step in and provide for us in all these ways. Community is the *way* that God's love sees to it that we are not separated from him.

Summary

As we experience suffering and evil, gospel faith sees the invisible God, able to create from nothing, raise the dead, and therefore work in ways that are good, sovereign, and inscrutable. Gospel love is God's unshakeable commitment to keep us in the salvation he has brought to us, no matter what past, present, and future throw our way. And gospel community is the way God's persevering love works to see to it that we do persevere, providing through others the comfort in affliction we cannot muster for ourselves. The gospel gives us good news in our suffering: God can raise the dead, nothing can separate us from his love, and we are not alone.

REFLECTION QUESTIONS

1. This chapter focused on the themes of faith, love, and community. Are there other gospel themes that you think are just as important to grasp if we are to overcome suffering and evil?

2. The focus of this chapter was on how *believers* can bear up under suffering and evil. But what about unbelievers? Is there anything in this chapter for them?

3. Though Abraham is "the paradigm example of gospel faith," his life was not free from stumbles. What does this say about God's willingness to persevere with us despite our faults?

4. Paul counsels the Romans through argument (in chapter 8, throughout the book, and throughout all his books). Why is argument an essential tool in his toolbox?

5. What are some ways that Christian community has been there for you, when your own suffering (or evil) compromised your ability to continue on as you would like?

Scripture Index

About the Author

Greg Welty (MPhil, DPhil in Philosophical Theology, Oriel College at the University of Oxford) was born and raised in Los Angeles, CA. In addition to his work at the University of Oxford, he is also a graduate of University of California, Los Angeles (BA, Philosophy) and Westminster Theological Seminary in California (MDiv). He was a teaching assistant for John Frame at Westminster; a stipendiary lecturer in philosophy at Regent's Park College, University of Oxford; Assistant Professor of Philosophy at Southwestern Baptist Theological Seminary; and is currently Professor of Philosophy at Southeastern Baptist Theological Seminary. He is also the program coordinator for the MA in Philosophy of Religion at Southeastern, has served as a pastor for more than ten years, and has written *Alvin Plantinga* in the Great Thinkers series.

4 0 QUESTIONS SERIES

40 QUESTIONS SERIES